THE EVER-DYING PEOPLE?

Canada's Jews in Comparative Perspective

Edited by Robert Brym and Randal F. Schnoor

Demise by assimilation or antisemitism is often held to be the inevitable future of Jews in Canada and other diaspora countries. *The Ever-Dying People?* shows that the Jewish diaspora, while often held to be in decline, is influenced by a range of identifiable sociological and historical forces, some of which breathe life into Jewish communities, including Canada's.

Bringing together leading Canadian and international scholars, *The Ever-Dying People?* provides a landmark report on Canadian Jewry based on recent surveys, censuses, and other contemporary data sources from Canada and around the world. This collection compares Canada's Jews with other Canadian ethnic and religious groups and with Jewish communities in other diaspora countries, including the United States, the United Kingdom, France, and Australia. It also sheds light on social divisions within Canadian Jewry: across cities, sub-ethnic groups, denominations, genders, economic strata, and political orientations. These bases of comparison usefully explain variation in a wide range of sociological phenomena, including ethnic identity, religiosity, acculturation, intermarriage, discrimination, economic achievement, and educational attainment.

ROBERT BRYM, FRSC, is a professor of sociology and an associate of the Centre for Jewish Studies at the University of Toronto.

RANDAL F. SCHNOOR is an adjunct professor at the Israel and Golda Koschitzky Centre for Jewish Studies at York University.

The Ever-Dying People?

Canada's Jews in Comparative Perspective

EDITED BY ROBERT BRYM AND
RANDAL F. SCHNOOR

UNIVERSITY OF TORONTO PRESS
Toronto Buffalo London

© University of Toronto Press 2023
Toronto Buffalo London
utorontopress.com

ISBN 978-1-4875-2876-8 (cloth)   ISBN 978-1-4875-2879-9 (EPUB)
ISBN 978-1-4875-2877-5 (paper)   ISBN 978-1-4875-2878-2 (PDF)

Library and Archives Canada Cataloguing in Publication

Title: The ever-dying people? : Canada's Jews in comparative
  perspective / edited by Robert Brym and Randal F. Schnoor.
Names: Brym, Robert J., 1951– editor. | Schnoor, Randal F., editor.
Description: Includes bibliographical references and index.
Identifiers: Canadiana (print) 2022047351X | Canadiana (ebook) 20220473544 |
  ISBN 9781487528775 (paper) | ISBN 9781487528768 (cloth) |
  ISBN 9781487528782 (PDF) | ISBN 9781487528799 (EPUB)
Subjects: LCSH: Jews – Canada. | LCSH: Jews – Canada – Identity. |
  LCSH: Jews – Canada – Social conditions. | LCSH: Jews –
  Canada – Economic conditions. | LCSH: Jewish diaspora.
Classification: LCC FC106.J5 E89 2023 | DDC 971/.004924–dc23

We wish to acknowledge the land on which the University of Toronto Press operates. This land is the traditional territory of the Wendat, the Anishnaabeg, the Haudenosaunee, the Métis, and the Mississaugas of the Credit First Nation.

University of Toronto Press acknowledges the financial support of the Government of Canada, the Canada Council for the Arts, and the Ontario Arts Council, an agency of the Government of Ontario, for its publishing activities.

For
Rhonda, Shira, Ben, Sophie, Molly, Talia, Jeff, Andie, Ariella, and Rick,
and
Marsha, Jaeli, and Shea

Contents

List of Tables xi

List of Figures xv

Part A. Introduction: Profiles of Canadian Jewish Life

1 The Ever-Dying People? Some Advantages of Comparative Analysis 5
ROBERT BRYM AND RANDAL F. SCHNOOR

2 Canadian Jewry since the Second World War 13
RICHARD MENKIS AND HAROLD TROPER

3 Demographic Overview 29
CHARLES SHAHAR

4 Antisemitism in Canada 39
MORTON WEINFELD

5 The Centrality of Jewish Education in Canada 56
RANDAL F. SCHNOOR

Part B. Comparing Canadian Jews across Social Characteristics

6 Twelve Degrees of Jewish Identity 73
ROBERT BRYM AND FENG HOU

7 Jewish Residential Patterns and Identity 85
JOSHUA HAROLD

viii Contents

8 Immigrant and Non-immigrant Household Income 100
NAOMI LIGHTMAN

9 Comparing Montreal and Toronto 114
IRA ROBINSON

10 Experiencing Race, Class, Ethnicity, and Gender: Jewish
Immigrants from the Former Soviet Union in Toronto 128
MARINA MORGENSHTERN

11 Attitudes and Activism concerning Israel 147
ELIZABETH MOORHOUSE-STEIN

Part C. Comparing Canadian Jews and Other Canadians

12 From the Jewish Question to the Muslim Question 165
ABDOLMOHAMMAD KAZEMIPUR

13 Jews and the Christian Goliath 179
REGINALD W. BIBBY

14 Are the Chinese Canada's New Jews? 195
FENG HOU AND ROBERT BRYM

15 Jews and Métis in Canada: Ethnic Mobility and the
Politics of Counting 214
DAVID S. KOFFMAN AND PAUL L. GAREAU

16 Jewish Intellectual Exceptionalism? Ethnic Representation at the
University of Toronto Medical School 230
JORDAN A. CHAD AND ROBERT BRYM

Part D. Comparing Jews in Canada and Other Countries

17 Jewish Demography and Identity in Nine Countries 249
SERGIO DELLAPERGOLA

18 Intermarriage in Canada and the United States: Déjà Vu or
Different? 267
FERN CHERTOK AND MATTHEW A. BROOKNER

19 Qualifying the Leading Theory of Diaspora Jewry: Jews from the
Former Soviet Union in Canada and the United States 283
ROBERT BRYM, ANNA SLAVINA, AND RHONDA LENTON

Contents ix

20 Perceptions and Realities of Antisemitism: Canadian,
British, and French Jews   300
L. DANIEL STAETSKY

21 Marriage and Mobility of Moroccan Jews in
Montreal and Paris   318
MARTIN MESSIKA AND YOLANDE COHEN

22 Jewish Engagement in Canada and Australia   332
ADINA BANKIER-KARP

List of Contributors   343

Index   347

Tables

3.1 Jewish population of Canada, 1901–2021   31
3.2 Canadian Jewish, non-Jewish, and total populations by age cohort, 2011   32
3.3 CMAs with a Jewish population of more than 1,000, 2011   33
4.1 Hate crimes by top ethnic, racial, or religious group, Canada, 2019, and Toronto, 2020   47
5.1 Enrolment in non-Orthodox and Orthodox Jewish day schools, Toronto and New York City, 2018   59
5.2 Participation in Jewish education, per cent by city and country   60
5.3 "How important is each of the following in what being Jewish means to you?" Toronto, 2018, in per cent   63
6.1 Jewish population of Canada by degree of Jewishness, 2011   76
6.2 Ordinary least squares (OLS) regression predicting degree of Jewishness for Canadians, ages 25–64, 2011 ($n = 26,660$)   80
7.1 Jewish socialization and residential concentration by city, 2018 ($n = 2,335$)   93
7.2 Per cent of Jews by density of Jewish population in city FSAs, 2018   94
7.3 General linear model (GLM) regression predicting Jewish residential clustering in Canada ($n = 1,740$)   94
8.1 Income measures for Jews and non-Jews after taxes and transfers, Canada, 2010   102
8.2 Self-reported gross annual income, 2017, and socio-economic characteristics, 2018, of Jewish immigrants and non-immigrants in four cities   105
8.3 Ordinary least squares (OLS) regression predicting household income after taxes and transfers by city, 2010   109

xii Tables

8.4   Ordinary least squares (OLS) regression predicting self-assessed gross household income of Jews by city, 2017   111
10.1 Self-reported annual household income of Jews born in Canada and the FSU, 2017, $000s, in per cent   133
10.2 Jewish identity and Jewish performance of FSU immigrant Jews and Canadian-born Jews, in per cent   137
11.1 Belief in the sincerity of Israel's peace effort and in the impact of settlements on Israel's security by selected variables, in per cent   149
11.2 Multinomial logistic regression predicting belief in the sincerity of Israel's peace effort   151
11.3 Multinomial logistic regression predicting belief in the impact of settlements on Israel's security   152
11.4 Multinomial logistic regression predicting belief in the sincerity of Israel's peace effort and in the security impact of settlements   155
13.1 Attitudes of Canadian Protestants and Catholics towards Jews, 1975 and 2000, in per cent   186
13.2 Negative attitudes towards select Canadian religious groups, 2019, in per cent   186
14.1 Educational attainment of Jewish, Chinese, and non-Jewish White Canadians between the ages of 25 and 34 by gender and immigration status, 1981–2016, in per cent   200
14.2 Jewish vs. Chinese representation by educational attainment category for men and women between the ages of 25 and 34, 1981 and 2016, in per cent   201
14.3 Jewish, Chinese, and non-Jewish White workers between the ages of 35 and 54 in the ten most common occupations in each ethnic group, by gender and immigration status, 1981–2016, in per cent   205
14.4 Top ten occupations for Jewish, Chinese, and non-Jewish White men and women between the ages of 35 and 54, 2016, in per cent   206
14.5 Median annual market income in dollars for Jewish, Chinese, and non-Jewish White workers between the ages of 35 and 54 by gender and immigration status, 2015 constant dollars   209
14.6 Sample 3 minus sample 1 Jewish–Chinese differences   210
16.1 Ethnic representation, University of Toronto Medical School, 1918–2018   233
17.1 Jewish population and HDI, Canada and eight other countries, 1980–2020   252

17.2 Age composition of Jews in Canada and eight other countries, 1925–2019, in per cent   257

17.3 Per cent stating items are a very important component of their Jewish identity, Canada and seven other countries, 2013–2018   260

18.1 Data collection by city   269

18.2 Indicators of Jewish communal connection in Canada and the US, in per cent   271

18.3 Jewish ethnic and religious capital-building in Canada and the US, in per cent   273

19.1 Indicators of Jewish religious and ethnic retention, Canada, 2018, and the US, 2013, in per cent   285

19.2 Indicators of religious assimilation, FSU Jews, Israel, 2014–2015, in per cent ($n \approx 568$)   288

19.3 Indicators of religious retention, FSU Jews in Canada and the US, in per cent ($n \approx 515$)   289

19.4 Indicators of ethnic retention, FSU Jews in Canada and the US, in per cent ($n \approx 515$)   290

19.5 Ordinary least squares (OLS) regression predicting Jewish religious retention and Jewish ethnic retention   296

20.1 Perception of the seriousness of discrimination against Jews/antisemitism by country, in per cent   307

20.2 Connection between antisemitic victimization and perception of discrimination against Jews/antisemitism as a problem   308

20.3 Connection between perception of discrimination against Jews/antisemitism as a problem and perception of discrimination against Blacks and Muslims   310

21.1 "How connected are you to Jewish life in your city?" 2018, in per cent   319

21.2 Occupational distribution of Moroccan-Jewish men in Montreal, 1969–2014, in per cent   327

21.3 Occupational distribution of Moroccan-Jewish women in Montreal, 1969–2014, in per cent   328

22.1 Difference between country means for Jewish social and religious capital scales   338

22.2 Ordinary least squares (OLS) regression predicting Jewish social and religious capital   339

Figures

5.1 Grade 9 enrolment at TanenbaumCHAT, by annual tuition in 2010 constant dollars, 2010–2020 66

6.1 Degree of Jewishness by socio-economic characteristics 77

6.2 A causal model of degree of identity 82

8.1 Distribution of household income for Jews and non-Jews after taxes and transfers, by decile, Canada, 2010 103

10.1 Connectedness to Jewish life in city by desire for more connectedness: three main Jewish sub-communities, 2018 138

12.1 Mean residential dissimilarity index by religion, 2001 and 2011 172

12.2 Residential dissimilarity index for Muslims vis-à-vis other religious groups, 2001 and 2011 173

13.1 Negative attitudes towards Jews by residence, in per cent 188

13.2 Importance of religion/identity, Canada, Jews 2018 and Christians 2019, in per cent 192

16.1 Ethnic over-representation among UTMS graduates, Jews vs. selected non-Jewish Asian and Middle Eastern groups, 1918–2018 234

17.1 Identity maps of Jewish identity markers, Canada and seven other countries, 2013–2018 262

20.1 Probability of believing that Jews in Canada often face discrimination, by sample category 312

20.2 Probability of believing that antisemitism in the UK is a very big problem, by sample category 312

20.3 Probability of believing that antisemitism in France is a very big problem, by sample category 313

THE EVER-DYING PEOPLE?

Canada's Jews in Comparative Perspective

PART A

Introduction: Profiles of Canadian Jewish Life

1 The Ever-Dying People? Some Advantages of Comparative Analysis

ROBERT BRYM AND RANDAL F. SCHNOOR

The Ever-Dying People?

Philosopher Simon Rawidowicz referred to the Jews as the "ever-dying people." He meant that, beginning with Moses, the demise of the Jews has been prophesied in every era, although the prophecies have often been accompanied by an escape clause. Thus, according to the Bible, as the Jews were about to cross the Jordan River and gain sovereignty, Moses proclaimed their certain destruction – unless they obeyed God's laws (Deuteronomy 8:19). Similarly, soon after the 1903 Kishinev pogrom, Chaim Nachman Bialik, who was to become Israel's national poet, warned that the annihilation of the Jews was imminent – unless they returned to the desert, that is, their Promised Land (Bialik [1904] 2005). Significantly, however, even when there was no apparent escape clause, Jewish communities remained vibrant: "Our incessant dying means uninterrupted living, rising, standing up, beginning anew" (Rawidowicz [1967] 2017, 63).

Given the trials of Jewish history, the fear of extinction persists. The perceived threats to diaspora Jews are assimilation in benign settings and antisemitism in hostile environments (Brym 1993; Dershowitz 1997; Friedmann 1967; Gitelman 1998; Gordon and Horowitz 2016; Wasserstein 1996). However, reality is more complicated than some observers suggest.

In 2000, demographers at the Hebrew University of Jerusalem projected the trajectory of the Jewish diaspora population to 2080. They anticipated a nearly 40 per cent drop in the diaspora population over that period, including a 34 per cent fall in the US and a 15 per cent decline in Canada (DellaPergola, Rebhun, and Tolts 2000, 120, 123). They may turn out to be right. Yet now, more than two decades into their projection, things seem to have moved in the opposite direction in countries that attract a considerable number of Jewish immigrants. Australia, Canada, Germany, Mexico, and the United States – countries that encompass more than 80 per cent of diaspora Jewry – have seen their Jewish populations grow.

Canada's Jewish population has in fact been growing since Canada's first national census in 1871, increasing 7 per cent between 2001 and 2021, when it reached an estimated 393,500 (DellaPergola 2022, 327; Shahar 2014, 6). Recent survey data show that, on a variety of measures, the Canadian Jewish community is more cohesive than are many other Canadian ethnic groups and some other Jewish diaspora communities, notably that of the United States (Brym 2022; Brym, Neuman, and Lenton 2019). Nonetheless, many Canadian Jews are like the Jewish optimist in the old joke that asks, "What's the difference between a Jewish pessimist and a Jewish optimist?" Answer: The Jewish pessimist says, "Things can't get any worse." The Jewish optimist says, "Yes they can."

This type of Jewish "optimist" tends to assume that the social cohesion of Canadian Jewry is necessarily waning among all but the most religious and nationalistic Jews. Danger supposedly lurks in the fact that Canada is one of the most socially welcoming, economically secure, and religiously tolerant countries for Jews, past or present (Koffman 2021). It follows that, with the exceptions noted earlier, post-immigration generations inevitably learn to speak unaccented English or French, study and work in ethnically and religiously heterogeneous educational institutions and workplaces, and form long-term intimate relationships with people from other ethnic and religious groups. From this point of view, they are bound to become like the blond, blue-eyed, athletic, Jewish high school student nicknamed "Swede" in Philip Roth's *American Pastoral*. "Swede," writes Roth, "was actually only another one of our neighborhood Seymours whose forebears had been Solomons and Sauls and who would beget Stephens who would in turn beget Shawns." (As if to prove his point, Roth forgets the Shloimes and Sruliks who begat the Solomons and Sauls.) "Where was the Jew in him?" Roth asks of Swede (Roth 1997, 20).

Towards a Comparative Sociology of Canadian Jews

Roth's view of diaspora life is too sweeping. The plain fact is that identifiable socio-economic, political, and cultural conditions are associated with the degree to which Jews interact with one another and thus remain ethnically cohesive. True, under some socio-economic conditions Jews disperse over many occupations, income strata, neighbourhoods, and cities. Dispersion diminishes interaction among them. However, under other conditions, they concentrate in few occupations, income strata, neighbourhoods, and cities. Concentration increases interaction among them. Government policies have a bearing on ethnic group cohesion too. Some governments provide a high level of symbolic and financial support for multiculturalism, thus enhancing ethnic group cohesion. Other governments provide less support or none at all, thus diminishing ethnic group cohesion. In addition, where Jews are highly ethnically cohesive, they tend to establish their own schools, summer camps, welfare agencies, governing bodies, and other institutions. These institutions take on a life of their own; their very operation increases interaction among Jews (Breton 1964).

It is also important to note the important role that cultural preferences play in this story. In a given time and place, the sum of all the social-structural and political forces listed earlier instills in Jews a degree of preference for interaction with other Jews. This degree of preference is part of their ethnic and religious culture. The degree of preference changes with alterations in the conditions listed earlier. However, like all components of culture, it does not transform overnight, typically lagging behind social-structural change (Ogburn 1964). Its core elements can endure, albeit with changes, for many generations. Finally, we note that no Jewish community is homogeneous. Different parts of the community are exposed to the conditions we have identified to varying degrees.

Taking these considerations into account, one may say that the comparative sociology of Jews identifies the socio-economic, political, and cultural conditions that influence ethnic group cohesion and examines how and why they vary over time and place.[1] Much of this volume thus seeks to answer the question posed in its title, and it does so in a typically Jewish way; that is, by asking another question: How does variation in the socio-economic, political, and cultural conditions of Jewish communities account for some communities withering and others fructifying? The chief contribution of many of the authors in this collection is that they identify those conditions and show how they operate.

Overview

Canadian sociologists who study Canadian Jewry are partly to blame for the absence of a comparative, sociological perspective concerning Canadian Jews. Few in number, we have focused our efforts on producing case studies highlighting the unique characteristics of Canadian Jewry rather than on comparative research. Moreover, nearly all our surveys have been based on non-representative samples of single communities (Berman Jewish Databank n.d.).

We designed this volume to promote a different approach. Specifically, we assembled a team of Canadian and international sociologists to analyse Canadian Jewry sociologically and comparatively. Many of us relied on data from the 2018 Survey of Jews in Canada (the first nationwide study of its kind) and Canadian census data. An admixture of historians and historically inclined social scientists helped to place our analyses in broader context.

Specifically, the contributors to this collection make comparisons across three types of analytical unit. First, we compare the Canadian Jewish community to Jewish communities in other countries – the United States, the United Kingdom, Australia, and France, among others. Second, we compare Canadian Jews with members of other Canadian ethnic and religious groups – Christians, Muslims, Chinese, and Métis. And third, we compare Canadian Jews across a variety of social characteristics – age, income, gender, denomination, and so on. Comparing across each type of analytical unit helps us describe and explain variation in a wide range of social phenomena including ethnic identity, religiosity, intermarriage, perceptions of discrimination, political involvement, educational attainment, occupational choice, and so on. In other words, our comparisons allow us to identify how Canadian Jewry is different than and similar to Jewries in other countries and other ethnic and religious groups in Canada; how various categories of Canadian Jews are different than and similar to other categories of Canadian Jews; and how certain features of socio-economic, political, and cultural life explain this variation (cf. Tilly 1984, 80–4).

Part A provides necessary background for our later comparative analyses. Richard Menkis and Harold Troper sketch the history of Canadian Jewry since the Second World War. Charles Shahar offers an overview of the main demographic features of Canadian Jewry. Morton Weinfeld and Randal Schnoor then focus on two of the issues that have done most to mobilize Canadian Jewry over the years – respectively, how to deal with antisemitism and how to provide youth with a Jewish education.

The authors make a few comparative observations in Part A, but our comparative analyses begin full force in Part B, where we compare different categories of Canadian Jewry. Robert Brym and Feng Hou identify multiple degrees of Jewish identity in Canada and show how they are linked to different locations in Canada's socio-economic structure. Then, Joshua Harold demonstrates how socialization into Jewish culture develops over the life course and influences Jewish residential patterns. Naomi Lightman compares the annual household income of Canadian Jews and non-Jews, and of Canadian Jewish immigrants and non-immigrants.

Next, Ira Robinson assesses the circumstances that make Montreal's Jewish community distinct from that of Toronto. This exercise is followed by Marina Morgenshtern's analysis of how the intersection of race, class, ethnicity, and gender affect the social statuses and self-conceptions of Jews from the former Soviet Union as they adapt to life in Toronto. An attitudinal cleavage is growing in the Canadian Jewish community concerning Israeli policy on the Palestinians; Elizabeth Moorhouse-Stein concludes Part B by examining the social bases of that division.

Part C compares Canadian Jews with other Canadian ethnic and religious groups. Abdolmohammad Kazemipur draws parallels and distinctions between antisemitism and Islamophobia, taking the opportunity to explore ways in which Jews and Muslims can identify and express common interests. Reginald Bibby provides an overview of Christian–Jewish relations in Canada and compares Christians and Jews in terms of their religiosity, internal polarization, and attitudes towards each other. Feng Hou and Robert Brym measure the degree to which Chinese Canadians are becoming the country's "new Jews" in the sense that their occupational profiles are converging. A comparison of the treatment of Jews and Métis in recent Canadian censuses by David Koffman and Paul Gareau follows. Part C ends with Jordan A. Chad and Robert Brym identifying the social forces underlying change in the proportion of Jews, East Asians, South Asians, and non-Jewish Middle Easterners among graduates of the University of Toronto medical school between 1918 and 2018.

Part D compares the Canadian Jewish community with Jewish communities in other countries. Sergio DellaPergola focuses on variation in population growth, migration to Israel, age composition, and type of Jewish identification in Canada, the United States, Australia, the United Kingdom, France, Germany, Russia, Argentina, and Israel. Fern Chertok and Matthew Brookner assess the degree to which Canada's Jewish intermarriage pattern differs from that of the United States or merely lags behind the United States by a generation or so. The varying impact of social structure and culture on religious and ethnic retention among Jews from the former Soviet Union in Canada and the United States is the subject of the next chapter by Robert Brym, Anna Slavina, and Rhonda Lenton. Then, Daniel Staetsky uses recent survey data to explore the nature of Jewish perceptions of antisemitism in Canada, France, and the United Kingdom. Martin Messika and Yolande Cohen compare marriage and mobility patterns among Jews of Moroccan origin in Montreal and Paris. Finally, the book concludes with Adina Bankier-Karp's analysis of factors accounting for varying degrees of Jewish engagement in Canada and Australia.

Acknowledgments

The contributors to this volume range from young scholars with freshly minted PhDs and much evident potential to senior academics with international reputations for the high quality of their scholarly work. Responding gracefully to our editorial suggestions even when they ultimately rejected them, the contributors produced a book that, in our opinion, makes a landmark contribution to the study of Canadian Jewry. We are grateful to them all.

Of the twenty-six contributors, six are historians and twenty are social scientists (fifteen sociologists, three demographers, one political scientist, and one academic social worker). Every discipline has its theories, concepts, and methods, but we have tried as much as possible to make this volume accessible to the educated, non-specialist reader. This involved a concerted attempt to avoid disciplinary jargon and technical discussions. Multivariate analyses will be found in nine chapters, but we have tried to explain them in plain English.

We are indebted to the Anne Tanenbaum Centre for Jewish Studies at the University of Toronto, the Israel and Golda Koschitzky Centre for Jewish Studies at York University, and two contributors who wish to remain anonymous for subventions that allowed this book to be published a year earlier than would have been otherwise possible.

It takes a family (or two) to write (or even edit) a book. Robert Brym dedicates this book to Rhonda Lenton, Shira, Ben, Sophie, and Molly Friedland, Talia, Jeff, and Andie Greenspoon, and Ariella and Rick Zeifman – all unstinting in their intellectual and/or emotional support. Randal Schnoor thanks his wife Marsha for her tremendous support and encouragement of his work and dedicates this volume to her and their two outstanding teenage children, Jaeli and Shea.

The two editors have thoroughly enjoyed working together and are delighted that what started as a professional collaboration resulted in friendship.

Finally, we acknowledge that we do not deliver all that comparative sociology promises. We have merely taken a modest first step in the comparative sociological analysis of Canadian Jewry. Our hope is that others will follow our lead.

NOTE

1 We base these observations partly on Goldscheider and Zuckerman (1984), an important work that has not enjoyed the influence it deserves. We depart

from Goldscheider and Zuckerman only insofar as we emphasize the enduring effect of cultural preferences on ethnic group cohesion, which they downplay. See chapter 6 in this volume.

REFERENCES

Berman Jewish Databank. n.d. "Canada." Jewish Federations of North America. Accessed 15 July 2022, https://bit.ly/2SIhtlI.

Bialik, Chaim Nachman. (1904) 2005. "Ba-ir ha-hariga: In the City of Slaughter." Translated by A.M. Klein. *Prooftexts* 25 (1–2): 18–29. https://doi.org/10.1353/ptx.2006.0003.

Breton, Raymond. 1964. "Institutional Completeness of Ethnic Communities and the Personal Relations of Immigrants." *American Journal of Sociology* 70 (2): 193–205. https://doi.org/10.1086/223793.

Brym, Robert. 1993. "The Rise and Decline of Canadian Jewry? A Sociodemographic Profile." In *The Jews in Canada*, edited by Robert Brym, William Shaffir, and Morton Weinfeld, 22–38. Toronto: Oxford University Press.

Brym, Robert. 2022. "The Occupational and Social Integration of Jews in Canada." In *American Jewish Year Book 2021*, edited by Arnold Dashefsky and Ira M. Sheskin, Vol. 120, 299–312. Cham, Switzerland: Springer.

Brym, Robert, Keith Neumann, and Rhonda Lenton. 2019. *2018 Survey of Jews in Canada*. Toronto: Environics Institute. https://bit.ly/3mdvMvg.

DellaPergola, Sergio. 2022. "World Jewish Population, 2021." In *American Jewish Year Book 2021*, edited by Arnold Dashefsky and Ira M. Sheskin, Vol. 121, 313–412. Cham, Switzerland: Springer.

DellaPergola, Sergio, Uzi Rebhun, and Mark Tolts. 2000. "Prospecting the Jewish Future: Population Projections, 2000–2080." In *American Jewish Year Book 2000*, Vol. 100, edited by David Singer and Lawrence Grossman, 103–20. New York: The American Jewish Committee.

Dershowitz, Alan M. 1997. *The Vanishing American Jew*. Boston: Little, Brown.

Friedmann, Georges. 1967. *The End of the Jewish People?* Garden City, NY: Doubleday.

Gitelman, Zvi. 1998. "The Decline of the Diaspora Jewish Nation: Boundaries, Content, and Jewish Identity." *Jewish Social Studies* 4 (2): 112–32. https://doi.org/10.2979/JSS.1998.4.2.112.

Goldscheider, Calvin, and Alan S. Zuckerman. 1984. *The Transformation of the Jews*. Chicago: University of Chicago Press.

Gordon, Antony, and Richard M. Horowitz. 2016. "Will Your Grandchildren Be Jews: Updated." *Aish*, 13 December 2016. https://bit.ly/3CS9Hu7.

Koffman, David, ed. 2021. *No Better Home? Jews, Canada, and the Sense of Belonging*. Toronto: University of Toronto Press.

Leshchinsky, Yakov. 1947. "Tzu der sotziologie fun poylishn yidntum" [Yiddish: On the sociology of Polish Jewry]. In *Oyfn rand fun opgrunt: Fun yidishn lebn in poyln (1927–1933)* [*At the edge of the abyss: On Jewish life in Poland (1927–1933)*], 15–54. Buenos Aires: Tsentral-farband fun poylishe yidn in argentina.

Ogburn, William. 1964. *On Culture and Social Change: Selected Papers*. Edited by Otis Dudley Duncan. Chicago: University of Chicago Press.

Rawidowicz, Simon. (1967) 2017. *State of Israel, Diaspora, and Jewish Continuity: Essays on the "Ever-Dying People."* Hanover, NH: Brandeis University Press and University Press of New England.

Roth, Philip. 1997. *American Pastoral*. Boston: Houghton Mifflin.

Shahar, Charles. 2014. *2011 National Household Survey Analysis: The Jewish Population of Canada*. Part 1, *Basic Demographics*. Part 2, *Jewish Populations in Geographic Areas*. Toronto: Jewish Federations of Canada – UJA. https://bit .ly/3zXU2VH.

Tilly, Charles. 1984. *Big Structures, Large Processes, Huge Comparisons*. New York: Russell Sage Foundation.

Wasserstein, Bernard. 1996. *Vanishing Diaspora: The Jews in Europe since 1945*. London: Hamish Hamilton.

2 Canadian Jewry since the Second World War

RICHARD MENKIS AND HAROLD TROPER

The Second World War catalyzed the transformation of Canadian Jewry. Before the war, many Canadian Jews retained close family ties to Europe, and the organized Jewish community drew deeply on Europe for religious and organizational guidance and leadership. The Holocaust shattered those bonds. Before the war, many Canadian Jews were made to feel they were in Canada by sufferance rather than by right. However, about 17,000 Canadian Jews served in the Canadian military between 1939 and 1945, and on the home front, Jewish entrepreneurship and labour – in the manufacture of clothing and food, scrap recycling, and urban land development – proved essential to the war effort (Bessner 2018). By war's end, Jews argued that their participation in the national war effort had earned them a seat at the national table.

In the war's aftermath, European Jewry decimated, Canadian Jewry entered more securely into the North American orbit. The war also moved the larger Canadian economy away from dependence on extractive industries and agriculture towards urban-based manufacturing, service, and professional sectors. Canadian Jews, just 1.5 per cent of Canada's population, were more urban than any other Canadian religious or ethnic group. Fully 80 per cent lived in Montreal, Toronto, Winnipeg, and Vancouver (Rosenberg 1965).

From the Second World War to Canada's Centennial

For Canadian Jews, opening immigration to Holocaust survivors was an urgent priority. In this effort, the Canadian Jewish Congress (CJC), a national Jewish umbrella organization widely regarded as the political voice of the Jewish mainstream, working in concert with Jewish Immigrant Aid Services (JIAS), could claim a modest record of achievement (Burgard 2019). In 1947, the government approved the admission of

1,000 Jewish orphans and then agreed to the reunification of survivors with Canadian family.

However, the opening of Canada to Jewish immigration was less a result of Jewish lobbying than domestic economic self-interest. Fearing a shortage of workers, labour-intensive industries pressed government to reopen immigration from Europe. As demand for labour grew, the clothing manufacturing industry won approval for the intake of several thousand Jewish clothing workers (Abella and Troper 1982; Knight, Draper, and Bryck 2020). As immigration grew, so too did pressure for progressive immigration policy. In the decade following passage of the 1952 Immigration Act, Canada gradually eliminated immigration restrictions based on race, ethnicity, and creed, first from Europe and then from the rest of the world.

The admission of 54,000 Jewish refugees and displaced persons brought Canada's Jewish population to 254,368 in 1961. This number included 35,000 Holocaust survivors and their children who entered Canada during the first decade after the war (Bialystok 2000; A. Goldberg 2015; Rosenberg 1965, 185). Another 7,000 survivors arrived among the Hungarian refugees admitted to Canada following the failed 1956 Hungarian uprising (Hidas 2007). Additional survivors came after first going to Israel. Holocaust survivors were younger than other Canadian Jews. They married and had children, so within a decade approximately one in three Canadian Jews was either a Holocaust survivor or the child of a Holocaust survivor. For many survivors, the legacy of the Holocaust lived on and separated survivors from Canadian Jews who did not share Holocaust memories or understand why survivors didn't just get over it.

With the collapse of France's Middle Eastern and North African colonial aspirations in the 1950s, tens of thousands of Iraqi and North African Jews, fearing an upsurge in nationalist-fed antisemitism, packed their bags. Most left for Israel and France, but approximately 15,000, most from Morocco, settled in Montreal between 1956 and 1967. A smaller number of Spanish-speaking Moroccan Jews settled in Toronto. The mainstream Montreal Jewish community soon learned that strategies employed to ease the integration of Holocaust survivors did not fit the Moroccan experience. The Moroccans – Sephardi, more religiously traditional, and French-speaking – saw themselves as different from and often at odds with the prevailing Ashkenazi and English-speaking Montreal Jewish community. As Moroccan numbers grew so too did Moroccan Jewish social, religious, educational, and business institutions that often paralleled those of the larger and more established Montreal Jewish community (Cohen 2010).

The CJC and other communal outreach to newly arrived groups may sometimes have been awkward, insensitive, and heavy-handed, but newcomers were welcomed. At the same time, the CJC was banishing others from the official Jewish community. Before the war, the mainstream Jewish community shunned Jewish communists for fear of legitimizing antisemitic accusations that Jews were communists. After June 1941, with the USSR now allied against Nazism, the CJC worked in solidarity with pro-Soviet Jewish organizations. After the war, many on the Jewish far left united to establish the United Jewish People's Order (UJPO), which in addition to its secular cultural programming and educational agenda expressed hostility to Zionism. The national executive of the CJC, influenced by Cold War fears, expelled UJPO and called on its regional offices to do the same. Although there was some resistance to the decision in Vancouver, UJPO was effectively frozen out of the mainstream of Jewish communal life (Jones 1998).

The main focus of the CJC was combating domestic antisemitism, especially in accommodation, employment, and education. Prior to federal enactment of the Charter of Rights and Freedoms in 1982, Parliament and provincial legislatures reigned supreme when it came to change in law and policy. To win support for legislative action, the mainstream Jewish community took an incremental approach and tried to build social and political consensus in favour of change. In this effort, the CJC often worked closely with organized labour and other victim minorities. The Jewish Labour Committee served as a bridge between the CJC and the labour movement.

In 1950, the Supreme Court of Canada ruled that restrictive covenants preventing Jews or others purchasing property were illegal (Walker 1996). A year later, the Jewish-led human rights coalition celebrated Ontario's passage of Canada's first Fair Employment Practices Act and, in 1954, a Fair Accommodation Practices Act, creating a legal framework for barring racial, ethnic, and religious discrimination in employment and accommodation. In other provinces, including Quebec, the campaign faced opposition. However, despite resistance, by the early 1960s a legal framework of human rights protections, if still patchy, was in place across Canada. The CJC and its constituent organizations and coalition partners played a major role in this outcome (Walker 2002; Clément, Silver, and Trottier 2012).

Underscoring growing public openness to Jewish participation in politics, Toronto, long regarded a North American outpost of Anglo-conformity, elected a Jewish mayor, Nathan Phillips, in 1954. Phillips remained in office until 1962. In 1964, Torontonians elected a second Jewish mayor, Phillip Givens. Unlike Phillips, Givens maintained a high profile in Jewish circles (Troper 2021).

Increased acceptance did not mean abandoning group solidarity. True, in the two decades after the war, many in the Jewish community relocated from the inner-city, immigrant-receiving neighbourhoods to new suburbs. But suburban Jewish neighbourhoods boasted large synagogues, a wide range of Jewish social agencies, and streetscapes filled with businesses and white-collar professionals that catered to a Jewish clientele (Diamond 2000).

In Quebec, interactions between Jews and non-Jews followed a similar trajectory. After the Second World War, new spaces for dialogue emerged. Jewish and non-Jewish intellectuals came together. Roman Catholic clergy increasingly embraced thinking that led to the Second Vatican Council, developing a respectful relationship with Judaism and the Jewish community (Lacasse 2020). The election of Jean Lesage in 1960 promised to set Quebec on a new path towards liberal politics, economic self-sufficiency, and away from Church dominance, especially in education. Many Jews welcomed these developments. However, because the Québécois emphasized the primacy of the French language, and separatist sentiment grew, many English-speaking Jews in Quebec worried they would become marginalized (Anctil 2011).

In 1963, the federal government under Lester Pearson, looking to address growing discord in Quebec, established a Royal Commission charged with recommending steps to develop an equal partnership between English and French while "taking into account the contribution made by the other ethnic groups to the cultural enrichment of Canada" (Royal Commission on Bilingualism and Biculturalism 1970, 3). From the outset, some ethnic groups, led by the Ukrainians, pressed Canada to move beyond bilingualism and biculturalism to multiculturalism. However, some Québécois were convinced that talk of multiculturalism distracted attention from the mistreatment of French Canada within Confederation (Lapointe-Gagnon 2018). The issue also divided Canadian Jews. While the CJC establishment in Montreal headquarters was reluctant to endorse multiculturalism when the Québécois demurred, Jews elsewhere in Canada, especially in the West, favoured state endorsement of ethnic pluralism.

Another concern for Canadian Jewry at war's end was the struggle for a Jewish homeland (Bercuson 1989). Before the war, Canadian Jewish support for a sovereign Jewish state in Palestine was somewhat divided. After the war, the Holocaust still fresh in mind, reservations about a sovereign Jewish state were largely cast aside. Once Israel declared its independence in 1948, the vast majority of Canadian Jews embraced the fledgling state as a symbol of Jewish continuity and, equally important, as a haven for persecuted Jews.

Although few Canadian Jews, even committed Zionists, seriously considered resettling in Israel, they followed events in the Jewish state keenly. In 1961, Israel apprehended Adolf Eichmann and secreted him out of hiding in Argentina to stand trial for crimes against humanity and against the Jewish people. The Eichmann trial, which turned the memory of the Holocaust from the private agony of survivors to the shared legacy of all Jews, was closely followed by Jews around the world. Holocaust memory emerged from the Eichmann trail as a pillar of Jewish identity (Lipstadt 2011).

Survivor activism soon played itself out on the streets of Canadian cities. In Montreal and Toronto, self-styled Canadian Nazis took to the streets in search of media attention. They openly pledged to continue the work that Hitler had begun and distributed antisemitic literature in school yards and Jewish neighbourhoods. The CJC publicly dismissed the group as publicity-seeking misfits and pleaded for community calm as it worked quietly behind the scenes to ensure the safety of the Jewish community. But to many survivors, the call for calm sounded little more than code for indifference and inaction and a betrayal of the memory of 6 million dead. When a Nazi march was announced for a public park in downtown Toronto in 1965, thousands of survivors and their supporters, ignoring CJC pleas to stay away, showed up with the intention of confronting any Nazi who dared appear. The Nazis did not march, but the chance appearance of several bikers mistaken for Nazis sparked a riot.

The CJC denounced both the riot and the rioters. Survivors, in turn, castigated CJC leadership as out of step with the Jewish street. A serious community rupture was averted only when a beleaguered CJC leadership hastily reached out to prominent survivor spokespersons, inviting them to join the CJC's inner circle, especially as related to Israel and Holocaust issues. This development brought survivor voices into CJC deliberations even as the CJC continued a policy of backroom activism in promoting legislation to make hate propaganda a criminal offence.

In 1965, the Pearson government appointed a Special Committee on Hate Propaganda, chaired by McGill professor Maxwell Cohen, to advise on legislation. In 1970, prohibitions against advocating genocide and inciting or promoting hate against an identifiable group were added to the Criminal Code (Bialystok 2000; Troper 2010).

From the Six Day War to the War in Lebanon

In the spring of 1967, as Canada celebrated its centennial, the Canadian Jewish community was gripped by fear of another Holocaust. In the Middle East, Egypt demanded the UN remove its peacekeepers from the Sinai Peninsula. The UN complied, and Egypt moved its military, well-armed by the Soviet Union, into Sinai. With artillery positioned on the Gulf of Aqaba, Egypt closed the Gulf to Israeli shipping, and Syria, Iraq, and Jordan pledged support to Egypt. As Western countries declared their neutrality, Israel mobilized its forces and pundits warned of massive Israeli loss – if not total annihilation – should war break out. Panicked Canadian Jews, including many who were disengaged from their Jewishness, reached into their pockets as never before. When rumours began to circulate that Israel needed volunteers to fill the labour gap created by mobilization, Jewish offices were besieged by those who wanted to go.

At dawn on Monday, 5 June, Israel launched a pre-emptive air strike on Egypt's military infrastructure. While maintaining strict secrecy, Israel took control of the sky and its ground forces pushed into Sinai. Canadian Jews, ignorant of the war's progress, were terrified that their worst fears were being realized. Only late in the afternoon of 5 June did Israel reveal the extent of its military success. In Canada, Jewish despair transformed into celebration. After six days of war, a ceasefire agreement left Israel in control of the Sinai Peninsula, the West Bank, the Golan Heights, and East Jerusalem.

The impact of the war on Canadian Jewish identity was dramatic. Israel's victory was for many a Holocaust averted. And with Canadian Jews feeling themselves stakeholders in Israel's security and Jewry's future, participation in Jewish service organizations and synagogues increased. So too did parental demand for Jewish parochial schooling, university student calls for Jewish content on Canadian campuses, participation in Canada–Israel student exchange programs, Canadian ethno-tourism to Israel, and even a short-lived increase in Canadian immigration to Israel. Increased street-level Jewish activism breathed new life into the Soviet Jewry campaign demanding freedom to emigrate for Soviet Jews. The campaign, embraced by Jewish youth and employing street-level tactics adopted from the American civil rights movement, organized anti-Soviet protests across Canada and lobbied government to engage with the Soviet Union on behalf of Soviet Jews (Averich-Skapinker 1993).

At the same time, Canadian Jewry experienced change in its relationship to Canadian society and politics. Pierre Elliot Trudeau, elected prime minister in 1968, was comfortable with Jews. He was the member of Parliament for Mount Royal, arguably the most Jewish of all federal ridings. He was also a staunch defender of meritocracy, and under his stewardship, Jews were for the first time appointed to the federal cabinet and welcomed into the highest ranks of the public service. The shattering of Ottawa's glass ceiling hastened a decline in anti-Jewish discrimination in boardrooms, university faculties, and professional groups. Many Jews also appreciated that Trudeau was a bedrock federalist who entered federal politics in 1965, together with several other prominent Quebec federalists, precisely to counteract what he saw as the separatist threat in Quebec.

Quebec nationalists were especially disappointed in 1971 when Trudeau declared Canada a multicultural society and implemented several modest cultural programs to support this new vision. For Quebec nationalists, multiculturalism seemed a federal ploy designed to devalue Quebec's national aspirations by treating the Québécois as simply another ethnic or immigrant group. Ironically, multiculturalism policy also frustrated many supporters of multiculturalism who were hoping for more recognition and greater financial support – especially for heritage language training – than was forthcoming.

Jews in Ontario and Western Canada, accustomed to a poly-ethnic environment, appreciated increased symbolic support for pluralism and material support for cultural programming. Many provinces also supported multicultural programming in areas of provincial jurisdiction. However, anglophone Jewish Montreal was more concerned with the rising tide of Quebec nationalism and erosion of the English language. Jewish Montrealers looked on with concern as Quebec's Liberal government passed its Official Language Act in 1974 (Bill 22), which made French the official language of Quebec. While the Quebec government reassured English speakers that their rights would be protected, the new law limited immigrant and francophone access to English-language public schools. Unilingual English-speaking Jews wondered how long it would be before French language fluency would become a legal prerequisite for participation in Quebec economic and professional life.

Their fears heightened in 1976, when Quebec elected a Parti Québécois (PQ) government. The PQ viewed Quebec as a nascent nation state and Quebec anglophones as a "national minority." Promising a future referendum on whether Quebec should pursue sovereignty, the new government replaced Bill 22 with a Charter of the French Language designed "to make French the language of Government and the Law, as well as the normal and everyday language of work, instruction, communication, commerce, and business (Coleman 1981). Thousands of Montreal Jews now felt they had no future in Quebec (Wisse 1977). In particular, many well-educated and unilingual young adults began packing their bags and leaving Montreal for Toronto or elsewhere in Canada or the United States. At the same time, new Jewish immigrants to Canada bypassed Montreal (Robinson 2021).

The promised referendum, calling for an independent Quebec in an economic union with the rest of Canada, was held in 1980. Voters rejected sovereignty-association by a margin of 59.56 per cent to 40.44 per cent, but Jewish Montrealers continued to leave. Upwards of 40,000 Montreal Jews eventually decamped for Toronto or elsewhere. As a result, the age distribution of anglophone Montreal Jews skewed towards the elderly. At the same time, the Sephardi proportion of the community increased, and Sephardim looked to assume a more important role in the Montreal Jewish community.

At roughly the same time, fissures over Israel appeared in the community. In 1979, with an election looming, Conservative leader Joe Clark visited Israel. In a meeting with Prime Minister Menachem Begin, Clark was pressed to move the Canadian embassy from Tel Aviv to Jerusalem. As the federal election campaign began, Clark promised that, if elected, he would make the move. Clark went on to form a minority government, promptly announcing he intended honour his pledge. A firestorm erupted. Arab governments threatened a boycott of Canadian goods and services. Canadian corporations with interests in the Middle East pressed Ottawa to reverse the decision. The press accused the Jewish community of putting Israel's interests ahead of Canada's. Clark, looking to backpedal, appointed Robert Stanfield to recommend a way out of the mess. Stanfield's report recommended that the embassy stay put (Flicker 2003). Partly as a result of the fiasco, the Clark government fell on a vote of non-confidence.

In the subsequent election, Trudeau's Liberals were re-elected with a majority. Trudeau continued to engage with Jews and the organized Jewish community but kept himself at arm's length from organized Jewish lobbying on Israel. His relationship with Begin, already tense because of the latter's perceived meddling in Canadian affairs, worsened in June 1982 with the Israeli invasion of Lebanon. On 12 June, as Israeli forces pushed towards Beirut, Trudeau remarked that "the death and destruction visited on innocent Lebanese civilians are unacceptable." Begin lashed back so harshly that Israel's ambassador to Canada at first refused to deliver his note (Miller 1991). As Israeli troops encircled Beirut, the Phalange, a predominantly Christian Lebanese right-wing militia, entered two Palestinian refugee camps and, in plain view of Israeli observers, murdered between 1,000 and 1,500 people. The Israeli public was horrified, and a peace movement, coalescing around Peace Now, organized an antiwar protest in Tel Aviv that mobilized 400,000 Israelis, 10 per cent of the country's population. In Canada, Jewish community support for Israel remained solid, but unquestioning support began to fray. Small groups of Canadian Jews came together to form chapters of

Canadian Friends of Peace Now. Some rabbis criticized Israel from the pulpit. Mainstream Jewish leaders prevaricated, wishing neither to become isolated on foreign policy issues nor elicit widespread anti-Israel sentiment (Weinfeld 2013).

From the Charter of Rights and Freedoms to the Early Twenty-First Century

A new era for Canada and Canadian Jews began in 1985, when the Charter of Rights and Freedoms became the supreme law of the land. In addition to enumerating core rights such as freedom of expression, assembly, religion, and the press, the Charter guaranteed "equal treatment before and under the law, and equal protection and benefit of the law without discrimination" (sec. 15.1). It also required that the Charter be interpreted in a multicultural context (Elman 1996).

The Charter raised the possibility of individuals or groups turning to the courts to seek remedy for violations of individual or collective rights. For example, for more than forty years the organized Jewish community had unsuccessfully lobbied the Ontario government to rescind a 1944 provision of the Ontario Education Act mandating compulsory religious instruction in Ontario public schools, but excusing individual children whose parents requested exemption. In 1990, a parent went to court claiming compulsory instruction violated freedom of religion and anti-discrimination. The Ontario Court of Appeal agreed, declaring the requirement unconstitutional (Sable 1998).

The Jewish community also learned that litigation in the age of the Charter could be problematic. The organized Canadian Jewish community supported the 1970 legislation against hate propaganda, but how would the courts balance freedom of speech with the requirement that the Charter be interpreted in a multicultural context? Two trials of Holocaust deniers in 1985, and their subsequent appeals, brought this question to the fore.

The first trial involved Ernst Zündel, a Toronto neo-Nazi Holocaust denier and publisher. Frustrated by Zündel's ongoing publications, members of the activist Holocaust Remembrance Association secured a temporary mail ban against Zündel in 1981. They unsuccessfully pressed the Attorney General of Ontario to prosecute Zündel based on the 1970 hate speech legislation. In November 1983, the Association's leader swore out a complaint under a seldom-used provision of the Criminal Code outlawing the dissemination of false news. The Attorney General of Ontario then instructed the Crown to take on the case. The trial's focus was *Did Six Million Really Die? The Truth at Last*, which reprinted a pamphlet claiming the Holocaust was a hoax and that Jews were using the Holocaust for financial and political gain.

The prosecution was required to satisfy the court that the Holocaust took place and that Zündel knew it. To makes its case, the Crown presented the testimony of Holocaust scholars and survivors' eye-witness accounts. The defence put its own "experts" on the stand while attempting to cast doubt on the veracity of survivor testimony. To Canadian Jews it was as if the Holocaust was on trial. Many were shocked not just by Zündel's attempted "assassination of memory" but also by the insensitivity of newspapers printing absurd claims by Zündel and his attorney that swimming pools could be found at Auschwitz but not gas chambers. In the end, Zündel was found guilty of spreading false news, but his conviction was overturned based on errors in jury selection and the judge's definition of the level of proof needed to establish guilt. Zündel was retried and again found guilty. On appeal, the Supreme Court of Canada quashed Zündel's second conviction, holding the law under which Zündel had been charged violated the Charter's guarantee of freedom of expression (Hill 1989).

While the activities of Zündel were distressing, many Canadians were even more horrified by the case of James Keegstra. The mayor of Eckville, Alberta, and a high school teacher, Keegstra brought his antisemitism into the classroom, teaching students that Jews were enemies of Christianity, created worldwide upheaval, and would stop at nothing for their cause, including fabricating the Holocaust to win sympathy (Bercuson and Wertheimer 1985). After a parent complained, Keegstra was charged under the 1970 law and found guilty of willfully promoting hatred of Jews. Keegstra's case dragged on for fourteen years, involving three appeals and two retrials. In the end, his conviction was upheld by the Supreme Court of Canada, which narrowly rejected the claim that hate speech was protected under the freedom of expression provision of the 1985 Charter of Rights and Freedoms.

Also in 1985, rumours circulated that Canada was harbouring Nazi war criminals, including the notorious Auschwitz doctor, Josef Mengele. Prime Minister Brian Mulroney established the Deschênes Commission to enquire into the presence of Nazi war criminals in Canada. The relationship between members of the Jewish and Ukrainian communities had been fraught for decades because Canadian Jews believed many Ukrainians who came to Canada after the war were Nazi collaborators who participated in the extermination of Jews. The Deschênes Commission heightened those tensions (Troper and Weinfeld 1988).

New challenges also emerged as the Canadian Jewish community continued to grow in size and diversity. Most population growth was due to immigration, not natural increase. From 1981 to 2021, the Jewish community grew by about 80,000 (26 per cent), largely as a result of intake from the Soviet Union, but also from Israel, South Africa, the United States, France, and Argentina (Shahar 2020). Like the surge of Sephardi immigration into Montreal during the late 1950s and 1960s, the integration of former Soviet Jews, approximately 70 per cent of whom settled in the Greater Toronto Area, became a focus of the organized Jewish community, but was not without its challenges (see chapter 10 in this volume). Some arrived in Canada directly from the Soviet Union. Others came via Israel. The latter included a large percentage of Jewish couples, the former a considerable percentage of intermarried couples. Consequently, the two groups tend to differ in their respective Jewish attachments and desire to engage with the Jewish mainstream (Brym, Neumann, and Lenton 2019).

Immigration was not the only demographic factor affecting the Jewish community. While Canadian Jews remained overwhelmingly urban, Montreal, Winnipeg, and small centres continued to lose Jewish population to Toronto, Ottawa, Calgary, and Vancouver, Canada's engines of economic growth. Toronto's Jewish population ballooned to almost twice the size of Montreal's, and the Vancouver community grew fastest in percentage terms, replacing Winnipeg as Canada's third-largest Jewish community.

The choice of Anglo-Jewish Montrealers to leave was difficult, but it was the choice that many felt forced to make. Even while Anglo-Jewish Montrealers increasingly learned French, for many the fear of being marginalized by Quebec nationalists did not subside. In the 1994 Quebec provincial election, the Parti Québécois under Jacques Parizeau won a majority. Parizeau pledged to hold another referendum on Quebec sovereignty within a year of his election. He kept his promise. The organized Jewish community joined the "no" campaign. Voting day, 31 October 1995, saw a turnout of more than 93 per cent of eligible voters. About 60 per cent of francophone voters cast their ballots in favour of sovereignty, but the "no" side managed a slim victory of just more than 1 per cent. In a bitter concession speech, Parizeau spoke about the "us" as the francophone voters who had voted "yes" and later said sovereignty had been defeated by "l'argent et les votes ethniques," money and ethnic votes. Quebec Jews had little doubt that Parizeau was pointing to them as responsible for the loss. While the loss came as a relief for the great majority of Jews in Quebec, it left many uneasy at their future prospects.

A sense of unease also developed among Canadian Jews about Canada–Israel relations. Canadian Jews, who sensed the chill between

Trudeau and Begin, were convinced that Brian Mulroney's election as prime minister in 1984 would translate into renewed warmth. And in the first few years of his government, Israel could count on Canadian government backing. Mulroney's appointment of Joe Clark – who had supported moving the Canadian embassy to Jerusalem – as secretary of state for external affairs also seemed to promise continuing Canadian support of Israeli policies. However, Clark, in concert with Middle East experts in the Department of External Affairs, set out to recalibrate Canada's relationship with Israel, the Palestine Liberation Organization (PLO), and Israel's Arab neighbours. Suddenly, to the consternation of the Israel lobby, Canada was no longer in lockstep with Israel at the United Nations, voicing opposition to Israeli settlement policies on the West Bank and providing funds to Palestinians in Lebanon and the West Bank (Miller 1991).

A greater shock to Canada's pro-Israel lobby was yet to come at the hands of Clark. The outbreak of the first intifada in late 1987 and Israel's suppression tactics provoked international concern. In late 1987, Mulroney allowed that in his view Israel was acting "with restraint." Clark disagreed. In an address to the annual meeting of the Canada-Israel Committee in Ottawa on 10 March 1988, Clark said it was time "to speak plainly." He shocked his audience by claiming "human rights violations such as we have witnessed in the West Bank and Gaza, in these past agonizing weeks, are totally unacceptable, and in many cases illegal under international law." Many booed Clark and/or walked out. Even more disconcerting was wide English and French press endorsement of Clark's remarks and cautions that Jews would do well to tone down their support for Israel lest they be suspected of dual loyalty (Miller 1991). Clark's often-cited speech represented a low point. More often than not, Canada stood with Israel, but an uncritical pro-Israel Canada response was no longer a given. When the Security Council of the United Nations voted to condemn Israel's handling of the second intifada in late 2000, Canada, a non-permanent member, voted with the majority while the Americans abstained (D. Goldberg 2001).

Although Canadian Jewish support for Israel remains solid, across-the-board community endorsement of every Israeli policy, especially among younger Jews, was by no means guaranteed. In the late 1980s, for example, the *Canadian Jewish News* reported a disagreement between a past and present president of the CJC over Israel's need to show more openness to the PLO. The paper subsequently described a rancorous Toronto synagogue debate between a representative of Peace Now and the president of the CJC (Taras and Weinfeld 1993). At the CJC triennial plenary held in Toronto in 1992, Canadian Friends of Peace Now moved a resolution calling for an end to "further settlement in the territories during peace negotiations" (Waller 1994). It was defeated handily, but it too underscored growing discord within the community as it neared the turn of the century.

Epilogue

The Canadian Jewish community has grown while most other diaspora communities have shrunk. Canada, thanks largely to ongoing immigration, is now home to the fourth-largest community in the Jewish diaspora – perhaps soon the third largest if out-migration from France continues at its present rate. In contrast to an earlier day, Canadian Jews enjoy greatly increased economic opportunity and wide public acceptance marked by high levels of social and economic mobility and expanding participation in Canadian social, cultural, and political life. However, for some, the widening circle of Jewish acceptance in Canada is accompanied by fear for the Jewish future.

As the organized Jewish community searches for ways to ensure continuity in the face of increasing out-marriage, division grows over Israel's policies regarding the Palestinians and other matters. We have seen how consensus on Israel has gradually shifted since the founding of the Jewish state in 1948 to a point where the 2018 Survey of Jews in Canada notes a widening generational rift over whether Jewish settlement in the West Bank is moral let alone legal under international law, whether settlements help or hurt Israel's security interests, and whether the Israeli government is sincere in its stated desire for peace and support of a two-state solution. Of late, intra-Jewish community discord has assumed institutional legitimacy with the establishment of competing fundraising and lobbying groups that challenge the historically strong Canadian Jewish accord in support of Israeli government policies.

Israel's policies regarding its Palestinian minority and Palestinians in the occupied territories threaten to divide Jew and non-Jew in Canada too. Many Canadian Jews are alarmed at what they see as increased levels of public and media censure of Israeli expansionism, an especially divisive issue on Canadian university campuses. According to many members of the Jewish community, a new antisemitism of the left has crystallized, an antisemitism of delegitimization that extends well beyond acceptable criticism of Israel, its leaders, parties, and policies to demonize the Jewish state and define Jews out of the family of nations. At the same time, the organized Jewish community in Canada is awake to the growth of right-wing nationalist jingoism that often embraces antisemitic tropes including Holocaust denial, not to mention desecration of synagogues and Jewish cemeteries.

There was a new dawn for Canadian Jews at the end of the Second World War. The Canadian Jewish community basked in the light and warmth of a new tolerance in the changing mosaic. Now, it cannot avoid seeing some dark omens for the future.

REFERENCES

Abella, Irving, and Harold Troper. 1982. *None Is Too Many: Canada and the Jews of Europe, 1933–1948*. Toronto: Lester & Orpen Dennys.

Anctil, Pierre. 2011. "A Community in Transition: The Jews of Montreal." *Contemporary Jewry* 31 (3): 225–45. https://doi.org/10.1007/s12397-011 -9067-6.

Averich-Skapinker, Mindy B. 1993. "Canadian Jewish Involvement with Soviet Jewry, 1970–1990: The Toronto Case Study." PhD diss., University of Toronto.

Bercuson, David. 1989. "The Zionist Lobby and Canada's Palestine Policy, 1941–1948." In *The Domestic Battleground: Canada and the Arab–Israeli Conflict*, edited by David Taras and David Goldberg, 17–36. Montreal: McGill-Queen's University Press.

Bercuson, David, and Douglas Lloyd Wertheimer. 1985. *A Trust Betrayed: The Keegstra Affair*. Toronto: Doubleday Canada.

Bessner, Ellen. 2018. *Double Threat: Canadian Jews, the Military, and World War II*. Toronto: University of Toronto Press.

Bialystok, Franklin. 2000. *Delayed Impact: The Holocaust and the Canadian Jewish Community*. Montreal: McGill-Queen's University Press.

Brym, Robert, Keith Neumann, and Rhonda Lenton. 2019. *2018 Survey of Jews in Canada: Final Report*. Toronto: Environics Institute for Survey Research. https://bit.ly/3mdvMvg.

Burgard, Antoine. 2019. "'The Fight on Educating the Public to Equal Treatment for All Will Have to Come Later': Jewish Refugee Activism and Anti-immigration Sentiment in Immediate Post-war Canada." *London Journal of Canadian Studies* 34 (1): 103–22. https://doi.org/10.14324/111.444.ljcs.2019v34.006.

Clément, Dominique, Will Silver, and Daniel Trottier. 2012. *The Evolution of Human Rights in Canada*. Ottawa: Canadian Human Rights Commission. http://bitly.ws/sMrU.

Cohen, Yolande. 2010. "The Jews in Morocco and Sephardic Jews in Canada: Migrations and Identity Creation." *Archives juives* 43 (2): 132–44. https:// doi.org/10.3917/aj.432.0132.

Coleman, William D. 1981. "From Bill 22 to Bill 101: The Politics of Language under the Parti Québécois." *Canadian Journal of Political Science* 14 (3): 33–44. https://doi.org/10.1017/S0008423900047053.

Diamond, Etan. 2000. *And I Will Dwell in Their Midst: Orthodox Jews in Suburbia*. Chapel Hill: University of North Carolina Press.

Elman, Bruce P. 1996. "The Constitutionalization of Multiculturalism in Canada: The Jewish Legal Role." In *Multiculturalism, Jews and Identities in Canada*, edited by Howard Adelman and John Simpson, 69–84. Jerusalem: Magnes Press.

Flicker, Charles. 2003. "Next Year in Jerusalem: Joe Clark and the Jerusalem Embassy Affair." *International Journal* 58 (1): 115–38. https://doi.org/10.1177/002070200305800106.

Goldberg, Adara. 2015. *Holocaust Survivors in Canada: Exclusion, Inclusion, Transformation, 1947–1955*. Winnipeg: University of Manitoba Press.

Goldberg, David. 2001. "The Post-statehood Relationship: A Growing Friendship." In *From Immigration to Integration: The Canadian Jewish Experience*, edited by Ruth Klein and Frank Dimant, 135–46. North York, ON: Institute for International Affairs, B'nai Brith Canada.

Hidas, Peter I. 2007. "Canada and the Hungarian Jewish Refugees, 1956–57." *East European Jewish Affairs* 37 (1): 75–89. https://doi.org/10.1080/13501670701197953.

Hill, Leonidas E. 1989. "The Trial of Ernst Zündel: Revisionism and the Law in Canada." *Simon Wiesenthal Center Annual* 6: 165–219.

Jones, Faith. 1998. "Between Suspicion and Censure: Attitudes towards the Jewish Left in Postwar Vancouver." *Canadian Jewish Studies* 6: 1–24. https://doi.org/10.25071/1916-0925.19832.

Knight, Andrea, Paula Draper, and Nicole Bryck. 2020. *The Tailor Project: How 2,500 Holocaust Survivors Found a New Life in Canada*. Toronto: Second Story Press.

Lacasse, Simon-Pierre. 2020. "Les Juifs de la Révolution tranquille: Regards d'une minorité religieuse sur le Québec de 1945 à 1976." PhD diss., University of Ottawa.

Lapointe-Gagnon, Valérie. 2018. *Panser le Canada: Une histoire intellectuelle de la Commission Laurendeau-Dunton*. Montreal: Boréal.

Lipstadt, Deborah E. 2011. *The Eichmann Trial*. New York: Schocken.

Miller, Ronnie. 1991. *From Lebanon to the Intifada: The Jewish Lobby and Canadian Middle East Policy*. Lanham, MD: University of America Press.

Robinson, Ira. 2021. "By the Rivers of the St. Lawrence: The Montreal Jewish Community and Its Postmemory." In *No Better Place: Canada, Its Jews, and the Question of Home*, edited by David Koffman, 161–76. Toronto: University of Toronto Press.

Rosenberg, Louis. 1965. "Two Centuries of Canadian Jewish Life." In *Canadian Jewish Reference Book and Directory, 1965*, edited by Eli Gottesman, 180–96. Montreal: Jewish Institute of Higher Research, Central Rabbinical Seminary of Canada.

Royal Commission on Bilingualism and Biculturalism. 1970. *Report of the Royal Commission on Bilingualism and Biculturalism*. Book IV, *The Cultural Contribution of the Other Ethnic Groups*. Ottawa: Queen's Printer for Canada. https://bit.ly/3P8e3B5.

Sable, Martin. 1998. "George Drew and the Rabbis: Religious Education in Ontario's Public Schools." *Canadian Jewish Studies* 6: 25–53. https://doi.org/10.25071/1916-0925.19833.

Shahar, Charles. 2020. "Canadian Jewish Population, 2019." In *American Jewish Year Book 2019*, Vol. 119, edited by Arnold Dashefsky and Ira M. Sheskin, 233–45. Cham, Switzerland: Springer.

Taras, David, and Morton Weinfeld. 1993. "Continuity and Criticism: North American Jews and Israel." In *The Jews in Canada*, edited by Robert Brym, Morton Weinfeld, and William Shaffir, 293–310. Toronto: Oxford University Press.

Troper, Harold. 2010. *The Defining Decade: Identity, Politics and the Canadian Jewish Community in the 1960s*. Toronto: University of Toronto Press.

Troper, Harold. 2021. "Nathan Phillips: The Election of Toronto's First Jewish Mayor." In *No Better Place: Canada, Its Jews, and the Question of Home*, edited by David Koffman, 147–60. Toronto: University of Toronto Press.

Troper, Harold, and Morton Weinfeld. 1988. *Old Wounds: Jews, Ukrainians, and the Hunt for Nazi War Criminals in Canada*. Toronto: Viking.

Walker, James W. St. G. 1996. "Canadian Anti-Semitism and Canadian Response: The Case of Nobel and Wolf." In *Multiculturalism, Jews and Identities in Canada*, edited by Howard Adelman and John Simpson, 37–68. Jerusalem: Magnes Press.

Walker, James W. St. G. 2002. "The 'Jewish Phase' in the Movement for Racial Equality in Canada." *Canadian Ethnic Studies* 34 (1): 1–30.

Waller, Harold M. 1994. "Canada." In *American Jewish Year Book 1994*, Vol. 94, edited by David Singer and Ruth R. Seldin, 229–47. New York: The American Jewish Committee.

Weinfeld, Morton. 2013. "If Canada and Israel Are at War, Who Gets My Support? Challenges of Competing Diaspora Loyalties: Marshall Sklare Award Lecture." *Canadian Jewish Studies* 21 (1): 28–50. https://doi.org/10.25071/1916-0925.39907.

Wisse, Ruth R. 1977. "Quebec's Jews: Caught in the Middle." *Commentary*, September 1977. http://bitly.ws/t2U5.

3 Demographic Overview

CHARLES SHAHAR

While the central data set for the purposes of this book is the 2018 Survey of Jews in Canada, this chapter paints a broad demographic profile of Canadian Jews by focusing mainly on the 2011 National Household Survey (NHS). The NHS, which replaced the previously scheduled 2011 Census of Canada, offers a starting point for considering later developments and thus provides a foundation for other chapters in this volume. The 2016 census did not include a question on religion and is therefore not useful for identifying Jews in a comprehensive fashion. Because of a change in question wording, it even undercounted the number of ethnically defined Jews in the country by a wide margin. Detailed results of the 2021 census will not be available until after the publication of this volume, so only a few preliminary results will be mentioned in this chapter.

Relying on the 2011 NHS, this chapter provides gender and age breakdowns, population distributions across provinces and major census metropolitan areas (CMAs), and analyses of seniors, low-income distribution, and intermarriage. The appendix outlines how Jewish identity is defined here, along with other methodological considerations related to the 2011 NHS.

Basic Demographics

Based on the NHS results and estimates of natural increase and net migration over the past decade, Sergio DellaPergola (2022, 327) puts Canada's core Jewish population at 393,500 in 2021, a 2.1 per cent increase since 2011 and an increase of 9.6 per cent since 1991 (see table 3.1). In contrast, Canada's total population grew 36.5 per cent between 1991 and 2021.

The Jewish population has been increasing since Jews began to settle in Canada in significant numbers at the turn of the last century. Peak

30   Charles Shahar

levels of growth occurred between 1901 and 1931, between 1945 and 1971, and between 1981 and 1991. On the other hand, the Jewish population declined from 1.3 per cent of the total Canadian population in 1991 to 1.1 per cent in 2021. In terms of size, Canadian Jewry ranked seventeenth among the country's ethnic groups in 2011.

On a broader scale, the estimated world Jewish population was 13,746,100 in 2012 and 15,166,200 in 2021 (DellaPergola 2013, 2022). Some 57.1 per cent of world Jewry lived in the diaspora in 2012, compared to 42.9 per cent in Israel. The corresponding percentages for 2021 were 54.7 per cent and 45.3 per cent.

In 2019, the Canadian Jewish community was the fourth largest in the world. Israel had the largest Jewish population (6.7 million), followed by the United States (5.7 million) and France (450,000). The Jewish populations of the United Kingdom (292,000), Argentina (180,000), Russia (165,000), Germany (118,000), Australia (118,000), and Brazil (92,600) ranked fifth through tenth. The Canadian Jewish community comprised 2.6 per cent of all Jews in the world in 2021 and 4.7 per cent of Jews in the diaspora.

Gender and Age

According to the NHS, there was a slightly higher proportion of females than males in the Canadian Jewish population in 2011 – 50.4 per cent female vs. 49.6 per cent male. Table 3.2 provides an age breakdown for Canadian Jews and non-Jews. In 2011, the Jewish population had a somewhat larger proportion of children 0–14 years of age than did the total population (18.2 per cent and 17 per cent, respectively). It had a similar percentage in the 15–24 age cohort compared with the total Canadian population (13.4 per cent and 13.2 per cent, respectively). In the 25–44 age cohort, the discrepancy between the two distributions was more marked. Some 23.5 per cent of Jews fell into this age cohort, compared to 26.7 per cent of Canada's total population. The Jewish community also had a smaller proportion in the 45–64 age cohort than did the Canadian population (28 per cent and 29.3 per cent, respectively). The Jewish community had a significantly larger proportion of seniors than did the total Canadian population (16.9 per cent vs. 13.9 per cent).

The median age of the Canadian Jewish population increased steadily from 33.6 years in 1971 to 40.5 years in 2011. Between 1991 and 2011, the Jewish community's median age increased at a significantly slower pace than that of the total Canadian population: 3.2 years for Jews compared to 6.9 years for the total Canadian population. The gap in the median ages of the two populations consequently narrowed considerably,

Demographic Overview 31

Table 3.1. Jewish population of Canada, 1901–2021

Year	Jewish population	Change from previous census	Change from previous census (%)
2021	393,500	+1,835	+2.1
2011	391,665	+17,605	+4.7
2001	374,060	+14,950	+4.2
1991	359,110	+45,245	+14.4
1981	313,865	+27,315	+9.5
1971	286,550	+32,182	+12.7
1961	254,368	+49,532	+24.2
1951	204,836	+36,251	+21.5
1941	168,585	+12,819	+8.2
1931	155,766	+30,321	+24.2
1921	125,445	+50,685	+67.8
1911	74,760	+58,267	+353.3
1901	16,493	–	–

Note: The 2021 estimate is from DellaPergola (2022, 327). The 2011 figure is from the NHS. Other figures are based on decennial Canadian censuses, 1901–2001. Figures for 1991, 2001, and 2011 are based on the Revised Jewish Definition described in Appendix 1 of Shahar (2014). Other census figures are based on the Jewish Standard Definition (1971 and 1981) or were derived from the religion or ethnicity variables individually (1901 to 1961). The Jewish Standard Definition was used to calculate population increase from 2011 (385,345) to 2021.
Source: Statistics Canada (2011).

standing at 4.1 years in 1991 and just 0.4 years in 2011. The ethnic groups with the highest median ages are the British (48.7 years), Americans (45.9 years), French (44.8 years), Germans (40.7 years), and Jews (40.5 years). These groups are generally established communities whose peak periods of immigration have long passed.

Population Distributions across Provinces

Jews live in every corner of Canada, but nearly six in ten reside in Ontario, one in four in Quebec, and one in ten in British Columbia. Fewer than 5 per cent of Canadian Jews live in the other provinces and territories.

In Ontario, Jews comprised slightly less than 2 per cent of the total population, in Quebec and Manitoba, 1.2 per cent, and in all the other provinces and territories combined less than 1 per cent. Jews constitute particularly small minorities in the Atlantic provinces and Saskatchewan (both 0.2 per cent), and a negligible percentage in the northern territories.

Of the ten provinces, six experienced population gain between 2001 and 2011 (Prince Edward Island, Saskatchewan, Newfoundland and

32 Charles Shahar

Table 3.2. Canadian Jewish, non-Jewish, and total populations by age cohort, 2011

Age cohort	Jews		Non-Jews		Total	
	Number	%	Number	%	Number	%
0–14	71,280	18.2	5,521,525	17.0	5,592,800	17.0
15–24	52,390	13.4	4,271,675	13.2	4,324,065	13.2
25–44	92,200	23.5	8,663,180	26.7	8,755,385	26.7
45–64	109,515	28.0	9,519,020	29.3	9,628,535	29.3
65+	66,280	16.9	4,485,260	13.8	4,551,535	13.9
Total	391,665	100.0	32,460,660	100.0	32,852,320	100.0

Note: The total per cent does not equal 100.0 due to rounding error.
Source: Statistics Canada (2011).

Labrador, British Columbia, Alberta, and Ontario). Two registered losses (Manitoba and Quebec), and two remained nearly the same (Nova Scotia and New Brunswick).

Population Distributions across CMAs

The great majority of Ontario Jews lived in the Toronto CMA in 2011 – 188,710 individuals, 83.3 per cent of the province's Jewish population. Ottawa had the next largest Jewish population with 13,355 individuals, or 5.9 per cent of the Jews in Ontario. Hamilton followed with 5,110 Jews, 2.3 per cent of the province's Jewish population. London had 2,675 Jews (1.2 per cent). CMAs with about 1,000–2,000 Jews included Kitchener-Cambridge-Waterloo, Oshawa, Windsor, Barrie, St. Catharines-Niagara, and Kingston.

In Quebec, nearly all Jews lived in the Montreal CMA in 2011: 90,780 individuals, or 97 per cent of all Jewish residents in the province. No other city in Quebec had a Jewish population approaching 1,000. In British Columbia, the Vancouver CMA had a Jewish population of 26,255 individuals in 2011, three quarters of all Jews residing in the province. The Victoria Jewish community numbered 2,740, comprising 7.8 per cent of Jews in British Columbia. Kelowna had the third largest Jewish population with 900 individuals, 2.6 per cent of Jews in this province. All other metropolitan areas in British Columbia numbered fewer than 500 Jews each.

The Winnipeg CMA had 13,690 Jews in 2011, 95.4 per cent of Jews in Manitoba. Regina had a Jewish population of 900, 47.2 per cent of the total Jews in Saskatchewan, while Saskatoon's 735 Jewish residents comprised 38.6 per cent of the province's Jewish population. Calgary had a Jewish population of 8,335, or 52.8 per cent of Alberta's Jewish residents. Edmonton had 5,550 Jews (35.1 per cent).

Table 3.3. CMAs with a Jewish population of more than 1,000, 2011

Census Metropolitan Area	Jewish Population	% of Canadian Jewish Population
Toronto, ON	188,715	48.2
Montreal, QC	90,780	23.2
Vancouver, BC	26,255	6.7
Ottawa-Gatineau, ON	14,010	3.6
Winnipeg, MB	13,690	3.5
Calgary, AB	8,335	2.1
Edmonton, AB	5,550	1.4
Hamilton, ON	5,110	1.3
Victoria, BC	2,740	0.7
London, ON	2,675	0.7
Halifax, NS	2,120	0.5
Kitchener-Cambridge-Waterloo, ON	2,010	0.5
Windsor, ON	1,515	0.4
Kingston, ON	1,185	0.3
Rest of Canada	26,975	6.9
Total	391,665	100.0

Source: Statistics Canada (2011).

Finally, in Atlantic Canada, Halifax had the largest number of Jews: 2,120 individuals, or 50.7 per cent of the total Atlantic Jewish community. All the other communities in Atlantic Canada had substantially smaller Jewish populations, with Moncton, Fredericton, Saint John, and St. John's having a combined population of 880 Jews, 21 per cent of the Jews in Atlantic Canada.

Table 3.3 shows the Jewish population distribution across the CMAs with the largest Jewish populations.

A cross-Canada comparison of Jewish populations within districts and municipalities reveals that the area with the highest density of Jews was Hampstead in the Montreal CMA, where Jews comprised 75.2 per cent of the total population. The next highest density is Côte Saint-Luc, also in the Montreal CMA, where Jews comprised 62.1 per cent of the total population. The district of Thornhill (Vaughan) in the Toronto CMA had the third highest Jewish density in the country, with Jews comprising 39.6 per cent of the total population.

Seniors

In 2011, there were 66,280 Jews over the age of 64 in Canada. This means that one in six Canadian Jews was a senior. Just over one half of elderly Canadian Jews were "young elderly" (less than 75 years of age), one third were between 75 and 84, and just over 15 per cent were 85+ years of age. The 85+ cohort increased from 7,985 in 2001 to 10,125 in 2011. This is the largest number of "older" elderly in the history of Canadian Jewry. Given the substantial number of Jews in the pre-elderly cohort (55–64 years) in 2011, the senior population now includes a large number of baby boomers. The increase in the "older" elderly reflects a bulge that has moved up the age distribution in the last few decades. Many of these individuals are parents of the baby boomers.

The largest number of Jewish elderly in the country (30,960) resided in the Toronto CMA. Montreal had 18,525 Jewish seniors, followed by Vancouver with 3,625, and Winnipeg with 2,580. Ottawa-Gatineau had 1,970 Jewish elderly, Calgary had 1,110, and Hamilton had 1,045.

Among metropolitan areas with Jewish populations of at least 1,500 people, Hamilton had the largest proportion of seniors (20.5 per cent), followed by Montreal (20.4 per cent), Windsor (19.8 per cent), and Winnipeg (18.8 per cent).

Low-Income Distribution

Statistics Canada has established a low income cut-off (LICO). It estimates that households spending 63.6 per cent or more of income on food, clothing, and shelter live in "straitened" circumstances. LICOs are adjusted for household size and the size of the community in which the household is located.

The LICO is not without weaknesses. It does not take into account information regarding a person's net worth; for instance, an individual can own a house and a car yet still be classified as living below the LICO. Moreover, the 63.6 per cent rule is somewhat arbitrary. It is also evident that the measure takes into account only food, shelter, and clothing. A more meaningful measurement would involve determining the cost of what Statistics Canada calls a "basket" of all necessities, including transportation, personal care, household supplies, recreation, health, and insurance. Finally, it must be noted that the LICO does not take into account the cost of living Jewishly, such as maintaining a kosher diet and paying synagogue dues.

Bearing these limitations in mind, about one in seven Canadian Jews (57,195 individuals, or 14.6 per cent) lived below the LICO in Canada in 2011, almost exactly the same proportion as for the Canadian population as a whole. This fact contradicts the widely held view that Jews are universally well-to-do. Jewish females were more likely than males to fall below the LICO, but the difference was not large (15.4 per cent vs. 13.8 per cent, respectively). Nor was there a large difference between the percentage of all Jews below the LICO and the 13.7 per cent of Jewish children (9,740 individuals) below the LICO.

The absolute number of disadvantaged Jews in a community was correlated with the community's size, but the correlation is not perfect. Montreal had the highest percentage of Jews living below the LICO in 2011: 20 per cent. The corresponding percentage was also relatively high in Regina (17.2 per cent), Vancouver (16.1 per cent), and London (15 per cent). The lowest percentages of Jews living below the LICO were in Kitchener-Cambridge-Waterloo (10.7 per cent), Kingston (9.3 per cent), and Ottawa-Gatineau (8.9 per cent).

In 2011, 10,395 seniors – 15.7 per cent of all seniors – lived below the LICO. Of all 57,195 Canadian Jews below the LICO, 18.2 per cent were seniors. Women were almost twice as likely as men to fall below the LICO (19.3 per cent vs. 11.6 per cent, respectively). Senior women were more inclined to experience low income because many lived alone; in 2011, 36.4 per cent of elderly women who lived alone were below the LICO.

Holocaust survivors in Canada numbered 17,300 in 2011, representing 28.2 per cent of Canada's Jewish seniors. Some 24.7 per cent of Holocaust survivors lived below the LICO, nearly twice the percentage for the rest of the Jewish population (12.6 per cent).

Some 24.9 per cent of Jews in single-parent households lived below the LICO in 2011, rising to 27.3 per cent among those living in female-headed single-parent families. The corresponding percentage for individuals living in couple arrangements was 8.8 per cent. In absolute terms, the number of Jews below the LICO was largest for those in couple arrangements (25,655), followed by unattached individuals (22,530), those living in female-headed single-parent families (7,170), those living in male-headed single-parent families (1,165), and those living with relatives (675).

The most vulnerable group consisted of individuals between the ages of 55 and 64 who relied on government social assistance or disability payments; of these individuals, 71 per cent lived below the LICO, many of whom encountered discrimination regarding their age, limiting their chance of finding adequate employment. Since they were too young to collect a pension, they struggled on meagre incomes that barely rose above subsistence levels. There were 2,725 such economically disadvantaged Jews in Canada. In fact, 56.4 per cent of all Canadian Jews receiving government social assistance or the like fell below the LICO in 2011.

In addition, 70.8 per cent of unattached Jews between the ages of 15 and 24 who lived alone or with non-relatives were below the LICO in

36   Charles Shahar

2011. Often, these individuals were students who had left their parents' home and were trying to make ends meet through part-time work, student loans, or bursaries. There were 3,245 such individuals in Canada in 2011.

Finally, among the most vulnerable segments in the community were the 540 children under 5 years of age living in female-headed single-parent families. Some 38.3 per cent of such children lived below the LICO.

Intermarriage

In 2011, there were 136,190 Canadian Jews who were married to or partnered with other Jews in Canada, and 48,515 Jews who were married to or partnered with non-Jews. The intermarriage rate was therefore 26.3 per cent, up from 16.8 per cent in 1991 and 9.0 per cent in 1981. Between 1981 and 2011, the intermarriage rate increased 3.9 percentage points for Catholics, 4.9 percentage points for Protestants, and 11.7 percentage points for Jews by religion (Brym and Lenton 2020, 73).

Some 54.4 per cent of intermarried spouses and partners lived in situations where the husband was Jewish and the wife non-Jewish, and 45.6 per cent lived in arrangements where the husband was non-Jewish and the wife Jewish.

Another way of looking at intermarriage focuses on the total number of Jews living in intermarried families, including children. In 2011, 72,370 Canadian Jews lived in intermarried households – about one in four individuals in households with couple arrangements.

The intermarriage rate was correlated with community size and the age of spouses or partners. Thus, the lowest intermarriage rates were in Montreal (15 per cent) and Toronto (17.3 per cent). The highest intermarriage rates were in Victoria (73.5 per cent), followed by Kingston (65 per cent), Regina (54.8 per cent), and Halifax (53 per cent). For spouses or partners under the age of 30, the intermarriage rate was 43 per cent.

About one in four Jewish children under the age of 15 who resided with both parents lived in an intermarried household in 2011. Of these children, 27 per cent (6,380) were identified by their parents as Jews by religion. Some 56.4 per cent (13,335) were identified as having no religion. The rest, 16.6 per cent (3,920), were identified as having a religion other than Judaism. In other words, nearly three quarters (73 per cent) of these children were not identified as belonging to the religious orientation of the Jewish spouse.

Whether a Jewish man or woman intermarries was a critical factor in the identification of the youngest child. For instance, in cases where Jewish men intermarry, 17.2 per cent of youngest children are identified as Jewish, 60.9 per cent as having no religious affiliation, and 22 per cent as having a different religion. In short, 82.9 per cent do not have the religious orientation of the Jewish father. In cases where Jewish women intermarry, 38.4 per cent of youngest children are identified as Jewish, 51.2 per cent as having no religious identification, and 10.3 per cent as having a different religion. Thus, more than six in ten (61.6 per cent) of the youngest children in the household are not identified as being Jewish. Although the latter figure was high, it was significantly lower than the comparable figure if the father married outside the faith (82.9 per cent).

Appendix: Definition of "Jewish" and Methodological Considerations

Since 1971, major analyses of the Canadian census have used the Jewish Standard Definition to distinguish Jews from non-Jews. Jim Torczyner of McGill University and the Jewish Federation of Montreal formulated this approach. They defined as Jewish people who specify that they identify as Jewish by (1) religion; or (2) ethnicity but identify with no religion. This means that people identifying as Jewish by ethnicity but indicating identification with a religion other than Jewish were designated as non-Jewish.

The two questions used to define who is Jewish in this chapter, namely religion and ethnicity, were included in the "long form" of the NHS, distributed to one third of Canadian households. The NHS was voluntary, and the weighted response rate was 73.9 per cent.

The extent to which non-response biased the results is unclear. It is possible that certain categories of the population, such as those below the LICO, individuals with few years of formal education, and recent immigrants were less inclined to answer the NHS than were other categories of the population. Statistics Canada applied sophisticated statistical treatments to deal with possible gaps in the data, but the change in methodology means it is difficult to determine margins of error for sample estimates.

A further issue is that, since the 2001 census, the number of Jews identifying as Jewish by ethnicity has declined dramatically. Accordingly, some individuals who said they had no religious affiliation might have fallen through the cracks because they did not identify themselves as Jewish by ethnicity.

The number of Canadians who indicated a Jewish ethnicity fell 54 per cent between 2011 and 2016, from 309,650 to just 143,660. The decline was mainly due to "Jewish" not being included as a response option in 2016 – the first time this occurred since the 1941 census.

Because the ethnicity variable has been slowly eroding in terms of its usefulness in identifying Jews, the Jewish Standard Definition was revised in 2011 and expanded to include a further set of variables, such as having an Israeli ethnicity and having knowledge of Hebrew or Yiddish. This Revised Jewish Definition increased the Jewish population in the NHS by 6,320.

REFERENCES

Brym, Robert, and Rhonda Lenton. 2020. "Jewish Religious Intermarriage in Canada." *Canadian Jewish Studies/Études juives canadiennes* 30: 67–82. https://doi.org/10.25071/1916-0925.40184.

DellaPergola, Sergio. 2013. "World Jewish Population, 2012." In *American Jewish Year Book 2012*, Vol. 109–12, edited by Arnold Dashefsky and Ira M. Sheskin, 213–83. Dordrecht, Netherlands: Springer.

DellaPergola, Sergio. 2022. "World Jewish Population, 2021." In *The American Jewish Year Book 2021*, Vol. 121, edited by Arnold Dashefsky and Ira M. Sheskin, 313–412. Cham, Switzerland: Springer.

Shahar, Charles. 2014. *2011 National Household Survey: The Jewish Population of Canada*. Part 1, *Basic Demographics*. Part 2, *Jewish Populations in Geographic Areas*. Toronto: Jewish Federations of Canada – UJA. https://bit.ly/3gSiWz1.

Statistics Canada. 2011. *2011 National Household Survey*. Catalogue no. 99-004-XWE. Ottawa: Statistics Canada.

4 Antisemitism in Canada

MORTON WEINFELD

Attending my Montreal synagogue for Rosh Hashana in 2019, I observed dramatically ramped-up security. Two large concrete slabs had been placed near the walkway leading into the building to prevent cars from approaching. Instead of the one young, unarmed guard we were used to seeing on the Sabbath, three experienced (but still unarmed) guards stood at the entrance. For years, synagogues in Europe have had far more security. In January 2020, the synagogue posted a sign near the entrance: "Do not hold the door open for a stranger. This is not being rude; it is being safe." These cautionary steps have become normalized in Canada as antisemitism has become more salient.[1]

Historical Background

Antisemitism dates back to the slavery of the Hebrews in Egypt, when Pharaoh regarded Jews as a suspect minority (Exodus 1:10). It continued through the Roman conquest, which put an end to Jewish sovereignty by means of murder, exile, enslavement, and the destruction of the Second Temple. The subsequent 2,000 years of minority diasporic experience, while by no means uniformly dismal, featured major eruptions of Jew hatred, murder, and exile, from the beginning of the First Crusade in 1096 through the Spanish Inquisition in the late 1400s and Eastern European massacres and pogroms from the seventeenth through the nineteenth and early twentieth centuries. The horror of the Holocaust casts a deep shadow on contemporary Jewish attitudes about antisemitism.

Because of this history, antisemitism, whether real or potential, is a constant feature of modern life for Jews. Hence the grim Jewish quip: "An antisemite is someone who hates Jews more than is necessary." Even before the recent talk of microaggressions, many Jews in North America kept their antennae tuned to high alert to possible slights and warning signals (Seeley, Sim, and Loosley 1956). Most Canadian Jews know that many Jews in Weimar Germany were highly assimilated and devoted to Germany and German culture. In 1933, the Jewish intermarriage rate was 28 per cent, higher than in Canada today (Lowenstein 2005, 26). None of this prevented the persecution of Jews under the Nazis. Jewish communal discourse is often shaped by post-Holocaust questions like, "Could it happen here?" and admonitions like "Never again."

With steady post–Second World War upward mobility, most North American Jews were seen as increasingly White, meaning they were less markedly Jewish, less frequently victimized than racialized minorities, and could enjoy the socio-economic benefits of their Whiteness (Brodkin 1998; Schraub 2019). Ironically, most Jews became White as the proportion of non-White Jews grew. Some are of Sephardic or Middle Eastern origin, others Ethiopian, and still others Black or Asian. The 2020 Pew survey of Jewish Americans found that about 8 per cent of Jewish adults are non-White, and the 2021 Canadian census placed the corresponding number for Canada at less than 4 per cent (Pew Research Center 2021; Brym 2023). Ultra-Orthodox Jews (particularly men) can perhaps qualify as a visible minority too because of their distinctive attire, making them more easily targeted for physical assault.

Antisemitism abroad helps to shape Canadian Jewish perceptions. The *Canadian Jewish News* features regular coverage of antisemitic incidents worldwide. Many Canadian Jews also follow such events in foreign publications, some of them online. When Jews are killed in Europe or while praying in an American synagogue – or by Hamas rockets in Israel – it resonates in Canadian Jewish life, just as mass murders in mosques or Black churches or police shootings resonate with worldwide Muslim and Black communities. That is part of the reason why Canadian synagogues and communal institutions heightened security measures well before the 2021 Gaza conflict.

Up through the 1960s, antisemitism was a prominent feature of Jewish life in Canada. It waned for three or four decades and resurfaced again around the turn of the twenty-first century, often linked to expressions of anti-Israel sentiment and right-wing populism. Jewish students claim to be affected by microaggressions and feel victimized by Israeli Apartheid Week and Boycott, Divestment, and Sanctions (BDS) campaigns on university campuses (Fleras 2016). Confrontation on the streets, some of them violent, broke out during and after the 2021 Gaza conflict (Bensadoun 2021).

Nonetheless, by some measures antisemitism in Canada today is far less salient than in the immediate post–Second World War period.

Antisemitism provided the context of Canada's closed-door policy towards Jewish refugees before and during the Second World War (Abella and Troper 1983). In the 1950s and into the 1960s, formal or informal quotas still operated in universities and corporate boardrooms. An effective legal structure in dealing with human rights, non-discrimination, and expressions of hate did not exist. Negative and demeaning stereotypes about Jews were widespread. Jews faced discrimination in employment, accommodation, and housing. Jewish children in public schools were usually expected to take part in all manner of Christian rituals and prayer. There were no human rights acts or human rights commissions, no hate literature laws, no constitutional protections. By choice and exclusion, Jews lived in solitude. *Crestwood Heights*, the pioneering study of Forest Hill in Toronto, described hesitant Jewish interactions with non-Jews; Canadian Jews in the 1950s played down their Jewish identity, still insecure in their new-found middle-class suburban status (Seeley, Sim, and Loosley 1956).

Notwithstanding such exclusions, Canadian Jews have not suffered enormously from antisemitism. There have been no forced conversions, expulsions, pogroms, Dreyfus affairs, Nuremberg Laws, or crematoria in this country. Jews were never the absolute Other they were in Europe and in Arab and Muslim countries. French–English polarization and the victimization of First Nations and non-White minorities assured Jews a margin of acceptability and buffered hatred. To date, Canadian Jews have not been murdered by antisemites, as they have been in the United States. Yet the Canadian case does not obscure the universal sense of Jewish insecurity.

Antisemitism in Canada dates back to before Confederation. Conflict over the 1807 election of Ezekiel Hart to the Legislative Assembly of Lower Canada included elements of antisemitism. Theological antisemitism existed throughout the pre-Confederation era, even in the near absence of Jews (Menkis 1992; Robinson 2013). In French Canada, a steady stream of antisemitic thought was present, some homegrown and some imported from France (Brown 1992). In English Canada, theological antisemitism was expressed in evangelical and missionary activity aimed at converting Jews and supporting such efforts elsewhere (Menkis 1992, 26–7). English Canada also developed a brand of "intellectual" antisemitism, typified by the writings of Goldwin Smith in the late nineteenth century (Tulchinsky 1992). Anglo antisemitism of this type helped feed into discrimination at Canadian universities. Jewish enrolment at McGill University declined between 1925 and 1935 from 25 to 12 per cent of the student population, and a Jewish quota at the University of Toronto Medical School was in place until the late 1950s (Anctil 1992; Levi 2003).

42   Morton Weinfeld

Canadian antisemitism reached its peak in the 1930s. Fascist organizations existed in both English and French Canada. In English Canada, antisemitism fed off Anglo-Saxon nativism and unemployment. Swastika clubs and associations were developed, and the swastika figured in the largest Jewish–Gentile riot in Canadian history, which broke out in 1933 in Toronto's Christie Pits after a baseball game between a largely Jewish team and an Anglo-Saxon club (Levitt and Shaffir 1987).

In Quebec, the situation was more serious. In the interwar period, French nationalism embraced three themes, all of which fed antisemitism: re-francization, with Jews identified with the English; the promotion of French entrepreneurs through the *achat chez nous* movement, which involved boycotting Jewish firms; and anti-immigration sentiment (Anctil 1992, 156). The conservative Catholic Church in Quebec opposed liberal and radical tendencies identified with Jews at home and abroad, and even more pronounced was the steady stream of antisemitism in articles, letters, and columns in the influential *Le Devoir* (Abella 1990, 180; Anctil 1992, 148). In 1934, Adrien Arcand formed the National Social Christian Party on a Nazi model. Arcand's movement numbered only in the hundreds and petered out during the war, but the fact that over 80 per cent of Quebec voters, and still more among francophones, rejected conscription in a 1942 referendum is revealing. In 1998, Esther Delisle's second book dealing with antisemitism and Nazi sympathizers in the post-war period was, like her first book in 1993, greeted with a blend of silence and contempt (Delisle 1998). The contrast with the mea culpas and enthusiastic reception in English Canada of Irving Abella and Harold Troper's *None Is Too Many* is stark. In any case, after the war, organized political antisemitism was largely discredited.

Types of Antisemitism

There are different ways of defining and measuring antisemitism. De jure antisemitism is explicitly mandated in, or permitted by, law, or so interpreted by the courts. The British North America Act contains a form of legal discrimination against Jews and other religious minorities in the area of educational rights. Protestants and Catholics enjoy educational rights to state funding unavailable to Jews and other religious minorities. (Some provinces – though not Ontario, with around 60 per cent of Canada's Jewish population – now partially fund Jewish schools.)

However, by and large, the force of law and jurisprudence in Canada today protects Jews (and other minorities) from discrimination and is a major impediment to antisemitism. This situation is typified by the adoption of the non-discriminatory immigration "points system" and the enactment of human rights legislation at provincial and federal levels. Nevertheless, there remain cases where law, or the interpretation of law, can harm Jewish interests. Quebec's Bill 21, passed in June 2019, curtails visible religious symbols in certain state-run professions or public situations. It therefore limits career opportunities for *kippah*-wearing Jews, among others. The law survived court challenge through its use of the "notwithstanding clause" of the Canadian Charter of Rights and Freedoms, which allows a temporary override of certain sections of the Charter.

De facto antisemitism involves acts by individual Canadians or institutions that harm Jews or hurt Jewish sensibilities although they may not be illegal. Some of these acts are motivated by anti-Jewish feeling, like an employer choosing not to hire a Jew. Others may be unintentional and systemic, like scheduling university exams on Passover.

Overt acts of antisemitism come in many forms. Acts of serious personal violence are rare in Canada; defacement of property or general vandalism is more common. Overt or covert discrimination in employment or in any other public domain is also rare today. In-person verbal insults and Internet postings are another form of antisemitism, the latter of which have become common with the flowering of social media. They can reflect stereotypes based on ignorance or malice, and some may not be intentionally hurtful. Many Jews see antisemitism as the subtext in criticism of Israel and Zionism (Brackman 2015).

Residential mixing, like other forms of social contact, is associated with lower levels of antisemitism. In 2009, 45 per cent of Canadians reported having Jewish friends, ranging from a high of 61 per cent in Ontario to a low of 20 per cent in Quebec (Geddes 2009). It is possible that the higher level of antisemitism among francophones, established in multiple surveys, may in part reflect a lack of contact (Brym and Lenton 1992).

Finally, antisemitism can permeate high culture and popular culture. Historically, this began as anti-Judaism and included the theological conviction that Jews were *collectively* responsible for killing Christ or that Judaism posed a threat to Christianity. Beyond that, it includes demeaning images of Jews in literature, intellectual discourse, and daily language, or the absence of Jewish themes in Canadian cultural production. The images of Shakespeare's Shylock or of rapacious Jewish businessmen or the use of "Jew" as an unflattering verb are well-known examples. This type of cultural antisemitism was more prevalent in the past.

The thematic content of traditional explicit antisemitism in the West can be reduced to four broad types (Wistrich 2010). First, religious *Christian antisemitism* feeds on the Christ-killer theme, or on claimed deficiencies in Judaic theology or ethics. A second type is *racist antisemitism*, rooted in biology. Proponents of this view argue that Jews are non-human, sub-human, or at the very least racially distinct from Aryans or non-Jews. Racist antisemitism also relates to Jews as a people or ethnic group with certain negative stereotypical traits.

Then there are two types of political or economic antisemitism. *Right-wing antisemitism* opposes Jews because they are seen to support liberalism, socialism, or communism. More recently, Jews have earned the enmity of the religious right by being identified with liberal or progressive positions – pro-choice, pro-sex education, pro-gay rights. *Left-wing antisemitism* opposes Jews because they are seen as arch-capitalists, greedy exploiters of the working class devoted to moneymaking and material pursuits. This strain goes back to the Middle Ages, when the image of the Jew as usurer or moneylender was widespread. A recent and controversial fifth variant attacks Zionism as reactionary nationalism, with Israel and its supporters an extension of Western colonialism and racism aimed at Arab or Muslim states.

How can Jews be simultaneously a religious group and a racial group, communists and capitalists, freethinkers and ultra-Orthodox? The myth of a Jewish conspiracy resolves all these contradictions. The *Protocols of the Elders of Zion*, fabricated by the Tsarist secret police in the early twentieth century, is the modern foundational document (Cohn 1967). It portrays all types of Jews as part of one overarching conspiracy, aided by the alleged Jewish control of the media, aimed at world domination.

The shadow of the Holocaust looms over Canadian Jewry, shaping attitudes about antisemitism. A 2018 survey found that 69 per cent of Canadian Jews regard "remembering the Holocaust" as essential to being Jewish, second only to "leading an ethical and moral life" at 72 per cent (Brym, Neuman, and Lenton 2019, 18). In contrast, a 2019 survey discovered that one fifth of Canadian young people had not heard of the Holocaust or were not sure what it was, and nearly two thirds of the sample did not know or underestimated the numbers of Jews killed (Arsenault 2019). Holocaust ignorance also resurfaced during the 2015 federal election campaign. Alex Johnstone, an NDP candidate from Ontario and a long-time school trustee and public school official, admitted that she was unfamiliar with the fact that Auschwitz was a Second World War death camp (Maloney 2015).

Two Canadian Holocaust denial cases in the 1980s were well publicized. Ernst Zündel, a German-born publisher of materials denying the

Holocaust and preaching a Jewish international conspiracy for world domination, was prosecuted under an obscure Criminal Code provision against the spreading of false news. He was eventually deported to Germany where he was convicted of Holocaust denial in 2007. James Keegstra was a social studies teacher in Alberta. He was prosecuted in 1985 under the hate literature laws in the Criminal Code for "willfully promoting hatred" against the Jewish people. He taught his high school students that the major events of Western history were largely the result of an international Jewish conspiracy (Bercuson and Wertheimer 1985; Mertl and Ward 1985). The case eventually wound up in the Supreme Court, which upheld the constitutionality of the hate speech laws as a legitimate restriction of free speech under section 1 of the Charter of Rights and Freedoms.

Tension between the right of free speech and hate speech will likely never be resolved (Lipstadt 1993). New cases with slightly different twists in new jurisdictions will arise. Hate messages on the Internet and on social media are a troubling new version (Lungen 2016). Canada's hate speech laws in the Criminal Code and in provincial statutes recognize that absolutes are rare, and that more often principles will jostle against one another. Depending on how courts adjudicate such cases, Canada's commitment to restrictions on hate speech, while troubling for civil libertarians, is an impediment to the growth of antisemitism.

Contemporary Canadian Antisemitism

In its most extreme form, anti-Zionism opposes the right of Jews to a state of their own. Given that nearly 6.9 million Jews now live in such a state and would defend its existence tooth and nail, denying the legitimacy of a Jewish state is for most Jews unambiguous antisemitism.

What about opposition to one or more Israeli *policies*? This is a more complex issue. Some critics of Israel consider anti-Zionism to be distinct from antisemitism and claim that the charge of antisemitism is often used by pro-Israel supporters to shield Israel from legitimate criticism. Nonetheless, as overt antisemitism has become unfashionable, some Jews and analysts have come to consider any harsh criticism of Israel a convenient substitute for antisemitism (Fulford 2018).

This issue is hotly debated in the Canadian Jewish community. In 2016, a conservative American Jewish newspaper published a list of the forty most hostile North American campuses for Jewish students. The University of Toronto ranked third, McGill University fourth (The Algemeiner 2016). Most of the incidents counted in the study involved anti-Israel activity. For example, at McGill University they included multiple attempts to pass BDS resolutions, the prohibition of pro-Israel articles in the campus paper, and a notorious tweet by a Jewish student involved in student government urging his colleagues to "punch a Zionist" (Fegelman 2015; Levitan 2015; Seidman 2016). Coverage of these incidents in the Jewish and general media magnified their impact on Canadian Jews.

One prominent source of data on antisemitism in Canada is the annual report on antisemitic incidents of the League for Human Rights of B'nai Brith Canada. The number of incidents reported for 2020 was 2,610 compared to 2,041 in 2019 and 240 in 1998. Most incidents involved harassment and vandalism. Much of the increase comes from more effective collection procedures and the inclusion of antisemitic comments online, with a single tweet now counting as an incident (Brym 2019). Still, one need not conclude that impactful antisemitism has increased ninefold over the past twenty years, as B'nai Brith Canada data claim (Alberta Jewish News 2015; B'nai Brith Canada 2010, 2019). Interestingly, the Anti-Defamation League (2021) in the United States reported 2,024 antisemitic incidents in 2020. The fact that the number of antisemitic incidents in the United States (a country with fifteen times as many Jews as Canada) is *less* than the number in Canada suggests that B'nai Brith is casting a much wider net in its definition of antisemitism.

What sorts of incidents are these? The following descriptions from the 2018 B'nai Brith report gives us a sense of the range: While treating a patient crying from severe sinus pain, an ER nurse in Ontario calls the patient "a spoiled rich Jewish [expletive] just looking for free meds." Graffiti reading "Kill the Jews" with a swastika was drawn on a bus stop in Kirkland, Quebec. Four religious Jewish teenagers out for a walk in Toronto were verbally abused and physically attacked by another group of teenagers (B'nai Brith Canada 2019).

Data on antisemitic acts are also available from official law enforcement records. The most recent reports as of this writing indicate that, in both absolute terms and relative to their population, Jews are the third most targeted ethnic, racial, or religious group in Canada after Blacks and Muslims. Metropolitan Toronto encompasses nearly one half of Canada's Jewish population but just one fifth of hate crimes against Jews. Still, Jews rank first among groups who are victimized by hate crimes in Toronto (see table 4.1). Most hate crimes against Jews are non-violent instances of what the police classify as "mischief." Hate crimes against Jews have been increasing since 2006, when country-wide statistics began to be collected.

Jewish Canadians do not seem to be penalized in terms of educational, occupational, and income attainment. This outcome does not

Table 4.1. Hate crimes by top ethnic, racial, or religious group, Canada, 2019, and Toronto, 2020

Group	Incidents	Approximate population	Rate per 100,000
		Canada	
Black	1,143	1,200,000	9.5
Muslim	1,037	1,100,000	9.4
Jewish	325	392,000	8.3
		Toronto	
Black	43	450,000	1.0
Muslim	9	470,000	0.2
Jewish	63	190,000	3.3

Note: "Muslims" include Arabs; Iranians and Afghanis ("West Asians"); and other non-Arab Muslims.
Source: Statistics Canada (2021); Toronto Police Service (2021).

prove the absence of antisemitism in the workplace, since it is possible that Jewish attainment (like the attainment of certain Asian groups) can take place despite prejudice or discrimination. Many Jews find employment in Jewish-owned firms or institutions, thus joining the Jewish "sub-economy," while many others are self-employed, mitigating the impact of any work-related antisemitism (Weinfeld with Schnoor and Shames 2018, 218–41).

Antisemitic Prejudice and Jewish/Non-Jewish Interactions

How extensive are antisemitic attitudes in Canada, and where are they concentrated? In the 2018 Survey of Jews in Canada, 34 per cent of respondents claimed there is "often" discrimination against Jews. The comparable figures were 60 per cent for discrimination against Indigenous Canadians, 51 per cent for Muslims, and 49 per cent for discrimination against Blacks. In this same survey, 38 per cent of respondents claimed personal experience of anti-Jewish discrimination. Orthodox and Sephardi Jews, and especially Jews between the ages of 18 and 29, report the highest level of discrimination based on religion. Sephardim and Jews in the 18–29 age cohort were among those most likely to experience discrimination based on ethnicity or culture (Brym, Neuman, and Lenton 2019, 47–55). It is probably significant that a 2015 survey of North American Jewish university students found that "hostility toward Jews and Israel appears to be particularly pronounced in specific schools, including a number in Canada" (Saxe et al. 2015, 23).

How do Jewish perceptions compare with Canadian popular attitudes? A 2008 poll found that 13 per cent of Canadians had an "unfavourable opinion" of Jews – 7 per cent in English Canada (the same as the United States) and 27 per cent in Quebec (about the same as in Germany). The national average was higher than the percentage for the US, the UK, and Australia, but lower than Germany, France, Spain, Poland, and Russia. On the other hand, the percentage of respondents with a "very favourable" attitude towards Jews was higher in Canada than in any of the other country except the United States (Jedwab 2008). A 2009 survey found that 53 per cent of Canadians had a positive view of Judaism, compared to 72 per cent for Christianity and 28 per cent for Islam. Respondents in Ontario were the most favourable towards Judaism at 59 per cent, while those from Quebec were least favourable at 36 per cent (Geddes 2009). Surveys conducted by the Anti-Defamation League used an eleven-item index to measure antisemitism in numerous countries in 2014 and 2020. Respondents who answered "true or probably true" to six of eleven anti-Jewish statements were classified as antisemitic. The survey found a 14 per cent antisemitic index score for Canada in 2014, which dropped down to 8 per cent in 2020, lower than the UK's 11 per cent. According to the 2020 survey, 17 per cent of Canadians believed Jews have too much power in the business world and 10 per cent believed Jews have too much control over global media (Anti-Defamation League 2014, 2021).

It is hard to interpret the importance of survey questions when they focus on attitudes rather than behaviour. Consider intermarriage, which can be seen as a sign of Jewish acceptance by non-Jews. There has been a clear increase among Canadians in the approval of Jewish/non-Jewish marriage (Bibby 1995). In a 2009 survey, 56 per cent of respondents found it acceptable for their child to marry a Jew (Geddes 2009). In terms of actual intermarriage rates, about 77 per cent of all married Canadian Jews in 2018 had a spouse who was Jewish by religion, with the level somewhat higher for older Canadians (Brym, Neuman, and Lenton 2019, 39–40, 45).

As noted, the link between antisemitism and opposition to Zionism (belief in Israel's right to exist as a Jewish state) or to Israeli policies is unclear and contentious in general and in Jewish political discourse. Social scientists have measured the correlation between anti-Israel attitudes and antisemitic attitudes. While there has been little research on this subject in Canada, a major survey in the UK found that "even harsh criticism of Israel was not necessarily antisemitic, but harsh criticism of Israel was likely to be associated with some level of antisemitism, in some cases a high level" (Brym 2019, 416).

Major Canadian Jewish organizations, notably B'nai Brith, as well as the Canadian Parliamentary Coalition to Combat Antisemitism, argue that many anti-Israel incidents justify conflating antisemitism and anti-Zionism (Brym 2019, 411). Indeed, Canadian Jewish organizations, as well as the Canadian Parliament, have adopted a definition of antisemitism developed by the International Holocaust Remembrance Association (IHRA) that includes elements of anti-Zionism or anti-Israelism. The definition was adopted by Canada's Parliament in 2019 and by the governments of Ontario and Quebec, but it has been met by criticism. Progressive Canadian groups like the New Democratic Party (NDP), civil liberties associations, Jewish and non-Jewish faculty petitions, and the BDS-supporting Independent Jewish Voices, argue the definition works to suppress criticism of Israel and limit free speech (Forrest 2019; Jewish Faculty Network 2020). Among the elements of the definition that refer to Israel are "denying the Jewish people their right to self-determination, e.g. by claiming that the existence of a State of Israel is a racist endeavour," or "applying double standards by requiring of [Israel] a behaviour not expected or demanded of any other democratic nation" (B'nai Brith Canada 2019, 8). More recently, some Jewish studies scholars critical of the breadth of the IHRA definition have proposed an alternate Jerusalem Declaration on Antisemitism less centred on criticism of Israel (Hensman 2021).

Support for Israel has become a wedge issue in the Jewish community. In the 2018 Survey of Jews in Canada, 82 per cent of Canadian Jews were willing to disclose their political party support. Of these respondents, 15 per cent supported the left-leaning NDP and Green parties, and 83 per cent supported the centrist and right-leaning Liberal and Conservative parties. About one quarter of Jews on the left and 3 per cent of Jews in the centre and on the right claimed that Canada is too supportive of Israel. Fully 60 per cent of Jewish supporters of the Conservative Party said that Canada's then-Liberal government was "not supportive enough" of Israel. That figure compares to 26 per cent of Liberal Party supporters. These fissures date back to the turn of the century, when some former Jewish Liberal Party supporters threw their support behind the Conservatives, who seemed more committed to Israel than the Liberals were. During and after the 2021 Gaza conflict, the Green Party, whose leader at the time was a Black Jewish woman, Annamie Paul, was torn by this debate. Paul resigned from her leadership position after facing the threat of being ousted from the party (Barry 2010; Brym, Neuman, and Lenton 2019, 63; Weinfeld with Schnoor and Shames 2018, 245–7; Thurton 2021).

Intersectionality and reciprocal solidarity play an important role in the make-up of contemporary antisemitism and anti-Zionism among liberal and progressive elements, many of whom see a parallel between the oppression of Indigenous and Black Canadians and the oppression of the Palestinians by Israel. Feminist groups and causes have attempted to vilify and exclude Jewish or Zionist women from gay pride parades. Opponents of Israel reject "pink-washing," that is, using relatively liberal attitudes towards LGBTQ+ individuals found in gay-friendly cities such as Tel Aviv to excuse or distract from Israeli mistreatment of Palestinians (Weinfeld with Schnoor and Shames 2018, 140). In 2019, Vegans for BDS organized a panel at the University of Toronto called "No Veganwashing Israeli Crimes." Speakers challenged the authenticity of Israel's vegan movement and voiced support for Palestine's animal rights movement (Fraiman 2019).

Prospects

Jews have long wrestled with the canard of dual loyalty, which fuels racism (Weinfeld 2015). The ease and relatively low cost of international travel and communication strengthens diaspora–homeland ties for many minorities (Satzewich and Wong 2006). Multicultural policy has a similar effect. While loyalty to a homeland does not necessarily challenge loyalty to Canada, it may be seen as a challenge to Canadian foreign policy; some minority groups who oppose the Canadian government's foreign policy or seek to change it may be seen as suspect or disloyal (Granatstein 2008; Satzewich 2007). Disagreement on foreign policy issues may thus become more salient in shaping domestic Canadian ethnic relations, including relations between Canadian Jews and Arabs or Muslims.

Finally, antisemitism in Quebec still has a distinctive edge. In Quebec today, antisemitism is more than the residue of staunch Catholicism. Jews in Quebec are overwhelmingly federalists and are perceived as such by Quebec nationalists and *independentistes*. In a 2007 poll, 41 per cent of French speakers in the province agreed with the statement, "Jews want to impose their customs and traditions on others," while just 31 per cent agreed that "Jews want to participate fully in society" (Robinson 2013). Pierre Péladeau, a prominent Quebec businessperson and father of former Parti Québécois leader Pierre Karl Péladeau, told a Quebec newsmagazine that he has great respect for Jews, but "they take up too much space" (Littman 1991). In 2014, the well-known Quebec radio host, Gilles Proulx, stated on air that Jews manipulate world governments and take economic control of the countries in which they live, while Louise Mailloux, a PQ candidate, publicly expressed her belief that kosher food is a scam and that its proceeds may be funding religious wars (Robinson 2013).

How do we understand the fact that many Canadian Jews believe themselves to be potential victims without having ever been seriously victimized? An ideology of omnipresent antisemitism is part of modern Jewish identity and international Jewish experience. It explains the enduring effect of the Holocaust on Jews far removed from the European death camps (Harold 2020; Harold and Fong 2018). It also explains why concern for the fate of Israel remains important, even as Israel appears militarily strong, and thus why apparent opposition to Israel's existence as a secure and Jewish state resonates for many Jews as antisemitic. Compared to other minorities, Canadian Jews are relatively affluent and well integrated socially and culturally. Yet in recent years, they have become increasingly concerned about antisemitism on the part of right-wing populists and left-wing anti-Zionists.

NOTE

1 I thank Mr. Jonah Levitt for his editorial and bibliographic assistance on this chapter. This is a revised and updated version of "Antisemitism in Canada: Past, Present and Future" (Weinfeld 2020), reprinted in part with permission of Robert Brym.

REFERENCES

Abella, Irving. 1990. *A Coat of Many Colours: Two Centuries of Jewish Life in Canada*. Toronto: Lester & Orpen Dennys.

Abella, Irving, and Harold Troper. 1983. *None Is Too Many: Canada and the Jews of Europe, 1933–1948*. Toronto: Lester & Orpen Dennys.

Alberta Jewish News. 2015. "B'nai Brith Audit Reveals Anti-Semitism in Canada Reaches an All-Time High." *Alberta Jewish News*, 11 June 2015. http://bitly.ws/t2Y7.

The Algemeiner. 2016. "The *Algemeiner*'s 1st Annual List of the US and Canada's Worst Campuses for Jewish Students." http://bitly.ws/t2Y5.

Anctil, Pierre. 1992. "Interlude of Hostility: Judeo-Christian Relations in Quebec in the Inter-War Period, 1919–1939." In *Anti-Semitism in Canada: History and Interpretation*, edited by Alan Davies, 135–66. Waterloo: Wilfrid Laurier University Press.

Anti-Defamation League. 2014. "ADL Global 100: An Index of Anti-Semitism." https://global100.adl.org/map.

Anti-Defamation League. 2021. "Audit of Antisemitic Incidents 2020." https://www.adl.org/audit2020.

Arsenault, Chris. 2019. "1 in 5 Canadian Youths Not Sure What Happened in the Holocaust, Survey Suggests." *CBC News*, 27 January 2019. http://bitly.ws/t2Y2.

Barry, Donald. 2010. "Canada and the Middle East Today: Electoral Politics and Foreign Policy." *Arab Studies Quarterly* 32 (4): 191–217. https://www.jstor.org/stable/41858634.

Bensadoun, Emerald. 2021. "Jewish Communities on Edge Amid 'Troubling Rise' of Anti-Semitism in Canada." *Global News*, 25 May 2021. http://bitly.ws/t2XZ.

Bercuson, David J., and Douglas Lloyd Wertheimer. 1985. *A Trust Betrayed: The Keegstra Affair*. Toronto: Doubleday Canada.

Bibby, Reginald W. 1995. *The Bibby Report: Social Trends Canadian Style*. Toronto: Stoddart.

B'nai Brith Canada. 2010. *2009 Audit of Antisemitic Incidents*. Toronto: League for Human Rights of B'nai Brith Canada.

B'nai Brith Canada. 2019. *2018 Annual Audit of Antisemitic Incidents*. Toronto: League for Human Rights of B'nai Brith Canada. http://bitly.ws/sLk7.

Brackman, Harold. 2015. "Regents Beware: You Are Already Under Attack for Calling Out 'Anti-Zionism.'" *Jewish Journal*, 11 June 2015. http://bitly.ws/t2XY.

Brodkin, Karen. 1998. *How Jews Became White Folks and What That Says about Race in America*. New Brunswick, NJ: Rutgers University Press.

Brown, Michael. 1992. "From Stereotype to Scapegoat: Anti-Jewish Sentiment in French Canada from Confederation to World War One." In *Anti-Semitism in Canada: History and Interpretation*, edited by Alan Davies, 239–66. Waterloo: Wilfrid Laurier University Press.

Brym, Robert. 2019. "Antisemitic and Anti-Israel Actions and Attitudes in Canada and Internationally: A Research Agenda." *Patterns of Prejudice* 53 (4): 407–20. https://doi.org/10.1080/0031322X.2019.1614295.

Brym, Robert. 2023. "Canadian Jewish Population 2021: New Estimates." In *American Jewish Year Book 2022*, edited by Arnold Dashefsky and Ira M. Sheskin. Cham, Switzerland: Springer.

Brym, Robert, and Rhonda Lenton. 1992. "Anti-Semitism in Quebec." *Canadian Journal of Sociology/Cahiers Canadiens de Sociologie* 17 (2): 179–83. https://doi.org/10.2307/3341195.

Brym, Robert, Keith Neuman, and Rhonda Lenton. 2019. *2018 Survey of Jews in Canada: Final Report*. Toronto: Environics Institute for Survey Research. https://bit.ly/3mdvMvg.

Cohn, Norman. 1967. *Warrant for Genocide: The Myth of the Jewish World Conspiracy and the Protocols of the Elders of Zion*. New York: Harper & Row.

Delisle, Esther. 1998. *Myths, Memory and Lies: Quebec's Intelligentsia and the Fascist Temptation, 1939–1960*. Montreal: Robert Davies Multimedia.

Fegelman, Mike. 2015. "When Criticism of Israel Becomes Anti-Semitism." *Huffington Post*, 31 August 2015. http://bitly.ws/t2XU.

Fleras, Augie. 2016. "Theorizing Micro-Aggressions as Racism 3.0: Shifting the Discourse." *Canadian Ethnic Studies* 48 (2): 1–19. https://doi.org/10.1353/ces.2016.0011.

Forrest, Maura. 2019. "There's a Debate over Canada's New Definition of Anti-Semitism, and It Might Sound Strangely Familiar." *National Post*, 27 June 2019. http://bitly.ws/t2Xr.

Fraiman, Michael. 2019. "Rise of the Vegan Jew." *Canadian Jewish News*, 2 October 2019. http://bitly.ws/t2XT.

Fulford, Robert. 2018. "The BDS Movement, Where the Anti-Semites Find Room to Flourish." *National Post*, 30 November 2018. http://bitly.ws/t2XR.

Geddes, John. 2009. "What Canadians Think of Sikhs, Jews, Christians, Muslims." *Maclean's*, 28 April 2009. http://bitly.ws/t2XP.

Granatstein, J.L. 2008. "Multiculturalism and Canadian Foreign Policy." In *The World in Canada: Diaspora, Demography, and Domestic Politic*, edited by David Bercuson and David Carment, 78–91. Montreal: McGill-Queen's University Press.

Harold, Josh. 2020. "A Genesis of Jewishness: Collective Memory, Identity Work, and Collective Boundary Making among Jews in Toronto." PhD diss., University of Toronto.

Harold, Josh, and Eric Fong. 2018. "Mnemonic Institutions and Residential Clustering: Jewish Residential Patterns in Toronto." *Canadian Review of Sociology/Revue Canadienne de Sociologie* 55 (2): 257–77. https://doi.org/10.1111/cars.12192.

Hensman, Rohini. 2021. "The Jerusalem Declaration on Antisemitism Is a Very Welcome Initiative." *The Wire*, 28 April 2021. https://bit.ly/3cdKeAd.

Jedwab, Jack. 2008. *Attitudes towards Jews and Muslims: Comparing Canada with the United States and Europe*. Montreal: Association for Canadian Studies.

Jewish Faculty Network. 2020. "Jewish Faculty in Canada against the Adoption of the IHRA Working Definition of Antisemitism." http://bitly.ws/t2Xd.

Levi, Charles. 2003. "'There Is a Definite Limitation Imposed' (Robin Ross to Claude Bissell, December 4, 1959): The Jewish Quota in the Faculty of Medicine, University of Toronto: Generational Memory Sustained by Documentation." *Historical Studies in Education/Revue d'histoire de l'éducation* 15 (1): 131–8. https://doi.org/10.32316/hse/rhe.v15i1.477.

Levitan, Tyler. 2015. "Criticizing Israel's Politics Isn't Anti-Semitism." *Huffington Post*, 14 August 2015. http://bitly.ws/t2Xh.

Levitt, Cyril, and William Shaffir. 1987. *The Riot at Christie Pits*. Toronto: Lester & Orpen Dennys.

Lipstadt, Deborah E. 1993. *Denying the Holocaust: The Growing Assault on Truth and Memory*. New York: Free Press.

Littman, Sol. 1991. *Quebec's Jews: Vital Citizens or Eternal Strangers: Analysis of Key Newspaper Coverage of Three Pertinent Incidents*. Los Angeles: Simon Wiesenthal Center.

Lowenstein, Steven M. 2005. "Jewish Intermarriage and Conversion in Germany and Austria." *Modern Judaism* 25 (1): 23–61. https://doi.org /10.1093/mj/kji003.

Lungen, Paul. 2016. "B'nai Brith Audit Finds Anti-Semitism Moving Online." *Canadian Jewish News*, 2 May 2016. http://bitly.ws/t2Xj.

Maloney, Ryan. 2015. "Alex Johnstone, NDP Candidate, Says She Didn't Know Auschwitz Was a Death Camp." *Huffington Post*, 23 September 2015. http://bitly.ws/t2Xk.

Menkis, Richard. 1992. "Anti-Semitism and Anti-Judaism in Pre-Confederation Canada." In *Anti-Semitism in Canada: History and Interpretation*, edited by Alan Davies, 11–28. Waterloo: Wilfrid Laurier University Press.

Mertl, Steve, and John Ward. 1985. *Keegstra: The Issues, the Trial, the Consequences*. Saskatoon, SK: Western Producer Prairie Books.

Pew Research Center. 2013. *A Portrait of Jewish Americans: Findings from a Pew Research Center Survey of U.S. Jews*. Washington, DC: Pew Research Center. http://bitly.ws/sMxz.

Pew Research Center. 2021. *Jewish Americans in 2020*. Washington, DC: Pew Research Center. http://bitly.ws/sMt9.

Robinson, Ira. 2013. "Reflections on Antisemitism in French Canada." *Canadian Jewish Studes/Études Juives Canadienne* 21 (1): 90–122. https://doi .org/10.25071/1916-0925.39911.

Satzewich, Vic. 2007. "Multiculturalism, Transnationalism, and the Hijacking of Canadian Foreign Policy: A Pseudo-Problem?" *International Journal* 63 (1): 43–62. https://doi.org/10.1177/002070200806300104.

Satzewich, Vic, and Lloyd L. Wong, eds. 2006. *Transnational Identities and Practices in Canada*. Vancouver: UBC Press.

Saxe, Leonard, Theodore Sasson, Graham Wright, and Shahar Hecht. 2015. *Antisemitism on the College Campus: Perceptions and Realities*. Waltham, MA: Maurice and Marilyn Cohen Center for Modern Jewish Studies, Brandeis University. https://bir.brandeis.edu/handle/10192/30810.

Schraub, David. 2019. "White Jews: An Intersectional Approach." *Association for Jewish Studies Review* 43 (2): 379–407. https://doi.org/10.1017 /S0364009419000461.

Seeley, John R., Robert A. Sim, and Elisabeth W. Loosley. 1956. *Crestwood Heights: A Study of the Culture of Suburban Life*. Toronto: University of Toronto Press.

Seidman, Karen. 2016. "BDS Vote Stirs Up Hostilities on McGill Campus." *Montreal Gazette*, 25 February 2016. http://bitly.ws/t2XK.

Statistics Canada. 2021. "Police-Reported Hate Crime, 2019." http://bitly.ws/t2XC.

Thurton, David. 2021. "Green Party's Annamie Paul Survives Emergency Meeting over Leadership." *CBC News*, 16 June 2021. http://bitly.ws/t2XA.

Toronto Police Service. 2021. *2020 Annual Statistical Report*. Toronto: Toronto Police Service.

Tulchinsky, Gerald. 1992. "Goldwin Smith: Victorian Canadian Anti-Semite." In *Anti-Semitism in Canada: History and Interpretation*, edited by Alan Davies, 67–92. Waterloo: Wilfrid Laurier University Press.

Weinfeld, Morton. 2015. "Canadian Jews, Dual/Divided Loyalties, and the Tebbit 'Cricket' Test." In *Revisiting Multiculturalism in Canada: Theories, Policies, and Debates*, edited by Shibao Guo and Llyod Wong, 141–58. Rotterdam: Sense Publishers.

Weinfeld, Morton. 2020. "Antisemitism in Canada: Past, Present and Future." In *Racism, Islamophobia, Antisemitism, and the Future of Canadian Society: Proceedings of the Fifth S.D. Clark Symposium on the Future of Canadian Society*, edited by Robert Brym, 57–78. Oakville, ON: Rock's Mills Press.

Weinfeld, Morton. 2021. "A Privileged Diaspora: Canadian Jewry in Comparative Perspective." In *No Better Home? Jews, Canada, and the Sense of Belonging*, edited by David S. Koffman, 19–32. Toronto: University of Toronto Press.

Weinfeld, Morton, with Randal F. Schnoor and Michelle Shames. 2018. *Like Everyone Else, but Different: The Paradoxical Success of Canadian Jews*. 2nd ed. Montreal: McGill-Queen's University Press.

Wistrich, Robert S. 2010. *A Lethal Obsession: Anti-Semitism from Antiquity to the Global Jihad*. New York: Random House.

5 The Centrality of Jewish Education in Canada

RANDAL F. SCHNOOR

Modes of Jewish Education

Jewish education has assumed much of the responsibility for creating and nurturing Jewish identity in the diaspora because of declining levels of synagogue attendance and religious observance. It achieves this goal formally by teaching Jewish languages, rituals, and secular culture, and informally by socializing Jews in their ethno-religious community. Formal education takes place mainly in full-time day schools and supplementary schools, including afternoon or Sunday schools, also called Hebrew schools. Informal socialization takes place in overnight summer camps, youth groups, and travel opportunities to Israel and Poland (including Birthright Israel and March of the Living), among other countries. This chapter focuses on Jewish day schools and overnight summer camps. Much of the analysis compares Canada and the United States, with detailed attention given to the situation in Toronto.[1]

All forms of organized Jewish education instill Jewish identity in youth, albeit in different ways and to varying degrees, with supplementary schools demonstrating the most mixed results due to their relatively non-intensive nature (Cohen 2007). Research shows that attending Jewish day school increases the likelihood of enrolling in Jewish Studies courses at university and participating in Jewish campus life. It is also associated with intensity of religious observance and sense of belonging to the Jewish community, among other indicators of Jewishness (Cohen 2007; Chertok et al. 2007; Horenczyk and Hacohen 2011). For instance, among Montreal Jews, attending a Jewish high school is the second strongest predictor of intensity of ritual observance later in life; only denominational affiliation is a stronger predictor (Shahar 2010). Jewish overnight camps are also effective in this regard (Cohen at al. 2011; Rothenberg 2016); providing a more experiential style of education, they engender positive feelings about Judaism and the Jewish community through pleasurable and meaningful activities and social interactions with other Jews (Cohen and Veinstein 2009).

Jewish Education in Canada and the United States

As a minority group deeply concerned with its continuity, the Canadian Jewish community devotes substantial resources to Jewish education. In fact, no ethnic or religious minority group in Canada has an educational system as extensive as that of the Jewish community. Moreover, Jewish education is more extensive in Canada than in the United States.

In the early twentieth century, Jewish youth in both countries typically attended full-time public school supplemented by Jewish school for a couple hours twice a week and/or on Sundays (Schoenfeld 1999). In the early 1940s, the parallelism weakened as Canada's first Jewish day schools were launched.

In Toronto, the first two full-time private Jewish schools were established in 1942 with the opening of Associated Hebrew School and Eitz Chaim School. Both were Orthodox in orientation and operated with no financial support from the Jewish Federation of Toronto, which was made up of non-Orthodox Jews who considered the schools too parochial. The schools were thus entirely funded by contributions from parents and private groups.

One challenge facing the graduates of the early Orthodox elementary day schools in the 1940s and 1950s was the lack of a Jewish high school in which to continue their Jewish education. As a result, the early graduates enrolled in public high schools. In the early 1960s, the Orthodox community addressed this challenge. For graduates of Associated Hebrew School, a modern Orthodox, co-educational, Zionist Jewish high school was established in 1960: the Community Hebrew Academy of Toronto (CHAT).[2] For the graduates of Eitz Chaim, more traditionally Orthodox, gender-segregated high schools were established – Ner Israel for boys in 1960, and Bais Ya'acov for girls in 1961.

In due course, non-Orthodox Jews also came to the conclusion that private, full-time Jewish schools with a less traditional curriculum were needed to ensure a Jewish future for their children (Diamond 2000). In 1961, the first two non-Orthodox day schools were established: United Synagogue Day School (now the Robbins Hebrew Academy), affiliated with the Conservative movement, and Bialik Hebrew Day School, a secular Yiddishist institution. Leo Baeck, the first day school under the umbrella of the Reform movement, was established in 1974. Beginning in the 1990s, non-denominational or community/pluralist schools flourished, beginning with the Toronto Heschel School (established 1996), the Paul Penna Downtown Jewish Day School (1998), and the Montessori Jewish Day School (2000).

For graduates of the non-Orthodox elementary schools in the 1960s, the relatively liberal CHAT was the high school of choice. However, as more non-Orthodox students enrolled in the school, some families became concerned about its less religious atmosphere. Looking for a school somewhere in the middle ground between CHAT and Ner Israel/Bais Ya'acov, these parents established gender-segregated, religious-Zionist schools: Yeshivat Or Chaim for boys, founded in 1973, and Ulpanat Orot for girls, founded in 1975.

The long history of internal jostling between different segments of the Jewish community notwithstanding, Toronto takes pride in housing the largest variety of Jewish day schools in Canada. They cover the full range of Jewish denominations including Orthodox, Conservative, Reform, secular, and non-denominational/community, among other designations. While in 1970 fewer than 3,000 students were enrolled in just a few Toronto Jewish day schools, by 1985 Toronto had more than a dozen Jewish day schools with close to 8,000 students at the elementary and high school levels (Pomson 2002; Shoub 1991). By 2002, there were twenty day schools with an elementary school population of close to 9,000, constituting 34 per cent of the total Jewish school-age population, and a high school population of more than 2,600 (Shoub and Levine 2002). The total was approximately 11,000 in 2013, dipping to about 10,000 in 2021.

Notwithstanding the recent decline (to be discussed below), what accounts for the dramatic rise of Jewish day school enrolment in Toronto over several decades? Two factors stand out. First, the crystallization of Canada's ethos of multiculturalism brought about new confidence for developing a comprehensive parochial school system; it became more acceptable for Jews to show interest in deepening their culture and identity through the development of private Jewish education (Schnoor 2011). Concern about assimilation accelerated this process. Second, upward mobility played a role in increasing Jewish day school enrolment. With average annual income well above the national average, many Canadian Jews have been in a position to finance new schools and pay private school tuition fees (Pomson 2002).

Jewish day school enrolment gained substantial momentum in the mid-to late 1970s – more than a decade before similar momentum was observed in the United States. Today, the popularity of Jewish day schools in Toronto for the non-Orthodox is striking when compared to the situation in New York City. Toronto Orthodox Jews attend Jewish

Table 5.1. Enrolment in non-Orthodox and Orthodox Jewish day schools, Toronto and New York City, 2018

	Non-Orthodox	
	Enrolment	Enrolment/10,000 Jews
Toronto	3,556	187.2
New York City	2,728	17.7
	Orthodox	
	Enrolment	Enrolment/10,000 Jews
Toronto	2,295	120.8
New York City	17,001	110.5

Note: The New York City data do not include 93,626 students in Hasidic schools or *yeshivas*. Similarly, the Toronto data do not include schools that are not affiliated with the UJA Federation of Toronto.
Sources: Besser (2020, 27); Held and Weber (2021); Shahar (2020); Sheskin and Dashefsky (2020).

day schools at only a slightly higher rate than New York Jews (120 students per 10,000 Jews in Toronto vs. 110 students per 10,000 Jews in New York). However, among the non-Orthodox, Toronto Jews are more than ten times more likely to attend Jewish day schools than New York Jews (see table 5.1). From 1998 to 2018, the number of non-Orthodox day schools in the United States fell from 158 to 134, and enrolment declined by 17 per cent (Wertheimer and Pomson 2021).

Table 5.2 demonstrates the prevalence of Jewish education in Canada compared to the United States. Some 43 per cent of adult Canadian Jews report having attended Jewish day schools compared to 24 per cent of American adults. In Montreal, the figure reaches 54 per cent, reflecting the traditionalism of that city's Jewish community and the partial subsidization of faith-based schools by the Quebec government – a key difference compared to Ontario. Similarly, 58 per cent of Canadian Jews have attended a Jewish overnight summer camp, compared to 40 per cent in the United States.

Why does Canada have a substantially higher rate of participation in Jewish education than the United States? The conventional argument is that Canadian Jews are twice as likely as US Jews to be immigrants (about 30 per cent versus 14 per cent), so they are arguably closer to the "old country" and therefore a step "behind" in the assimilation process. The argument has some validity. Thus, Canada has a considerably higher proportion of Holocaust survivors than the US does. The

60   Randal F. Schnoor

Table 5.2. Participation in Jewish education, per cent by city and country

Attended	All four Canadian cities	Toronto	Montreal	Winnipeg	Vancouver	US
Jewish day school	43	43	54	44	33	24
Jewish summer camp	58	61	59	52	44	40
Other type of Jewish education	67	73	58	67	61	61

Sources: Brym, Neuman, and Lenton (2019); Pew Research Center (2021).

survivors and their offspring have left an indelible imprint on the Canadian Jewish mindset. On the other hand, in recent decades most Jewish immigrants were more likely to be fairly assimilated Jews from the former Soviet Union or the United States than Yiddish-speaking Jews from Poland or Ladino-speaking Jews from Morocco. Therefore, the time-lag argument holds less sway than it once did. We must dig deeper into the socio-historical context of North American Jewry to fully understand why US Jews are less likely than Canadian Jews to pursue Jewish education (Abella 1998; Menkis 2008; Schnoor 2011; Tulchinsky 2001; chapter 19 in this volume).

Europeans began settling the United States a century earlier than Canada. By the second half of the eighteenth century, a strong American national identity had developed in armed rebellion against British rule. A weaker national identity emerged from Canada's later, gradual, and relatively peaceful road to independence from Britain a century later. Consequently, for immigrants, Americanization has been and continues to be a more potent assimilatory force than Canadianization. One upshot of this divergent history is that the liberal Reform movement found more fertile soil for growth in the United States than in Canada, where the more traditional Orthodox and especially Conservative denominations have flourished. The stronger tendency of Canadian Jews to attend Jewish day schools today is partly a result of these different paths of historical development.

A related circumstance leading to divergence concerns the manner in which Canada and the United States have dealt with minority groups. When the British conquered the northern part of the continent, the French population was sufficiently large that they had to be accommodated, that is, given substantial political and cultural authority. By the second half of the twentieth century, Canada was officially declared a bilingual and bicultural country. Pressure from non-French minority groups subsequently led to the institutionalization of multiculturalism as state policy. Symbolic and financial state support for minority cultures, languages, and educational institutions is thus stronger in Canada than in the United States.

Finally, it should be noted that by the middle of the nineteenth century, Jews in the US had spread out over numerous metropolitan areas. Today, fewer than half of US Jews live in the four US cities with the largest Jewish populations. In contrast, more than 80 per cent of Canada's Jews are concentrated in Toronto, Montreal, Vancouver, and Winnipeg. With substantially higher geographical concentration, Canadian Jews have been able to develop a more cohesive national community infrastructure. This circumstance is yet another factor that has made the Canadian Jewish day school system stronger than its American counterpart.

Impact of Jewish Education

According to the 2018 Survey of Jews in Canada, attending a Jewish day school is partly a function of denominational affiliation: 67 per cent of Orthodox/Modern Orthodox Jews say they have attended Jewish day school, compared to 43 per cent of Conservative Jews, 38 per cent of unaffiliated Jews, and 24 per cent of Reform Jews. Day school attendance is also a function of age cohort, with attendance levels more than twice as high among Jews eighteen to twenty-nine (68 per cent) than among those fifty-five and older (31 per cent). This circumstance reflects the growing popularity of Jewish day school over the last few decades. On average, Jews who have attended a Jewish day school or yeshiva have done so for nine years. Average years of attendance is highest among the Orthodox/Modern Orthodox denomination (eleven years).

Summer camps provide one of the most popular forms of Jewish education in Canada. In 2018, 58 per cent of Canadian Jews had attended an overnight summer camp with Jewish content at least once. Summer camp attendance is most prevalent among those living in Toronto (61 per cent) and Montreal (59 per cent), and among those who are Orthodox/Modern Orthodox (69 per cent). It is less common in Vancouver (44 per cent), among Jews who are not affiliated with any denomination or movement (44 per cent), and among those who do not belong to any type of Jewish organization (45 per cent).

In that same survey, 67 per cent of Canadian Jews said that when growing up they participated in other kinds of Jewish educational programs, such as Hebrew school, Sunday school, or a Jewish teen program. This type of educational experience is most common in Toronto

(73 per cent) and among those affiliated with the Conservative or Reform denominations (75 per cent for both). Participation in this type of Jewish education is notably low among first-generation Canadians from the former Soviet Union (34 per cent) and those who were not raised in the Jewish religion (22 per cent).

Table 5.3 lists thirteen factors associated with the influence of day school and summer camp attendance on Jewish engagement and identity. It demonstrates a substantial positive association between attendance and stronger engagement in Jewish life. For example, 46 per cent of those who attended Jewish day school light Shabbat candles every week, compared to 25 per cent of respondents who did not go to Jewish day school. Of those who attended Jewish summer camp, 86 per cent contribute to Jewish charities compared to 71 per cent of those who did not attend. In general, the influence of summer camp attendance is weaker than the influence of Jewish school.

Attending day school and attending summer camp are correlated; some individuals attended both. However, because some individuals did not attend both, some factors are substantially different between their effect on those who said they attended Jewish day school and those who said they attended Jewish overnight camp. Those factors are shaded grey in table 5.3. Most of the factors on which day school has the largest positive influence are expressions of religiosity.

Affordability Crisis and Response

While Jewish day schools and summer camps have a positive effect on Jewish identity, their cost is a barrier to access. Between 2001 and 2011, average household income in Toronto rose 11 per cent. Jewish elementary school tuition rose 61 per cent. The average elementary Jewish day school tuition in Toronto was $16,737 in 2019–20 (Grassroots for Affordable Jewish Education [GAJE] n.d.).[3] This is a major financial commitment for non-affluent families, especially when there is more than one child attending school. The Jewish community provides substantial tuition subsidies for low-income families,[4] but middle-class families are financially squeezed (Brym and Lenton 2020; Kotler-Berkowitz, Adler, and Kelman 2016). They may want their children to be exposed to Jewish life and culture and to develop a strong Jewish identity through Jewish schooling, but high and rising costs are prohibitive. When added to the onerous cost of home ownership in Toronto, especially in a Jewish neighbourhood, and maintaining a Jewish household and Jewish way of life, the cost of day school tuition is increasingly out of reach for many families.

Table 5.3. "How important is each of the following in what being Jewish means to you?" Toronto, 2018, in per cent

Jewish day school				Jewish overnight camp		
	Attended	Did not attend	Difference		Attended	Did not attend	Difference
Light Shabbat candles every week	46	25	21	Being Jewish is very important	71	56	15
Religion is very important	40	23	17	Synagogue member	57	42	15
Being part of Jewish community (essential)	50	33	17	Donation to Jewish charity in last year	86	71	15
Being Jewish is very important	73	58	15	Religion is very important	35	25	10
Observing Jewish Law (essential)	30	16	14	Celebrating Jewish holidays (essential)	62	52	10
Attend synagogue once/week or more	22	10	12	Married to a Jew	79	69	10
Synagogue member	57	45	12	Light Shabbat candles every week	38	29	9
Donation to Jewish charity in last year	86	76	10	Leading an ethical and moral life (essential)	75	68	7
Celebrating Jewish holidays (essential)	63	53	10	Being part of Jewish community (essential)	43	37	6
Married to a Jew	80	71	9	Observing Jewish Law (essential)	24	18	6
All friends are Jewish	14	6	8	Attend synagogue once/week or more	18	12	6
Caring about Israel (essential)	46	40	6	All friends are Jewish	12	6	6
Leading an ethical and moral life (essential)	75	70	5	Caring about Israel (essential)	44	41	3
Average			12				9

Note: Shaded cells indicate factors that are at least 5 percentage points different between their effect on those who said they attended Jewish day school and those who said they attended Jewish overnight camp.
Source: Brym, Neuman, and Lenton (2019).

According to Grassroots for Affordable Jewish Education (GAJE), a Toronto organization formed in 2015 to address the affordability crisis, the proportion of families in Toronto who are willing to continue Jewish education after the elementary level has decreased significantly. In 2006, 79 per cent of students graduating from non-Orthodox Jewish elementary day schools went on to TanenbaumCHAT. In 2015, the figure was 52 per cent. Directly related to this phenomenon is the dramatic overall decrease in TanenbaumCHAT enrolment, from a high of 1,530 in 2008–9 to 875 in 2017–18, a 42 per cent reduction.

As tuition increases have far surpassed household income increases, affordability of Jewish day schools in Toronto, particularly in York Region, has reached near-crisis proportions, with several schools merging or closing down. In 2017, the north campus of TanenbaumCHAT closed and merged with the south campus, a sudden move that was met with great frustration from parents living in the northern suburbs. In 2019, three elementary Jewish day schools in Thornhill were forced to close due to decreasing enrolment: Leo Baeck Day School (Reform), Associated Hebrew School (community), and Eitz Chaim School (Orthodox). Elementary enrolment continued its decline and dropped by 272 students in 2019–20 from the previous year.

How has the Jewish community of Toronto responded to this challenge? In partnership with other faith-based communities (Muslim, Hindu, etc.), the Jewish community has for many years lobbied the Ontario provincial government for financial support of community educational institutions, but with little success. The United Nations High Commissioner for Refugees declared in 1999 that funding Ontario's Catholic schools to the exclusion of all others is discriminatory and violates the International Covenant on Civil and Political Rights. As a result, the Ontario Jewish Association for Equity in Education together with the Alliance of Christian Schools (a Protestant school body) filed a lawsuit against the province. The lawsuit was unsuccessful in the Supreme Court of Canada. The court ruled that while the province was indeed guilty of discriminatory behaviour, its policies were based on a constitutional provision, and therefore the province was under no legal obligation to modify this policy (Brown 2011). As a result of this perceived injustice, some Jews in Ontario feel that their rights of equal citizenship are being violated. In 2021, GAJE initiated a new legal attempt to have the court reassess and reconsider the Supreme Court decision on which Ontario relies to justify its lack of funding.

Meanwhile, in March 2017, a surprise announcement was made by TanenbaumCHAT and the UJA Federation of Toronto that private donations of $14 million ($10 million from alumni Edie Neuberger and

Norm Jesin and $4 million from the Granovsky family) would reduce the tuition of the high school by approximately 30 per cent, from $28,000 per year to $18,500–$19,000 for the five-year period 2017–22. This move dramatically affected enrolment. In the first two years of the program, Grade 9 entry-level enrolments rose by more than 50 per cent from 190 to 300 students, and the school population increased from 875 to 1,017 students (see figure 5.1). While cost is not the only factor keeping families from choosing Jewish day schools – another factor is a decrease in perceived value (see Goldsweig 2020; Rosov Consulting 2017) – the results at TanenbaumCHAT are noteworthy.

While increasing high school enrolment is an important accomplishment, the drop in elementary school enrolment means that the pool of potential high school recruits will shrink, notwithstanding "new stream" students who enter high school from outside the Jewish day school system. Accordingly, building on the successful experiment at Tanenbaum-CHAT, the Jewish Foundation of Greater Toronto in partnership with leading community philanthropists launched the Generations Trust Scholarship in 2021. It focuses on students from Junior Kindergarten to Grade 8, supplementing the standard tuition assistance program that has been in place in Toronto for many years. The advantage of the Generation Trust Scholarship is that the application process is much less intrusive, burdensome, and off-putting than the traditional subsidy process. Rather than asking for a detailed accounting of monthly expenses, the value of cars, vacation expenditures, and so on, the Generations Trust Scholarship supplies a simple online calculator that asks a few questions about income and provides the result of the application within a few weeks. In 2021, the program offered a tuition cap for up to three children of $16,500–$21,000. With average tuitions around $17,000, this is a small benefit for one child, but with two or three children the savings can be substantial. To eliminate uncertainty for families, tuition rates are guaranteed for the full period that the children are in elementary Jewish day school. Nine schools are included in the program. The hope is to include more in the future.

The new subsidy programs signal a turning point in addressing the financial challenges that Toronto Jewish families have been facing for many years. They supplement successful overnight camp subsidies such as One Happy Camper, which offer reduced rates for first-time campers in one of the Federation-affiliated Jewish overnight camps in the Toronto area. In 2021, the average fee for a six-week Jewish overnight camp was approximately $7,500, significantly less than Jewish day school tuition, but certainly a challenge for many families. Since 2012, Montreal has developed its own Generations Fund Scholarship to reduce Jewish day school tuition and camp fees.

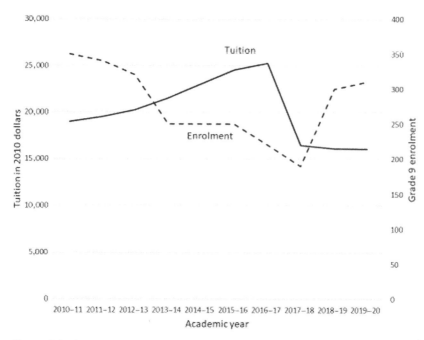

Figure 5.1. Grade 9 enrolment at TanenbaumCHAT, by annual tuition in 2010 constant dollars, 2010–2020
Sources: Bank of Canada (n.d.); Generations Trust (2020); Goldsweig (2020).

Education, Intermarriage, and Assimilation

Many Jewish community leaders worry about intermarriage because they tend to believe that it leads inexorably to assimilation. They also believe that Jewish education is the best safeguard against intermarriage. Both beliefs contain some truth – and more than a little oversimplification.

While the Jewish intermarriage rate has been rising in Canada since the early 1930s, it is not the case that assimilation is the inevitable outcome. Today, students are graduating from liberal Jewish day schools strongly committed to identifying as Jews, more Jewishly literate than their parents, but at the same time *less* committed to in-marriage than their parents (Pomson and Schnoor 2018; Rosov Consulting 2017). Because of their rich Jewish education and the multicultural milieu in which they have grown up, students today are typically proud of who they are as Jews and report that they look forward to raising Jewish children whether they marry a Jew or not. Moreover, although intermarriage often leads to assimilation, multivariate analysis of data from the 2018 Survey of Jews in Canada shows that "relatively intensive secondary socialization [i.e., attending a Jewish day school] not only lowers the likelihood of intermarriage in the children's generation but can overwhelm the effect of intermarriage in the parents' generation" (Brym and Lenton 2020, 75). One may feel justified in concluding that the main threat to the continuity of the Canadian Jewish community is not intermarriage but the affordability of Jewish education.

NOTES

1 Some sections of this chapter are revised and updated from "Jewish Education in Canada and the United Kingdom: A Comparative Perspective" (Schnoor 2021).
2 In 2008, the school was renamed TanenbaumCHAT.
3 Ontario pays the full cost of Roman Catholic schools but nothing for other religious day schools and independent schools. Quebec, British Columbia, Alberta, and Manitoba pay 50–60 per cent of the costs of secular subjects in Jewish day schools. This makes a significant difference in affordability. Average Jewish day school tuition is about $13,000 in Vancouver, $11,000 in Montreal, $9,000 in Winnipeg, and $8,400 in Calgary (GAJE n.d.). In some countries, such as the United Kingdom, Jewish day schools are considered state schools and are thus fully funded by the government (Schnoor 2021).
4 In 2018–19, the UJA Federation allocated $18.5 million to Jewish education, 31 per cent of its annual allocations. Of that, $11.6 million was designated for day school tuition assistance, providing subsidies for 2,377 students. It is the highest share allocated to Jewish education of any Jewish community in North America but accounts for just 10 per cent of the operational costs of the affiliated Jewish schools in Toronto. The UJA allocation to day schools has not increased in the last few years (GAJE n.d.).

REFERENCES

Abella, Irving. 1998. "Canadian Jewry: Past, Present and Future." Inaugural Lecture, J. Richard Shiff Chair for the Study of Canadian Jewry. Toronto: Centre for Jewish Studies, York University.

Bank of Canada. n.d. "Inflation Calculator." Accessed 14 July 2022, https://www.bankofcanada.ca/rates/related/inflation-calculator/.

Besser, Mordechai. 2020. *A Census of Jewish Day Schools in the United States, 2018–2019*. New York: Avi Chai Foundation. http://bitly.ws/sMte.

Brown, Michael. 2011. "Canada: Jewish Education in Canada." In *International Handbook of Jewish Education*, edited by Helena Miller, Lisa D. Grant, and Alex Pomson, 1141–53. Dordrecht, Netherlands: Springer.

Brym, Robert, and Rhonda Lenton. 2020. "Jewish Religious Intermarriage in Canada." *Canadian Jewish Studies/Études juives canadiennes* 30: 67–82. https://doi.org/10.25071/1916-0925.40184.

Brym, Robert, Keith Neuman, and Rhonda Lenton. 2019. *2018 Survey of Jews in Canada: Final Report*. Toronto: Environics Institute for Survey Research. https://bit.ly/3mdvMvg.

Chertok, Fern, Leonard Saxe, Charles Kadushin, Graham Wright, Aron Klein, and Annette Koren. 2007. *What Difference Does Day School Make? The Impact of Day School: A Comparative Analysis of Jewish College Students*. Waltham, MA: Maurice and Marilyn Cohen Center for Modern Jewish Studies, Brandeis University.

Cohen, Steven M. 2007. "The Differential Impact of Jewish Education on Adult Jewish Identity." In *Family Matters: Jewish Education in the Age of Choice*, edited by Jack Wertheimer, 34–56. Waltham, MA: Brandeis University Press.

Cohen, Steven M., Ron Miller, Ira M. Sheskin, and Berna Torr. 2011. *Camp Works: The Long-Term Impact of Jewish Overnight Camp*. New York: Foundation for Jewish Camp. http://bitly.ws/sMth.

Cohen, Steven M., and Judith Veinstein. 2009. *Jewish Overnight Camps: A Study of the Greater Toronto Market*. Toronto: UJA Federation of Greater Toronto. http://bitly.ws/sMtc.

Diamond, Etan. 2000. *And I Will Dwell in Their Midst: Orthodox Jews in Suburbia*. Chapel Hill: University of North Carolina Press.

Generations Trust. 2020. *Investing in the Future of Our Jewish Community*. Toronto: UJA Federation of Greater Toronto and Julia and Henry Koschitzky Centre for Jewish Education, York University.

Goldsweig, Seth J. 2020. "Leadership Perspectives on the Financial Sustainability of Non-Orthodox Jewish Day Schools in Toronto." *Journal of Jewish Education* 87 (3): 226–61. https://doi.org/10.1080/15244113.2020.1847005.

Grassroots for Affordable Jewish Education (GAJE). n.d. "Home." Accessed 14 July 2022, https://gaje.ca.

Held, Daniel, and Tanya Weber. 2021. "Special Tabulation of Enrolment in Toronto Jewish Day Schools." UJA Federation of Greater Toronto.

Horenczyk, Gabriel, and Hagit Hacohen Wolf. 2011. "Jewish Identity and Jewish Education: The Jewish Identity Space and Its Contribution to Research and Practice." In *International Handbook of Jewish Education*, edited by Helena Miller, Lisa D. Grant, and Alex Pomson, 183–201. Dordrecht, Netherlands: Springer.

Kotler-Berkowitz, Laurence, Chaim Adler, and Ari Y. Kelman. 2016. "Financial Constraints on Intensive Jewish Education: The Interactive Effects of Financial Capacity and Jewish Connections." *Contemporary Jewry* 36 (1): 125–50. https://doi.org/10.1007/s12397-016-9159-4.

Menkis, Richard. 2008. "North of the Border." *AJS Perspectives: The Magazine of the Association for Jewish Studies* (Fall): 26–8. http://bitly.ws/sMt6.

Pew Research Center. 2021. *Jewish Americans in 2020*. Washington, DC: Pew Research Center. http://bitly.ws/sMt9.

Pomson, Alex. 2002. "Jewish Day-School Growth in Toronto: Freeing Policy and Research from the Constraints of Conventional Sociological Wisdom." *Canadian Journal of Education/Revue canadienne de l'education* 27 (4): 379–98. https://doi.org/10.2307/1602241.

Pomson, Alex, and Randal F. Schnoor. 2018. *Jewish Family: Identity and Self-formation at Home*. Bloomington: Indiana University Press.

Rosov Consulting. 2017. *Challenges and Opportunities on the Jewish Day School Landscape: A Thought and Action Paper for Jewish Federations*. Toronto: The Jewish Federations of North America. http://bitly.ws/sMtj.

Rothenberg, Celia A. 2016. *Serious Fun at a Jewish Community Summer Camp: Family, Judaism, and Israel*. Lanham, MD: Lexington Books.

Schnoor, Randal F. 2011. "The Contours of Canadian Jewish Life." *Contemporary Jewry* 31 (3): 179–97. https://doi.org/10.1007/s12397-011-9075-6.

Schnoor, Randal F. 2021. "Jewish Education in Canada and the United Kingdom: A Comparative Perspective." In *No Better Home? Jews, Canada and the Sense of Belonging*, edited by David Koffman, 70–80. Toronto: University of Toronto Press.

Schoenfeld, Stuart. 1999. "Jewish Education and Jewish Continuity in the United States and Canada: A Political Culture Perspective." *Journal of Jewish Education* 65 (1–2): 60–71. https://doi.org/10.1080/0021624990650107.

Shahar, Charles. 2010. *Jewish Life in Montreal: A Survey of the Attitudes, Beliefs and Behaviours of Montreal's Jewish Community*. Montreal: Federation CJA.

Shahar, Charles. 2020. "Canadian Jewish Population, 2019." In *American Jewish Year Book 2019*, Vol. 119, edited by Arnold Dashefsky and Ira M. Sheskin, 233–45. Cham, Switzerland: Springer.

Sheskin, Ira M., and Arnold Dashefsky. 2020. "United States Jewish Population, 2019." In *American Jewish Year Book 2019*, Vol. 119, edited by Arnold Dashefsky and Ira M. Sheskin, 135–231. Cham, Switzerland: Springer.

Shoub, Barry. 1991. *Day School Enrolment*. Toronto: UJA Federation of Greater Toronto, Board of Jewish Education.

Shoub, Barry, and Joyce Levine. 2002. *Population Survey*. Toronto: UJA Federation of Greater Toronto, Board of Jewish Education.

Tulchinsky, Gerald. 2001. "The Canadian Jewish Experience: A Distinct Personality Emerges." In *From Immigration to Integration: The Canadian Jewish Experience*, edited by Ruth Klein and Frank Dimant, 19–30. Toronto: Institute for International Affairs, B'nai Brith Canada.

Wertheimer, Jack, and Alex Pomson. 2021. "Jewish Education and the Pandemic: The Surprising Success of Day Schools in a Time of Crisis." *Commentary* 151 (1). http://bitly.ws/sMtp.

PART B

Comparing Canadian Jews across Social Characteristics

6 Twelve Degrees of Jewish Identity

ROBERT BRYM AND FENG HOU

Defining Jewish

Binary conceptualizations of Jewishness are common in some types of religious, legal, political, and sociological thinking. In such cases, distinct criteria for establishing Jewishness allow any individual to be definitively declared either Jewish or non-Jewish. Intermediate gradations are denied.

We wish to avoid binary definitions, focusing instead on the demonstrable fact that individuals identify as Jewish to varying degrees (DellaPergola 2015). Moreover, we emphasize that Jewishness, like all identities, is viscous. Although "sticky," it can flow, varying by social, economic, and political circumstances at a given point in time and, as circumstances change, over time.

For Sergio DellaPergola, the dean of Jewish demography, the chief determinant of Jewishness is familial proximity to what he calls "core" Jews. Core Jews identify with the Jewish religion and Jewish ethnicity, or with Jewish ethnicity and no religion. Applying that definition allows him to arrive at a count of 393,500 core Jews in Canada in 2021. According to DellaPergola, this inner circle is embedded in circles of increasing circumference. The second circle includes people who identify as either partly Jewish or who have a Jewish parent although they do not consider themselves to be Jewish (56,500 additional Canadians). The two outermost circles include all members of households containing at least one core Jew (another 100,000 Canadians) and individuals with a Jewish grandparent (yet another 150,000 Canadians) (DellaPergola 2022, 385). As one moves from the innermost to the outermost circle, familial proximity to core Jews and, with it, strength of Jewish identity, tend to decline.

Familial proximity to core Jews is not the only factor influencing degree of identification with Jewishness. For example, Jean-Paul Sartre ([1946] 1965, 143) famously wrote that "it is the anti-Semite who creates the Jew." He was reflecting on how the application of the 1935 Nuremberg Laws forced a recrudescence of Jewish identity on the part of many German citizens who had previously considered themselves barely or not at all Jewish. Another circumstance that may be associated with Jewishness is one's occupation. For instance, sociologists have shown that the concentration of American Jews in relatively high-status socio-economic locations has increased opportunities for intra-ethnic interaction and thus moderated assimilation (Goldscheider and Zuckerman 1984; Hartman and Hartman 2009; Rebhun 2015; for similar research on various ethnic groups in Canada, see Reitz 1980).

This chapter is the first systematic attempt to demonstrate how important socio-economic characteristics are associated with different degrees of identification with Jewishness in Canada at a single time point. We first identify twelve degrees of Jewishness. We then analyse how education, occupation, annual income, religious intermarriage, and residential concentration vary by degree of Jewishness.

Data Source and Categorization

Canada's 2016 census did not include a question on religion and is therefore not useful for assessing the issues just outlined. Data from the 2021 census were unavailable when this chapter was written. Therefore, this paper focuses on data from the 2011 National Household Survey (Statistics Canada 2011).

The 2011 National Household Survey (NHS) included two questions that permit the categorization of Canadian Jews:

(1) What were the ethnic or cultural origins of this person's ancestors? An ancestor is usually more distant than a grandparent. For example, Canadian, English, French, Chinese, East Indian, Italian, German, Scottish, Irish, Cree, Mi'kmaq, Salish, Métis, Inuit, Filipino, Dutch, Ukrainian, Polish, Portuguese, Greek, Korean, Vietnamese, Jamaican, Jewish, Lebanese, Salvadoran, Somali, Colombian, etc.

(2) What is this person's religion? Indicate a specific denomination or religion even if this person is not currently a practicing member of that group. For example, Roman Catholic, United Church, Anglican, Baptist, Lutheran, Muslim, Presbyterian, Pentecostal, Jewish, Buddhist, Hindu, Sikh, Greek Orthodox, etc.

Respondents could select one religion or no religion. They could also select one to six ethnic labels. These options permit multiple cross-classifications of religion and ethnicity.

We propose a scale of twelve gradations of Jewishness based partly on DellaPerrgola's work and partly on the structure of the 2011 NHS. In this schema, the strongest level of Jewishness involves identifying with the Jewish religion and one or more ethnicities including Jewish. The weakest level involves identifying with a non-Jewish religion and multiple ethnicities, with Jewish ethnicity ranked fourth to sixth. Table 6.1 displays the full scale and the estimated frequency for each category in Canada's 2011 population.

We anticipated that certain socio-economic characteristics would be associated with position on this scale. That is, we expected strength of Jewish identification to vary with socio-economic location.

Figure 6.1 substantiates that expectation. It displays eight graphs. Respectively for each of the twelve categories defined earlier, graphs A through E indicate the percentage of Canadian Jews between the ages of twenty-five and sixty-four who, in 2011, had completed a university degree, completed a law degree, completed a medical degree, were employed in a managerial occupation, or were employed in an occupation requiring low skill.[1] Graph F displays the percentage of married and cohabiting Canadian Jews of all ages whose partner was not a Jew by religion. Graph G shows the average market income in dollars of Jews between the ages of twenty-five and sixty-four in 2010. The 2011 NHS allows us to identify the census tract in which each respondent lived.[2] Graph H indicates the mean percentage of core Jews residing in census tracts for each of our twelve categories.

The solid, jagged line in each graph is the curve for Jews across the twelve degrees of Jewishness. The straight, sloped, dotted line in each graph illustrates the linear trend for the curve. The horizontal, dashed line indicates the mean (or in the case of annual income, the median) for Canada's non-Jewish population (or in the case of census tract residents, for Canada's population of non-core Jews) in the equivalent age cohort.[3] The zero-order correlation is in the upper right corner of each graph.

The graphs show that individuals who identify most strongly as Jewish tend to have completed a university degree, a law degree, or a medical degree; to have a managerial job; to not have a job requiring little skill; to earn relatively high annual income; to not be religiously intermarried; and to live in Toronto or Montreal and in census tracts with a relatively high percentage of core Jews. Although none of the curves rises or descends perfectly smoothly, seven of the eight correlations

76 Robert Brym and Feng Hou

Table 6.1. Jewish population of Canada by degree of Jewishness, 2011

	Core	Non-core	Total
1. Jewish religion and single or multiple ethnicities including Jewish	206,530	0	206,530
2. Jewish religion and no ethnicity or non-Jewish ethnicity/ies	122,970	0	122,970
3. No religion and single Jewish ethnicity	9,790	0	9,790
4. No religion and multiple ethnicities, Jewish ethnicity ranked 1	11,040	0	11,040
5. No religion and multiple ethnicities, Jewish ethnicity ranked 2	17,150	0	17,150
6. No religion and multiple ethnicities, Jewish ethnicity ranked 3	9,710	0	9,710
7. No religion and multiple ethnicities, Jewish ethnicity ranked 4–6	8,160	0	8,160
8. Non-Jewish religion and single Jewish ethnicity	0	2,620	2,620
9. Non-Jewish religion and multiple ethnicities, Jewish ethnicity ranked 1	0	5,480	5,480
10. Non-Jewish religion and multiple ethnicities, Jewish ethnicity ranked 2	0	15,950	15,950
11. Non-Jewish religion and multiple ethnicities, Jewish ethnicity ranked 3	0	13,010	13,010
12. Non-Jewish religion and multiple ethnicities, Jewish ethnicity ranked 4–6	0	10,210	10,210
	385,350	47,270	432,620

Source: Statistics Canada (2011).

associated with the graphs are strong (with magnitudes ranging from 0.718 to 0.867), and one is moderately strong (with a magnitude of 0.471).[4]

Specifically, in graphs A through E (per cent completing a university degree, per cent completing a law degree, per cent completing a medical degree, per cent with a managerial occupation, and per cent with a low-skill occupation), the score for Jews approaches the mean for non-Jews as one moves from the first to the twelfth degree of Jewishness. In graph F (median annual income), the curve for Jews ends just below the median for non-Jews.

Graph F (rate of religious intermarriage) and graph H (per cent core Jews in census tract) may seem anomalous insofar as moving from the first to the twelfth degree of Jewishness is associated with *increasing* distance from the mean score for non-Jews. However, this trend is an artifact of the way the data are coded. Graphs F and H show that a higher rate of religious intermarriage and a smaller percentage of core

Twelve Degrees of Jewish Identity

Figure 6.1. Degree of Jewishness by socio-economic characteristics

Jews in a respondent's census tract are associated with a weaker Jewish identity.

Level of education, type of occupation, amount of income, rate of intermarriage, and residential concentration are not just characteristics of individuals or groups; they represent bases of association – social settings in which people meet, date, and procreate. Depending on their social composition, these settings influence the efficiency with which religious and ethnic identities are reproduced. The greater the religious and ethnic heterogeneity of educational institutions, workplaces, professional associations, voluntary organizations, neighbourhoods, and families – that is, the greater the degree to which bases of association are populated by people of different religions and ethnicities – the less efficiently they reproduce religious and ethnic identities. Contrariwise, reproductive efficiency increases with the religious and ethnic homogeneity of myriad bases of association. At the cultural level, Jewishness varies with level of adherence/non-adherence to certain practices, values, and beliefs. Our graphs imply that, at the social-structural level, Jewishness varies with the religious and ethnic homogeneity/heterogeneity of identifiable socio-economic settings.

Multivariate Analysis

The graphs in figure 6.1 illustrate that strong Jewish identity is associated with social settings that are relatively homogeneous in their religious and ethnic composition. However, the indicators of religious and ethnic composition are themselves correlated. For example, people who complete a law degree generally earn relatively high income. Knowing both these factors are associated with relatively strong Jewish identity says nothing about their independent effects, that is, how much each factor contributes to strength of Jewish identity on its own. Nor does it say anything about their joint effect, that is, the effect of both factors combined.

To discover the independent effects of the two factors on strength of Jewish identity one must examine the association between one of the factors and strength of Jewish identity while controlling for the other factor. For example, simplifying somewhat, we can examine the association between completing a law degree and strength of Jewish identity for high- and low-income earners separately. At one extreme, if the association between completing a law degree and strength of Jewish identity disappears for high- and low-income earners examined separately, we are obliged to conclude that completing a law degree has no direct effect on strength of Jewish identity. However, it has an indirect effect on strength of Jewish identity that operates through its effect on income. At the other extreme, if the initial association remains the same for high- and low-income earners examined separately, we are obliged to conclude that completing a law degree is solely responsible for the initial association; income has no effect. These are extreme outcomes. Usually, statistical control produces results between the extremes.

If the exercise just described is conducted for multiple factors simultaneously, one is engaged in multivariate analysis. Multivariate analysis also tells us the likelihood that, after controls, associations are statistically significant – that is, not due to chance. Moreover, it reveals the combined effect of all factors on the phenomenon of interest.

Table 6.2 summarizes the results of our attempt to discover the independent and joint effects on strength of Jewish identity of five sets of factors associated with social settings that vary in their religious and ethnic composition. We measured strength of Jewish identity using our twelve-point scale of degree of Jewishness. We hypothesized that strength of Jewish identity decreases with religious intermarriage and increases with high levels of academic attainment, occupational skill level, annual market income, and residential concentration. We expected to find that non-intermarried individuals with advanced degrees, high occupational skill, and high income who reside in areas with a relatively high concentration of core Jews would have the strongest Jewish identity, while individuals without these attributes would have the weakest Jewish identity. That is just what we discovered.

Model 1 examines only the effect of various levels of educational attainment on strength of Jewish identity. Model 2 controls for occupational skill level. Model 3 adds controls for annual market income. Intermarriage is controlled in model 4. And model 5 introduces controls for residency in areas of high Jewish concentration: whether one lives in Montreal or Toronto (which together account for about three quarters of Canada's Jewish population) and the percentage of core Jews who reside in the census tract where an individual lives.

Each successive model improves on its predecessor. Thus, as one moves from model 1 to model 5, the percentage of explained variation in strength of Jewish identity increases from 1.8 per cent to 25.2 per cent. Additional analysis of change in the amount of variation explained by each model (R^2) shows that intermarriage has by far the strongest independent effect on strength of Jewish identity, followed by residential concentration. Education, annual market income, and occupational skill level have little independent effect. Changes in the regression coefficients from model 1 to model 5 further suggest that the effect of education on strength of Jewish identity works indirectly through

80 Robert Brym and Feng Hou

Table 6.2. Ordinary least squares (OLS) regression predicting degree of Jewishness for Canadians, ages 25–64, 2011 (n = 26,660)

	Model 1	Model 2	Model 3	Model 4	Model 5
Education (ref.: high school or less)					
Some post-secondary education	−0.164***	−0.125*	−0.127*	−0.038	−0.022
	(0.056)[a]	(0.056)	(0.056)	(0.049)	(0.049)
Bachelor's degree	−0.758**	−0.639***	−0.601***	−0.355***	−0.317***
	(0.052)	(0.054)	(0.054)	(0.048)	(0.048)
Master's degree	−0.662***	−0.511***	−0.449***	−0.186***	−0.159**
	(0.054)	(0.058)	(0.058)	(0.052)	(0.051)
Doctoral degree	−0.436***	−0.265**	−0.100	−0.130	−0.220*
	(0.094)	(0.099)	(0.098)	(0.088)	(0.088)
Degree in medicine	−1.243***	−1.076***	−0.813***	−0.315***	−0.328***
	(0.090)	(0.096)	(0.098)	(0.087)	(0.086)
Degree in law	−1.261***	−1.093***	−0.862***	−0.502***	−0.488***
	(0.087)	(0.092)	(0.094)	(0.083)	(0.082)
Occupational skill level (ref.: low-skilled)					
Technical		−0.209***	−0.193**	−0.183**	−0.179***
		(0.054)	(0.054)	(0.046)	(0.047)
Professional		−0.380***	−0.326***	−0.372***	−0.374***
		(0.054)	(0.055)	(0.047)	(0.048)
Managerial		−0.524***	−0.380***	−0.368***	−0.353***
		(0.058)	(0.060)	(0.052)	(0.053)
Annual market income (ref.: > $0 to < = $19,999)					
$20,000 to $49,999			0.031	0.027	0.029
			(0.052)	(0.046)	(0.045)
$50,000 to $79,999			0.044	−0.011	−0.018
			(0.055)	(0.049)	(0.048)
$80,000 to $99,999			−0.017	−0.043	−0.059
			(0.068)	(0.060)	(0.059)
$100,000+			−0.477***	−0.317***	−0.279***
			(0.058)	(0.051)	(0.050)
Non-Jewish partner (0 = yes; 1 = no)				2.707***	2.370***
				(0.032)	(0.035)
Residential concentration					
Montreal or Toronto (0 = no; 1 = yes)					−0.525***
					(0.037)
Per cent (%) core Jews in census tract					−0.009***
					(0.001)

(Continued)

Table 6.2. Ordinary least squares (OLS) regression predicting degree of Jewishness for Canadians, ages 25–64, 2011 (n = 26,660) (Continued)

	Model 1	Model 2	Model 3	Model 4	Model 5
Intercept	3.069***	3.272***	3.266***	2.176***	2.807***
	(0.041)	(0.050)	(0.059)	(0.054)	(0.060)
R^2	0.018	0.022	0.027	0.236	0.252

*p < 0.05, **p < 0.01, ***p <0.001
[a] Standard errors (se) in parentheses.
Source: Statistics Canada (2011).

occupation, earnings, and intermarriage; the effect of occupation works partly indirectly through earnings, intermarriage, and residential concentration; and the effect of earnings works partly indirectly through intermarriage and residential concentration.[5]

Model 5 includes all controls. It indicates that earning a bachelor's degree, a medical degree, or a law degree are more statistically significant than earning a master's degree and a PhD. This finding may reflect a decline since the 1970s in the percentage of academics who are of Jewish origin, a phenomenon that has been documented for the United States but not for Canada (Chiswick 2009). For occupational skill level, the most significant effects are for professional and managerial occupations, while for annual income only the highest bracket (earnings of $100,000+ per year, more than twice the median for all Canadians in 2011) is statistically significant in the full model.

How to Think about Degrees of Identity

Our analysis examines the relationship between (1) the homogeneity/heterogeneity of various bases of association as indexed by individuals' socio-economic characteristics and (2) degree of Jewish identity. However, two variables not examined here stand behind this relationship in time and causal priority. Specifically, every household is characterized by the cultural preferences of its adult members and the structure of opportunities they face (see figure 6.2).

Structures of opportunities are governed by power relations – the capacity of dominant groups to permit or obstruct entry by subordinate groups to educational institutions, jobs of varying quality, and positions of political authority. Opportunities may be abundant or few, and adult household members respond accordingly (Goldscheider and Zuckerman 1984). At one extreme – say, Canada today – Jews can relatively

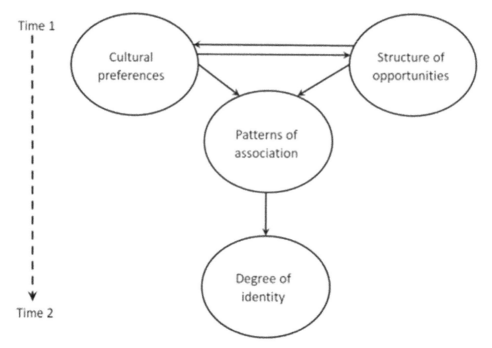

Figure 6.2. A causal model of degree of identity
Note: Solid lines represent causal paths, with arrowheads indicating the direction of causation. The dashed line indicates the passage of time between the formation of a household and the maturation of the household's offspring.

easily gain a higher education, advance in the occupational hierarchy, participate fully in the political life of the nation, and live where they please. At the other extreme – say, Nazi Germany – they enjoy none of these advantages, so they migrate, if possible, to a country with more structural opportunities or otherwise confront their fate.

Past generations developed cultural preferences for particular types of education, occupations, political involvement, and residential patterns based on the structure of opportunities *they* faced. For instance, Jews invited by Western European aristocrats and members of royalty to perform middleman functions in pre-modern Western Europe developed a certain disdain for physical labour, a preference for relative occupational autonomy, and a tendency to live in ghettos (Leshchinsky [1928] 2020). They also developed a political tradition of petitioning and interceding with higher powers to achieve political aims. These cultural preferences were reinforced beginning in the thirteenth century, when

Jews were being expelled by Western European rulers while Polish rulers invited them to perform similar economic functions in Eastern Europe. The standards were passed down until late nineteenth- and early twentieth-century socialists and Zionists began emphasizing the virtues of physical labour, national–cultural autonomy, and, in the case of the Zionists, sovereignty.

The structure of opportunities and historically conditioned cultural preferences in Canada today influence one's choice of social settings, which are in turn characterized by varying degrees of ethnic and religious homogeneity/heterogeneity. These settings then reinforce or weaken ethnic and religious identification. In this manner, cultural preferences, opportunity structures, and patterns of association combine to influence the various ways in which one can identify as a Jew. Ultimately, they influence the cohesiveness and therefore the degree and character of the Canadian Jewish community's continuity.

NOTES

1 We focus on individuals twenty-five to sixty-four years of age because most people in that age cohort are in their prime working years.
2 Census tracts are divisions of 2,500–8,000 people located in centres with an urban core population of 50,000 or more. More than 95 per cent of Canadian Jews live in census tracts.
3 The central tendency tends to be better represented by the median than the mean because of the upward skew typically associated with income distributions.
4 By far the smallest of the twelve categories ($n = 480$ in the sample, an estimated 2,620 in the population) include people with a non-Jewish religion and single Jewish ethnicity. Their characteristics are somewhat anomalous given the observed trends in the data. Specifically, they have an unexpectedly low rate of intermarriage (a surprisingly high number of them are married to a Jew by religion), an unexpectedly high percentage of them have a law degree or work in a low-skilled occupation, their median annual income is unexpectedly low, they are disproportionately in the 45–64 age cohort, and they are somewhat more likely to live in areas with a high concentration of Jews than one would expect.
5 For instance, in model 1 the difference between individuals with a law degree and those with a high school diploma or less is 1.261 on the twelve-point scale of Jewish identity. The difference falls to 1.093 in model 2 when occupational skills are controlled. Because $|-1.261| - |-1.093| = 0.168$, and $|0.168| \div |-1.261| = 13.3\%$, the decrease suggests that about 13 per cent of the effect of education on Jewish identity is indirect in the sense that it works

through the achievement of higher occupational status. In model 3, which controls for annual market income, the difference between a law degree and a high school diploma or less falls to 0.862, implying that the effect of education also works partly through higher annual income. Furthermore, when intermarriage and residential concentration are controlled in model 5, only about 39 per cent of the observed difference in model 1 remains: $(-0.488) \div (-1.261) = 38.7\%$. Similar patterns are evident at other educational levels. In short, most of the effect of education on Jewish identity works indirectly through the achievement of relatively high occupational status, earnings, and residential concentration, and a relatively low intermarriage rate.

REFERENCES

Chiswick, Barry. 2009. "The Rise and Fall of the American Jewish PhD." *Contemporary Jewry* 29 (1): 67–84. https://doi.org/10.1007/s12397-008-9000-9.

DellaPergola, Sergio. 2015. "End of Jewish/Non-Jewish Dichotomy? Evidence from the 2013 Pew Survey." In *American Jewish Year Book 2014*, Vol. 114, edited by Arnold Dashefsky and Ira M. Sheskin, 33–9. Cham, Switzerland: Springer.

DellaPergola, Sergio. 2022. "World Jewish Population, 2021." In *American Jewish Year Book 2021*, edited by Arnold Dashefsky and Ira M. Sheskin, Vol. 121, 313–412. Cham, Switzerland: Springer.

Goldscheider, Calvin, and Alan S. Zuckerman. 1984. *The Transformation of the Jews*. Chicago: University of Chicago Press.

Hartman, Harriet, and Moshe Hartman. 2009. *Gender and American Jews: Patterns in Work, Education and Family in Contemporary Life*. Hanover, NH: Brandeis University Press.

Leshchinsky, Yakov. (1928) 2020. "The Development of the Jewish People over the Last 100 Years." Translated by Robert Brym. *East European Jewish Affairs* 50 (1/2): 157–242. https://doi.org/10.1080/13501674.2020.1793279.

Rebhun, Uzi. 2015. "*Assimilation in American Life*: An Empirical Assessment of Milton Gordon's Multidimensional Theory." *Journal of Contemporary Religion* 30 (3): 473–96. https://doi.org/10.1080/13537903.2015.1081350.

Reitz, Jeffrey G. 1980. *The Survival of Ethnic Groups*. Toronto: McGraw-Hill.

Sartre, Jean-Paul. (1946) 1965. *Anti-Semite and Jew*. Translated by George J. Becker. New York: Schocken.

Statistics Canada. 2011. *2011 National Household Survey*. Catalogue no. 99-004-XWE. Ottawa: Statistics Canada.

7 Jewish Residential Patterns and Identity

JOSHUA HAROLD

Cultural Preference and Neighbourhood Choice

In chapter 6 of this volume, Brym and Hou show that strength of Jewish identity is associated with the social locations individuals occupy. After predicting variation in strength of Jewish identity using occupational, educational, residential, and other indicators of social location, they conclude with a theoretical statement. They propose that people choose to enter one social location or another depending on how power relations structure their opportunities, with cultural preferences leading them to favour particular social locations (see figure 6.2).

Brym and Hou do not, however, examine empirically how either of these factors impact the decision to enter one social location or another. In this chapter, I add empirical substance to their theoretical claim by examining how cultural preferences influence whether individuals choose to reside in a Jewish neighbourhood. Specifically, using data from the 2018 Survey of Jews in Canada and the 2011 National Household Survey, I measure the effect of a series of variables on residential choice. These variables tap the cultural heritage that Canadian Jews learn as they proceed through the life course.

The decision to reside in one neighbourhood or another is influenced by many social forces other than those I examine here, among them affordability of housing, quality and type of schools and natural environment, and proximity to work, relatives, shopping, and recreational facilities. Given the myriad factors that come into play, I do not expect to be able to explain a high percentage of the variation in choice of neighbourhood. But that is not my aim. Here, I seek only to identify some of the social sources of the cultural preference to reside in a Jewish neighbourhood and then assess the strength of their effects.

Life Is with People

For centuries, internal and external forces caused Jews to reside closely clustered. On the one hand, living in proximity to one another was desirable insofar as it facilitated communal and institutional life, friendships, and a sense of togetherness. A famous anthropological study of the Eastern European *shtetl* (a small, predominantly Jewish town), appropriately titled *Life Is with People*, emphasized the centrality of sociability as a cultural principle of Jewish life (Zborowski and Herzog 1952). The historical record shows that, even in the first decades of the twentieth century, segregated Jewish neighbourhoods provided Jewish immigrants in Canada with a sense of security and access to social networks for jobs, religious and cultural amenities, and mutual aid societies (Tulchinsky 2008).

On the other hand, the clustering of Jews in ghettos, *shtetlekh*, and segregated neighbourhoods was also the result of discrimination and restrictions imposed by the outside world. For example, in the first decades of the twentieth century, deeply antisemitic Poland stands out as the country with the highest degree of Jewish residential segregation. Jews composed 80–90 per cent of certain sections of Warsaw, Lodz, Pinsk, Grodno, Bialystok, and other Polish cities and towns (Leshchinsky 1947). But even in Canada, the early establishment of densely populated Jewish areas was influenced by discrimination and regulations restricting where Jews could live (Harris 2004).

In the 1910s, the overwhelming majority of Toronto's 18,000 Jews lived in the southern half of what is today Toronto's downtown – a rectangle bounded on the east by Yonge Street, on the west by University Avenue, on the north by College Street, and on the south by Queen Street. "The Ward" or "St. John Shtetl," as it was commonly known, boasted four synagogues and countless mutual benefit societies, *cheders* (Jewish primary schools), *landsmanshaftn* (fraternal organizations of immigrants from the same city or region), clothing workshops and factories, and of course houses – although "boasted" is perhaps an inappropriate verb in the case of the houses, nearly one third of which lacked plumbing and 108 of which were declared unfit for human habitation by the city's medical officer of health in 1911. As modern buildings replaced old structures, Jews moved westward en masse to Kensington Market and Spadina Avenue, which became equally well known for their vibrant Jewish life – and crowded and unsanitary conditions (Speisman 1979). The downtown areas of St. Louis and Laurier were to Montreal what Kensington and Spadina were to Toronto (Weiser 2021).

As housing restrictions eased and educational and occupational opportunities increased, Jews gradually moved out of the inner city. However, most of them did not scatter. It is more accurate to say that most of them moved collectively to a few new locations. Consequently, although about two thirds of Canadian Jews are non-immigrants, Jews remain among the most residentially concentrated ethnic groups in Canada and the most residentially concentrated religious group; residential concentration is higher only among a few racially distinct groups composed largely of recent immigrants (Fong and Chan 2011; Balakrishnan and Gyimah 2003; Fong and Wilkes 2003; see also chapter 20 of this volume). Jews no longer live in the unsanitary and crowded conditions of The Ward, but they continue to cluster in certain sections of Canada's largest cities.

The persistence of Jewish residential concentration across generations runs counter to conventional thinking about immigrant settlement and integration. The frequently employed sociological theory of spatial assimilation emphasizes how socio-economic factors shape residential patterns. Simplifying somewhat, the idea is that as a minority group's socio-economic status improves, its members disperse spatially, integrating into the larger society and maximizing their chances of further improving their socio-economic status (Mendez 2009). The socio-economic position of Jews has improved considerably over the last century. Jews have higher levels of education than most other ethnic groups and tend to be overrepresented in professional occupations (see chapter 6 in this volume). They have dispersed spatially, but much less than one would expect given their rate of upward mobility. Jews remained relatively concentrated as they moved into middle-class suburban neighbourhoods. Bathurst Street in Toronto exemplifies this phenomenon. Jews migrated northward from Spadina and Kensington along Bathurst Street to Forest Hill, the Bathurst and Lawrence area, and then into Vaughan (Thornhill). The flow is evident from the age of synagogues, Jewish community centres, and Jewish schools as one proceeds north on Bathurst Street (Schoenfeld 2020; Harold and Fong 2018a).

What accounts for the relative continuity of Jewish residential concentration across generations? Historically, restricted opportunities for residential choice loomed large in the ghettoization and residential segregation of Jews. In Brym and Hou's terminology, given the distribution of power between Jews and non-Jews, there were relatively few opportunities for Jews to live outside ghettoes and strictly circumscribed neighbourhoods. However, in a relatively tolerant, free, and high-mobility society like Canada today, such restrictions exist barely if at all. It follows that cultural preferences have come to play a proportionately larger causal role in choice of residence than they did in the past.

In this chapter, I identify several indicators of cultural preference and assess their influence on Jewish residential concentration. My approach borrows from life course theory, which focuses on how events and processes early in the life course influence later life events (Elder, Johnson, and Crosnoe 2003). For example, primary socialization in the family introduces a child to certain cultural preferences. Then, as ethnic and religious aspects of identity crystallize during adolescence and early adulthood, they are painted not just by contemporaneous experiences but also by the cultural preferences one learned earlier in the life course. Subsequently, in adulthood, one's social environment is characterized by supportive forces (such as the hardening of friendship circles) and hostile forces (such as perceived group threats). The perception of threats is influenced not just or even mainly by the objective and concurrent level of threat but also and perhaps mostly by cultural predispositions learned earlier in life. Likewise, the composition of one's adult friendship circle is influenced by the inclusion of childhood friends (Bar-Tal and Antebi 1992; Harold and Fong 2018b; Kouvo and Lockmer 2013; Peach 1996; Tavory 2016; chapter 19 in this volume).

The decision to live in one neighbourhood or another is influenced by the cumulative and interacting effects of all the preceding and concomitant events and processes just listed. Specifically, I expect that primary socialization, the crystallization of ethnic and denominational identities, the ethnic composition of one's friendship network, and perceptions of the severity of antisemitism influence the decision to live in a Jewish neighbourhood.

Before testing my argument, I offer a thumbnail sketch of how the pattern of Jewish residential concentration has changed over time.

Canadian Jewish Geography

Jewish residential settlement in Canada has been an uneven process, with the Jewish population clustering in just a few areas. Jews can be found in all Canadian provinces and territories, but 85 per cent of them are concentrated in the metropolitan areas of Toronto, Montreal, Vancouver, Winnipeg, and Ottawa. Even in Atlantic Canada, over one half of the region's 4,000 Jews live in metropolitan Halifax (Shahar 2014).

Jewish residential patterns are continuously shifting and tied to broader processes of immigration, urbanization, and suburbanization. Large waves of Jewish migration to Canada from Central and Eastern Europe in the second half of the nineteenth century saw Jewish populations in Toronto, Montreal, and Winnipeg grow substantially. Nevertheless, a small number of Jewish immigrants settled in smaller cities and even rural settings. In the 1870s, nearly all Jews in Canada lived in Ontario and Quebec, but by the 1930s about 20 per cent had moved westward (Rosenberg [1939] 1993). The influx of Jewish immigrants to Toronto ultimately made it home to the country's largest Jewish community, the population of which now accounts for nearly one half of Canadian Jewry.

It was around the 1930s that Jews in Toronto and Montreal began moving out of inner-city areas into new suburbs. The movement intensified in the years following the Second World War. In Toronto, Jews began moving into Forest Hill and then into York Region. The suburban Jewish population grew from 2.1 per cent of the City of Toronto's total (Jewish and non-Jewish) population in 1951 to 7.2 per cent a decade later (Klaff 1983). A similar trend was apparent in Montreal as Jews increasingly settled in Outremont and Westmount. In Vancouver, early immigrants who settled in the East End moved to the West End, and in Winnipeg, Jews increasingly moved out of the North End to the city's southern neighbourhoods.

At the turn of the twentieth century, Toronto's Jewish community was about one-half the size of Montreal's, but by 1981 Toronto was home to more than 40 per cent of the country's Jews while Montreal was home to 34 per cent of them. In 2011, the last year for which there is reliable data as of this writing, Toronto accounted for 48 per cent of Canadian Jews, with Montreal at 23 per cent, Vancouver at 7 per cent, and Winnipeg and Ottawa each at 3.5 per cent.

Within census metropolitan areas (CMAs), Jews are concentrated in a number of areas. With a Jewish population of more than 70,000, York Region is home to 37 per cent of Jews in the Toronto CMA (Shahar, Gofine, and Pelly 2015), and Vaughan is home to 67 per cent of Jews in York Region. Even so, Jews form a minority in Vaughan, accounting for about 16 per cent of its residents. Richmond Hill has the second largest Jewish population in York Region at 17 per cent. While the more northern parts of York Region – King, Aurora, and Newmarket – have smaller numbers of Jews, the Jewish populations there grew considerably after 1991. For example, Newmarket witnessed Jewish population growth of 117 per cent between 1991 and 2011, while Aurora's Jewish population grew by 180 per cent (Shahar, Gofine, and Pelly 2015).

In the Montreal CMA, 21 per cent of Jews live in Côte Saint-Luc and 13 per cent in the West Island (Shahar 2014). In terms of population density, Hampstead and Côte Saint-Luc are in the lead; Jews compose 75 per cent and 62 per cent of the total population in these areas, respectively. While Toronto's Jewish population continues to grow (as does that of Calgary, Ottawa, and Vancouver, the last of which witnessed 30 per cent growth in its Jewish population between 1991 and 2011), the Jewish population of Montreal has been declining for several decades – by more than 10 per cent from 1991 to 2011 alone. A similar decline is evident in Winnipeg.

The 2018 Survey of Jews in Canada explored this issue in Montreal and Winnipeg. It found that many Jews are leaving for better career opportunities, to be closer to family or friends in other cities, and to be part of a larger or different Jewish community (Brym, Neuman, and Lenton 2019a, 70–1). Of the Jews remaining in Winnipeg, more than one half live in the southern part of the city, particularly in the neighbourhoods of Tuxedo and River Heights (Rosenberg-Cohen 2016).

The Jewish community of Vancouver, although twice the size of its Winnipeg counterpart, is anomalous in terms of clustering. There are no distinctly Jewish neighbourhoods in Vancouver similar to Tuxedo and River Heights in Winnipeg (Shahar and Rivkin 2014). Nonetheless, parts of the Vancouver CMA have larger Jewish populations than others. Some 55 per cent of Jews in the Vancouver CMA live in the City of Vancouver, and 23 per cent call Greater Richmond their home. The West Side of Vancouver has the highest density of Jews at 4 per cent of the total population (Shahar and Rivkin 2014).

Measuring Jewish Cultural Preferences and Residential Concentration

To better understand how cultural preferences shape Jewish residential clustering in Canada, I examined several aspects of socialization as they develop over the life course using data from the 2018 Survey of Jews in Canada.

Primary socialization in the family introduces children to the cultural norms, beliefs, values, and practices of their parents. It acts as a kind of filter later in the life course, establishing cultural predilections that structure receptivity to subsequent influences. Accordingly, I distinguished respondents who do not have two Jewish parents (coded 0) from those with two Jewish parents (coded 1), expecting the latter to be more inclined to choose to live in a Jewish neighbourhood.

Jewish identity becomes fully crystallized as one approaches and enters adulthood. Influenced by earlier cultural preferences, Jewish identity also influences the probability of choosing to live in a Jewish neighbourhood. Jewish identity is double-faceted, combinatorial, and variable:

- *Double-faceted*. For some people, Jewishness is tied to a particular religious denomination, which reflects patterns of ritual observance and belief to varying degrees. Alternatively, Jewishness may be a cultural or ethnic identity that does not include religion. Here, Jewishness may centre on feeling part of the Jewish people, attachment to Israel, or supporting community organizations.
- *Combinatorial*. An individual's Jewish identity may include one or both of the elements just listed.
- *Variable*. The strength of Jewish identity, however an individual defines it, varies from one person to the next.

To account for the double-faceted, combinatorial, and variable aspects of identity, I created a scale of ethnic identity and a measure of denominational identification. I constructed the ethnic identity index from items in the 2018 Survey of Jews in Canada including how emotionally attached respondents are to Israel, how connected they feel to Jewish life in the city where they live, and how important being Jewish is to them. Available responses to these items ranged from "not at all" to "very." The scale items also included measures of whether respondents made a financial donation to a Jewish charity or cause in the year before the survey, and whether they know the Hebrew alphabet; these last two variables are binary (yes or no).

Items in the ethnic identity scale were standardized to account for questions having different numbers of response options, and the standardized values were added together. The result was an approximately three-point scale with a range of −2.55 to 0.692 (sd = 0.682). Higher scores on the scale indicate a stronger Jewish ethnic identity. The bottom third of the scale may be said to correspond to weak identity, the middle third to moderate identity, and the top third to strong identity. Cronbach's alpha is 0.696 for the ethnic identity scale, indicating acceptable reliability. I expected that higher scores would be associated with an increased likelihood of choosing to live in a Jewish neighbourhood.

The religious denomination variable is based on the denomination respondents identified with, if any. I divided the denomination variable into four categories: no affiliation = 1, liberal = 2, Conservative = 3, and traditional = 4. Respondents were coded as liberal if they identified with the Reform, Reconstructionist, or Humanist branches of Judaism, as Conservative if they identified with the Conservative denomination, and as traditional if they identified as Orthodox, Modern Orthodox, Chasidic, or Yeshivish. I expected Jewish residential clustering to increase with higher scores on the denomination variable.

A questionnaire item in the 2018 Survey of Jews in Canada asked, "How many of your close friends are Jewish? Would you say: all of them, most of them, some of them, hardly any of them, or none of them?" I coded responses as follows: none of them = 1, hardly any of them = 2, some of them = 3, most of them = 4, and all of them = 5. I expected that people with higher scores would be more inclined to choose to live in a Jewish neighbourhood.

I also anticipated that choosing to live in a Jewish neighbourhood would be more likely for adults who think antisemitism is widespread than for adults who think it is circumscribed. A questionnaire item that asked respondents how often they think Jews are the subject of discrimination in Canada measured this variable (rarely or never = 0, sometimes or often = 1).

The dependent variable in my analysis is the percentage of Jews in a census forward sortation area (FSA) based on the 2011 National Household Survey. On average, about 20,000 people reside in an FSA, which corresponds to the first three characters of a person's postal code. About nine of ten respondents in the 2018 Survey of Jews in Canada supplied the first three characters of their postal code. Hereafter I refer to FSAs as "neighbourhoods," and FSAs in which 10 per cent or more of the population is Jewish as "Jewish neighbourhoods." I define Jews as those who identify with the Jewish religion and those who identify with no religion but identify as Jewish by ethnicity. It was necessary to estimate the percentage of Jews who identify with no religion but identify as Jewish by ethnicity. To do so, I subtracted the number of Jews by religion from the total Jewish population in a CMA and calculated the difference as a percentage of the total. This percentage was then added to each FSA.

Table 7.1 shows the percentage of respondents in each city who scored high on each of the measures just described. Even this crude array shows that the cities with the strongest levels of Jewish socialization have the largest percentage of Jews living in Jewish neighbourhoods. Thus, the average score on the five indicators of Jewish socialization in table 7.1 is 42 per cent for Vancouver, 48 per cent for Winnipeg, 55 per cent for Toronto, and 57 per cent for Montreal. The proportion of Jews living in Jewish neighbourhoods is zero in Vancouver, about three in ten in Winnipeg, and about seven in ten in both Toronto and Montreal.

Table 7.2 provides additional details on the density of the Jewish population in the four cities of interest. On average, Jews compose a small percentage of neighbourhood populations in the four cities. Among all FSAs in the census metropolitan area of Montreal, the average percentage of Jews is 4 per cent. Among all FSAs in the census metropolitan area of Toronto, the comparable figure is 2 per cent. In Winnipeg and Vancouver, the comparable figure is 1 per cent. Still, as described earlier, there are some neighbourhoods where the density of Jews is much higher. About one quarter of Montreal's Jews live in neighbourhoods

Table 7.1. Jewish socialization and residential concentration by city, 2018 (n = 2,335)

	Toronto	Montreal	Winnipeg	Vancouver
Per cent living in a Jewish neighbourhood*	73	69	31	0
Average of the five indicators listed below	55	57	48	42
Per cent with both parents Jewish	91	91	81	75
Per cent with strong Jewish ethnic identity	25	26	23	24
Per cent with traditional denominational identity	16	29	6	9
Per cent who think antisemitism is widespread	85	82	80	77
Per cent with most or all Jewish friends	59	59	50	27

* Jewish neighbourhoods are defined as Statistics Canada's forward sortation areas (FSAs) when ten per cent or more of the inhabitants are identified as Jewish by religion or ethnicity. FSAs that passed this threshold were identified from the 2011 National Household Survey. "Per cent living in a Jewish neighbourhood" is based on the 2,079 respondents in the 2018 Survey of Jews in Canada who supplied postal code information that allowed us to identify their FSAs. All other variables are based on the 2,335 respondents in the 2018 Survey of Jews in Canada. Jewish ethnic identity was coded as strong if a respondent scored among the top 25 per cent on the Jewish ethnic identity scale.
Sources: Brym, Neuman, and Lenton (2019b); Statistics Canada (2014).

where more than six in ten residents are Jewish, and about one fifth of Toronto's Jews live in neighbourhoods where five in ten residents are Jewish. Montrealers are most likely and Vancouverites least likely to live in neighbourhoods densely populated by Jews, with a relatively small difference between residents of Montreal and Toronto. Winnipeggers occupy roughly the mid-point between those two cities and Vancouver in terms of Jewish population density.

Choosing Whether to Live in a Jewish Neighbourhood

How much do each of the factors I have identified contribute to the decision to live in a Jewish neighbourhood in Canada? To answer this question, I conducted multiple regression analyses, the results of which are reported in table 7.3.

Table 7.3 displays three regression models that represent successive stages in the life course. Model 1 measures only the effect of having two Jewish parents on the decision to live in a Jewish neighbourhood. It shows that being raised by two Jewish parents significantly increases the likelihood of making that choice. Specifically, having two Jewish parents increases Jewish residential concentration by exactly 100 per cent.[1] Put differently, the percentage of Jews living in an FSA is twice as high for those whose parents are Jewish than for those who have fewer than two Jewish parents.

Table 7.2. Per cent of Jews by density of Jewish population in city FSAs, 2018

Density of Jewish population in %	Toronto	Montreal	Winnipeg	Vancouver
<5%	14	23	48	90
5–9%	13	7	21	10
10–14%	5	9	15	0
15–19%	9	10	0	0
20–24%	11	8	16	0
25–29%	8	4	0	0
30–34%	5	3	0	0
35–39%	9	0	0	0
40–44%	4	11	0	0
45–49%	0	0	0	0
50–54%	21	0	0	0
55–59%	0	0	0	0
60–64%	0	0	0	0
65%+	0	24	0	0
Total	100	100	100	100
Average	2	4	1	1

Note: Columns may not total 100 per cent due to rounding.
Source: Harold (2023).

Table 7.3. General linear model (GLM) regression predicting Jewish residential clustering in Canada ($n = 1,740$)

	Model 1	Model 2	Model 3
Both parents Jewish	0.692***	0.454***	0.343***
	(0.068)[a]	(0.074)	(0.074)
Ethnic identity scale		0.276***	0.171***
		(0.036)	(0.036)
Denominational identity		0.112***	0.069**
		(0.023)	(0.022)
Proportion of Jewish friends			0.381***
			(0.031)
Perception of antisemitism			0.203***
			(0.061)
Constant	2.491***	2.410***	1.035***
	(0.065)	(0.088)	(0.140)
Log likelihood	−7158.085	−7100.969	−7044.167
Aikake information criterion (AIC)	8.220	8.167	8.104

**$p < 0.01$, ***$p < 0.001$
Note: The dependent variable is a percentage. Ordinary least squares regression can predict values less than 0 or more than 100, so I used a general linear model with a gamma distribution, which models skewed and truncated distributions.
[a] Standard errors (se) in parentheses.
Source: Brym, Neuman, and Lenton (2019b).

Model 2 moves beyond the key circumstance influencing primary socialization to include the crystallization of ethnic identity and religious denominational identity, presumably in late adolescence and early adulthood. I found that people with a stronger ethnic Jewish identity and a more traditional religious affiliation are significantly more likely to live in a Jewish neighbourhood than are others. Specifically, moving from the bottom third of the ethnic identity scale to the middle third (or from the middle third to the top third) increases Jewish residential clustering by 32 per cent. Similarly, moving "up" one rung in denominational affiliation increases Jewish residential clustering by 12 per cent. The percentage of Jews living in an FSA is thus 64 per cent higher for Jews with a strong Jewish ethnic identity (the top third of the ethnic identity scale) than those with a weak Jewish identity (the bottom third of the scale), and 36 per cent higher for Jews who identify with traditional denominations than those who do not identify with any denomination.

Notably, once the ethnic identity scale and the religious denomination variable are added to the regression model, the effect of having two Jewish parents weakens but remains statistically significant. This result implies that having two Jewish parents is both directly and indirectly associated with choosing to live in a Jewish neighbourhood. That is, primary socialization by itself influences neighbourhood choice (this is the direct effect), but it also increases the influence of ethnic identity and religious denomination on neighbourhood choice (this is the indirect effect). This finding is consistent with the argument that events and processes at different stages of the life cycle are not merely additive in their effects. Rather, early events and processes filter the effect of later events and processes. In the case at hand, they magnify them.

Model 3 adds two more variables to the regression equation: the proportion of respondents' Jewish friends and respondents' perception of antisemitism at the time of the survey. Since 89 per cent of respondents in the weighted sample were thirty years or older, I believe these measures adequately tap circumstances at a later stage of the life cycle than the measures in models 1 and 2 do.

I found that with each increase in the ethnic homogeneity of the friendship network – from no Jewish friends to hardly any, from hardly any to some, from some to most, or from most to all – Jewish residential concentration increases by 46 per cent. The difference between having no Jewish friends and all Jewish friends is therefore associated with a 184 per cent increase in the percentage of Jews residing in one's neighbourhood.

Jewish residential clustering also increases significantly when antisemitism is perceived to be a widespread problem for Jews in Canada. That is because living in a Jewish neighbourhood increases one's sense of security by reducing the feeling that one is an outsider and increasing one's sense of belonging (Alper and Olson 2011; Harold and Fong 2018b). The percentage of Jews living in a neighbourhood is 23 per cent higher for those who view antisemitism as a persistent problem in Canada than for those who believe antisemitism is rare or non-existent.

In model 3, the effects of variables introduced earlier once again weaken but remain statistically significant, supporting the life-course argument that earlier events and processes filter the effects of later ones. Model 3 also permits ranking the predictors in order of their independent effects. That is, it is possible to measure and rank the effect of each predictor controlling for all other predictors. With all variables in the equation, the percentage of Jews in one's neighbourhood increases by 46 per cent as one moves from no Jewish friends to hardly any, from hardly any to some, from some to most, or from most to all; by 41 per cent if one has two Jewish parents as opposed to fewer than two; by 23 per cent for those who view antisemitism as a persistent problem in Canada as opposed to those who think antisemitism is rare or non-existent; by 19 per cent as one moves one third of the way up the ethnic identity scale; and by 7 per cent as one moves from no denominational affiliation to liberal affiliation, from liberal to Conservative, or from Conservative to traditional. Finally, I note that model 3 fits the data better than the preceding models, as indicated by the declining Aikake information criterion (AIC) statistic across models.

Culture and Place

The decision to live in a Jewish neighbourhood stems from a range of socio-economic and cultural factors. On average, Jews in Canada enjoy a relatively high level of university education and annual income. The concentration of the Jewish community in metropolitan areas and specific neighbourhoods within metropolitan areas is partly a reflection of socio-economic differences between Jews and other minority groups (Fong and Wilkes 2003; cf. Schoenfeld 2020 for a similar argument regarding Jews in the United States). However, as I have illustrated, a well-rounded picture of the desire for residential propinquity also requires understanding the role of cultural preferences. This chapter shows how different stages of socialization into the community's culture over an individual's life course play an important role in shaping the Jewish residential landscape of Canadian cities.

My analysis nonetheless suffers from shortcomings, not the least of which is that I have ignored the ethnic, racial, and sexual diversity of Canada's Jewish community and the variation in socialization experiences associated with this variation. Canadian Jews trace their origins to many countries with distinct cultures, and converts to Judaism come from myriad religious, ethnic, and racial groups. Moreover, LGBTQ+ Jews have socialization experiences that differ from those of the heterosexual majority (Weinfeld with Schnoor and Shames 2018). Surely information on the socialization experiences of the ethnic, racial, and sexual subgroups that compose Canadian Jewry – and the way those subgroups intersect and interact – would enrich our understanding of how Canadian Jewishness is associated with variation in residential concentration (Gonzalez-Lesser 2020). Future researchers may even be obliged to conclude that fractalization is a more appropriate term than clustering as a description of Jewish residential patterns in Canada.

NOTE

1 Table 7.3 presents log transformed coefficients. I exponentiated the coefficients so results could be expressed in percentage terms.

REFERENCES

Alper, Becka A., and Daniel Olsen. 2011. "Do Jews Feel Like Outsiders in America? The Impact of Anti-Semitism, Friendships, and Religious Geography." *Journal for the Scientific Study of Religion* 50 (4): 822–30. https://doi.org/10.1111/j.1468-5906.2011.01599.x.

Balakrishnan, T.R., and Stephen Gyimah. 2003. "Spatial Residential Patterns of Selected Ethnic Groups: Significance and Policy Implications." *Canadian Ethnic Studies* 35 (1): 113–34.

Bar-Tal, Daniel, and Dikla Antebi. 1992. "Beliefs about Negative Intentions of the World: A Study of the Israeli Siege Mentality." *Political Psychology* 13 (4): 633–45. https://doi.org/10.2307/3791494.

Brym, Robert, Keith Neuman, and Rhonda Lenton. 2019a. *2018 Survey of Jews in Canada: Final Report*. Toronto: Environics Institute for Survey Research. https://bit.ly/3tGZACg.

Brym, Robert, Keith Neuman, and Rhonda Lenton. 2019b. *2018 Survey of Jews in Canada*. Toronto: Environics Institute for Survey Research. Machine readable file.

Elder, Glen H., Monica Kirkpatrick Johnson, and Robert Crosnoe. 2003. "The Emergence and Development of Life Course Theory." In *Handbook of the Life Course*, edited by Jeylan T. Mortimer and Michael J. Shanahan, 3–19. New York: Kluwer Academic/Plenum Publishers.

Fong, Eric, and Elic Chan. 2011. "Residential Patterns among Religious Groups in Canadian Cities." *City and Community* 10 (4): 393–413. https://doi.org/10.1111/j.1540-6040.2011.01383.x.

Fong, Eric, and Rima Wilkes. 2003. "Racial and Ethnic Residential Patterns in Canada." *Sociological Forum* 18 (4): 577–602. https://doi.org/10.1023/B:SOFO.0000003004.78713.2e.

Gonzalez-Lesser, Emma. 2020. "Jewishness as *sui generis*: Extending Theorizations beyond the Debate of Race, Ethnicity, or Religion." *Ethnic and Racial Studies* 43 (3): 479–500. https://doi.org/10.1080/01419870.2019.1643487.

Harold, Joshua, and Eric Fong. 2018a. "Mnemonic Institutions and Residential Clustering: Jewish Residential Patterns in Toronto." *Canadian Review of Sociology* 55 (2): 257–77. https://doi.org/10.1111/cars.12192.

Harold, Joshua, and Eric Fong. 2018b. "Mobilizing Memory: Collective Memory Schemas and the Social Boundaries of Jews in Toronto." *Ethnic and Racial Studies* 41 (2): 343–61. https://doi.org/10.1080/01419870.2017.1344719.

Harris, Richard. 2004. *Creeping Conformity: How Canada Became Suburban, 1900–1960*. Toronto: University of Toronto Press.

Klaff, Vivian. 1983. "The Urban Ecology of Jewish Populations: A Comparative Analysis." In *Papers in Jewish Demography, 1977*, edited by Uziel O. Schmelz, Paul Glikson, and Sergio DellaPergola, 343–61. Jerusalem: Hebrew University of Jerusalem.

Kouvo, Antti, and Carita Lockmer. 2013 "Imagine All the Neighbours: Perceived Neighbourhood Ethnicity, Interethnic Friendship Ties and Perceived Ethnic Threat in Four Nordic Countries." *Urban Studies* 50 (19): 3305–22. https://doi.org/10.1177/0042098013484538.

Leshchinsky, Yakov. 1947. "Tzu der sotziologie fun poylishn yidntum" [Yiddish: On the sociology of Polish Jewry]. In *Oyfn rand fun opgrunt: Fun yidishn lebn in poyln (1927–1933)* [At the edge of the abyss: On Jewish life in Poland (1927–1933)], 15–54. Buenos Aires: Tsentral-farband fun poylishe yidn in argentina.

Mendez, Pablo. 2009. "Immigrant Residential Geographies and the 'Spatial Assimilation' Debate in Canada, 1997–2007." *Journal of International Migration and Integration* 10 (1): 89–108. https://doi.org/10.1007/s12134-008-0090-8.

Peach, Ceri. 1996. "Good Segregation, Bad Segregation." *Planning Perspectives* 11 (4): 379–98. https://doi.org/10.1080/026654396364817.

Rosenberg, Louis. (1939) 1993. *Canada's Jews: A Social and Economic Study of Jews in Canada in the 1930s*. Montreal: McGill-Queen's University Press.

Rosenberg-Cohen, Faye. 2016. *Jewish Winnipeg Demographics*. Winnipeg: Jewish Federation of Winnipeg. https://bit.ly/3jCgGhf.

Schoenfeld, Stuart. 2020, "Jews, Jewish Institutions, and the Construction of Identity in Changing American Cities and Urban Neighborhoods."

Contemporary Jewry 40 (3): 323–65. https://doi.org/10.1007/s12397
-020-09332-4.

Shahar, Charles. 2014. *2011 National Household Survey: The Jewish Population of Canada*. Part 1, *Basic Demographics*. Part 2, *Jewish Populations in Geographic Areas*. Toronto: Jewish Federations of Canada – UJA. https://bit.ly/3gSiWz1.

Shahar, Charles, Robin Gofine, and Sandi Pelly. 2015. *2011 National Household Survey: The Jewish Community of Toronto*. Part 1, *Basic Demographics*. Part 2, *Jewish Populations in Demographic Areas*. Toronto: Jewish Federations of Canada – UJA. http://bitly.ws/suYH.

Shahar, Charles, and Shelley Rivkin. 2014. *2011 National Household Survey: The Jewish Community of Greater Vancouver*. Part 1, *Basic Demographics*. Part 2, *Jewish Populations in Geographic Areas*. Vancouver: Jewish Federations of Canada – UJA. http://bitly.ws/suYG.

Speisman, Stephen A. 1979. *The Jews of Toronto: A History to 1937*. Toronto: McClelland & Stewart.

Statistics Canada. 2014. "Individuals File, 2011 National Household Survey (Public Use Microdata File)." Catalogue no. 99M0001X2011001. http://bitly.ws/t36i.

Tavory, Iddo. 2016. *Summoned: Identification and Religious Life in a Jewish Neighbourhood*. Chicago: University of Chicago Press.

Tulchinsky, Gerald. 2008. *Canada's Jews: A People's Journey*. Toronto: University of Toronto Press.

Weinfeld, Morton, with Randal F. Schnoor and Michelle Shames. 2018. *Like Everyone Else but Different: The Paradoxical Success of Canadian Jews*. 2nd ed. Montreal: McGill-Queen's University Press.

Weiser, Kalman. 2021. "Vilna on the St Lawrence: Montreal as the Would-Be Haven for Yiddish Culture." In *No Better Home? Jews, Canada, and the Sense of Belonging*, edited by David Koffman, 56–69. Toronto: University of Toronto Press.

Zborowski, Mark, and Elizabeth Herzog. 1952. *Life Is with People: The Culture of the Shtetl*. New York: Schocken Books.

8 Immigrant and Non-immigrant Household Income

NAOMI LIGHTMAN

Introduction

Historical and contemporary discrimination notwithstanding, Canada's Jews are often considered a model minority. Members of the community are said to prioritize education, achieve a high level of integration in the labour market, and enjoy above-average family income (see chapters 6 and 14 in this volume). Yet little is known about how the economic standing of Canadian Jews compares to that of other Canadians. The economic situation of Jewish immigrants in Canada – about one third of the country's Jewish population – is an especially unexplored area.

I shed light on these issues using data from the 2018 Survey of Jews in Canada and the 2011 National Household Survey. I focus on Jewish households in Toronto, Montreal, Vancouver, and Winnipeg, where more than eight in ten Canadian Jews live, and pay particular attention to how Jewish immigrants fare financially. My aim is to examine variation in household income between Jews and non-Jews and among various categories of the Jewish population while highlighting the effects of immigration status and city of residence. Three sets of questions structure the analysis:

1 How do Jews compare with non-Jews in terms of household income attainment, low income, and inequality in the country as a whole, and in the country's four cities with the largest Jewish populations?
2 How do Jewish immigrants compare to Jews born in Canada in terms of household income attainment and related socio-demographic factors?
3 Controlling for other relevant factors (age, gender, educational level, and so on), do Jewish immigrants experience a household income disadvantage in Canada?

I begin with an overview of the annual household income distribution of Jews and non-Jews in each city and then compare Jewish immigrants and non-immigrants. Finally, I turn to a multivariate analysis with relevant controls that assesses the determinants of annual household income for Canadian Jews.

Immigrants in Canada's Labour Market

Across Canada, discernible patterns exist in who gets ahead and who falls behind in the labour market, with inequalities sometimes leading to multigenerational disadvantages (Lightman et al. 2021; Lightman and Good Gingrich 2018; Pendakur and Pendakur 2015). In addition to a persistent and substantive wage gap between men and women, racial minorities and immigrants tend to earn less than their White or Canadian-born compatriots, and on average, immigrants tend to retire with less wealth than those who are Canadian-born (Block, Galabuzi, and Weiss 2014; Galabuzi and Teelucksingh 2010; Javdani and Pendakur 2014).

Across Canada, immigrants, especially racialized immigrants who arrived recently from "non-traditional" source countries, are consistently found to earn less than comparable Canadian-born workers. Over the past four decades, Canadian immigrants have seen a consistent and disproportionate decline in their earnings upon entering the workforce and are increasingly concentrated in part-time, contractual, seasonal, and other precarious labour market segments (Banerjee and Lee 2015; Hira-Friesen 2018; Lightman 2021). Immigrants tend to have a higher level of education than Canadian-born workers, but they are nearly twice as likely to experience low income and suffer the negative impacts of recessions first and for longer (Good Gingrich and Mitchell 2020; Picot and Sweetman 2012; Shields et al. 2011).

While most Jewish immigration occurred before the Second World War, significant immigrant waves arrived from Eastern Europe in the late 1940s and 1950s, North Africa beginning in the late 1950s, the former Soviet Union beginning in the late 1970s, South Africa in the 1980s and 1990s, and France in the 2000s. Israelis and Americans also form substantial parts of the Canadian Jewish immigrant community, although it is difficult to associate them with particular waves of immigration (Abella and Troper 1979; Reimers and Troper 1992; Troper 1993; Weinfeld with Schnoor and Shames 2018). Let us then compare the household income of Canadian-born Jews and non-Jews, and of Canadian-born Jews and Canadian Jewish immigrants.

102   Naomi Lightman

Table 8.1. Income measures for Jews and non-Jews after taxes and transfers, Canada, 2010

	Jews (n = 6,833)	Non-Jews (n = 688,189)	Difference (%)
Median total household income before tax ($)			
Toronto	32,000	25,000	28
Montreal	27,000	24,000	13
Vancouver	36,000	25,000	44
Winnipeg	30,000	26,000	15
Canada	31,000	26,000	19
Per cent in a low-income household before tax (%)			
Toronto	11	15	4
Montreal	17	18	1
Vancouver	10	17	7
Winnipeg	10	16	6
Canada	12	15	3

Note: Medians are significantly different based on a two-sample Wilcoxon rank-sum (Mann-Whitney) test. Small discrepancies in differences are due to rounding. Sample *ns* are shown.
Source: Statistics Canada (2011).

Jewish Income Inequality in Canada

Table 8.1 and figure 8.1 help to answer the first of the three questions I posed earlier: How do Jews compare with non-Jews in terms of household income attainment, low income, and inequality in the country as a whole and in the country's four cities with the largest Jewish populations?

Table 8.1 displays median household income and the proportion of the population below the Statistics Canada low income measure before tax (LIM-BT) in 2010, a full year before the 2011 National Household Survey was in the field. The LIM-BT is one-half the Canadian median household income multiplied by the square root of household size, adjusted to take into account that household needs increase with family size, but at a decreasing rate with each additional family member. The figures are for income after payment of income tax and receipt of transfer payments such as employment insurance and old age security.

Table 8.1 informs us that Jews earn higher income than non-Jews across Canada and in each of the four cities of interest here. For Canada as a whole, median total income before tax is more than 19 per cent higher for Jews. However, the inter-city difference ranges substantially from 13 per cent higher in Montreal to 44 per cent higher in Vancouver. In cities where Jewish households earn relatively high median

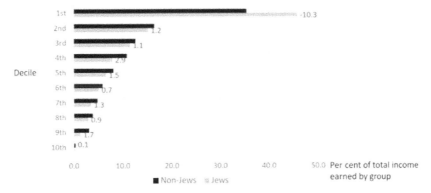

Figure 8.1. Distribution of household income for Jews and non-Jews after taxes and transfers, by decile, Canada, 2010
Note: The number beside each pair of bars indicates the difference between the share of total household income for Jews and the share of total household income for non-Jews. Positive numbers indicate the share is greater for non-Jews. The negative number indicates the share is greater for Jews. Sample n for Jews = 6,833; sample n for non-Jews = 688,189.
Source: Statistics Canada (2011).

household incomes (Toronto and Vancouver), we observe greater disparity in median household income between Jews and non-Jews.

The percentage of households earning low income is 3 points lower for Jews than for non-Jews, with differences in the four cities of interest ranging from 1 percentage point in Montreal to 7 percentage points in Vancouver. For Jews, the percentage of the population in a low-income household is by far the highest in Montreal at 17 per cent. In the other cities of interest, 10–11 per cent of the Jewish population are in low-income households.

Figure 8.1 illustrates income inequality. It shows how the percentage of total household income earned by all Jews is divided among the bottom 10 per cent (decile) of Jewish households, the next 10 per cent, and so on. It follows the same procedure for non-Jews. Figure 8.1 says that, for the bottom 90 per cent of Jewish and non-Jewish households, the share of total income earned by non-Jewish households is between 0.1 per cent and 2.9 per cent more than the share of income earned by Jewish households. However, for the top 10 per cent of Jewish households, the share of income earned by Jewish households is 10.3 per cent higher than the share earned by non-Jewish households. In other words, the level of household income inequality is much higher among Jews than non-Jews. The higher the ratio of the top decile's income share to the bottom decile's income share, the greater the level of income inequality for the group in question. The ratio is 229 for Jews and 118 for non-Jews. This difference is largely due

104   Naomi Lightman

to the relatively large proportion of Jewish professionals and managers compared to the corresponding proportion in the non-Jewish population.

The 2018 Survey of Jews in Canada provides details on the immigrant Jewish population over the age of seventeen in the four cities of interest. Some 29 per cent of respondents in the weighted sample were born outside of Canada. The percentage of Jewish immigrants in Toronto, Montreal, and Winnipeg is very close to the national average but stands at 36 per cent in Vancouver.

Table 8.2 helps answer the second question I posed: How do Jewish immigrants compare to Jews born in Canada in terms of household income attainment and related socio-demographic factors? It presents information on how Jewish immigrants compare to Jewish non-immigrants in terms of income and a variety of socio-demographic characteristics. Two measures of income are given. The first measure is self-rated income ranging from 1 to 6, with 1 = under \$50,000; 2 = \$50,000–\$74,999; 3 = \$75,000–\$109,999; 4 = \$110,000–\$149,999; 5 = \$150,000–\$299,999; and 6 = \$300,000+. The second measure derives from a question asking, "Which of the following best describes your total household income at the present time? Would you say it is good enough for you and you can save from it; just enough for you, so that you do not have major problems; not enough for you and you are stretched; or not enough for you and you are having a hard time?" I combined the last two responses to form a new category, "not enough," which is found in table 8.2.

In the 2018 Survey of Jews in Canada, the mean difference in household income is statistically significant (at $p < .05$) in the total sample and in Toronto and Winnipeg, but is not statistically significant in Montreal and Vancouver. In terms of the proportion of respondents who felt their household income was "not enough," statistically significant differences are observed again in Toronto and Winnipeg, but not in the total sample or in Vancouver or Montreal. The biggest difference is in Winnipeg, where one-third more immigrant Jews identified as having "not enough" income as compared to non-immigrant Jews (20 per cent versus 15 per cent). Thus, immigrant Jews in Toronto and Winnipeg, and in Canada as a whole, depending on the measure examined, earn significantly less than Jewish non-immigrants and feel they do not earn enough to get by without stress.

With respect to socio-demographic characteristics, no statistically significant differences are observed between immigrant and non-immigrant Jews in terms of gender distribution, or in terms of those who felt connected to their city's Jewish community or city of residence. However, Jewish non-immigrants are significantly more likely to be under the age of thirty while Jewish immigrants are significantly

Immigrant and Non-immigrant Household Income 105

Table 8.2. Self-reported gross annual income, 2017, and socio-economic characteristics, 2018, of Jewish immigrants and non-immigrants in four cities

	Immigrants (n = 693)	Non-immigrants (n = 1,635)
	Mean	*Mean*
Total household income before tax (on a six-point scale)		
Four cities*	3.16	3.49
Toronto*	3.41	3.78
Montreal	2.96	3.23
Vancouver	3.50	3.18
Winnipeg*	2.53	3.22
	Per cent	*Per cent*
Household income is "not enough"		
Four cities	17	15
Toronto*	18	14
Montreal	14	14
Vancouver	13	16
Winnipeg*	20	15
Feel Jewish connection in city of residence	79	80
Gender		
Male	40	43
Female	60	57
City of residence		
Toronto	48	49
Montreal	27	28
Vancouver	10	8
Winnipeg	15	15
Age		
18–29*	9	13
30–44	23	23
45–54	16	15
55–64	10	21
65+*	34	27
Educational attainment		
Some or completed high school or GED	23	20
Some university	5	7
Completed bachelor's degree or some graduate/ professional school	36	37
Completed graduate/professional school	36	36

Note: *Percentages or means statistically different at p < .05. The *ns* are for the samples.
Source: Brym, Neuman, and Lenton (2019).

more likely to be older than sixty-four. This pattern is similar to trends in the country's general immigrant population (Statistics Canada 2017). The Jewish immigrant population is also significantly more likely to have completed high school or received a Graduate Equivalency Degree (GED) as their highest level of education. In contrast, the general trend in Canada is for immigrants to be more highly educated than non-immigrants (Turcotte 2019). This pattern is likely associated with the older age profile of the immigrant Jewish population compared to that of the immigrant population as a whole.

Income Determinants for Immigrant and Non-immigrant Jews

Multivariate analysis permits the assessment of the unique and combined effects of multiple factors on income for Jewish immigrants and non-immigrants in Canada. The models I present examine whether, on average, Jewish immigrants are disadvantaged in terms of household income Canada-wide and in the four cities of interest, while parcelling out effects tied to gender, whether one is racialized, one's level of education, one's occupation, and so on. This approach allows me to answer my third research question: Controlling for other relevant factors, do Jewish immigrants experience a household income disadvantage in Canada?

Using 2011 National Household Survey data, table 8.3 in the appendix examines determinants of income for Canadian Jews by religion for the four cities of interest and the country as a whole. In all models, I find a substantive and positive effect of being Jewish on household income, ranging from over $8,000 annually Canada-wide to approximately $5,200 annually in Montreal. This translates to an approximately 11 per cent advantage in median household income for Jews as compared to non-Jews Canada-wide, taking into account financial implications tied to immigration status, gender, race, age, marital status, highest level of education, occupation, and city of residence. Within the four cities of interest, being Jewish translates to an approximately 9 per cent advantage in household income in Winnipeg, a 10 per cent advantage in Toronto, and an 8 per cent advantage in Vancouver and Montreal, holding other factors constant.

In these models, I find a consistent negative effect of immigrant status on income, controlling for other factors in the regression models. The largest effects are in Toronto (-$9,644) and Montreal (-$8,563). In contrast, being a child of immigrants (a second-generation Canadian) has a positive effect on household income Canada-wide and in all cities of interest besides Toronto, where it continues to have a small negative effect. This finding suggests an encouraging story of upward mobility for Jewish immigrants in Canada over generations, net of other factors.

When similar multivariate analyses are run using data from the 2018 Survey of Jews in Canada, I find a negative effect of being a first-generation immigrant for Jews Canada-wide and in all cities except Vancouver. The largest negative effect is found in Winnipeg, followed by Montreal, holding other factors constant (see table 8.4 in the appendix).

However, in all models apart from Winnipeg's, second-generation Jews (born in Canada with one or both parents born outside of the country) are not found to have statistically significant lower household income than those with both parents born in Canada, all else the same. Thus, outside of Vancouver, Jewish immigrants are found to fare worse than non-immigrant Jews, but second-generation Canadian Jews have no financial advantage or disadvantage relative to non-immigrant Jews outside of Winnipeg.

Three main conclusions follow from my analysis. First, Jews in Canada have an income advantage over and above what one would expect given their socio-demographic characteristics as measured here. Future research will have to explore the factors responsible for this advantage. They may include concentration in high-paying occupations such as medicine and law (see chapter 6 in this volume) and above-average weekly hours of work and access to social and cultural capital. Second, Jewish immigrants tend to experience a substantial income disadvantage even taking into account the other socio-demographic characteristics measured here. Third, the income disadvantage of the immigrant generation largely disappears for the children of immigrants.

Conclusion

My analysis delves beyond assumptions of Jews as a model minority by examining income disparities tied to city of residence and immigration status. Clearly, "the notion of one homogeneous mainstream Canadian Jewish community does not hold" (Weinfeld with Schnoor and Shames 2018, 106). Labour market supports are needed to assist low-income and first-generation Jewish immigrants in achieving their full economic potential. Thus, the data demonstrate that despite above-average income, Jewish Canadian income inequality is substantial, and the level of low income is of particular concern for Jews in Montreal. As well, immigrant Jews, like non-Jewish immigrants in Canada, experience negative economic effects in the labour market, regardless of their level of education or connection to their ethnic community in their city of residence. Research is needed to unpack the challenges and opportunities Jewish immigrants face in Canada's labour market. Only research can determine the degree to which lack of English or French

108   Naomi Lightman

language proficiency, lack of Canadian work experience, unrecognized educational credentials earned abroad, and outright discrimination are responsible for Jewish immigrants' relatively low level of household income and how these barriers may be overcome.

Appendix: 2011 National Household Survey Regression Results

Table 8.3 provides multivariate regression findings from the 2011 National Household Survey. The dependent variable is household income before tax in 2010. The focal independent variables are (1) the effect of being Jewish as compared to non-Jewish (the reference category); and (2) the effect of generational status, disaggregated by first-generation immigrants (born outside Canada) and second-generation immigrants (born in Canada with at least one parent born outside Canada), compared to those who are Canadian-born and have parents who are both Canadian-born (the reference category).

Model 1 tests for effects on the total Canadian population, while models 2–5 test for effects within the four cities of interest. Controls are included for gender, race, age, and marital status (with "male," "White," "married," and "age 45–64" as the reference categories). The potentially mediating effects of human capital and type of employment are captured using respondent's highest level of educational attainment (with "university completion" as the reference category) and broad occupational category (with "business, finance, and administrative occupations" as the reference category). In model 1, the respondent's city of residence is controlled (with "Toronto" as the reference category).

The larger a sample, the more likely one will discover statistically significant findings, all else the same. Given the hundreds of thousands of respondents in the 2011 National Household Survey sample, I therefore focus on effect sizes rather than statistical significance. In table 8.3, mostly consistent trends are observed across the five models. In all models, being Jewish exerts a substantively positive effect on household income, controlling for the other factors. Canada-wide, the constant term ($72,685) is the estimated average income for someone who is in the reference group for all variables (a non-Jewish, non-immigrant who is male, White, between the ages of forty-five and sixty-four, married, completed university, works in business/finance, and lives in Toronto). The positive coefficient of $8,006 for being Jewish suggests an 11 per cent increase in average household income for Jews, as compared to non-Jews, all else the same.

Controlling for other variables, a negative effect on household income of being a first-generation immigrant is evident across all models,

Immigrant and Non-immigrant Household Income 109

Table 8.3 Ordinary least squares (OLS) regression predicting household income after taxes and transfers by city, 2010

	Model 1	Model 2	Model 3	Model 4	Model 5
	Canada	Toronto	Montreal	Vancouver	Winnipeg
	$n = 467,861$	$n = 83,372$	$n = 57,063$	$n = 34,145$	$n = 10,535$
Religion (ref.: non-Jewish)					
Jewish	8,006***	7,762***	5,228***	6,184***	5,562***
Immigration status (ref.: non-immigrant)					
First generation	−5,260***	−9,644***	−8,563***	−6,896***	−5,981***
Second generation	2,001***	−919***	501***	1,898***	1,359***
Gender (ref.: male)					
Female	−13,066***	−12,782***	−9,527***	−14,602***	−10,398***
Race (ref.: White)					
Racialized	−6,332***	−7,413***	−4,198***	−9,127***	−5,233***
Age (ref.: 45–54 years)					
<30 years	−20,130***	−25,898***	−20,174***	−20,010***	−16,661***
30–44 years	−5,807***	−7,741***	−6,953***	−5,456***	−5,196***
55–64 years	−716***	−354***	275***	2,753***	395***
65+ years	−34***	7,475***	3,853***	4,860***	−540***
Marital status (ref.: married)					
Not married	−6,053***	−6,060***	−6,435***	−7,505***	−6,128***
Educational attainment (ref.: completed university)					
High school/GED or less	−18,133***	−18,025***	−16,905***	−14,622***	−11,016***
Some university	−11,335***	−11,569***	−10,807***	−8,375***	−5,662***
Completed postgraduate/ professional school	13,366***	11,227***	10,887***	7,505***	16,512***
Sector (ref.: business, finance, administration)					
Sales and service	−7,735***	−9,563***	−5,495***	−10,547***	−6,979***
Trades, transport, equipment operation, etc.	−4,162***	−9,361***	−4,159***	−9,507***	−3,677***
Other	3,120***	3,877***	3,955***	2,874***	3,355***
City of residence (ref.: Toronto)					
Montreal	−6,927***				
Vancouver	−697***				
Winnipeg	−6,179***				
Other	−4,003***				
Constant	72,685***	78,474***	63,525***	74,025***	58,576***
Adjusted R^2	0.18	0.16	0.21	0.17	0.23

***$p < 0.001$
Note: Sample ns are shown.
Source: Statistics Canada (2014).

but a positive effect can be observed for being a second-generation immigrant Canada-wide, as well as in all cities aside from Toronto, where a small negative effect remains. Thus, in all models, the negative effect of being an immigrant is either eliminated and becomes a positive determinant of income or is substantively diminished for the second generation born in Canada.

Control variables demonstrate anticipated effects. Women earn less than men across all models, as do racialized individuals and people who are not married. Those between the ages of forty-five and sixty-four (typically considered peak earning years) have the highest income on average, and higher levels of education and professional occupations are associated with higher household income.

2018 Survey of Jews in Canada Regression Results

Table 8.4 provides regression analyses similar to those in table 8.3, but this time using the 2018 Survey of Jews in Canada data set, which permits assessment of income disparities between immigrant and non-immigrant Jews in Canada, again controlling for relevant factors. As in table 8.2, the dependent variable is a six-point categorical measure of self-assessed household income, with higher values representing higher income. The independent variable captures the effect of immigrant generational status, measured similarly to the 2011 National Household Survey to assess the effect of being a first-generation or second-generation immigrant compared to being Canadian-born with parents born in Canada (the reference category).

Model 1 tests the effects on the total sample, while models 2–5 test for effects in the four cities of interest. Controls are included for sex (with "male" as the reference category), age (with "45–54 years old" as the reference category), and marital status (with "married" as the reference category). To measure connectedness to the Jewish community, I used a questionnaire item that asked respondents how connected they feel to the Jewish community of the city in which they reside, with the reference category, "connected," combining responses for those who said they were "very" or "somewhat" connected. A control is included for highest level of education attained, with "completed university" as the reference category. In model 1, city of residence is controlled, with "Toronto" as the reference category. The sample size in the Vancouver and Winnipeg models are small, so results for those cities should be treated cautiously.

In model 1, a substantial negative effect of being a first-generation Jewish immigrant is found, demonstrating an approximately 10 per cent lower average income than comparable Canadian-born Jews. No

Table 8.4. Ordinary least squares (OLS) regression predicting self-assessed gross household income of Jews by city, 2017

	Model 1	Model 2	Model 3	Model 4	Model 5
	Four cities	Toronto	Montreal	Vancouver	Winnipeg
	$n = 1,464$	$n = 712$	$n = 375$	$n = 133$	$n = 244$
Immigration status (ref.: non-immigrant)					
First generation	−0.49***	−0.44**	−0.65**	−0.12	−1.04***
Second generation	−0.17	−0.02	−0.35	0.01	−0.46*
Gender (ref.: male)					
Female	−0.32***	−0.19	−0.55***	−0.76**	−0.08
Connected to city's Jewish community (ref.: yes)					
No	−0.34***	−0.25	−0.78**	−0.51	−0.03
Age (ref.: 45–54 years)					
18–29 years	−0.66***	−0.33	−1.06***	−1.34**	−0.85**
30–44 years	−0.59***	−0.41	−0.66**	−0.67	−0.72**
55–64 years	−0.59***	−0.49**	−0.99***	−0.34	0.00
65+ years	−0.94***	−0.92***	−1.08***	−0.86*	−0.45
Marital status (ref.: married)					
Not married	−1.08***	−1.13***	−0.52**	−1.24***	−1.06***
Highest level of education (ref.: university)					
High school/GED or less	−0.49***	−0.42**	−0.53**	−0.01	−0.78**
Some university	−0.37*	−0.52*	−0.60	0.87	−0.01
Completed postgraduate/ professional school	0.32***	0.23*	0.32	0.08	0.04
City of residence (ref.: Toronto)					
Montreal	−0.41***				
Vancouver	−0.53*				
Winnipeg	−0.21				
Constant	4.98***	4.76***	4.91***	4.84***	4.36***
Adjusted R^2	0.25	0.20	0.21	0.30	0.27

*$p < 0.05$, **$p < 0.01$, ***$p < 0.001$
Note: Sample ns are shown. Household income is coded as 1 = <$50,000; 2 = $50,000–$74,999; 3 = $75,000–$109,999; 4 = $110,000–$149,999; 5 = $150,000–$299,999; and 6 = $300,000+.
Source: Brym, Neuman, and Lenton (2019).

significant effect of being a Jewish immigrant is evident in the Vancouver model, but in Montreal, Toronto, and Winnipeg a significant negative effect is observed, with immigrant Jews faring worst, on average, in Winnipeg, controlling for other factors. On average, immigrant Jews in Winnipeg are found to earn 24 per cent less household income than Jewish non-immigrants. The comparable figure is 13 per cent less for Montreal and 9 per cent less for Toronto. Thus, table 8.4 demonstrates that Jews born outside Canada have, on average, lower self-rated household income than Canadian-born Jews, with larger effects in Winnipeg and Montreal. However, in all models beside Vancouver's, the negative "immigrant effect" is not significant for second-generation Jews.

The rest of the variables in table 8.4 find similar effects as in table 8.3. Among Jews, women have significantly lower household income than men in the four-city model, as do Jews who are not married. Those between the ages of forty-five and fifty-four say they fare best financially, and higher education overall is associated with higher household income. From model 1, respondents in Montreal and Vancouver have significantly lower household income than those in Toronto. In the total sample, as well as in Montreal, a significant negative effect is found for those who do not feel connected to their city's Jewish community.

REFERENCES

Abella, Irving, and Harold Troper. 1979. "'The Line Must Be Drawn Somewhere': Canada and Jewish Refugees, 1933–9." *Canadian Historical Review* 60 (2): 178–209. https://doi.org/10.3138/CHR-060-02-04.

Banerjee, Rupa, and Byron Y. Lee. 2015. "Decreasing the Recent Immigrant Earnings Gap: The Impact of Canadian Credential Attainment." *International Migration* 53 (2), 205–18. https://doi.org/10.1111/j.1468-2435.2012.00775.x.

Block, Sheila, Grace-Edward Galabuzi, and Alexandra Weiss. 2014. *The Colour Coded Labour Market by the Numbers*. Toronto: Wellesley Institute. http://bitly.ws/sMuN.

Brym, Robert, Keith Neuman, and Rhonda Lenton. 2019. *2018 Survey of Jews in Canada*: *Final Report*. Toronto: Environics Institute for Survey Research. https://bit.ly/3tGZACg.

Galabuzi, Grace-Edward, and Cheryl Teelucksingh. 2010. *Social Cohesion, Social Exclusion, Social Capital*. Brampton, ON: Region of Peel, Human Services.

Good Gingrich, Luann, and Andrew Mitchell. 2020. "The Story So Far: COVID-19, the Canadian Labour Market, and Immigrants." COVID-19: Disruption, Denudation and Dawning Series, York University, Toronto, ON. http://bitly.ws/sMuQ.

Hira-Friesen, Parvinder. 2018. "Immigrants and Precarious Work in Canada: Trends, 2006–2012." *Journal of International Migration and Integration* 19 (1): 35–57. https://doi.org/10.1007/s12134-017-0518-0.

Javdani, Mohsen, and Krishna Pendakur. 2014. "Fiscal Effects of Immigrants in Canada." *Journal of International Migration and Integration* 15 (4): 777–97. https://doi.org/10.1007/s12134-013-0305-5.

Lightman, Naomi. 2021. "Does Care Count for Less? Tracing the Income Trajectories of Low Status Female Immigrant Workers in Canada, 1993–2015." *Canadian Studies in Population* 48: 29–57. https://doi.org/10.1007/s42650-021-00040-4.

Lightman, Naomi, Rupa Banerjee, Ethel Tungohan, Conely de Leon, and Philip Kelly. 2021. "An Intersectional Pathway Penalty: Filipina Immigrant Women inside and outside Canada's Live-In Caregiver Program." *International Migration* 60 (2): 29–48. https://doi.org/10.1111/imig.12851.

Lightman, Naomi, and Luann Good Gingrich. 2018. "Measuring Economic Exclusion for Racialized Minorities, Immigrants and Women in Canada: Results from 2000 and 2010." *Journal of Poverty* 22 (5): 398–420. https://doi.org/10.1080/10875549.2018.1460736.

Pendakur, Krishna, and Ravi Pendakur. 2015. "The Colour of Money Redux: Immigrant/Ethnic Earnings Disparity in Canada, 1991–2006." Department of Economics Working Papers, Simon Fraser University, Burnaby, BC. https://EconPapers.repec.org/RePEc:sfu:sfudps:dp15-13.

Picot, Garnett, and Arthur Sweetman. 2012. "Making It in Canada: Immigration Outcomes and Policies." *Institute for Research on Public Policy Study* 29 (April). https://irpp.org/research-studies/making-it-in-canada.

Reimers, David M., and Harold Troper. 1992. "Canadian and American Immigration Policies since 1945." In *Immigration, Language and Ethnicity: Canada and the United States*, edited by Barry R. Chiswick, 15–65. Washington, DC: AEI Press.

Shields, John, Philip Kelly, Stella Park, Nathan Prier, and Tony Fang. 2011. "Profiling Immigrant Poverty in Canada: A 2006 Census Statistical Portrait." *Canadian Review of Social Policy/Revue canadienne de politique sociale* 65–6: 92–111. https://crsp.journals.yorku.ca/index.php/crsp/article/view/35245.

Statistics Canada. 2011. *2011 National Household Survey*. Catalogue no. 99-004-XWE. Ottawa: Statistics Canada.

Statistics Canada. 2017. "Focus on Geography Series, 2016 Census." Catalogue no. 98-404-X2016001. http://bitly.ws/t37N.

Troper, Harold. 1993. "Canada's Immigration Policy since 1945." *International Journal* 48 (2): 255–81. https://doi.org/10.1177/002070209304800204.

Turcotte, Martin. 2019. "Results from the 2016 Census: Education and Labour Market Successes and Challenges for Children of Immigrant Parents." Statistics Canada Catalogue no. 75-006-X. http://bitly.ws/t37S.

Weinfeld, Morton, with Randal F. Schnoor and Michelle Shames. 2018. *Like Everyone Else but Different: The Paradoxical Success of Canadian Jews*. 2nd ed. Montreal: McGill-Queen's University Press.

9 Comparing Montreal and Toronto

IRA ROBINSON

Comparisons

In any attempt to evaluate contemporary Jewish Montreal, comparison with Toronto Jewry is relevant insofar as Toronto took Montreal's place as the largest and most influential Jewish community in Canada in the 1970s. Nonetheless, the comparison has attracted little scholarly attention. As David S. Koffman and Morton Weinfeld (2011, 201) note, "comparing Jewish life in Montreal and Toronto remains a theme of anecdotal interest, but no systematic scholarly comparisons between Jewish Montreal and Jewish Toronto have been published."

This chapter will undertake the beginnings of such a comparison to better understand contemporary Montreal. This chapter will also cite survey data from the Jewish communities of Winnipeg and Vancouver where relevant. A brief study can hardly represent the last word on the topic, but it will point to significant social, cultural, and religious areas of comparison that need to be explored in detail.

Jews in Quebec share much with Jews in Ontario and the rest of Canada. Like other Canadian Jews, they are highly urbanized; 97 per cent of the Jews in Quebec live in the Greater Montreal area. This closely resembles the living pattern of Canadian Jews as a whole, more than 87 per cent of whom live in just six metropolitan areas (Brym, Neuman, and Lenton 2019, 6).

Montreal Jews have a reputation for being socially cohesive across generations – a reputation borne out by the 2018 Survey of Jews in Canada. Forty-eight per cent of Montrealers feel "very connected" to the Jewish community of their city, followed by 37 per cent of Winnipeggers, 34 per cent of Torontonians, and 21 per cent of Vancouverites. However, a similar percentage of Jewish Montrealers (80 per cent) and Torontonians (83 per cent) donated to a Jewish organization other than a synagogue in

2018, compared with 73 per cent in Winnipeg and 54 per cent in Vancouver. Some 60 per cent of Jews in both Montreal and Toronto report that most or all of their close friends are Jewish. The comparable figures are 49 per cent in Winnipeg and 27 per cent in Vancouver. Almost identical percentages of Jewish Montrealers (62 per cent) and Torontonians (61 per cent) are synagogue members, compared to 46 per cent of Winnipeggers and 37 per cent of Vancouverites. The same pattern is evident in other aspects of Jewish involvement. Though Montreal has historically tended to have the lowest intermarriage rate in Canada, as of 2018, at 26 per cent, it has ceded that title to Toronto, whose intermarriage rate was 22 per cent. Importantly, however, both Montreal and Toronto have significantly lower intermarriage rates than Ottawa (40.4 per cent), Winnipeg (49 per cent) and Vancouver (60 per cent) (Brym, Neuman, and Lenton 2019, 65, 30; Shahar and Schnoor 2015, iv).

Despite social and religious similarities between Jews in Montreal and Toronto, Montreal Jewry has developed a unique way of being Jewish in the past century. This distinctiveness stems from an environment in which sizeable English- and French-speaking communities live their own, largely separate linguistic and cultural lives while, to a limited degree, engaging with the languages and cultures of other Montrealers (Lacasse 2020, 2–3; Anctil 2011). Residential patterns reflect this reality. In 2001, across Canada's largest cities, Jews were the most highly segregated non-Indigenous ethnic or racial group, and their level of residential segregation was higher in Montreal than in other large Canadian cities (Balakrishnan, Maxim, and Jurdi 2005; chapter 7 in this volume). Consequently, while the English and the French are often said to form two solitudes in Quebec, Montreal's Jews have been accurately characterized as a third solitude, an experience that is not shared by Jews in Toronto or elsewhere in Canada (Greenstein 1989; Tulchinsky 1984).

This circumstance likely explains why the English-language literary works of leading Montreal Jewish authors A.M. Klein, Irving Layton, Mordecai Richler, and Leonard Cohen express "Jewish exclusion from a culturally elite subset of society" marked mainly by "tradition and ancestry" – a sense of exclusion that is largely foreign to the Jewish experience in other Canadian cities (Gomery 2016, 16). Significantly, Baghdad-born, French-speaking Naïm Kattan took a different approach. Rather than expressing isolation, he succeeded admirably in promoting dialogue with francophone Quebecers (Arnold 2021). In any case, one academic authority on Jewish literature mentions authors from numerous cities who have contributed unique insights on Canadian Jewish life. Montreal leads the list. Toronto is conspicuous by its absence (Brenner 1998, 284).

It is thus foundational to understanding the situation of contemporary Montreal Jews that they constitute a significant part of a unique multilingual and multicultural urban milieu embedded in an overarching bilingual and bicultural urban environment. It is equally important to recognize that Montreal Jews have not only been significantly influenced by their urban milieu but have also exercised a discernable influence on the ethos of Montreal as a whole, including its foodways (O. Bauer 2014). Finally, one must recognize that the Montreal Jewish community has significantly influenced Jews elsewhere in Canada and, indeed, throughout the Jewish world (Robinson 2021).

Community Survey

Founded in the eighteenth century in the wake of the British conquest of New France, the Montreal Jewish community for its first two centuries constituted the largest and most religiously, culturally, and philanthropically active Jewish community in Canada. Montreal Jews take pride in their comprehensive system of communal organizations (Robinson n.d.). Surveys consistently show Montreal's Jewish community having among the highest levels of Jewish education, ritual observance, synagogue affiliation, volunteerism, and ties to Israel of any Jewish community in North America (Brym, Neuman, and Lenton 2019; Koffman and Weinfeld 2011; Shahar 2015b).

Until the late twentieth century, the organizational life of Canadian Jewry as a whole was headquartered in Montreal, and Jewish Canadians often looked to Montreal's leadership for guidance (Elazar and Waller 1990). Although Toronto surpassed Montreal in the size of its Jewish population in the 1970s, Montreal continued to be celebrated throughout the world for its vibrant communal and cultural Jewish life (Wisse 1977, 56).

The fate of Montreal's Jewish community in the 1970s and thereafter closely paralleled that of anglophone Quebec as a whole, and was directly connected to arguably the most important trend in twentieth-century Canadian economic history: the replacement of Montreal by Toronto as the country's economic centre (Levine 1990). It is likely that the Jewish population of Montreal began to decline some time prior to the victory of the nationalist Parti Québécois (PQ) in the 1976 provincial election (S. Cohen 1977, 12; Robinson 2021). The Jewish population of Quebec reached its peak in the 1971 census. By 2011, the Jewish population of Montreal was about 80 per cent of its size four decades earlier (Shahar 2014a, 85, 49). During the 1970s and 1980s, approximately 10,000 Jews left Montreal for Toronto (Lacasse 2020, 29);

since 1976, some 30,000–40,000 Jews have left the province (Csillag 2013; Knelman 2016).

Economic motivations certainly played an important role in the decision to leave. Thus, in the 1970s and following decades, Jews did not leave Montreal for elsewhere at a uniform rate across the age and economic spectrum. Upwardly mobile young adults and professionals predominated among the migrants. Jews whose economic prospects outside the province were less promising tended to remain behind (Shahar 2014a, 39). The hypothesis that economic factors loomed large in the exodus is consistent with the 2018 Survey of Jews in Canada, which found that 14 per cent of 18–44-year-old Jews in Toronto and 52 per cent in Vancouver reported that they had moved from another part of Canada as an adult. Of this group, 35 per cent had moved from Montreal, followed by Ottawa (21 per cent). No other place in Canada was mentioned by more than 5 per cent of this group. When asked why they chose to leave Montreal, 70 per cent said they moved for better career opportunities. Another survey of Jews who moved from Quebec found that fewer than 4 per cent had done so because of inadequate French (Read 2018).

It is thus reasonable to assume that much of the out-migration of Jews from Montreal is a movement of upwardly mobile individuals seeking to better their careers. The deciding factor with respect to the demographic trend in Jewish Montreal is more likely to be that Bill 101, by restricting access to English education, mandating French examinations for professional licensing, and creating a work environment in which fluency in French is an exceedingly important job qualification, serves as a brake on people from most of the rest of the world, including Jews, who might otherwise consider moving to Montreal.

Beyond economic factors, the emigration of Montreal Jews was also strongly motivated by Quebec's Quiet Revolution of the 1960s, which involved the rapid modernization and francization of Quebec's state institutions, the passage of the 1977 Charter of the French Language (Bill 101), and the 1980 and 1995 referenda on Quebec separation from the rest of Canada (Lacasse 2020; Troper 2010). Many Montreal Jews evidently feared for their future in a Quebec that seemed bent on changing the conditions that had hitherto fostered the development of the Jewish community, and they struggled with new provincial language policies that challenged the viability of the Jewish community's extensive educational system, one of its major institutional priorities, and its long-established way of operating in English. Many Jews read these new government language policies as "anti-Semitic in tone" (Read 2018, 35). Issues related to language persist in the Montreal Jewish community; a significant number of its Jews (32 per cent) reported concerns regarding language discrimination in the 2018 Survey of Jews in Canada. This concern is unique to the Quebec experience; reports of language discrimination are negligible in Toronto (4 per cent), Vancouver (3 per cent), and Winnipeg (7 per cent) (Brym, Neuman, and Lenton 2019, 49).

The emigration of large numbers of Jews from Montreal was hardly the sole major repercussion of the Quiet Revolution for the Montreal Jewish community. Its organizational structure had evolved in the early to mid-twentieth century in reaction to the established faith-based institutionalization of health, education, and social services in Quebec until the 1960s. The Jewish community thus heavily invested in its own complex institutional structure that included numerous schools, social service agencies, and medical facilities (Rosenberg and Jedwab 1992). The Jewish community continued to maintain this institutional structure long after earlier discriminatory attitudes and faith-based institutionalization of education and social services in Quebec had significantly abated, and it strongly defended its autonomy in the face of Quebec government takeovers of faith-based educational, health, and social service institutions (Weinfeld 1980, 7).

On issues related to antisemitism, Montreal Jews report levels of antisemitism similar to those of Toronto Jews. The same percentage of Montreal and Toronto Jews think they are often the object of discrimination (33 per cent, versus 23 per cent in Winnipeg and 22 per cent in Vancouver). This similarity is surprising to some researchers who posit a historically higher level of antisemitism in Quebec than in Ontario (Brym, Neuman, and Lenton 2019, 9). Indeed, as recently as the 1980s, the level of antisemitism was twice as high in Quebec as in the rest of Canada (Brym and Lenton 1991, 1992). As well, in 2009, just 36 per cent of Quebecers held a favourable opinion of Judaism, though that number increased to 45 per cent in 2017. The comparable figure for the rest of Canada is 59 per cent (Brym, Neuman, and Lenton 2019, 55).

In general, tolerance of religious and ethnic minorities in Quebec has remained an issue. In 2019, for example, the Quebec government passed Bill 21 banning Quebec teachers, police officers, judges, and lawyers working in public services from wearing religious symbols such as crosses, hijabs, turbans, and yarmulkes. On the other hand, the Quebec government has taken steps to distance itself from the historical antisemitism of Quebec nationalism and has facilitated the continuation of Jewish identity in Quebec by partially financing Jewish schools (something the Ontario government has yet to do) and supporting Jewish social service agencies. While antisemitism represents an ongoing and currently growing concern among Jews in Quebec, it has been argued that the similar level of perception of antisemitism by Montreal and Toronto Jews may reflect growing comfort on the part of Jews in Quebec. Increasingly at ease in French, they may have begun to think of themselves as a permanent and accepted part of Quebec society (Read 2018; Robinson 2013).

The priority and concern of the Montreal Jewish community for Jewish education has expressed itself in the community's significant emphasis on Jewish day schools (Brym, Neuman, and Lenton 2019, 43). In recent decades, the Jewish community of Montreal has experienced a steadily rising level in day school enrolment (Read 2015, 66–7). Quebec currently has the highest rate of students enrolled in Jewish day schools in Canada, particularly in secondary education (Read 2018) Enrolment in Montreal Jewish day schools steadily increased between 1971 and 2011, a period in which the Jewish population of Montreal was declining. Thus, participation in day school education involves an increasing percentage of the community. Though Toronto has more students attending elementary day schools than Montreal does, as well more Jewish day schools, attendance in Jewish secondary schools in Montreal as a proportion of the community far surpasses all other Canadian cities. Interestingly, the rising rate of Jewish day school enrolment in Toronto since the 1980s is due in part to the migration of Montreal Jews to Toronto, many of whom continued the Montreal Jewish community's preference for sending their children to Jewish day schools (Pomson and Schnoor 2008, 20).

Whatever in-migration to Montreal occurred in the past half century has been insufficient to offset out-migration. Nonetheless, Jewish migration to Montreal has been significant. Census data show that in 2011, 33.9 per cent of Montreal Jews were born outside of Canada, a figure that does not take into consideration immigration to Montreal from elsewhere in Canada. Most of Montreal's Jewish foreign-born immigrated since the beginning of the Quiet Revolution, notably Sephardim (mainly Moroccan Jews) who started arriving in the late 1950s, and Jews from France who started arriving in the 2000s (Shahar 2014a, iii, 9, 13).

Sub-Communities

The Montreal Jewish community as it existed prior to the Quiet Revolution was strongly dominated by people of Eastern European Ashkenazi ancestry. Ashkenazi Jews remain the most numerous and influential component of the Jewish community today (Teboul 2001, 22). However,

Ashkenazim in Montreal are in relative decline numerically. In 2011, they numbered 65,920, or 72.6 per cent of the Jewish community, down from 74.6 per cent a decade earlier (Shahar 2015b, 8). If Ashkenazim had formed the sole major component of the Montreal Jewry, the community's viability would have been considerably compromised by the emigration of Jews from Quebec (Shahar 2014b, 33). In this respect, Montreal is like Winnipeg, which also experienced a significant decline in its Jewish population in the same period.

The fact that Montreal still houses Canada's second largest Jewish community by a wide margin is largely because, by the 1970s, two substantial sub-communities had established themselves in the city: ultra-Orthodox (Haredim, predominantly Hasidic[1]), and Sephardim (Anctil and Robinson 2019; Brym, Neuman, and Lenton 2019, 31; Y. Cohen 2017; Shahar 2003). Neither the Hasidic nor the Sephardi sub-communities completely identify with the mainstream Ashkenazim, and tensions have existed between both of these sub-communities and the communal leadership. However, neither is positioned to supplant the mainly Ashkenazi leadership of the Jewish community.

The two sub-communities are especially important because Montreal did not attract a large sub-community of Jews of Israeli origin, as did Toronto; although a few thousand Jews of Israeli origin live in Montreal, this is less than half the number of Israeli Jews living in Toronto. As well, Jews from the former Soviet Union are not as well represented in Montreal as in Toronto, where about 70 per cent of Canada's Jewish immigrants from the former Soviet Union reside (Remennick 2006).

While not constituting a distinct sub-community the way the Hasidim and Sephardim do, Holocaust survivors form an important part of the Montreal Jewish community, engendering a strong Holocaust consciousness among Montreal Jews (Shahar 2015d, iii). The percentage of the city's population comprising Holocaust survivors is higher in Montreal than in any other Canadian city, and when it comes to servicing Holocaust survivors in Canadian areas of sparse Jewish population, Jewish organizations direct them to contact the Cummings Centre for Jewish Seniors in Montreal.

While some strictly Orthodox Jews, including Hasidim, lived in Montreal prior to the 1940s, the growth of this sub-community commenced in earnest after the Second World War, concomitant with the settlement of Holocaust survivors in the city (Lapidus 2004; Read 2017, 7; Shahar 2015d). Today, about one quarter of Montreal Jews classify themselves as Orthodox or Modern Orthodox, and another 6 per cent classify themselves as Hasidic/Chabad. The percentage of Orthodox Jews is large compared to Toronto (16 per cent), Winnipeg (6 per cent), and Vancouver (9 per cent) (Brym, Neuman, and Lenton 2019, 23). It is perhaps indicative that in Toronto, the flagship "establishment" synagogue is a Reform Temple, Holy Blossom, similar to the situation in many Jewish communities in the United States, whereas the Montreal equivalent is Shaar Hashomayim, a traditional Ashkenazi synagogue (J. Bauer 2011).

As the Haredi sub-community developed, it did not share the Montreal Jewish communal ethos as it had developed in the twentieth century, in which Orthodox Judaism was publicly respected so long as Orthodox synagogues and rabbis did not overtly impinge on the lifestyle choices of community members. Montreal's Haredi community developed and expanded mostly separately from the established Jewish community. It nonetheless managed to establish a close, symbiotic relationship with the community, which gives it significant support. The Haredi sector has come to dominate Montreal's kosher food industry, including the Jewish Community Council, which supervises kosher food in the city (Lapidus 2011).

The separation of the Hasidic sub-community from the rest of Montreal Jewry is marked linguistically by its adoption of Yiddish as a means of internal communication, an identity marker, and a barrier mechanism. According to the 2016 Canadian census, Quebec has more people with Yiddish as their mother tongue and more who speak Yiddish at home than the rest of Canada combined (Statistics Canada 2018). In the rest of the Canadian Jewish community, Yiddish is now largely vestigial and "post-vernacular," but Montreal possesses substantial institutional remnants of its once-robust Yiddish-speaking Jewish community, such as the Jewish People's and Peretz Schools and the Jewish Public Library (Margolis 2021).

The Hasidim do not constitute a single, unified community. They are divided into several groups, including strong representation from Chabad, Satmar, Vizhnits, Belz, Tash, and other sects. Contrary to the trend in the rest of Jewish Montreal, their sub-community is growing quickly because of in-migration and a high fertility rate (Shahar 2014a, 32). Suburban Boisbriand is the home of the Tasher Hasidim, whose enclave, Kiryas Tash, was established in the 1960s (Lacasse 2017). Tash experienced remarkable population growth of 66.8 per cent between 2001 and 2011. The adjacent Montreal neighbourhoods of Park Avenue/Park Extension and Outremont, containing the majority of Montreal's Hasidic communities, also experienced a large increase in population in that decade, 58.6 per cent and 28.8 per cent, respectively. Tash boasts a total fertility rate of 5.03 and an extraordinarily low median age of 13.5 years (Shahar 2015a, 3). Outremont and the neighbouring district of Park Extension also have very low median ages because they are populated mainly by Haredi Jews (19.6 years and 25.6 years, respectively) (Shahar 2014b, 91–3). Beyond the already-mentioned Hasidic districts, the Snowdon neighbourhood houses a concentration of Chabad/Lubavitch Hasidim, and the Belz Hasidic community has established a branch in the heavily Jewish suburb of Côte Saint-Luc.

Starting in the late 1950s, and peaking between 1965 and 1967, thousands of North African Jews arrived in Montreal, spurred by the decolonization of North Africa and growing antipathy to Jews in North Africa following Israel's declaration of independence. Their arrival roughly coincided with Quebec's Quiet Revolution. Like the Haredim, this sub-community has strongly influenced the demography of Montreal Jewry and its linguistic composition. By the end of the 1970s, more than 11,000 Jews of North African origin had settled in Montreal (Lacasse 2020, 255; Read 2017, 12) and in 2011, 22,225 Sephardim lived in Montreal, comprising 24.5 per cent of the Jewish community (Shahar 2015b, iii). Clearly, Sephardim, like the Haredim, helped replace the demographic losses the Montreal Jewish community experienced since the 1970s. Also like the Haredim, the Sephardi sub-community significantly changed the linguistic profile of the community, since most North African Jewish immigrants to Montreal were more at home in French than in English.

For the Montreal Jewish community, the Sephardim posed both a problem and an opportunity. From the perspective of the exclusively Ashkenazi-origin Jewish leaders of the 1960s, the problem was clear. Sephardim seemed to pose an assimilatory problem, partly inherent in the educational choices Jewish parents then faced. Almost all francophone Sephardim faced "a choice of identifying either with the existing Anglophone Jewish community and probably losing [their] language and [their] unique French-Sephardic cultural heritage or with a non-Jewish francophone community and thus probably losing [their] Jewish religious connections" (Rosenberg 1972, 420). Moreover, early Sephardi efforts to create their own communal institutions were not always well received by the Ashkenazi communal leadership. In particular, the founding of the first francophone Jewish school in Montreal, l'École Maïmonide in 1969, did not occur without a certain irritation on the part of the established Jewish leadership (Teboul 2001, 61–3). The Sephardim had to negotiate their place in the larger Jewish community.

However, the opportunity the Sephardic Jewish immigrants presented Montreal Jewry when they arrived was equally clear. As francophones, Sephardim could serve as a bridge between the anglophone-dominated Jewish community and the francophone majority in Quebec. Their presence in the Jewish community was evidence that Montreal Jewry had not turned its back on the francophone reality of the province.

A substantial Sephardi community is found in Toronto, too, but it consists mainly of Spanish-speaking Moroccan Jews, especially from Tangiers, rather than French-speaking Moroccan Jews, who tended to settle in Montreal (Y. Cohen 2020).

As Montreal's Sephardim increasingly established themselves and their communal institutions in the late twentieth century, the organized Jewish community understood the necessity of accommodating them. By the early twenty-first century, the communal leadership met with considerable success in its efforts to co-opt Sephardim into its leadership circles. For its part, the Sephardi community in the past half century has increasingly accommodated itself to the anglophone environment of the Montreal Jewish community as well as to the francophone environment of Quebec as a whole. Thus, 30.7 per cent of Sephardim spoke English at home in 2011, though only 9.2 per cent reported English as their mother tongue. Moreover, use of English in Sephardic homes between 2001 and 2011 increased from 26.5 per cent to 30.7 per cent, whereas the use of French as a home language decreased from 67.8 per cent to 62.3 per cent (Shahar 2015b, 27). As well, the birth rate of the Sephardi sub-community, which at the time of its arrival exceeded that of the Ashkenazi-origin Jews, has declined, and other characteristics of this sub-community have converged with those of Ashkenazi-origin Jews over time (Shahar 2014c, 7).

Towards a Conclusion

Gershom Scholem (1971, 350) famously wrote that predicting future trends "is the task of prophets, not of professors." I will nonetheless end this preliminary comparative survey of the Montreal Jewish community with some observations on a likely trajectory for this community in the coming years, as well as some ideas for future research in this area.

It would seem that prospects for Montreal Jewry will largely depend on the way that Montreal, and Quebec as a whole, evolve with respect to inclusivity for anglophones and religious and racial minorities. In its official statements, the Quebec government affirms that "the terms 'Québec nation' and 'the people of Québec' are not limited to Francophones; they include all individuals residing in Québec" (Secrétariat du Québec aux relations canadiennes 2015). However, the concern that has been widely expressed in the province regarding the apparently increasing use of the English language, particularly on the Island of Montreal, suggests that, in case of conflict, it is the health of the French language that will be prioritized over that of Quebec's "cultural communities." It seems equally clear that legislative restrictions on the use of religious symbols by public servants remain popular in the province as a whole. These factors will likely result in continuing demographic decline for the Jewish community as young anglophone Jews, most of them bilingual, contemplate where they wish to establish their homes and careers.

Future research in this area should investigate several dynamics relative to the two important sub-communities that have helped to significantly mitigate the Montreal Jewish community's demographic decline – the Sephardim and the Hasidim. With respect to the Sephardim, it would be interesting to research the apparently growing phenomenon of Sephardic–Ashkenazic intermarriage. It would also be useful to examine the impact of integration of Sephardim into leadership circles of Montreal's Federation CJA. In particular, researchers could shed light on how this integration has impacted both the Sephardic community's institutions and those of the Jewish community as a whole. Further research on the Hasidim of Quebec is needed to investigate the widespread custom of Hasidic grooms from outside Montreal marrying women from Montreal and moving to their wives' city. How does this continuing influx of young men integrate into the local Hasidic and Jewish community and the Quebec job market? Another fascinating topic concerns whether the current symbiotic relationship between the Hasidic community and the Jewish community as a whole can be sustained if the Hasidim continue to constitute an ever-growing proportion of the community.

NOTE

1 While "Haredi," often translated as "ultra-Orthodox," comprises Hasidic and non-Hasidic communities, Hasidic communities predominate in Montreal. In this chapter, I use the terms interchangeably.

REFERENCES

Anctil, Pierre. 2011. "A Community in Transition: The Jews of Montréal." *Contemporary Jewry* 31 (3): 225–45. https://doi.org/10.1007/s12397 -011-9067-6.

Anctil, Pierre, and Ira Robinson. 2019. *Les Juifs hassidiques de Montréal.* Montreal: Les Presses de l'Université de Montréal.

Arnold, Janice. 2021. "Obituary: Iraqi-born Naïm Kattan Brought Cultures Together in Quebec." *Canadian Jewish News*, 6 July 2021. http://bitly.ws /sMvZ.

Balakrishnan, T.R., Paul Maxim, and Rozzet Jurdi. 2005. "Social Class versus Cultural Identity as Factors in the Residential Segregation of Ethnic Groups in Toronto, Montreal and Vancouver for 2001." *Canadian Studies in Population* 32 (2): 202–27. https://doi.org/10.25336/P6930T.

Bauer, Julien. 2011. "Jews as Symbols and Reality in Multicultural Canada." *Jerusalem Center for Public Affairs* 67 (April): 1–23. http://bitly.ws/sw9W.

Bauer, Olivier. 2014. "Bagel, Bagelry, Smoked Meat, and Deli as the Jewish Part of Montreal's Culinary Heritage." Paper presented at Food Heritage, Hybridity & Locality: An International Conference, Brown University, Providence, RI, 23 October 2014. https://core.ac.uk/download/pdf/228378547.pdf.

Brenner, Rachel Feldhay. 1998. "Canadian Jews and Their Story: The Making of Canadian Jewish Literature." *Prooftexts* 18 (3): 283–97. https://www.jstor.org/stable/20689525.

Brym, Robert, and Rhonda Lenton. 1991. "The Distribution of Anti-Semitism in Canada in 1984." *Canadian Journal of Sociology* 16 (4): 411–18. https://doi.org/10.2307/3340962.

Brym, Robert, and Rhonda Lenton. 1992. "Anti-Semitism in Quebec: Reply to Langlois." *Canadian Journal of Sociology* 17 (2): 179–83. https://doi.org/10.2307/3341195.

Brym, Robert, Keith Neuman, and Rhonda Lenton. 2019. *2018 Survey of Jews in Canada: Final Report.* Toronto: Environics Institute for Survey Research. https://bit.ly/3qS0ees.

Cohen, Stanley M. 1977. "Jewish Concerns in Quebec." *Canadian Zionist,* January–February 1977, 10–12, 15.

Cohen, Yolande, ed. 2017. *Les Sépharades du Québec: Parcours d'éxils nord-africains.* Montreal: Del Busso.

Cohen, Yolande. 2020. "Enclaves ethniques et stratégies residentielles des juifs à Toronto et Montréal." *Canadian Jewish Studies* 30: 83–114. https://doi.org/10.25071/1916-0925.40185.

Csillag, Ron. 2013. "Will Rising Nationalism Renew Montreal Jewish Exodus?" *Jewish Telegraphic Agency,* 8 October 2013. https://bit.ly/36jnF73.

Elazar, Daniel, and Harold Waller. 1990. *Maintaining Consensus: The Canadian Jewish Polity in the Postwar World.* Lanham, MD: University Press of America.

Gomery, Madeleine. 2016. "To Emerge from the Ghetto Twice: Anti-Semitism and the Search for Jewish Identity in Post-War Montreal Literature" *DOROT: The McGill Undergraduate Journal of Jewish Studies* 15: 1–19. http://bitly.ws/sMwt.

Greenstein, Michael. 1989. *Third Solitudes: Tradition and Discontinuity in Jewish-Canadian Literature.* Montreal: McGill-Queen's University Press.

Knelman, Martin. 2016. "Director Revisits Exodus from Quebec in Documentary." *Toronto Star,* 29 April 2016. https://bit.ly/36kjub8.

Koffman, David S., and Morton Weinfeld. 2011. "Recent Developments in the Social Scientific Study of Canadian Jews." *Contemporary Jewry* 31 (3): 199–221. https://doi.org/10.1007/s12397-011-9066-7.

Lacasse, Simon-Pierre. 2017. "À la croisée de la Révolution tranquille et du judaïsme orthodoxe: L'implantation de la communauté hassidique des

Tasher au cœur du Québec francophone et catholique (1962–1967)." *Histoire Sociale* 50 (102): 399–422. https://doi.org/10.1353/his.2017.0041.

Lacasse, Simon-Pierre. 2020. "Les Juifs de la Révolution tranquille: Regards d'une minorité religieuse sur le Québec de 1945 à 1976." PhD diss., Université d'Ottawa. http://dx.doi.org/10.20381/ruor-24678.

Lapidus, Steven. 2004. "The Forgotten Hasidim: Rabbis and Rebbes in Prewar Canada." *Canadian Jewish Studies* 12: 1–30. https://doi.org/10.25071/1916-0925.22624.

Lapidus, Steven. 2011. "Orthodoxy in Transition: The Vaad Ha'ir of Montreal in the Twentieth Century." PhD diss., Concordia University. https://spectrum.library.concordia.ca/7228/.

Levine, Marc V. 1990. *The Reconquest of Montreal: Language Policy and Social Change in a Bilingual City*. Philadelphia: Temple University Press.

Margolis, Rebecca. 2021. "*In der heym in Kanade*: A Survey of Yiddish Today." In *No Better Home? Jews, Canada, and the Sense of Belonging*, edited by David S. Koffman, 261–83. Toronto: University of Toronto Press.

Pomson, Alex, and Randal F. Schnoor. 2008. *Back to School: Jewish Day School in the Lives of Adult Jews*. Detroit: Wayne State University Press.

Read, Jamie Anne. 2015. "'J'y suis. Pour de Bon.': Montreal Jewish Education and the Social Construction of Diaspora Identity." PhD diss., University of Waterloo. http://hdl.handle.net/10012/9716.

Read, Jamie Anne. 2018. "The Precarious History of Jewish Education in Quebec." *Religion and Education* 45 (1): 23–51. https://doi.org/10.1080/15507394.2017.1367595.

Remennick, Larissa. 2006. "Russian Jews in the Global City of Toronto: A Pilot Study of Identity and Social Integration." *Space, Populations, Societies* 1: 61–81. https://doi.org/10.4000/eps.1235.

Robinson, Ira. n.d. "Historical Introduction to the Jewish Community of Quebec." Federation CJA. Accessed 29 June 2022, http://bitly.ws/t38E.

Robinson, Ira. 2013. "Reflections on Antisemitism in French Canada." *Canadian Jewish Studies* 21 (1): 90–122. https://doi.org/10.25071/1916-0925.39911.

Robinson, Ira. 2021. "'By the Rivers of the St. Lawrence': The Montreal Jewish Community and Its Postmemory." In *No Better Home? Jews, Canada, and the Sense of Belonging*, edited by David S. Koffman, 161–76. Toronto: University of Toronto Press.

Rosenberg, M. Michael, and Jack Jedwab. 1992. "Institutional Completeness, Ethnic Organizational Style and the Role of the State: The Jewish, Italian and Greek Communities of Montreal." *Canadian Review of Sociology* 29 (3): 266–87. https://doi.org/10.1111/j.1755-618X.1992.tb02439.x.

Rosenberg, Stuart E. 1972. "French Separatism: Its Implications for Canadian Jewry." *American Jewish Year Book* 73: 407–27. https://www.jstor.org/stable/23603467.

Scholem, Gershom. 1971. *Major Trends in Jewish Mysticism*. New York: Schocken Books.

Secrétariat du Québec aux relations canadiennes. 2015. "Recognition of the Québec Nation." Government of Québec. https://bit.ly/36iPjRA.

Shahar, Charles. 2003. *A Comprehensive Study of the Frum Community of Greater Montreal*. Montreal: Federation CJA.

Shahar, Charles. 2014a. *2011 National Household Survey: The Jewish Community of Montreal*. Part 1, *Basic Demographics*. Part 9, *Jewish Populations in Geographic Areas*. Montreal: Jewish Federations of Canada – CJA. http://bitly.ws/sw5I.

Shahar, Charles. 2014b. *2011 National Household Survey: The Jewish Population of Canada*. Part 1, *Basic Demographics*. Part 2, *Jewish Populations in Geographic Areas*. Toronto: Jewish Federations of Canada – CJA. https://bit.ly/3qRivJ4.

Shahar, Charles. 2014c. *2011 National Household Survey: The Jewish Population of Canada*. Part 3, *Jewish Seniors*. Part 4, *The Jewish Poor*. Toronto: Jewish Federations of Canada – CJA. https://bit.ly/3wgFdve.

Shahar, Charles. 2015a. *2011 National Household Survey Brief: Fertility Rates of Montreal's Jewish Community*. Montreal: Jewish Federations of Canada – CJA. https://bit.ly/36kO2JQ.

Shahar, Charles. 2015b. *2011 National Household Survey: The Jewish Community of Montreal*. Part 7, *The Sephardic Community*. Montreal: Jewish Federations of Canada – CJA. http://bitly.ws/sw5h.

Shahar, Charles. 2015c. *2011 National Household Survey: The Jewish Community of Montreal*. Part 8, *Immigration and Language*. Part 9, *Core FSU Jews*. Montreal: Jewish Federations of Canada – CJA. http://bitly.ws/sw5m.

Shahar, Charles. 2015d. *2011 National Household Survey: The Jewish Community of Montreal*. Part 10, *Holocaust Survivors*. Montreal: Jewish Federations of Canada – CJA. https://bit.ly/3xsOrGk.

Shahar, Charles, and Randal F. Schnoor. 2015. *2011 National Household Survey: The Jewish Community of Ottawa*. Part 5, *The Jewish Family*. Part 6, *Intermarriage*. Toronto: Jewish Federations of Canada – UJA. https://bit.ly/3yvHSTu.

Statistics Canada. 2018. "Data Tables, 2016 Census." https://bit.ly/3wtIBDU.

Teboul, Victor. 2001. *René Lévesque et la communauté juive*: *Entretiens*. Montreal: Editions des Intouchables.

Troper, Harold. 2010. *The Defining Decade: Identity, Politics, and the Canadian Jewish Community in the 1960s*. Toronto: University of Toronto Press.

Tulchinsky, Gerald. 1984. "The Third Solitude: A.M. Klein's Jewish Montreal, 1910–1950." *Journal of Canadian Studies* 19 (2): 96–112. https://doi .org/10.3138/jcs.19.2.96.

Weinfeld, Morton. 1980. "The Jews of Quebec: Perceived Anti-Semitism, Segregation, and Emigration" *Jewish Journal of Sociology* 22: 5–19.

Wisse, Ruth R. 1977. "Quebec's Jews: Caught in the Middle." *Commentary*, September 1977. http://bitly.ws/t38J.

10 Experiencing Race, Class, Ethnicity, and Gender: Jewish Immigrants from the Former Soviet Union in Toronto

MARINA MORGENSHTERN

Intersectionality

This chapter analyses how the ethnic, gender, and occupational roles and identities of Jews from the former Soviet Union (FSU) changed in response to historical and structural pressures associated with immigration.[1] It is a story of how White, middle-class, professional, presumably heterosexual, immigrant Jews, socialized in a non-Western society, worked towards achieving social privilege and a sense of belonging to the dominant group.[2] It is a complex story of life-long simultaneous participation in the experiences of social privilege and oppression. Although these experiences are specific to FSU Jewish immigrants in Toronto, they bear witness to broader issues in Canadian Jewish experience that require the community's consideration. My interest in this subject derives from my being an immigrant twice over, first from the FSU to Israel, and later from Israel to Canada.

Toronto hosts the largest FSU Jewish community in Canada, numbering about 40,000, roughly one fifth of Toronto Jewry (Shahar 2015).[3] They constitute Canada's third-largest Jewish community; only Canadian-born Jews in Toronto and Canadian-born Jews in Montreal form larger communities. Most FSU Jews are relatively recent arrivals. Some 9,175 arrived between 1990 and 1999, and 7,965 between 2000 and 2010. Some came directly from the FSU, others via Israel. Like other immigrants, they sought to improve living standards and quality of life for themselves and their children. Their immigration to Canada was influenced by socio-economic and political upheaval and the rise of antisemitism in the FSU in the 1980s, as well as by Canadian immigration policy, which favoured skilled immigrants.

I use the lens of intersectionality to fully understand the experiences of FSU immigrant Jews. Intersectionality refers to how multiple social markers – including race, ethnicity, class, gender, sexuality, and geographical origin – combine and become embodied in the lives of individuals, resulting in unique experiences and outcomes (Crenshaw 1989). From this perspective, individual identity is a product of simultaneously participating in different levels and types of privilege and oppression, which vary by social context and throughout the life course (Hulko 2009). Examining the interplay of these facets of social life allows one to develop a complex understanding of individuals' unique social trajectories and experiences.

I interviewed a sample of twenty-two FSU immigrants in Toronto in depth using research methods well suited to eliciting previously unknown narratives of the resettlement experience and its social context.[4] The sample consisted of ten couples and two single people. Interviews first allowed subjects to serve as witnesses to the collective socio-political experience of FSU Jewish immigration to the West. The first round of interviews was then used as a backdrop for oral history interviews that explored individual experiences. The following general probes were used in the first set of interviews:

- Can you talk about the experiences of FSU Jews who immigrated to Canada?
- What was their situation like in the FSU?
- What do you think it is like for them in Toronto?

In the oral history interviews, participants were asked the following:

- What was your life like in the Soviet Union?
- What has life been like for you since immigrating to Canada?
- What helps/helped you build your life in Canada?

I used additional probes to explore participants' education, economic situation, relationship to the labour market, and differences they may have noticed between life in the FSU and in Canada.

I begin by summarizing the participants' accounts of race, class, and ethnic identities and experiences of Jews in the FSU. I then discuss the unique ethnic and class trajectories of individuals in my sample, followed by a depiction of their gender experiences, focusing on their gender roles and identities. Although these issues are presented separately, they are intertwined, creating complex links between subjectivity, nationhood, culture, race, class, gender, and sexuality.

Class Privilege and Ethnic Subordination

Race, class, and gender identities are products of social and economic conditions and individuals' social locations in relation to the allocation of resources by societal institutions. One must appreciate pre-migration life to understand how these identities were formed in the country of origin and later negotiated in the country of immigration.

Jews in the Soviet Union experienced a peculiar combination of class privilege and ethnic marginalization. With the rise of the Soviet state, they were able to take advantage of unprecedented educational and employment opportunities, with more than 60 per cent of men and women attaining academic degrees and professional experience in the 1990s (Gitelman 2010; Brym with Ryvkina 1994; Remennick 2006). Alesha,[5] one of the study participants, remarked that Soviet Jews' collective narrative is based on two motives: *zhazhda uchit'sya* (a thirst for study) and *zhelaniye prodvinut'sya v zhizni* (a drive to get ahead in life). The participants considered investment in higher education and belonging to the intelligentsia as fundamental parts of Soviet-Jewish identity and survival strategies to facilitate social mobility and maintain a place in the social elite: "Russian Jews, they are *ish ha-sefer* ["people of the book" in Hebrew]. From generation to generation, they got through using their brains, not muscles. ... That's how you survive" (Janna). Some mentioned that working-class Jews were more an exception than a rule. For them, Jews were typically professionals: "I've never seen a Jew who sells potatoes. Jews were doctors, engineers, or musicians" (Stella). Education, professional status, and economic privilege were seen as inherent Jewish characteristics everywhere, not only in the FSU: "Privileged status, despite antisemitism ... Jewish resourcefulness, intelligence, and education ... talent to fight for themselves and achieve something. And study better than others. And bright minds. In any country that has even a small Jewish community, this community is wealthy and lives very well there, and rich; best houses, best streets" (Volodya). Thus, this group of Jews equated education with economic privilege and success and with being a worthy Jew.

However, the experience of upward mobility and economic privilege was negotiated in the context of state-sponsored antisemitism. Soviet leaders, to create a new ethnic formation – "the Soviet people" – aimed to force assimilation and eradicate Jewish identity. Jews were restricted from practising their religion and keeping ethnic and religious traditions and rituals. State antisemitism was expressed first by Lenin's insistence that the Jews were not a nation and the hope that they would assimilate and disappear, followed by Stalin's personal paranoia directed at

Jews, the denial of the Holocaust by Soviet leaders, and the imposition of quotas for Jews in Soviet higher education institutions. While many Jews took on the role of supporters of the early Soviet state, by the late 1960s many saw themselves as a people whose participation in society had been marginalized, their contribution silenced, and their presence undesirable (Brym with Ryvkina 1994; Gitelman 2010). Some participants stressed the dehumanizing experience of being "othered," being treated as strangers who do not belong: "We felt like strangers there, despite the fact we were not strangers. Our native tongue is Russian, our second language was Ukrainian.... They stressed often to us that we were not like others. It was hurtful and offensive.... Sometimes, these antisemitic statements were made, and you couldn't object to them because you're afraid!" (Lora).

Others spoke about Soviet practices of silencing expressions of Jewishness. In this context, those who happened to know/retain Yiddish would secretly use it only in the privacy of their home: "Antisemitism was in the air. The Jew was a curse.... When my Mom and my Grandma spoke Yiddish to each other, they would tell me it's French. I realized it wasn't French but couldn't understand why they hid it from me" (Larissa).

State antisemitism was most harshly experienced in access to higher education and hiring – a consequence of the 2 per cent quota established by the Soviet state. As a result, many Jews failed their university entrance exams: "I knew from my father, who worked at the university, that for every "5" received by a Jewish applicant, examiners were personally accountable to the rector.... I have seen people fainting after being questioned two or three hours on the entrance exam, just to find a reason to fail them" (Lora).[6] Others were denied a job once their Jewish surname was confirmed, or their ethnicity was checked; Jewish ethnicity was recorded in the fifth line of the Soviet internal passport and was referred to by many participants as a "blackening under the fifth rib" (Leon).

The exclusionary treatment of the Soviet state became the foundation for a community based on bonding through exclusion: "We were tied together by the attitude towards us. We felt united just because we were all treated as strangers. In all other instances, we were completely assimilated" (Eric). Jewishness was fixed, not chosen; it was "on the face and in the passport" (Volodya). Jewish identity "revolved around domestic rather than communal practices" (Gershenson and Shneer 2011, 102), although for many it was also grounded in "being in touch, connections, communication, mutual aid, advice" (Sveta). The experience of social subordination became an important characteristic of the Jewish community insofar as it facilitated the emergence of a strong Jewish identity. The informal Jewish community was the main support for maintaining middle-class, professional status despite state marginalization.

Race and Class Trajectories

FSU Jews arrived in Canada like other skilled immigrants from non-Western economies. They often faced significant problems of occupational readjustment because their educational and professional credentials were not recognized, and they had limited English proficiency. Although one half of FSU Jewish immigrants arrived with a university degree and more than one quarter with a graduate degree, they experienced economic vulnerability, especially in the decade after arrival (Shahar and Rosenbaum 2005). Thus, in 2011, FSU immigrants had the lowest annual median income in the Jewish community at under $27,000; the highest proportion, nearly one half, with annual individual earnings of less than $25,000; and the lowest proportion in high-income brackets (Shahar 2015).

Economic advancement was evident from the get-go. Analysis of 1996 Canadian census data revealed as much (Brym 2001). Similarly, data from the 2018 Survey of Jews in Canada suggest that economic differences between FSU-born and Canadian-born Jews have diminished over time (see table 10.1). In 2017, FSU immigrant Jews still formed a substantially higher percentage of households with annual income less than $75,000 (30 per cent, compared to 19 per cent for Canadian-born Jews) and a lower percentage earning $150,000 or more (13 per cent compared to 24 per cent). However, they also had a somewhat higher percentage earning mid-level annual household income of $75,000–$150,000, suggesting progress towards the middle class (28 per cent versus 25 per cent for Canadian-born Jews).

In Canada, where values of individual responsibility and competition are paramount and official antisemitism does not exist, the main goal of FSU immigrants is to regain middle-class, professional status. This aim is perceived as an individually driven endeavour, where success depends purely on one's own skills, aspirations, talents, creativity, and willingness to work hard. As Stass put it: "For us, communism ended the moment we left, and there began a marathon of who achieves what. So, I achieved, and you are a loser if you are still running." Many concentrated on securing Canadian academic credentials to advance their chance to regain their privileged status. Stella saw her academic studies as "an oasis among the vulgar. It saved me morally." Alesha shared

Table 10.1. Self-reported annual household income of Jews born in Canada and the FSU, 2017, $000s, in per cent

	Low		Middle		High			
	<$50	$50–75	$75–110	$110–150	$150–300	$300+	No answer	Total
FSU (n = 148)	16	14	15	13	11	2	30	101
Canada (n = 1,633)	10	9	13	12	16	8	33	101

Note: With few FSU-born Jews in the sample, results must be interpreted cautiously. Respondents were asked to report household income in the full year preceding the survey. Rows do not total 100 due to rounding.
Source: Brym, Neuman, and Lenton (2019).

his thoughts: "Get education in the country where you live. Finding a survival job in construction won't take you anywhere. Education is a means of getting ahead." Acknowledging the disadvantage of being an immigrant professional, he also recognized that one needs "to stand out," to out-perform others – the same way Jews in the Soviet Union used to overcome subordination.

The participants viewed systemic barriers as normal. They were not shocked by rejection. Janna likened the barriers to "bullying in the Soviet Army – there were novices and those 'veterans' ... If she has a comfy spot, why would she give it away to someone?" This metaphor implies keen awareness of the existence of a hierarchy of statuses based on ethnicity, race, class, and tenure, as well as acceptance of the individual's responsibility for finding the means to advance. To reaffirm their professional/middle-class identity, some participants distinguished themselves from those who did not or could not improve their lives. They thus helped to reproduce the socio-economic hierarchy and its supporting values, which regulate and devalue working-class jobs as undignified and regard ordinary workers as people engaged in the rat race and leading meaningless lives. It should also be noted that, for many participants, Israel was an important mid-point in their move to the West, equipping them with life experience, work experience, and material resources facilitating their embrace of the opportunities Canada offered.

The immigrants – who had been able to achieve high educational credentials and professional jobs in a society characterized by blatant state-sponsored antisemitism – could see no reason not to be able to make it in a country full of opportunity and free from the only oppression they knew. However, while the oppressive framework of state antisemitism is absent in Canada, the experience of marginalization as a Jew remains relevant. In this context, it is situated in the strained relationship with the Canadian Jewish community.

Experience with the Jewish Community

When FSU Jewish immigrants began to arrive in Canada in significant numbers in the early 1980s, they were seen as not conforming to Canadian Jewish expectations. For example, the group was characterized as "lacking the impulse for ethnic and religious survival so characteristic of their North American counterparts" (Glickman 1996, 209). This deficiency was perceived as threatening to the cultural-religious distinctiveness of Canadian Jews, who had struggled to preserve their ethnic identity while becoming an integral part of Canadian society. FSU Jewish identity was judged against the Canadian Jewish norm of communal performance, deemed "not Jewish enough," and labelled "Russian" (Avrich-Skapinker 1993, 197). Recent scholarship has a more nuanced perspective on the subject, extending the discourse about a single, stable Jewish identity to a perspective stressing multiplicity, flexibility, and constant renegotiation. It sees Soviet Jewish identity as blending Judaism and Jewish history with secular Russian culture (Basok 2002). This discursive shift coincided with the political shift in the global Jewish polity initiated by Natan Sharansky, who, as chair of the Jewish Agency for Israel from 2009 to 2018, championed the strengthening of secular Jewish identity around the world, bringing FSU Jews from the margins to the centre of the global Jewish experience.

Even so, study participants revealed the immense influence of othering discourses and encounters with Canadian Jews. They wanted to be seen as intelligent, educated, and well-respected professionals. Instead, they often felt devalued, alienated, and insulted by a patronizing attitude. They were hurt by not being perceived as equals. They also spoke about the difference between themselves and Canadian Jews in their ways of expressing Jewish identity. Finally, they spoke about class differences being a reason for the paucity of shared spaces in which the two Jewish sub-communities could interact.

When speaking about the Canadian Jewish community, participants discussed it primarily through the lens of Jewish social and communal services that assisted immigrants during the initial stages of resettlement. They spoke extensively about instrumental assistance they received in legal services, discounts at the Jewish community centre gym, and help with basic furniture and referrals to the Jewish store for second-hand goods. But when it came to interests beyond basic material needs, services were in many cases experienced as inappropriate, degrading, or paternalistic. For example, Sveta was dismayed by the lack of Jewish solidarity and disinterest in her professional future on the part of her settlement worker. As an English teacher, she was seeking guidance to continue her professional career in Canada. Instead, she was discouraged and sent to a non-professional job: "The settlement worker suggested I should get a job at a Russian delicatessen, I can cut sausage there.... I was told plainly that becoming a teacher in Canada is almost impossible. I mean, she practically said, 'Get it straight: You are nobody here, you're nothing, remember it once and for all.'" Sveta expected settlement services to recognize and value her proven professional skills and experience. Instead, her professionalism was devalued and forgotten. She experienced this encounter as degrading.

Similarly, Alla spoke about her family's experience with a host family program that aimed to connect newcomers with established families and in this way help newcomers become part of the community. Alla and her family joined their host family's Passover Seder. They brought gifts to show appreciation for the hosts' invitation and to position themselves as equals "of the same kind." Instead, they experienced humiliation by being treated as a charity case:

> They [the host family] apparently thought of us as a poor, primitive family. So, she shows me a turkey and says, "This is turkey, so here I am measuring the temperature, so this is a thermometer, and now I cut slices of turkey, and this is how I serve it to the table." They behaved like they were going to acculturate us poor, poor relatives. ... And they were disappointed that we were not shocked, that we had seen a bird called turkey before and had eaten it before coming to Canada. It was a terrible experience. It was very, extremely patronizing.

Such experiences produced a sense of alienation and not belonging.

Although some participants noted shared interests and participation in events and campaigns organized by the mainstream Jewish community, such as "rallies in support of Israel … a big rise during this Lebanon war," the discord in definitions of Jewish identity between the two sub-communities was another impediment to building connections. Canadian Jews, who often define their Jewishness as a religious identity, expected FSU Jews to be intensely aware of Jewish identity and possess a strong desire to enhance it through participation in Jewish community life; they experienced FSU Jewish immigrants as "too different, too disinterested or distant to ever become part of the mainstream community" (Avrich-Skapinker 1993, 154).

The participants, while possessing a strong sense of Jewish identity, explained their lack of participation in Jewish community life by their different socialization and class differences. Some, although impressed by the visibility and power of the Jewish community, commented on the different ways of performing Jewishness, contrasting the confident ways of Canadian Jews, who were open about their Jewishness, with the discreet Jewishness of Soviet Jews, who "learned not to stand out too much" (Inna). Many perceived the Canadian Jewish community revolving around Jewish religious practices and gatherings in synagogues and saw a clear separation, having been "taught from childhood totally different concepts" (Volodya), pointing to anti-religious socialization in the FSU and stressing their Jewishness revolving around home, family, and friends. Alla, whose Jewishness was based on a sense of belonging to the Jewish people, especially coming from "a family of *tzaddikim*," shared that feeling when community leaders offered to have her marriage religiously sanctioned. It left her feeling inadequate and not "properly" Jewish. Others contested the adoption of dominant ways of Canadian Jewish performance as an expression of "double morality" and a sign of assimilation and conformity to the mainstream, even though they realized the benefits achieved by "establishing connections," especially for finding a job. Finally, they mentioned social inequality between the two communities as a reason for performing their Jewishness differently; they could hardly afford high synagogue membership fees and tuition for Jewish day schools, having to work long hours to pay the bills, and they for the most part had insufficient mastery of English to engage in communal religious practice.

These accounts are supported by findings from the 2018 Survey of Jews in Canada displayed in table 10.2. I divided twenty-three survey items into two panels, fourteen in the top panel pertaining to Jewish identification, and nine in the bottom panel pertaining to Jewish behaviour. I then calculated percentages for each item separately for respondents born in the FSU and for those born in Canada. Differences between FSU- and Canadian-born Jews were subsequently arrayed so big differences appear at the top and bottom of each panel, while small differences appear in the middle. Positive differences indicate preferences of Canadian-born Jews, negative numbers preferences of FSU-born Jews.

Canadian- and FSU-born Jews have much in common. For instance, for both groups, Holocaust remembrance is the single most important component of Jewish identification, and making financial donations to a Jewish charity or cause is the most important component of Jewish behaviour. However, differences between the subgroups are

Table 10.2. Jewish identity and Jewish performance of FSU immigrant Jews and Canadian-born Jews, in per cent

	Birth country		
	FSU (n = 148)	Canada (n =1,633)	Difference
Jewish identification			
How important is religion in your life? (very + somewhat important)	47	69	22
How important is working for justice and equality for your Jewish identity? (essential + important)	82	88	6
How important is celebrating Jewish holidays with family for your Jewish identity? (essential + important)	91	95	4
How important is leading an ethical and moral life for your Jewish identity? (essential + important)	91	94	3
How important is being Jewish in your life? (very + somewhat)	89	92	3
How important is being intellectually curious for your Jewish identity? (essential + important)	85	84	−1
How important is remembering the Holocaust for your Jewish identity? (essential + important)	99	96	−3
How often are you attracted to Jewish content when choosing a book (frequently + occasionally)	72	69	−3
How important is having a good sense of humour for your Jewish identity? (essential + important)	75	71	−4
How important is caring about Israel for your Jewish identity? (essential + important)	91	86	−5
How often are you attracted to Jewish content when choosing a movie or a play? (frequently + occasionally)	74	66	−8
How important is being part of the Jewish community for your Jewish identity? (essential + important)	95	85	−10
How emotionally attached to Israel do you feel (very + somewhat)	90	78	−12
How important is participating in or attending Jewish cultural activities for your Jewish identity? (essential + important)	79	67	−12
Jewish behaviour			
Being member of a synagogue, temple, or other prayer group (oneself or someone in the household)	32	58	26
Making a financial donation to any Jewish charity or cause (oneself or someone in the household)	65	81	16
How connected do you feel to Jewish life in the city where you live? (very + somewhat)	68	78	10
Lighting Sabbath candles (always + usually)	34	44	10
Being member of a Jewish organization other than a synagogue or temple (oneself or someone in the household)	36	46	10
Attending synagogue (essential + important)	53	62	9
Attending Jewish religious services twice a month or more	23	28	5
Observing Jewish law (essential + important)	58	62	4
Having Jewish friends (all of them or most of them)	64	57	−7

Note: Attending religious services excludes weddings, funerals, and bar/bat mitzvah ceremonies. Results should be interpreted cautiously due to the small sample size for FSU Jews.
Source: Brym, Neuman, and Lenton (2019).

also evident. While Canadian-born Jews are much more inclined to view religion as an important basis for Jewish identification than are FSU-born Jews, FSU-born Jews are significantly more inclined to regard attending secular Jewish cultural activities in that way. Making donations to Jewish charities and causes is the most important form of Jewish behaviour for Canadian-born Jews. Although it ranks near the top for FSU-Jews, too, significantly fewer of them select it as an important form of Jewish behaviour for themselves – probably because they are economically less secure than their Canadian-born co-religionists, as we have seen. Similarly, having Jewish friends is an important form of Jewish behaviour for both subgroups, but it is significantly more important for FSU-born than for Canadian-born Jews. A final, poignant difference worth mentioning concerns connectedness to Jewish life. FSU-born Jews are substantially more likely than Canadian-born Jews to regard being part of the Jewish community as a key component of Jewish identification. At the same time, they feel much less connected to Jewish life in their city than do Canadian-born Jews. In fact, despite their relatively high regard for the importance of Jewish community, FSU-born Jews appear to feel more alienated from Jewish life in their city than either self-identified Sephardi or Israeli-born Jews in Canada (see figure 10.1).

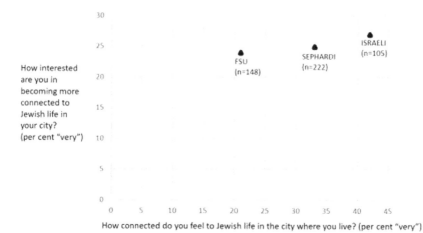

Figure 10.1. Connectedness to Jewish life in city by desire for more connectedness: three main Jewish sub-communities, 2018
Note: Some overlap exists among the three groups portrayed here. Three per cent of FSU Jews identify as Sephardim; 2 per cent of Sephardim identify as FSU Jews and 15 per cent as Israelis; and 31 per cent of Israeli Jews identify as Sephardim.
Source: Adapted from Brym, Neuman, and Lenton (2019, 74–5).

Gender Trajectories

With immigration, familiar gender practices are both challenged and reinforced. In the FSU, despite the rhetoric of equality between men and women, gender roles and identities were informed by patriarchal and heteronormative values. Men played the dominant economic role. Women's universal full-time employment did not change the common perception of their domestic role as a core aspect of their female identity. Men's roles in the domestic sphere were mostly marginal. The support of parents (mainly mothers) was the main strategy that allowed women to balance employment and domestic responsibilities. It meant that women enjoyed economic privilege generated by their partners' position and income and help from their parents and in-laws. In Canada, these gendered arrangements are complicated by impaired mobility due to limited English proficiency and lack of recognition of education and professional credentials. Moreover, support from the extended family is rarely available for two reasons. First, Canadian immigration policy prefers younger, skilled immigrants while limiting sponsorship of older family members. Second, extended family members are often elderly, thus becoming consumers rather than providers of care. They create heavier workloads and responsibilities for women, especially in dual-earner families. These changes often dictate changes in gender roles; as Volodya put it, "the rules of the game change depending on the game's course." While such changes were grudgingly accepted, their effects on the distribution of power in the family and on gender identity were difficult to negotiate.

The Effect of Declining Power of Male Roles

The Canadian socio-economic and labour market context played an important role in the gender experiences and identities of immigrant men. As a result of challenging educational and credential recognition practice, both men and women participants initially found themselves demoted to semi-professional or unskilled jobs.

Both men and women participants closely associated masculine identity with the ability to provide for one's family, referring to it as "innate," "natural," "in-born," and "normal." Thus, for men, the burden of social expectations (as well as their own expectations) caused them to seek paid jobs immediately following immigration. Such employment resulted in further marginalization because the men tended to work with other immigrants and were therefore seldom able to advance their English language skills. Having to work long hours to provide for their families, they also had little time or opportunity to invest in developing their cultural capital to fit the requirements of the labour market by taking a professional course. Experience at work further challenged their masculinity insofar as men saw their jobs as boring, dehumanizing, and deskilling, "like a robot put there for a specific task" (Tolik). They were disappointed about having to descend the career ladder and stymied by the lack of opportunities to demonstrate their professionalism. Men who had professional jobs or owned businesses had to work long and hard to maintain their middle-class status. They expected their wives to be supportive and understanding and shoulder the responsibility of caring for the family. Change in occupational trajectory did not always alter gender identity. Some men maintained familiar patriarchal expectations, believing the men's role was to be a breadwinner, and that taking up household and caring responsibilities was "against nature ... a little bit of nonsense" (Tolik). Adherence to the familiar gender identity patterns, compounded by the adoption of dominant neo-liberal constructions of individual merit, caused them to feel in limbo with no clear masculine identity or anchor in life. Some women also revealed discontent about their partners' inability to fulfil career ambitions, "giving up, not wanting to go study, not [being] prepared to fight the circumstances, to keep going at any cost" (Sveta).

Yet other men, especially younger ones, who emigrated from the FSU in their early twenties and lived in Israel prior to coming to Canada, gave up thinking in dichotomous categories of traditional male/female roles, extended their masculine identities, and challenged the status quo by performing household duties: "I understand that she might be tired. So, I will take a chicken out of the freezer, or fry potatoes, and will put shirts in the laundry so she can have some rest by the TV.... This 'manly, not manly' – it's nonsense. Manliness is not about 'I never cook,' 'I never clean.' Manliness is about being able to endure difficulties, taking responsibility. And machismo is about getting on one's high horse" (Stass). These men also stressed that their wives never blamed them for not being able to find a well-paying job nor referred to them as "an exception."

The Effect of Employment and Care Demands on Female Roles

The trajectory followed by women was different. They were also demoted to dead-end factory jobs or relegated to feminized low-wage jobs at first. For example, Lora, who had been an electronic engineer in Ukraine, was forced to take a part-time position as a childcare assistant in Toronto. This traditional female occupation was more accessible to her than one in the male-dominated niche of the labour market in which she was qualified but where her professional credentials were not acknowledged. However, this low-wage and physically and emotionally demanding job provided income that was crucial to her family's ability to achieve and maintain its middle-class status: "If I didn't work, we wouldn't be able to afford this condo. My earnings, although not big, contribute a lot" (Lora).

However, since the pressure to provide was weaker on women than on men, and because their feminine identity was constructed mostly around caring roles, women had more opportunity to access Canadian education. All women in the sample earned Canadian educational credentials, facilitating professional employment compatible with middle-class status. Once women overcame the hurdle of finding a job, they experienced the demands of the labour market as much higher than in the FSU, describing their jobs as being "hard, very hard" (Stella), "not a job for a woman" (Tanya), and feeling their "skills were put to the fullest of tests" (Natasha).

As a result of landing a professional role, these women often became de facto family breadwinners, a dramatic change and/or turning point in their lives. In the FSU, although employed full-time in professional jobs, the women had often been poorly paid and accorded subordinate status, with their social status deriving from their husbands' professional careers and income. Professional employment in Canada provided them not only with higher income, but also with higher status, thereby enhancing personal autonomy and paving the way for them to become their families' means of achieving middle-class status. It also required them to negotiate their families' contacts with the external environment and to invest in the building of their families' social networks and connections. Combining ambitious and demanding employment with the "natural" role of social reproduction and caring, with no support available, often became "a horror," forcing women "to burn the candle at both ends" (Stella), leaving them limited opportunity for leisure. Thus, women found themselves dealing with the multiple burdens of professional employment and household and caring responsibilities for the survival, well-being, and happiness of their family members because transformations in gendered employment arrangements were rarely accompanied by a redistribution of domestic labour. Both men and women, for the most part, continued to maintain patriarchal, heterosexual, bourgeois ideals regarding women's social reproduction responsibilities, with women often yearning for being "creators of a peaceful and decorous home" (Hyman 2002, 155) and their male partners being the breadwinners. Immigration for these women was a mixed blessing: the material conditions of many women's lives may

Bridging the Gap

Participating in a variety of statuses embedded in changing hierarchies causes individuals to face opportunities and constraints that force their roles and identities to change over time. I have examined the interactive effects of status hierarchies based on race, class, ethnicity, gender, and immigration status as the only way to offer a fully rounded picture of role and identity change among FSU Jews in Toronto.

Michele Byers suggests that Jewishness, once identified, becomes an inescapable marker of difference that undermines myths of meritocracy. She stresses that "Jews have been both ... the ultimate insiders and forever outsiders; they are always parvenus, but also always pariahs as well" (Byers 2009, 48). This interpretation can be also applied to the experience of FSU Jewish immigrants. It advances the understanding that although FSU Jewish immigrants achieve and benefit from social privilege, they also experience oppression.

Specifically, FSU immigrants' Jewish identities are informed by White and professional privilege and marginalization as Jews and immigrants. Their class identities and experiences make little sense without considering their Jewish experience in the FSU and structural realities in Canada. Education was their strategy to deal with oppression and achieve social status in the FSU; in the Canadian context, it reinforced their belief in individual responsibility for economic and professional success and became the means for seeking social recognition. Their gender identities and experiences cannot be understood without reference to their White, professional, and heterosexual privilege and immigrant subordination. Heterosexual privilege and patriarchal values, which form the foundation of their gender identities both in the FSU and in Canada, were coupled in Canada with the values of individual responsibility and meritocracy, reinforcing class identity – a process that variously maintained and challenged familiar gender arrangements. Finally, immigrants' social experiences with native Canadian Jews cannot be understood without taking White and professional identities into consideration. Because these immigrants identify as White professionals and subscribe to the dominant notion of Canadian Jewish success and power, they want to be recognized and legitimized as such. Yet, as FSU Jews who were stripped of the freedom to embrace Jewishness in their country of origin, and whose ways of Jewish performance are different from those of Canadian-born Jews, they are reminded by the mainstream Jewish community, which itself struggles with the tension between assimilation and preserving ethnic identity, that they are not quite White, not quite professional, and not quite Jewish. The relationship between the two sub-communities resembles Bauman's (1997, 72) discussion of Jewish status within the broader society:

> Wherever they come and dearly wish to stay, the nomads find themselves to be parvenus. Parvenu, *arriviste*; someone already *in*, but not quite of, the place; an aspiring resident without a residence permit. Someone reminding the older tenants of the past which they want to forget and the future they would rather wish away. ... The older tenants hate the parvenus for awaking the memories and premonitions they struggle hard to put to sleep. But they can hardly do without parvenus, without some of them being branded parvenu, set apart, charged with carrying the bacillus of restlessness in their bodies; it is thanks to such a branded part, and them only, that the whole may think that the bad dreams and the morbid premonitions are other people's tales and do not quite apply to themselves. The parvenu needs a parvenu in order not to feel a parvenu.

Indeed, the expression of Jewish identity is the most prominent reason for the tension between the two Jewish sub-communities. FSU Jews experience a dearth of valued recognition by the mainstream Jewish community, both professionally and culturally. They are expected to assimilate to the Jewish community and to retain only a Canadian-style Jewish identity. The paucity of shared spaces further contributes to the lack of involvement and engagement between the two Jewish sub-communities.

My analysis highlights the structural boundaries and social inequalities that limit FSU Jewish immigrants' community integration. Class, race, ethnicity, and gender are all factors that shape social connectedness within a community and so illuminate the political dimensions of inclusion and well-being. Recognition and validation of diverse ways in which FSU Jewish immigrants express their Jewish identity is essential for the future relationship between the two Jewish sub-communities.

Facilitating FSU Jewish immigrants' membership in the mainstream Jewish community in Canada, and developing a stronger sense of connectedness to it, will be impossible without purposive effort on the part of the organized Jewish community to legitimize, engage, and include FSU Jewish ways in local norms of Jewish conduct – and to adapt local norms to those of FSU Jews. This effort must aim to educate members of the mainstream Jewish community about FSU Jews and their experiences, sensitize community-based organizations to issues

144 Marina Morgenshtern

of diversity, and eliminate systemic barriers that prevent bridging the two sub-communities.

Finally, although the experiences I have outlined are specific to FSU Jewish immigrants in Toronto, they bear witness to broader issues in the Canadian Jewish experience that require the community's thoughtful consideration.

NOTES

1 This chapter is in part a composite sketch based on research reported more extensively in Morgenshtern and Pollack (2014, 2016).
2 North American Jews came to be considered White because they were granted legal and property rights, especially after the Second World War, and achieved rapid upward mobility (Kaplan 1998).
3 This number includes individuals who self-identified as Jewish by religion or ethnicity or as having no religion but Jewish ethnicity, and who were born in the FSU, had parents who were born in the FSU, or were children in a household where the parents met any of these criteria.
4 The methodologies include testimonio, the "first-person narration of socially significant experiences in which the narrative voice is that of a typical or extraordinary witness or protagonist who metonymically represents others who have lived through similar situations and who have rarely given written expression to them" (Zimmerman 2011, 119), and oral history, which records "what has often been defined as 'history from below,' allowing for a multitude of points of view and giving a voice to individuals and groups who have been marginalized in conventional histories" (Hajek 2014, 771).
5 All names of study participants are pseudonyms.
6 The Soviet Union implemented a 5-point grading system: 5 = excellent, 4 = good, 3 = satisfactory, 2 = unsatisfactory, and 1 = complete failure.

REFERENCES

Avrich-Skapinker, Mindy. 1993. "Canadian Jewish Involvement with Soviet Jewry, 1970–1990: The Toronto Case Study." PhD diss., University of Toronto.
Basok, Tanya. 2002. "Fragmented Identities: The Case of Former Soviet Jews in Toronto." *Identity: An International Journal of Theory and Research* 2 (4): 341–60. https://doi.org/10.1207/S1532706XID0204_04.
Bauman, Zygmunt. 1997. *Postmodernity and Its Discontents*. Cambridge, UK: Polity Press.

Brym, Robert. 2001. "Jewish Immigrants from the Former Soviet Union in Canada, 1996." *East European Jewish Affairs* 31 (2): 36–43. https://doi.org/10.1080/13501670108577948.

Brym, Robert, Keith Neuman, and Rhonda Lenton. 2019. *2018 Survey of Jews in Canada: Final Report.* Toronto: Environics Institute for Survey Research. https://bit.ly/3qS0ees.

Brym, Robert, with Rozalina Ryvkina. 1994. *The Jews of Moscow, Kiev and Minsk: Identity, Antisemitism, Emigration.* New York: New York University Press.

Byers, Michele. 2009. "The Pariah Princess: Agency, Representation, and Neoliberal Jewish Girlhood." *Girlhood Studies* 2 (2): 33–54. https://doi.org/10.3167/ghs.2009.020204.

Crenshaw, Kimberlé. 1989. "Demarginalizing the Intersection of Race and Sex: A Black Feminist Critique of Antidiscrimination Doctrine, Feminist Theory and Antiracist Politics." *University of Chicago Legal Forum* 1: 139–67. https://chicagounbound.uchicago.edu/uclf/vol1989/iss1/8.

Gershenson, Olga, and David Shneer. 2011. "Soviet Jewishness and Cultural Studies." *Journal of Jewish Identities* 4 (1): 101–19. https://doi.org/10.1353/jji.2011.0005.

Gitelman, Zvi. 2010. "A Jagged Circle: From Ethnicity to Internationalism to Cosmopolitanism – and Back." *European Review of History* 17 (3): 523–39. https://doi.org/10.1080/13507486.2010.481956.

Glickman, Yakov. 1996. "Russian Jews in Canada." In *Multiculturalism, Jews, and Identities in Canada*, edited by Howard Adelman and John H. Simpson, 192–218. Jerusalem: Magnes Press.

Hajek, Andrea. 2014. "Oral History." In *SAGE Encyclopedia of Research Methods*, edited by Michael S. Lewis-Beck, Alan Bryman, and Time Futing Liao, 771–2. London: Sage.

Hulko, Wendy. 2009. "The Time- and Context-Contingent Nature of Intersectionality and Interlocking Oppression." *Affilia: Journal of Women and Social Work* 24 (1): 44–55. https://doi.org/10.1177/0886109908326814.

Hyman, Paula. 2002. "Gender and the Shaping of Modern Jewish Identities." *Jewish Social Studies* 8 (2/3): 153–61. https://doi.org/10.2979/JSS.2002.8.2-3.153.

Kaplan, Caren. 1998. "'Beyond the Pale': Re-Articulating U.S. Jewish Whiteness." In *Talking Visions: Multicultural Feminism in a Transnational Age*, edited by Ella Shohat, 451–9. Cambridge, MA: Massachusetts Institute of Technology.

Morgenshtern, Marina, and Shoshana Pollack. 2014. "Changing the Rules of the Game: Experiences of Jewish Immigrants from the Former Soviet Union." *Journal of Feminist Family Therapy* 26 (3): 117–37. https://doi.org/10.1080/08952833.2014.917571.

Morgenshtern, Marina, and Shoshana Pollack. 2016. "Stories of (Be)longing to the Center: Race, Class and Ethnicity in FSU Jewish Immigrant Experiences." *The International Journal of Diversity in Organizations, Communities and Nations: Annual Review* 16 (1): 19–35. https://doi.org/10.18848/1447-9532/CGP/19-35.

Remennick, Larissa. 2006. "Russian Jews in the Global City of Toronto: A Pilot Study of Identity and Social Integration." *Espace, Populations, Sociétés* 1: 61–81. https://doi.org/10.4000/eps.1235.

Shahar, Charles. 2015. *2011 National Household Survey: The Jewish Community of Toronto*. Part 8, *Immigration and Language*. Part 9, *Core FSU Jews*. Toronto: Jewish Federations of Canada – UJA. http://bitly.ws/sw5m.

Shahar, Charles, and Tina Rosenbaum. 2005. *2001 Census Analysis Series: The Jewish Community of Toronto*. Part V, *Immigration and Language*. Toronto: UJA Federation of Greater Toronto. https://bit.ly/3hocYGP.

Zimmerman, Marc. 2011. "Testimonio." In *SAGE Encyclopedia of Research Methods*, edited by Michael S. Lewis-Beck, Alan Bryman, and Tim Futing Liao, 118–19. London: SAGE.

11 Attitudes and Activism concerning Israel

ELIZABETH MOORHOUSE-STEIN

Introduction

Canadian Jews are strongly emotionally attached to Israel. Nonetheless, fewer than one in four Canadian Jews think the Israeli government is making a serious effort at a peace agreement with the Palestinians, and just over one in four think West Bank settlements are *not* illegal under international law (Brym, Neuman, and Lenton 2019, 59–60). These findings challenge conventional wisdom. Canadian Jews are often said to be conservative minded with regard to Israel. However, empirical analysis reveals attitudinal fissures regarding Israeli policy. These divisions are associated with different age cohorts, denominations, party support, and type of community involvement.

This chapter seeks to describe these divisions and explain why relatively young Canadian Jews who are politically liberal or left-leaning and identify with the Reform denomination or are non-denominational tend to be more critical of Israeli policy regarding West Bank settlements and Israel's approach to the peace process – and, conversely, why Canadian Jews who are politically conservative, older, and identify with the Orthodox or Conservative denominations tend to be less critical. I also compare Canadian-Jewish attitudes towards Israel with similar attitudes in the United States, and in relation to organized Jewish advocacy pertaining to Israel in Canada over the last decade.

Attachment and Attitudes towards Israel

The 2018 Survey of Jews in Canada found that 48 per cent of Canadian Jews are "very" emotionally attached to Israel, 31 per cent are "somewhat" emotionally attached, and 19 per cent are "not very" or "not at all" emotionally attached. It is often said that this strong emotional connection has led to a strong consensus on matters related to Israel. However, this judgment has been based mainly on Jewish community newspapers, national news coverage predicting how Canadian Jews will vote in federal elections, and statements released by the Jewish community's primary advocacy institutions – the Centre for Israel and Jewish Affairs (the advocacy arm of the Jewish Federations of Canada) and the former Canadian Jewish Congress.

There can be little doubt that the highly centralized community infrastructure presents an image of communal consensus when it comes Canadian Jews' opinions on Israel (Schnoor 2011; Waller 1993; Brym 1993). However, according to the 2018 Survey of Jews in Canada, just 35 per cent of Canadian Jews believe the Israeli government is making a sincere effort to establish a peace agreement with the Palestinians, only 14 per cent think continued settlement building in the West Bank helps Israel's security, and 43 per cent think West Bank settlements are not illegal under international law. Despite the prevailing public image, multiple studies conducted since the early 1980s document criticism in the Jewish community of Israel's 1982 invasion of Lebanon, the expansion of settlements in the West Bank, and permanent Israeli occupation of that territory (Habib 2004; Haklai 2008; Taras and Weinfeld 1990; Brym 1983, 1993; Sucharov 2011; Waller and Weinfeld 1987).

Among Canadian Jews, the main factors that account for differences of opinion towards these aspects of Israeli policy are age, denominational identification, political party support, and type of community involvement (see table 11.1). Fewer significant differences are associated with variation in educational attainment, and fewer still with differences in household income and gender (the last two factors are therefore not shown in table 11.1).

Specifically, 50 per cent of Orthodox Jews think Israel is making a sincere effort at a peace agreement, and 57 per cent think continued settlement building either helps Israel's security or makes no difference to it. In contrast, just 36 per cent of Reform Jews think the Israeli government is making a sincere effort at a peace settlement with the Palestinians, and a mere 8 per cent think continued settlement building helps Israel's security. Only about 10 per cent of Orthodox Jews think Israeli settlements in the West Bank are illegal under international law, compared to almost 30 per cent of Reform Jews (not shown in table 11.1). The views of Conservative Jews are roughly in between those of Orthodox and Reform Jews, and the views of non-denominational Jews resemble those of Reform Jews.

Some 59 per cent of Canadian Jews who support the Conservative Party think the Israeli government is making a sincere effort at peace,

Table 11.1. Belief in the sincerity of Israel's peace effort and in the impact of settlements on Israel's security by selected variables, in per cent

	Is the current Israeli government making a sincere effort to bring about a peace settlement with the Palestinians?[a]	Does the continued building of Jewish settlements in the West Bank help or hurt the security of Israel?[b]		
	Yes	Help	Hurt	No difference
Age (years)				
18–29	30	13	40	17
30–44	27	9	43	22
45–54	37	14	43	24
55–64	38	18	37	24
65–74	38	12	40	30
75+	46	16	28	28
Denomination				
Orthodox/Modern Orthodox	50	27	20	30
Conservative	43	12	32	29
Reform	36	8	51	21
Non-denominational	28	10	53	20
Party support				
Conservative	59	31	26	43
Liberal	25	11	61	28
New Democratic	11	4	86	10
Green	19	11	66	24
Education				
High school	43	19	31	23
College	42	14	29	27
Undergraduate	34	15	38	24
Graduate	31	11	47	23
All				
Canadian Jews	35	14	39	24
US Jews[c]	35	19	40	31

[a] "No" and "Don't know" are omitted.
[b] "It depends" and "Don't know" are omitted.
[c] By religion only. The first column is for 2020, the remaining columns for 2013.
Sources: Brym, Neuman, and Lenton (2019); Pew Research Center (2013; 2021).

compared to just 25 per cent of Liberal Party supporters and 11 per cent of NDP supporters. Jewish supporters of the Conservative Party are also far more likely than Jewish supporters of the Liberal and New Democratic parties to think continued settlement building helps Israel's security, and they are far less likely to think settlements are illegal according to international law.

Finally, Canadian Jews under the age of forty-five are significantly less likely to think the Israeli government is making a sincere effort at a peace agreement and more likely to think Israeli settlements are illegal under international law. In particular, about one half of those under the age of thirty do not agree with the view that Israel is making a sincere effort to arrive at a peace settlement with the Palestinians, and almost one third think Israeli settlements are illegal under international law. Among members of this youngest age cohort, the share of those who think settlements are illegal under international law is larger than the share who think they are legal.

Predicting Attitudes towards Peace Efforts and Settlements

Multivariate analysis permits an assessment of the unique influence of various factors on attitudes. Such an assessment is important because if, for example, Conservative supporters tend to be elderly, we cannot know how much of their attitude on a particular issue is due to their Conservative Party support and how much is due to their age. Multivariate analysis allows us to separate these effects. For instance, we have seen that denominational identification, political party support, and age are all associated with the policy items I have been discussing. Multivariate analysis tells us the effect of denominational affiliation alone for individuals matched in terms of their political party support and age; the effect of political party support alone for individuals matched in terms of denominational affiliation and age; and so on.

Tables 11.2 and 11.3 present multivariate analyses showing the unique effect of various socio-demographic factors on Canadian Jews' opinions of Israel's efforts to construct West Bank settlements and achieve peace with the Palestinians.

Denomination, political partisanship, and age have the largest impact on opinions concerning the Israeli government's sincerity in attempting to bring about a peace agreement and the security implications of continued settlement building in the West Bank. Gender and household income do not have an independent effect.

Orthodox Jews are more than four times more likely than non-denominational Jews to think continued settlement building helps

Table 11.2. Multinomial logistic regression predicting belief in the sincerity of Israel's peace effort

	Not making a sincere effort	
	B (se)	Exp (B)
Age (ref.: 75+ years)		
18–29	0.777* (0.342)	2.175
30–44	0.852** (0.304)	2.345
45–54	0.418 (0.315)	1.519
55–64	0.104 (0.308)	1.109
65–74	0.422 (0.327)	1.526
Denomination (ref.: non-denominational/just Jewish)		
Orthodox/Modern Orthodox	−0.948*** (0.239)	0.387
Conservative	−0.519* (0.217)	0.595
Reform	−0.255 (0.237)	0.775
Party support (ref.: liberal)		
Conservative	−1.635*** (0.175)	0.195
New Democratic	0.787** (0.301)	2.197
Green	0.922 (0.637)	2.514
Education (ref.: graduate degree)		
High school	−0.375 (0.325)	0.687
College	−0.683* (0.269)	0.505
Undergraduate	−0.012 (0.177)	0.988
Household income (ref.: $150,000+)		
Under $50,000	−0.602* (0.272)	0.548
$50–74,999	−0.083 (0.263)	0.920
$75–109,999	−0.481* (0.225)	0.618
$110–149,999	0.005 (0.235)	1.005
Gender (ref.: female)		
Male	0.376* (0.161)	1.456
Constant	0.943** (0.357)	
n	1,022	
−2 log likelihood	1,489.117	
Nagelkerke R^2	0.285	

*$p < 0.05$; **$p < 0.01$; ***$p < 0.001$

Note: This table reports multinomial logit coefficients (B), standards errors (se), and odds ratios (Exp[B]). The reference category is "Yes, the current Israeli government is making a sincere effort." The "Don't know" category is omitted.

Source: Brym, Neuman, and Lenton (2019).

Table 11.3. Multinomial logistic regression predicting belief in the impact of settlements on Israel's security

	Helps security		No difference/it depends	
	B (se)	Exp (B)	B (se)	Exp (B)
Age (ref.: 75+ years)				
18–29	−1.287** (0.479)	0.276	−0.393 (0.362)	0.675
30–44	−1.098** (0.404)	0.334	−0.489 (0.323)	0.613
45–54	−0.884* (0.422)	0.413	−0.388 (0.338)	0.679
55–64	−0.230 (0.395)	0.795	−0.267 (0.336)	0.765
65–74	−1.082* (0.438)	0.339	−0.669 (0.346)	0.512
Denomination (ref.: non-denominational /just Jewish)				
Orthodox/Modern Orthodox	1.414*** (0.309)	4.111	1.115*** (0.257)	3.051
Conservative	0.124 (0.301)	0.884	0.352 (0.223)	1.422
Reform	0.345 (0.341)	0.708	−0.049 (0.239)	0.952
Political party (ref.: liberal)				
Conservative	1.771*** (0.238)	5.878	0.935*** (0.182)	2.547
New Democratic	−1.983** (0.686)	0.138	−1.234*** (0.303)	0.291
Green	0.066 (0.675)	1.068	−1.198 (0.678)	0.302
Education (ref.: graduate degree)				
High school	0.189 (0.425)	1.208	0.050 (0.339)	1.052
College	0.373 (0.352)	1.452	−0.028 (0.290)	0.972
Undergraduate	0.082 (0.241)	1.085	−0.041 (0.183)	0.960
Household income (ref.: $150,000+)				
Under $50,000	0.607 (0.364)	1.835	0.557* (0.280)	1.745
$50–74,999	−0.029 (0.367)	0.972	0.219 (0.269)	1.244
$75–109,999	0.491 (0.302)	1.635	0.391 (0.233)	1.479
$110–149,999	0.147 (0.311)	1.158	−0.180 (0.247)	0.835
Gender (ref.: female)				
Male	0.454* (0.216)	1.575	0.077 (0.165)	1.080
Constant	−1.621** (0.479)		− 0.544 (0.374)	
n	1,022			
−2 log likelihood	1,939.016			
Nagelkerke R^2	0.302			

*$p < 0.05$; **$p < 0.01$; ***$p < 0.001$
Note: This table reports multinomial logit coefficients (B), standards errors (se), and odds ratios (Exp[B]). The reference category is "Continued settlement building in the West Bank hurts the security of Israel." The "Don't know" category is omitted.
Source: Brym, Neuman, and Lenton (2019).

rather than hurts Israel's security, and more than three times more likely to think it helps Israel's security rather than making no difference. Orthodox Jews are also an estimated 2.5 times more likely than non-denominational Jews to think the Israeli government is making a sincere effort at peace, holding other predictors constant.

Conservative Jews are more likely than Orthodox Jews to hold critical positions, but less likely to do so than non-denominational Jews are. They are an estimated 1.7 times more likely than non-denominational Jews to think the Israeli government is making a sincere effort at peace. However, the results show that, regarding the perceived security implications of West Bank settlements, identifying with Conservative or Reform Judaism does not have a statistically significant impact when compared to identifying as non-denominational.

The political party that Canadian Jews support has a significant influence on opinions regarding peace efforts and settlements. When all other variables are held constant, Jews who support the Conservative Party are an estimated five times more likely than Jews who support the Liberal Party to think the Israeli government is making a sincere effort at peace, and almost six times more likely than Liberals to think continued settlement building helps rather than hurts Israel's security. They are also more likely than Liberal Jews are to think continued settlement building makes no difference to Israel's security rather than thinking it hurts Israel's security. However, NDP supporters are twice as likely as Liberal supporters to think Israel is not making a sincere effort at peace, and fully seven times more likely than Liberals are to think settlement building hurts Israel's security rather than helps it.

Being under the age of forty-five is also a significant predictor of critical positions regarding Israel settlement policy and peace initiatives. When holding all other factors constant, Canadian Jews under the age of forty-five are more than twice as likely as those seventy-five years and older to think the Israeli government is not making a sincere effort at peace. Those younger than thirty are an estimated 3.6 times more likely than those seventy-five years and older to think settlement building hurts rather than helps Israel's security, and those between thirty and forty-four years of age are an estimated three times more likely than those aged seventy-five years and older to think settlement building hurts rather than helps Israel's security. Only those between the ages of fifty-five and sixty-four are not significantly more critical of West Bank settlements than those above the age of seventy-four are.

Differences in level of household income, educational attainment, and gender are less consistent and statistically significant predictors. However, the patterns point towards higher income being linked with more critical positions on the sincerity of Israel's peace efforts, as well as women being significantly more likely than men to doubt that the Israeli government is making a sincere effort at peace and to think that settlement building helps Israel's security.

The influence of synagogue membership, membership in other Jewish organizations, donating to Jewish charities or causes, and having attended a full-time Jewish school were also examined (see table 11.4). Attending religious services at least once a week and donating to Jewish charities are significantly associated with believing that Israeli peace efforts are sincere and that West Bank settlements help or have no impact on Israel's security. The 15 per cent of Canadian Jews who attend services at least weekly are an estimated 2.5 times more likely than those who seldom attend to think the Israeli government is making a sincere effort at peace. They are also nearly four times more likely than the latter to think settlements help rather than hurt Israel's security. Donors to Jewish causes are significantly more likely than non-donors to think the Israeli government is making a sincere effort at peace, that settlement building helps Israel's security rather than hurts it, and that the construction of Jewish settlements on the West Bank makes no difference to Israel's security. Being a member of a synagogue and having attended a full-time Jewish school are not statistically significant predictors of attitudes towards West Bank settlements but are statistically significantly associated with belief in the sincerity of Israel's peace efforts. Finally, membership in a Jewish organization other than a synagogue and attending religious services monthly are not statistically significantly associated with attitudes on either issue.

Canadian and American Jews

Denomination, political party support, and age go a long way towards explaining Canadian Jews' differences of opinion on the sincerity of Israel's peace efforts and West Bank settlement construction. The findings on denomination and age mirror research on American Jews' opinions

Table 11.4. Multinomial logistic regression predicting belief in the sincerity of Israel's peace effort and in the security impact of settlements

	Peace effort		Impact of settlements on Israel's security			
	No sincere effort		Help Israel's security		No difference/depends	
	B (se)	Exp (B)	B (se)	Exp (B)	B (se)	Exp (B)
Household member is synagogue member	−0.341* (0.153)	0.711	−0.035 (0.218)	0.966	0.210 (0.162)	1.234
Household member is member of other Jewish organization	0.169 (0.131)	1.184	−0.046 (0.183)	1.047	−0.060 (0.140)	0.942
Donated to Jewish charity	−0.464* (0.198)	0.628	0.679* (0.282)	1.971	0.806*** (0.215)	2.240
Attended full-time Jewish school	−0.320* (0.129)	0.726	0.343 (0.178)	1.409	0.144 (0.138)	1.155
Attends services (ref.: seldom, few times a year, never)						
At least once weekly	−0.880*** (0.189)	0.415	1.348*** (0.241)	3.849	0.411 (0.211)	1.508
Once or twice monthly	−0.054 (0.178)	0.947	0.134 (0.260)	1.143	−0.030 (0.187)	0.971
Age (ref.: 75+ years)						
18–29	1.158*** (0.267)	3.183	−1.456***(0.371)	0.233	−0.919** (0.295)	0.399
30–44	0.982*** (0.235)	2.671	−1.092** (0.315)	0.336	−0.549* (0.260)	0.578
45–54	0.294 (0.247)	1.342	−0.684* (0.335)	0.505	−0.312 (0.278)	0.732
55–64	0.180 (0.240)	1.197	−0.248 (0.310)	0.780	−0.358 (0.273)	0.699
65–74	0.395 (0.257)	1.485	−0.949** (0.352)	0.387	−0.491 (0.284)	0.612
Household income (ref.: $150,000+)						
Under $50,000	−0.398* (0.202)	0.671	0.586* (0.278)	1.797	0.350 (0.217)	1.419
$50–74,999	−0.289 (0.201)	0.749	0.417 (0.279)	1.517	0.216 (0.216)	1.241
$75–109,999	−0.500** (0.178)	0.607	0.487* (0.245)	1.627	0.345 (0.190)	1.413
$110–149,999	−0.080 (0.181)	0.932	0.021 (0.254)	1.021	−0.241 (0.195)	0.786
Gender (ref.: female)						
Male	0.239 (0.126)	1.270	0.636*** (0.176)	1.889	0.194 (0.134)	1.214
Constant	0.658* (0.306)		−1.915*** (0.429)		−0.989** (0.339)	
n	1,451		1,451			
−2 log likelihood	1.973.500		2585.223			
Nagelkerke R^2	0.112		0.147			

*$p < 0.05$; **$p < 0.01$; ***$p < 0.001$

Note: This table reports multinomial logit coefficients (B), standards errors (se), and odds ratios (Exp[B]). Reference category for "Peace effort" is "Israeli government is making a sincere effort." The "Don't know" category is omitted. Reference category for "Impact of settlements on Israel's security" is "Continued settlement-building in the West Bank hurts Israel's security." The "Don't know" category is omitted.

Source: Brym, Neuman, and Lenton (2019)

on the same issues. Analysis of data from the 2013 Pew Research Center survey of American Jews reveals that denominational differences, followed by age, are the strongest and most consistent sources of division among American Jews regarding the peace process and settlements. Also consistent with the findings reported here is that household income is not a highly significant or consistent predictor of American Jews' opinions on these issues (Kotler-Berkowitz 2017).

Canadian Jews' relatively deep emotional attachment to Israel does not prevent most of them from holding critical or ambivalent views of Israel's policies regarding the peace process and West Bank settlements. This conclusion calls into question the view that Canadian Jews are more conservative than are American Jews with respect to the attitudes analysed here. In both countries, 35 per cent of Jews think the Israeli government is making a sincere effort at peace, and about 40 per cent think continued settlement building in the West Bank hurts Israel's security (see table 11.1).

The Canadian findings reported earlier on the effects of denominational affiliation and participation in Jewish life also mirror research on American Jews (Waxman 2017). This fact presents us with a paradox. The Orthodox and especially Conservative denominations are much more numerous in percentage terms in Canada than in the United States, and their rate of participation in Jewish organizations and full-time Jewish schooling is much higher. One might therefore expect Canadian Jews to hold more positive views of Israel's West Bank settlement policy and the sincerity of its peace efforts than American Jews do. How, then, can one explain the fact that the distribution of critical and non-critical opinions regarding the attitudes analysed here is almost identical in the two countries?

The unexpectedly similar distribution may be a function of Canadian Jews feeling less inhibited than Americans do about expressing their views. One is typically more frank about family matters with a close relative than with a stranger. Analogously, the fact that Canadian Jews are about twice as likely as American Jews to say they are "very attached" to Israel emotionally, less than half as likely to say they feel "not very attached" or "not at all attached," and around twice as likely to have visited Israel may make them more likely to express critical opinions of certain Israeli policies (Brym, Neuman, and Lenton 2019, 57–8, 73; Pew Research Center 2021, 36, 138, 179). It may also be relevant that Canada's foreign aid and diplomatic support of Israel is minute compared to US military aid and diplomatic support. Consequently, Canadian Jews may on average consider it less risky to express critical judgments than American Jews do.

Conservative and Liberal Party Support

The findings reviewed earlier show that Conservative Party support significantly predicts favourable opinions on settlement construction and efforts to reach a peace agreement, with support weaker among Liberal Party supporters and weaker still among supporters of the NDP. While 60 per cent of Jews who support the Conservatives think the Canadian government does not support Israel enough, 59 per cent of Liberal supporters think Canada's support for Israel is about right (Brym, Neuman, and Lenton 2019, 63). And although 47 per cent of Jews supporting the New Democratic Party think Canada's support for Israel is about right, 27 per cent think it is too supportive, with just 4 per cent of Liberals and merely 1 per cent of Conservatives sharing that view.

In Canada and the United States, Jewish political behaviour is shaped by immediate political contexts and particular Jewish values and ideas, with the latter having a strong impact on issues pertaining to Israel (Barnett 2016; Haklai 2008; Habib 2004; Safran 1991; Shain 1999; Sucharov 2011; Waxman 2016; Wald 2019; Weinfeld 2014; Weisberg 2019). More than a decade ago, an historic shift occurred among Canadian Jews away from the Liberals and towards the Conservatives (Offman 2013; Martin 2015). Throughout the 2000s, and against the backdrop of the Liberal sponsorship scandal, many Canadian Jews grew dissatisfied with the party's response to anti-Israel advocacy on campuses and the nuclear threat from Iran. Conservatives promised greater support for Israel. In 2006, Prime Minister Stephen Harper cut funding to the Hamas-led government in Gaza and defended Israel in its war with Hezbollah. At the same time, Liberal leader Michael Ignatieff criticized Harper for not playing a mediating role and accused Israel of war crimes. Over the next couple of years, others in the Liberal Party leadership criticized the Conservatives' unreserved support for Israel in the UN and other international forums (Martin 2015). An apology from Ignatieff and a change of party leader did not mend the rift between many Canadian Jews and the Liberals in advance of the 2011 election. Since 2015, however, both parties' official positions on Israel have been similar, with the exception of Conservative support for relocating the Canadian embassy to Jerusalem. It is likely that the lack of substantive difference partly explains why, as of 2018, Canadian Jews' support for the Liberal and Conservative parties is almost equal – 36 per cent for the Liberals and 32 per cent for the Conservatives.

Advocacy Organizations

Advocacy organizations are the main actors in minority political activism, engaging in political activism and claiming to speak on behalf of the minority population (Haklai 2011). The principal Jewish and Israel advocacy organization in Canada is the Centre for Israel and Jewish Affairs (CIJA), the advocacy arm of the Jewish Federations of Canada. CIJA's mandate is, inter alia, to advocate for public policies in the interests of the organized Jewish community, fight antisemitism and anti-Zionism, and promote support for Israel among all political parties (CIJA 2020). It does not comment on events in Israel other than to support an end to the Israel–Palestine conflict, defend Israel during conflicts and wars, and advocate that Canada recognize Jerusalem as the capital of Israel. It advocates that the Canadian government encourage Israeli and Palestinian leaders to negotiate directly with each other towards a two-state solution, but it has also called on the government to "draw a clear moral distinction" between "the defensive actions of Israelis" and "the illegal aggression of banned terror groups such as Hamas and Hezbollah" (CIJA 2020, 13; Fogel 2018b; Smith 2017). In both the *Globe and Mail* and *National Post*, CIJA leadership has also argued that Israel's occupation of the West Bank is not an impediment to resolving the conflict or to a future Palestinian state, but rather that the Palestinian leadership is responsible for rejecting peace proposals and for failing to end the violence of Hamas and Hezbollah towards both Israelis and Palestinians (Fogel 2010, 2014, 2017, 2018a, 2018b).

Even before the former Canadian Jewish Congress and the Canada–Israel Committee were absorbed by CIJA in 2010–11, many Canadian Jews were dissatisfied with their community's major advocacy organizations. They believed that an increasingly consolidating and centralizing Jewish advocacy structure misrepresented the diversity of Canadian-Jewish perspectives on Israel, represented an increasingly right-leaning point of view, and did not welcome criticism of the Israeli government or of Canadian government support for it from the Jewish community (Levy-Ajzenkopf 2013).

About 20 per cent of Canadian Jews that identify with a Jewish religious denomination are aligned with the Reform movement, and some liberal and left-leaning Jews have found a basis of support in Reform synagogues. In addition, four left-leaning alternatives to the major advocacy organizations exist in Canada. Canadian Friends of Peace Now (n.d.) was founded in the early 1980s in response to Israel's war in Lebanon and in alliance with the large and influential

Shalom Achshav movement in Israel. The New Israel Fund (NIF) of Canada was founded in 1986 to raise money for Israeli organizations that support "economic equality, religious freedom, civil and human rights, shared society and anti-racism, Palestinian citizens, and democracy itself" (NIF Canada n.d.). It is affiliated with sister organizations in Israel, the US, the UK, Australia, Germany, and Switzerland. Both organizations advocate a two-state solution and oppose West Bank settlements and Israeli occupation of the West Bank and Gaza. Two other Canadian advocacy organizations were founded around the time CIJA became the primary national Jewish and Israel advocacy organization. JSpaceCanada characterizes itself as a progressive organization focusing on issues of social justice and human rights in Israel (JSpaceCanada n.d.). It favours a two-state solution and opposes Israel's occupation of the West Bank. Independent Jewish Voices (IJV) is the most left-wing Jewish organization in Canada. It supports the Boycott, Divestment and Sanctions (BDS) movement and Palestinians' right of return – red lines that cannot be crossed for the rest of the organized Jewish community (IJV n.d.). All four organizations seek to engage young Jews who feel little or no affinity with the major Jewish advocacy organizations or campus Hillels.

An Uncertain Future

As noted earlier, older Canadian Jews are significantly more inclined than younger Canadian Jews to support Israeli West Bank settlement policy and believe that Israel's peace efforts are sincere. This tendency may derive from their vivid memories of the Holocaust and the fears they experienced during Israel's 1948, 1967, and 1973 wars. For older Canadian Jews, Israel's vulnerability is palpable. In contrast, the events just listed are more distant for younger Canadian Jews; the slice of history they have experienced may incline them to see Israel as a strong, militarily advanced, occupying power (Cohen and Kelman 2010). As older generations pass from the scene, it is thus possible that a critical stance towards Israeli policy will become more widespread in the Canadian Jewish community. However, that outcome is not certain. As members of younger generations age, their attitudes may shift. Unpredictable political and military events in the Middle East may push them to the right. Based on the preceding analysis, what can be said with more confidence is that, at present, debate among Canadian Jews about important aspects of Israeli government policy has become more fractious than at any time in the past.

REFERENCES

Barnett, Michael N. 2016. *The Star and the Stripes: A History of the Foreign Policies of American Jews*. Princeton, NJ: Princeton University Press.

Brym, Robert. 1983. "Israel in Lebanon." *Middle East Focus* 6 (1): 14–19.

Brym, Robert. 1993. "Politics: Introduction." In *The Jews in Canada*, edited by Robert Brym, Morton Weinfeld, and William Shaffir, 250–3. Toronto: Oxford University Press.

Brym, Robert, Keith Neuman, and Rhonda Lenton. 2019. *2018 Survey of Jews in Canada: Final Report*. Toronto: Environics Institute for Survey Research. https://bit.ly/3mdvMvg.

Canadian Friends of Peace Now. n.d. "About Us." Accessed 30 June 2022, https://www.peacenowcanada.org/about-us-2/.

Centre for Israel and Jewish Affairs (CIJA). 2020. "Federal Issues Guide." Accessed 8 May 2021, http://bitly.ws/sMxp.

Cohen, Steven M., and Ari Y. Kelman. 2010. "Thinking about Distancing from Israel." *Contemporary Jewry* 30 (2/3): 287–96. https://doi.org/10.1007/s12397-010-9053-4.

Fogel, Shimon Koffler. 2010. "Abbas Must Prepare His People for Peace with Israel." *National Post*, 1 September 2010, A17.

Fogel, Shimon Koffler. 2014. "Israel-Gaza Must Be Viewed from a Bigger Mideast Lens." *Globe and Mail*, 31 July 2014. http://bitly.ws/t3bY.

Fogel, Shimon Koffler. 2017. "Paris Summit: Building Israeli-Palestinian Peace from the Ground Up." *Globe and Mail*, 15 January 2017. http://bitly.ws/sMxu.

Fogel, Shimon Koffler. 2018a. "Gazans Deserve a Better Future – without Hamas." *Globe and Mail*, 17 May 2018, A15.

Fogel, Shimon Koffler. 2018b. "25 Years after Oslo, Lessons for Achieving Israeli-Palestinian Peace." *Globe and Mail*, 13 September 2018. http://bitly.ws/sMxx.

Habib, Jasmin. 2004. *Israel, Diaspora, and Routes of National Belonging*. Toronto: University of Toronto Press.

Haklai, Oded. 2008. "Helping the Enemy? Why Transnational Jewish Philanthropic Foundations Donate to Palestinian NGOs in Israel." *Nations and Nationalism* 14 (3): 581–99. https://doi.org/10.1111/j.1469-8129.2008.00333.x.

Haklai, Oded. 2011. *Palestinian Ethnonationalism in Israel*. Philadelphia: University of Pennsylvania Press.

Independent Jewish Voices (IJV). n.d. "About IJV." Accessed 30 June 2022, https://www.ijvcanada.org/about-ijv/.

JSpaceCanada. n.d. "What We Do." Accessed 30 June 2022, https://www.jspacecanada.ca/about.

Kotler-Berkowitz, Laurence. 2017. "The Structure of Political Divisions among American Jews." *Contemporary Jewry* 37 (1): 5–27. https://doi.org/10.1007/s12397-016-9180-7.

Levy-Ajzenkopf, Andy. 2013. "Is CIJA Better or Worse Than What Came Before?" *Canadian Jewish News*, 27 March 2013. http://bitly.ws/t3bZ.

Martin, Patrick. 2015. "Diverse Jewish Views Come to the Fore: Despite the Tories' Realignment of the Political Landscape in 2006, Liberals and NDP Are Back as Kosher Options for Many." *Globe and Mail*, 17 October 2015, A14.

New Israel Fund (NIF) Canada. n.d. "About Us." Accessed 30 June 2022, https://nifcan.org/about/.

Offman, Craig. 2013. "Jewish Community Finds a Friend in Harper." *Globe and Mail*, 30 November 2013. http://bitly.ws/sMxy.

Pew Research Center. 2013. *A Portrait of Jewish Americans: Finding from a Pew Research Center Survey of U.S. Jews*. Washington, DC: Pew Research Center. http://bitly.ws/sMxz.

Pew Research Center. 2021. *Jewish Americans in 2020*. Washington, DC: Pew Research Center. http://bitly.ws/sMt9.

Safran, William. 1991. "Diasporas in Modern Societies: Myths of Homeland and Return." *Diaspora* 1 (1): 83–99. https://doi.org/10.1353/dsp.1991.0004.

Schnoor, Randal F. 2011. "The Contours of Canadian Jewish life." *Contemporary Jewry* 31 (3): 179–97. https://doi.org/10.1007/s12397-011-9075-6.

Shain, Yossi. 1999. *Marketing the American Creed Abroad: Diasporas in the U.S. and Their Homelands*. Cambridge, UK: Cambridge University Press.

Smith, Marie-Danielle. 2017. "Canada Careful on Jerusalem Policy; Liberal Regime Avoids Criticism of U.S. Decision." *National Post*, 7 December 2017, A11.

Sucharov, Mira. 2011. "Values, Identity, and Israel Advocacy." *Foreign Policy Analysis* 7 (4): 361–80. https://doi.org/10.1111/j.1743-8594.2011.00145.x.

Taras, David, and Morton Weinfeld. 1990. "Continuity and Criticism: North American Jews and Israel." *International Journal* 45 (3): 661–84. https://doi.org/10.1177/002070209004500307.

Wald, Kenneth D. 2019. *The Foundations of American Jewish Liberalism*. Cambridge, UK: Cambridge University Press.

Waller, Harold. 1993. "The Canadian Jewish Polity: Power and Leadership in the Jewish Community." In *The Jews in Canada*, edited by Robert Brym, Morton Weinfeld, and William Shaffir, 254–69. Toronto: Oxford University Press.

Waller, Harold, and Morton Weinfeld. 1987. "A *Viewpoints* Survey of Canadian Jewish Leadership Opinion." *Viewpoints* 15 (4), S1–S3.

Waxman, Dov. 2016. *Trouble in the Tribe: The American Jewish Conflict over Israel*. Princeton, NJ: Princeton University Press.

Waxman, Dov. 2017. "American Jews and the Israeli-Palestinian Conflict: Part of the Problem or Part of the Solution?" *Political Science Quarterly* 132 (2): 313–40. https://doi.org/10.1002/polq.12617.

Weinfeld, Morton. 2014. "If Canada and Israel Are at War, Who Gets My Support? Challenges of Competing Diaspora Loyalties: Marshall Sklare Award Lecture." *Contemporary Jewry* 34 (3): 167–87. https://doi.org/10.1007/s12397-014-9126-x.

Weisberg, Herbert F. 2019. *The Politics of American Jews.* Ann Arbor: University of Michigan Press.

PART C

Comparing Canadian Jews and Other Canadians

12 From the Jewish Question to the Muslim Question

ABDOLMOHAMMAD KAZEMIPUR

Five Questions

When I suggested in *The Muslim Question in Canada* (Kazemipur 2014) that the Jewish Question of the late nineteenth century seemed to have been replaced by a Muslim Question of similar nature, I received two unhappy reactions: one from Jewish friends, the other from Muslim friends. My Jewish friends were unhappy that the Jewish Question might have been replaced by any other question, particularly a Muslim one; my Muslim friends were unhappy that I had likened them to Jews. Those reactions alerted me to deep-seated beliefs and stereotypes prevalent in the Jewish and Muslim communities towards each other. Since then, I have been reflecting on the nature of those perceptions, their sources, and possible remedies.

Several issues of interest to the Canadian public would inevitably bring up Canadian Muslims and Jews simultaneously: the issue of the largest non-Christian religious minority in the country, the Israel–Palestine conflict, and the issue of rising Islamophobia and antisemitism. That last issue is recent and of enormous significance for both the national identity of Canadians and the image of Canada worldwide. Nationally, it defines the image of Canada that Canadians hold. Internationally, it determines the fate of the ideals of tolerance and multiculturalism that Canada has championed for the past half-century. But there is yet another, less explored issue that I will focus on in this chapter: the relationship between the Canadian Muslim and Jewish communities. In particular, I will address the following questions:

1 What are the general demographic and socio-economic profiles of Canadian Jews and Muslims?

166   Abdolmohammad Kazemipur

2 Are antisemitism and Islamophobia two different phenomena or aspects of the same phenomenon?
3 How do Muslims' and Jews' patterns of inter-group relations contribute to the amelioration or exacerbation of the problems they face as religious minorities?
4 How can history help us understand and address antisemitism and Islamophobia?
5 How can one help to create better relations between the Muslim and Jewish communities in Canada?

Demographic and Socio-economic Profiles

The roughly 2 million Muslims and 393,000 Jews in Canada have very different demographic and socio-economic profiles. The Canadian Muslim population is still largely an immigrant population; most of its members arrived after 1970 (Kazemipur 2014). In contrast, only about one third of Canadian Jews are immigrants. The level of educational attainment of the two groups also displays a fairly stable gap. In 2001, about 28 per cent of Muslims and 40 per cent of Jews held university degrees. A decade later, the figures had risen to 35 per cent and 47 per cent, respectively. A gap also exists with regards to income. Median income for the entire population of Canadian Muslims over the age of fourteen in 2001 was around $11,000 and for Jews around $29,000, rising in 2011 to $16,000 and $34,000, respectively (Statistics Canada 2003, 2013).[1] (The Canadian census includes the religion variable once every decade, and the 2021 data had not been released at the time of this writing.)

While both groups' educational attainments are higher than the average Canadian population and their educational and income gaps may narrow as Muslims become more settled in Canada, current differences in their educational and income profiles can lead to two other major differences between the Jewish and Muslim communities: their occupational profiles and their distribution in Canadian urban space. Compared to Muslims, Jews are more heavily concentrated in senior and middle management, professional, administrative, and senior clerical positions. Muslims are more concentrated in clerical, sales and service, skilled crafts, and semi-skilled manual jobs. This pattern was stable between 2001 and 2011. As for the distribution of the population of each group in urban neighbourhoods, Jews have a much higher level of ethnic concentration, mostly in higher-income neighbourhoods, while Muslims are more dispersed and reside mostly in lower-income neighbourhoods (Statistics Canada 2003, 2013).

Differences in the profiles of Canadian Muslims and Jews have significant implications for their experiences, as well as the ways in which they are perceived by others. For instance, they can lead to differences in the nature of antisemitic and Islamophobic opinions in circulation: while both groups are targets of hate-based attitudes and actions, Jews are generally considered part of the existing order, and Muslims a subversive force bent on disrupting it; one is seen as a threat from above, the other a threat from below. This is probably reflected in the fear expressed mainly in Europe of a Muslim demographic and cultural takeover, as opposed to the fear of Jewish dominance over media and financial institutions that is often associated with antisemitism.

Antisemitism and Islamophobia: The Same or Different?

The recent rise of anti-Muslim and anti-Jewish rhetoric and physical assaults against members of these communities in Canada and elsewhere raises questions about the relationship between Islamophobia and antisemitism. Are they manifestations of the same problem or distinct phenomena in need of distinct conceptualizations? Existing research is inconclusive, but some European and comparative studies offer useful hints.

On one side of these debates are those who consider Islamophobia and antisemitism recent manifestations of old forms of racism and anti-minority sentiment, akin to anti-communism, anti-Black racism, and anti-Mormonism in the US in the nineteenth and early twentieth centuries (Aschauer 2016). From this perspective, Islamophobia and antisemitism are fundamentally similar. Other scholars argue that racism explains antisemitic prejudice more than it explains anti-Muslim and anti-Islam sentiments (Unal 2016), although the much larger proportion of immigrants among Muslims than Jews in Canada may also suggest that, while antisemitism may be more strongly associated with racism, Islamophobia may be more heavily affected by anti-immigrant sentiments. Yet another position is that, "because anti-Semitism is taboo in Germany, and because anti-Semites cannot openly utter anti-Semitic statements anymore, Islamophobia may have become an outlet for hidden or latent anti-Semitism" (Hafez 2016, 20). Expressing Islamophobic views may also be less punitive compared to expressing antisemitic views because "some find it difficult to sympathize with a minority that is perceived to be disloyal or associated with terrorism, a view that leads to a perception of Muslims as a threat rather than as a disadvantaged minority" (Meer and Modood 2009, 335).

The above arguments point to the fact that the conceptualization of Islamophobia and antisemitism need to move away from simplified classifications and become more nuanced and better contextualized to reflect the complexity of this field of study. One example of this complexity is the strategic adoption by some far-right groups of Jewish-friendly or Muslim-friendly positions, playing them off each other for political gain. Hence the recent emergence of a type of "philosemitism" among European far-right groups that see Jews as "European, pro-Israel and anti-Muslim" and "as part of an imagined Judeo-Christian civilization"; these groups use Jewish people "as a shield against the accusations of racism," which allows "the election of many such parties to legislative bodies and the implementation of far-right policies under the guise of liberalism" (Rose 2020, i–ii). Similar to this type of "philosemitism," a type of "Islamophilia" has emerged. It creates an imagined category of "good Muslim" to oppose the "bad Muslim." When this happens, "'friendship' is subordinated to the demands of sameness – whether conceived in national or human terms … [and] can be just as coercive, just as prone to misrecognition, as the sentiments of hostility it is meant to correct" (Shryock 2010, 9).

Against this background, what is the nature of the antisemitism and Islamophobia that is emerging in Canada? Does it look more like the American version – in which both Muslims and Jews are seen as Others – or the European variant, with a combination of relatively mild antisemitism and strong Islamophobia? Available data cannot provide a convincing answer to this question. Recent Canadian surveys show that the level of self-reported experiences of discrimination is similar among Muslims and Jews – about one fifth of each group report discrimination related to their religion, another fifth due to their ethnicity or culture (Brym, Neuman, and Lenton 2019, 50). However, Canadian Muslims are about five times more numerous than Canadian Jews, implying that discriminatory actions are five times more frequent among them in absolute terms. Moreover, two of the most extreme acts of violence against Muslims living in any Western country took place in Canada: the 2017 murder of six Muslims in the Quebec City mosque shooting, and the 2021 murder of four members of a Muslim family in a deliberate hit and run incident in London, Ontario. Only the 2019 mosque massacre in Christchurch, New Zealand, which left fifty-one people dead, exceeds these incidents in the destruction of human life. No acts of extreme violence have been perpetrated against Canadian Jews. In addition, one must take into account that Canada's Muslim community has a lower economic status and more of its members are visibly distinct than is the case for Canada's Jews. Hence, its members are more likely to become targets for hate-motivated attacks. Finally, negative mass media content about Muslims flows steadily, reenergizing extremist elements, while such content about Jews is markedly less evident. Social media balances matters somewhat, but, taken together, the information just cited points to a higher likelihood of a European-style far right emerging in Canada.

Jewish–Muslim Relations

An unfortunate fact about antisemitism and Islamophobia is that Jewish and Muslim communities have themselves contributed to the problem. Widespread unease about each community on the part of the other is evident. The sources of discomfort include the Israel–Palestine conflict and anxiety over loss of status as the most victimized group. The former issue is of course much better known and more visible than the latter, but both are serious.

For a long time, some elements on both sides have framed the Israel–Palestine conflict as religious in nature. On the Muslim side, many religious leaders try to depict the conflict as a modern-day manifestation of animosity between Muslims and Jews that dates back to the time of the Prophet Muhammad and is captured in some anti-Jewish verses in the Quran. On the other side, some Jews justify the settlement of Jews and the formation of a Jewish state in Palestine as the fulfillment of a destiny promised by God. Some 42 per cent of Canadian Jews believe that "the land was given to the Jewish people by God" (Brym, Neuman, and Lenton 201, 61). The disagreement and deadlock over the fate of Jerusalem/Al-Quds is a symbolic exhibition of the efforts to religionize this political conflict; and the expansion of Jerusalem's symbolic role surely deepens the conflict's religious dimension (Shikaki 2021). This mode of conceptualization has turned a primarily political matter into a religious issue, which, by definition, makes it an issue for all co-religionists on both sides of the conflict. It is similar to what happened in the conflict between Sunni and Shia Muslims, which began as a political disagreement over the issue of the Prophet Muhammad's successor, but then turned into deeply held religious beliefs expressed in huge corpora of jurisprudential teachings – so much so that, even if people on both sides would be willing to let go of the political problem, they would remain unsure of what to do with the extensive collection of religious teachings on the subject.

Contrary to what many people outside the Muslim community think, the Israel–Palestine conflict does not occupy a central place in the minds of many Muslims. It may be central for Arab Muslims, who have been involved in the conflict for a century – or even longer, at least for Arab elites if not Arab masses (Mandel 1965) – but it is less salient for Canadian Muslims who have migrated to Canada from other parts of the Muslim world. For Muslims from the Indian subcontinent, for example, a much larger issue is the partition of India–Pakistan in 1947 and the status of Kashmir. For many Muslims from Afghanistan and Iran, the Israel–Palestine conflict, while heartbreaking, is either a secondary or non-issue. Canadian Muslim immigrants from the Far East or Africa also have other major concerns besides the Middle East conflict. In short, the centrality of the Israel–Palestine conflict in the Muslim psyche is a perception that does not match the reality of many Canadian Muslim lives.

To be sure, many members of the Muslim community (not to mention people outside the community) are critical of some of the policies of the State of Israel, particularly with regard to Jewish settlements in the West Bank, the use of disproportionate force and violence in the treatment of Palestinians, and the economic sanctions and siege imposed on Gaza. For those critics, what is unfathomable is the view of a large portion of the Jewish community who equate criticism of Israel with antisemitism; and this outlook has doubtless hindered the development of cordial Muslim–Jewish relations. What is particularly confusing for many Muslims (and non-Muslims) is that such critical views and positions vis-à-vis Israel's policies exist within Canada's Jewish community, putting many Canadian Jews "in a difficult position when these controversies become a topic of conversation or debate" (Brym, Neuman, and Lenton 2019, 52; chapter 11 in this volume). A critical view of Israel's West Bank policies is shared by most Israelis too (Gross 2020). No one can reasonably accuse them of being antisemites.

A much subtler issue is the question of who is the prime target of bigotry. Considerable anxiety seems to exist among some members of the Jewish community that a disaster like the Holocaust may recur if the focus on antisemitism is lost. Some observers have said so explicitly, remarking that it is dangerous to compare antisemitism and Islamophobia, and criticizing people for "downplaying anti-Semitism and exaggerating Islamophobia" (Cesarani 2011, 8). While it is easy to understand and empathize with the fear that genocidal actions may recur, I believe we need a different approach than trying to argue that nothing has changed for Jewish communities in the West since the Nazi era. Americans, for instance, give the highest favourability ratings to Jews over all other religious groups (Masci 2019), and as the Director of Communications and Public Affairs for Canada's Centre for Israel and Jewish Affairs (CIJA) noted, "public opinion studies consistently show that Jews enjoy higher favourability ratings than adherents of almost every other religion" (quoted in Lungen 2017). I will return to this topic later.

A serious communal divide exists between Jews and Muslims. There is little interaction between them. A large body of research shows that interaction between people of different backgrounds generally weakens their negative stereotypes and results in warmer inter-group relationships (Masci 2019; Gardner and Evans 2018). I have found this dynamic at work for Canadian Muslims (Kazemipur 2014). Similarly, Brym, Neuman, and Lenton (2019) report that the Canadian Jews most likely to say that Indigenous peoples, Muslims, and Black people experience discrimination are those with more non-Jewish friends.

The Jewish and Muslim communities in Canada are a prime example of low inter-group contact. In general, inter-group interactions occur in schools, workplaces, neighbourhoods, and friendship circles. The distinct occupational profiles of Canadian Muslims and Jews, noted earlier, militate against such interactions at work. Friendship circles on both sides also incline towards exclusion of non-group members. Thus, nearly 60 per cent of Jews in Toronto and Montreal, home to three quarters of Canada's Jews, have friendship networks composed mostly or completely of other Jews (Brym, Neuman, and Lenton 2019, 28).

The most consequential environment for interaction might be neighbourhoods, due to the voluntary nature of interactions in these settings and the fact that a shared neighbourhood gives all members of a family ample opportunity to interact with members of other groups and develop sociable and emotional ties to them. However, existing information suggests that Muslim–Jewish contact at the neighbourhood level is highly limited.

The index of dissimilarity is a measure of segregation. Its value ranges from 0 to 1, with 0 representing the lowest and 1 the highest levels of segregation between groups. Figure 12.1 reports the index of dissimilarity for eight Canadian religious groups, averaged for all census metropolitan areas (CMAs), in 2001 and 2011.

In figure 12.1 we find eight religious groups, each labelled on the x-axis. Each group is represented by seven pairs of bars. The grey bar in each pair represents 2001, the black bar, 2011. The seven pairs of bars for each religious group show the index of dissimilarity between the labelled religious group and the seven other religious groups.

Note first that, for all religious groups save the Sikhs, the 2011 bars are longer than the 2001 bars. This patterns signifies that, over the decade under consideration, opportunities for inter-group interaction at the neighbourhood level diminished for seven of the eight religious

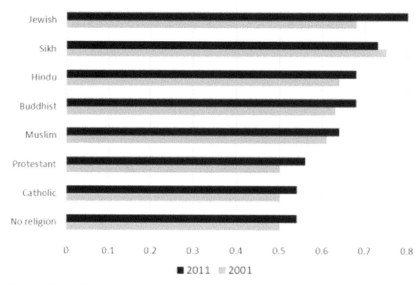

Figure 12.1. Mean residential dissimilarity index by religion, 2001 and 2011
Source: Statistics Canada (2003; 2013).

groups. Then note that the bars representing Jews are on average longer than the corresponding bars representing other religious groups. The implication of this pattern is that Jews have the highest level of neighbourhood segregation (see chapters 6 and 7 in this volume). Finally, observe in figure 12.2 that Muslims are more segregated from Jews than from any other religious group, and their level of segregation from Jews increased substantially between 2001 and 2011. The paucity and lessening of interaction between Muslims and Jews at the neighbourhood level means that personal and empathic contacts have little – and lessening – opportunity to counter negative stereotypes held by members of one group about the other.

History Lessons

In the history of the relationship between Jews and Muslims one can find three master narratives. The first narrative is promoted by extremist Islamists, particularly in the Arab world, who start by citing anti-Jewish verses from the Quran and end by recounting the Israel–Palestine conflict. The second narrative is espoused mostly by moderate Muslims. It focuses on the relatively warm reception Jews experienced in Muslim-controlled Andalusia (the Iberian Peninsula)

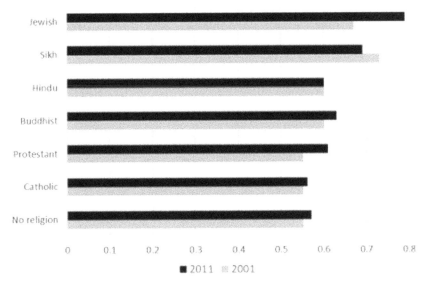

Figure 12.2. Residential dissimilarity index for Muslims vis-à-vis other religious groups, 2001 and 2011
Source: Statistics Canada (2003; 2013).

and later in Muslim North Africa after they were expelled in the *reconquista* (the wars through which Christians reconquered Andalusia from Muslim rule). The third narrative is favoured by some contemporary, liberal-minded intellectuals in the West, who refer to the simultaneous rise of Islamophobia and antisemitism in Western countries as a sign of shared fate and an echo of the similar experience of Muslims and Jews under Christian rule in Andalusia.

Today, Islamophobia in the West resembles the antisemitism of late nineteenth-century Europe around the time of France's Dreyfus affair. The discovery of hidden (and not-so-hidden) anti-Jewish sentiment in France, the centre of European intellectualism and the Enlightenment, made the Dreyfus affair particularly shocking for many. However, the identity politics created to serve the state building projects of late nineteenth-century Europe generated that wave of antisemitism – and simultaneously, Islamophobia. The two ideologies "have a connected history that is rooted in the formative period of European modernity," in which "the formation of homogeneous Christian nations within ... Europe ... was achieved through the 'exclusion' of Jews and Moors" (Hafez 2016, 21). Today, a similar dynamic is at work in response to the forces of globalization that have been undermining state sovereignty and national identity. The difference is that nineteenth-century nationalism was largely opposed to the sub-national forces of feudalism, while today we are witnessing a reaction against supra-national forces of a global nature.

Accordingly, just as the defence of Jews against late nineteenth-century European antisemitism was not just about the defence of Jews, the defence of Jews and Muslims against twenty-first-century antisemitism and Islamophobia is not just about the defence of Jews and Muslims either. Rather, it is an effort to influence the kind of identity that a nation adopts: a nativist identity revolving around the superiority of one group, versus an inclusivist identity centred on the values of justice, liberty, and solidarity. To choose the latter option, and to defend Muslims and Jews against the discriminatory forces ranged against them, does not require affection for Muslims and Jews. Support for the principles of justice, freedom, and solidarity is sufficient reason – and it is a responsibility for all people of good will, regardless of religion or non-religion.

Improving the Inter-group Relationship

If my diagnosis of the state of the Canadian Muslim–Jewish relationship is accurate, how can it be improved? This is an open question for the members of the two communities, as well as for those outside them. Solutions must come out of collective thinking, but I offer some initial thoughts to get the thinking started. In the following, I use two organizing concepts that I have borrowed from a Quranic verse: "Indeed Allah enjoins justice and kindness, and generosity towards relatives, and He forbids indecency, wrongdoing, and aggression" (Quran 16:90). The two keywords, "justice" and "kindness," have been interpreted by scholars of Islam as meaning, respectively, "giving everything and everyone what they rightfully deserve" and "being generous and giving them more than what they deserve." Trying to find equivalents of these two concepts in today's thought, I feel that they correspond, respectively, with language centred on rights and justice, and language centred on solidarity, empathy, and civility. Most current social justice–oriented scholarship revolves around the concept of right, but I think this by itself is inadequate, and needs to be supplemented by a focus on the concept of solidarity. An example of this two-pronged approach can be found in Simone Chambers' article, written in the aftermath of the Islamists' bloody attack on the office of the magazine *Charlie Hebdo* in France. Talking about the "Je suis Charlie" and "Je ne suis pas Charlie" slogans in the aftermath of the attack, Chambers (2015, 13) wrote:

"'Je suis Charlie' certainly defended the right to freedom of speech. 'Je ne suis pas Charlie' did not challenge this right but rather defended the value of civility. Free speech and civility do not have to be at odds. … Civility is the appropriate principle to defend if the goal is an integrated pluralism."

Informed by the principles of justice and empathy, I can think of five ideas that may help to improve the relationship between Canadian Jewish and Muslim communities. All require changes on both fronts.

First, drawing on the principle of fairness, Jews need to abandon the view that criticism of Israel means antisemitism. This view has been strategically adopted for political purposes, and hence has no roots in a fair assessment of the reality discussed earlier. On the flip side, Muslims must stop seeing the Israel–Palestine conflict as a religious one and as a continuation of the relationship between the Muslim and Jewish tribes of early Islam. This view also lacks a fair reading of history. In other words, fighting antisemitism and Islamophobia should allow a critique of Israeli policy, as well as a critique of the politics and culture of Muslim societies and communities.

Second, informed by the principle of empathy, Muslims should begin to acknowledge the historical injustices that have been inflicted on Jews in almost every society they have lived in as a minority (including many Muslim societies); moreover, against this background, Muslims should understand the symbolic and practical significance of having Israel as a sovereign state for the Jews, as a place from which they will not be expelled every time a new ruler comes to power. Jews should also begin to acknowledge the similar humiliation that Palestinians have endured in the lead-up to and following the creation of the State of Israel by Israel and many Arab countries and fellow Muslims. Jews should also be aware of the fact that many Muslims view the formation of Israel as part of a broader colonial project by the West – as reflected, for example, in the mandate and activities of the Jewish Colonisation Association, and implemented in ways resembling the methods by which Europeans took over many countries, including Canada. The fact that today, in Canada, the land treaties of European colonizers and Indigenous peoples are considered faulty raises at least the possibility that a similar thing could happen in the case of Palestinians.

Third, competition over who is the top victim of hatred – what Neiman (2019) calls an "Olympics of suffering" – is fruitless, if not harmful. Instead, one can adopt a different approach, suggested by Bulgarian-French philosopher Tzvetan Todorov's consideration of how the Holocaust should be viewed by Germans and Jews: "Germans should talk about the singularity of the Holocaust, Jews should talk about its universality" (quoted in Neiman 2019, 28). In other words, Germans should take responsibility for what happened in Germany and not trivialize that responsibility by arguing that similar things have happened and do happen elsewhere. Jews should recognize that it might happen again not just to Jews but to others as well; and if it happens to others, it does not end with them, because the impetus in much antisemitism is not to exclude just Jews but all Others, including Muslims. The fight against Islamophobia from this point of view is not a defence of Islam nor even of Muslims. Rather, it is opposition to the forces that create both Islamophobia and antisemitism.

Fourth, the principles of fairness and empathy will not grow deep roots unless awareness of them is accompanied by social interaction between members of the two communities. One significant outcome of such interaction is that it turns demographic categories into real humans. While the former is easily subjected to stereotypes and generalized judgements, the latter presents so much diversity and complexity that it brings about individualized assessments and humility in judgement. Muslims and Jews are probably the two groups that need such interactions the most and enjoy them the least.

Fifth, Muslims and Jews have much in common and much they can learn from one another. For example, Muslims' strong sense of social justice has been built into their faith from the very beginning of Islam. It can serve as a resource for finding allies in fighting against injustice. Jews have shown remarkable resilience during their history and have flourished in the face of omnipresent adversaries. This should serve as a source of inspiration for other minorities, including the Muslim community.

Conclusion

The recent rise of antisemitism and Islamophobia in Canada and elsewhere in the West motivates one to rethink the sources of such hatred. It should also prompt the Jewish and Muslim communities to reflect more deeply on their own experiences, particularly in relation to one another, and on how they can create a friendlier and more respectful relationship with one another. Such a need has been recognized for a long time by some moderate and progressive religious leaders. Interfaith initiatives have been introduced to remedy the situation. Here and elsewhere, I have talked about the ineffectiveness of such initiatives, the main problems with them being that, first, they engage only those who are already promoting better relationships, and second, they give religion a central place in the discussion (Kazemipur 2014). In this chapter, I have offered broad contours of a diagnosis and a solution, informed by sociological insight, in the hope that they will serve as the start of a larger conversation.

NOTE

1 Among the myriad factors responsible for the gap is the fact that the Muslim population is younger than the Jewish population, is composed of a larger proportion of immigrants, and faces a higher level of discrimination in employment (Evra and Kazemipur 2019; Kazemipur 2020).

REFERENCES

Aschauer, Wolfgang. 2016. "The Multidimensional Nature of Islamophobia: A Mixed Method Approach to Constructing the Attitudes toward Muslims Scale (ATMS)." *Islamophobia Studies Journal* 3 (2): 131–58.

Brym, Robert, Keith Neuman, and Rhonda Lenton. 2019. *2018 Survey of Jews in Canada: Final Report*. Toronto: Environics Institute for Survey Research. https://bit.ly/3mdvMvg.

Cesarani, David. 2011. "Are Muslims the New Jews? Comparing Islamophobia and Anti-Semitism in Britain and Europe." Yale Initiative for the Interdisciplinary Study of Antisemitism Discussion Paper. https://bit .ly/3ATr2T0.

Chambers, Simone. 2015. "Free Speech and Civility in Pluralist Societies." In *After the Paris Attacks: Responses in Canada, Europe, and around the Globe*, edited by Edward M. Iacobucci and Stephen J. Toope, 13–20. Toronto: University of Toronto Press.

Evra, Rose, and Abdolmohammad Kazempipur. 2019. *The Role of Social Capital and Ethnocultural Characteristics in the Employment Income of Immigrants over Time*. Ottawa: Statistics Canada. https://bit.ly/3CUwTVQ.

Gardner, Scott, and Jonathan Evans. 2018. "In Western Europe, Familiarity with Muslims Is Linked to Positive Views of Muslims and Islam." Pew Research Center. 24 July 2018. https://pewrsr.ch/3tAQoit.

Gross, Judah Ari. 2020. "Nearly Half of Jewish Israelis Oppose Unilateral West Bank Annexation – Poll." *Times of Israel*, 29 January 2020. https://bit .ly/3EemXHU.

Hafez, Farid. 2016. "Comparing Anti-Semitism and Islamophobia: The State of the Field." *Islamophobia Studies Journal* 3 (2): 16–34.

Kazemipur, Abdolmohammad. 2014. *The Muslim Question in Canada: A Story of Segmented Integration*. Vancouver: UBC Press.

Kazemipur, Abdolmohammad. 2020. "Islamophobia in Canada between Populism and Political Correctness." In *Racism, Islamophobia, Antisemitism, and the Future of Canadian Society: Proceedings of the Fifth S.D. Clark Symposium on the Future of Canadian Society*, edited by Robert Brym, 7–27. Oakville, ON: Rock's Mills Press.

Lungen, Paul. 2016. "One in Five Canadians See Judaism Benefiting Canada: Study." *Canadian Jewish News*, 12 September 2016. https://bit.ly/3z6Nd3a.

Mandel, Neville J. 1965. "Turks, Arabs and Jewish Immigration into Palestine, 1882–1914." PhD diss., University of Oxford.

Masci, David. 2019. "In U.S., Familiarity with Religious Groups Is Associated with Warmer Feelings toward Them." Pew Research Center. 31 October 2019. https://pewrsr.ch/3k0Zjqj.

Meer, Nasar, and Tariq Modood. 2009. "Refutations of Racism in the 'Muslim Question.'" *Patterns of Prejudice* 43 (3–4): 335–54. https://doi.org/10.1080/00313220903109250.

Neiman, Susan. 2019. *Learning from the Germans: Race and the Memory of Evil*. New York: Farrar, Straus and Giroux.

Rose, Hannah. 2020. *The New Philosemitism: Exploring a Changing Relationship between Jews and the Far-Right*. London: International Centre for the Study of Radicalisation, King's College London. https://bit.ly/3CQmudz.

Shikaki, Khalil. 2021. "Fighting in Gaza Marks the Start of a More Violent Era: The Search for a Two-State Solution Is Over." *Foreign Affairs*, 19 May 2021. https://fam.ag/3Ej6qTt.

Shryock, Andrew. 2010. "Introduction: Islam as an Object of Fear and Affection." In *Islampohobia/Islamophilia: Beyond the Politics of Enemy and Friend*, edited by Andrew Shryock, 1–25. Bloomington: Indiana University Press.

Statistics Canada. 2003. Nesstar Data Portal, Statistics Canada Data Liberation Initiative.

Statistics Canada. 2013. Nesstar Data Portal, Statistics Canada Data Liberation Initiative.

Unal, Fatih. 2016. "Islamophobia and Anti-Semitism: Comparing the Social Psychological Underpinnings of Anti-Semitic and Anti-Muslim Beliefs in Contemporary Germany." *Islamophobia Studies Journal* 3 (2): 35–55.

13 Jews and the Christian Goliath

REGINALD W. BIBBY

Christian Canada

Until about 1950, religion was exceedingly important to most Canadians. To know one's religious affiliation was to have an important clue about one's moral and political leanings, school system preferences, and even one's favourite newspaper (Grant 1988).

Among Christians, conformity to French-rooted Catholicism and British-rooted Protestantism was pervasive. Compliance with Christian expectations regarding practices, beliefs, and lifestyle was high. Surveys show that, in 1945, some 60 per cent of Canadians were attending religious services on close to a weekly basis. In Quebec, where Catholicism had an especially strong grip on the population, the attendance figure was closer to 80 per cent through the early 1960s. Core beliefs about God, the divinity of Jesus, and life after death were all extremely high as Canada entered the second half of the twentieth century (Bibby 2002).

Beyond identification, practices, and belief, social life in much of Canada was also influenced by religion. Religious groups played an influential role in business, labour, education, health, social services, leisure, and the media. In Quebec, public education, for example, was offered to students through two systems, one Catholic, the other Protestant. Jews, by default, were slotted in the latter. That situation fostered the growth of a private Jewish school system and other Jewish community institutions that promoted the retention of Jewish ethnic identity (Brym, Slavina, and Lenton 2020, 371).

In other parts of the country, religion also had a significant presence. Many politicians, including Premiers William Aberhart and Ernest Manning in Alberta, Tommy Douglas in Saskatchewan, and, federally, Prime Minister John Diefenbaker, were openly Christian and devout. Universities, including Acadia, Mount Allison, St. Francis Xavier,

180 Reginald W. Bibby

Ryerson, McMaster, Wilfrid Laurier, Winnipeg, Brandon, Regina, and Victoria were founded and run by religious groups, as were Laval and Montreal in Quebec. Social services, hospitals, youth activities, and an array of charitable organizations likewise had religious roots and support. Laws and regulations at federal, provincial, and local levels dealing with a wide range of moral and lifestyle issues and reflecting everything from sexuality and abortion through appropriate holidays and Sunday activities frequently reflected Christian values.

A high level of religious participation continued through the 1950s and 1960s. Weekly attendance of religious services among Catholics held steady at about 85 per cent, and remained strong for Protestants at around 45 per cent. The membership of the United and Anglican churches peaked at over 1 million each in 1965 (Grant 1988, 161). This was a time when Cardinal Léger would say of Montreal, "When I bow to say the evening rosary, all of Montreal bows with me" (quoted in Poulin and Dufresne 1973). The cardinal overlooked the fact that Jews were not among them.

Life in the Land of the Christian Goliath

That's not to say that a rich religious mosaic was emerging in Canada. On the contrary, respectful coexistence with other groups was hardly the Christian mindset. The numerical dominance of Protestants and Catholics meant that Jews, along with other small religious groups, were relegated to the sacred sidelines. Life was not easy for outsiders in a "Christian country."

Christianity was widely viewed as the one true religion with a mandate to evangelize pretty much anyone who was not a Christian. By the time of Confederation in 1867, Christian missionary work – particularly on the part of Catholics, Anglicans, and Methodists – saw large numbers of Indigenous people become at least nominally Christian (Grant 1988, 8). The national expectation of Christian compliance was evident in the establishment of residential schools (1847–1996), which had an explicit purpose: "to indoctrinate children into a new culture – the culture of the legally dominant Euro-Christian Canadian society" (Truth and Reconciliation Commission 2015, v).

Other non-Christians were regarded as "religious outsiders" and therefore targets of proselytism. Those with "no religion," to the extent they could be identified, were also viewed as "lost" and in need of salvation, Christian-style. Thus, in the early part of the twentieth century, Anglicans maintained active Jewish missions in Montreal and Toronto, staffing them with ordained converts. Presbyterians likewise had a special interest in Jewish missions, who felt Christians had a solemn duty to reach "the lost children of Israel" (Davies and Nefsky 1997, 635, 673).

Still, there were some positive developments. In the 1920s, Rabbi Ferdinand Isserman of Holy Blossom Temple and Reverend Ernest Hunter of the Carlton Street United Church in Toronto made history as a rabbi and minister exchanging pulpits at a time when it was rare for even Protestant and Catholic clergy to interact professionally (Eliefja 1987, 1). A range of prominent Protestant and Catholic leaders joined government officials in a public service in 1936 celebrating the eightieth anniversary of the Holy Blossom congregation. An article in *The Canadian Baptist* trumpeted that such a service could not have taken place in Europe (Davies and Nefsky 1997, 706).

In addition to the proselytizing inclinations of Christians, an extremely important additional issue for Christian–Jewish relations was the rampant and overt antisemitism in Europe. Anti-Jewish sentiment in Europe set the stage for early Christian–Jewish relations in Canada, arriving with the first European settlers, especially those from Britain and France (Davies and Nefsky 1997, 274; Robinson 2015, 25). In the first half of the twentieth century, while Canada's Jewish population increased from approximately 15,000 to 200,000, about 4 million other, mostly Christian, immigrants arrived from Europe, often bringing with them hostile attitudes and behaviours towards Jews. In the period spanning the two World Wars, anti-Jewish sentiment peaked, inflamed as it was by Nazi propaganda (Betcherman 1975, 100, 132). Irving Abella (1990, v–vi) described Canada during this period as "a benighted, xenophobic, anti-Semitic country" where "Jews were excluded from almost every sector of Canadian society and some were even excluded from the country itself by a government and a people who felt there were already too many Jews here." At best, Jews were viewed as culturally and religiously different outsiders in need of conversion. At worst, they were treated with blatant hostility, disdain, and discrimination by Christian groups and individuals, including Catholic and Protestant politicians.

The desire on the part of Catholics and Protestants to retain their monopoly was sometimes draconian, particularly when supplemented with antisemitism. Some quick examples:

- As recently as the 1930s and 1940s in Quebec, no mass medium would broadcast opinions contrary to those of the Roman Catholic Church, whose favourite scapegoats for all societal ills were communists and Jews (Bibby 1987, 18).
- Parish priests often made use of fascist hate propaganda to update prejudices against Jews, with one 1937 parish newspaper noting that "all countries are unanimous in recognizing that we have no greater enemy than the Jews. They are the source of all great cataclysms. They are promoters of discord" (quoted in Bibby 1987, 123).

182   Reginald W. Bibby

- In the minds of some Christians, the age-old idea of Jews as "Christ-killers" persisted and took extremely cruel forms. Poet Irving Layton recalled growing up Jewish in Montreal in the 1920s this way: "The strongest memory I have is of clashes. Around Easter ... something seemed to happen to the gentiles. They took it as a cue to come and beat up on the Jews. So, without fail, every Easter, they would descend on the embattled Jews with bottles and bricks, and we'd be waiting for them on the roofs, like an army, with sticks, and stones, with anything" (quoted in Robinson 2015, 59).
- In June 1939, the government of William Lyon Mackenzie King decided to turn away the MS *St. Louis* carrying 900 Jewish refugees who had boarded weeks earlier in Hamburg, Germany. Forced to return to Europe, 254 ended up dying in the Holocaust. True, the Anglican and United Churches campaigned on behalf of Jewish refugees. However, "most Canadians were indifferent to the suffering of German Jews and hostile to their admission to Canada" (Abella and Troper 1982, 51). It took the Holocaust and anti-Christian Nazis to stir the conscience of some Christian theologians to reflect on their past and condemn antisemitism (Baum 1975, 314).

Following the Second World War, relations between Christians and Jews improved significantly. In 1947, the Canadian Council for Christians and Jews (now the Canadian Centre for Diversity) was established, accompanied by a large number of municipal, dialogue-oriented associations of Christians and Jews and, increasingly, other faith groups as well. It was a signal of things to come.

Two Transformative Developments

Two largely unanticipated developments – perhaps correlated, perhaps not – took place in Canada from the 1960s onward that transformed relations between Christians and Jews and, for that matter, relations among everyone else too. First, participation in Christian religious groups dropped off dramatically. Second, Canada embarked on a highly conscious and ambitious effort to become a far more just, equitable, and compassionate society.

Decline in Religious Participation

On the religious front, national weekly service attendance that had been around 60 per cent in 1945 dipped to about 30 per cent in 1975, and 20 per cent in 2000. It stands at around 15 per cent today. In 1971, 4 per cent of Canadians indicated they had "no religion." According to Statistics Canada (2022), in 2021 that figure had risen to nearly 35 per cent. Recent analyses of Canadians generally and Catholics specifically have found a strong tendency for individuals to continue to identify with religions, but to have very much of an à la carte posture towards their groups' beliefs, practices, and teachings. Deference has given way to defiance and discernment. Religious groups and their leaders have lost much of their authority.

In the early decades of the twenty-first century, Christianity no longer occupies centre stage in Canada. Protestantism is not a pivotal feature of Anglo culture, while Catholicism is no longer at the heart of Québécois culture. Religious diversity reigns: other, relatively small groups – Muslims, Hindus, Sikhs, Buddhists, and Jews – have gained admission to the religious mosaic along with its attendant rights and privileges.

Equal recognition aside, it seems apparent that religion's importance for adherents of all religious groups has declined as individuals have increasingly shared in dominant cultural values, including individualism, diversity, and choice. As of the mid-1970s, regular synagogue attendance in Toronto, for example, was over 50 per cent among Orthodox Jews, but had fallen to below 25 per cent for those who were Conservative or Reform (Kallen 1977, 80). Today, weekly synagogue attendance is about 15 per cent (Brym, Neuman, and Lenton 2019, 25). One of the challenges facing minority religious groups that have grown primarily through immigration is how to retain the interest and involvement of second- and third-generation Canadians. The problem is hardly new. We tend to forget that the people who founded Canada's Christian groups were immigrants who were not very successful in retaining the adherence of subsequent generations.

Religion obviously continues to have a presence in Canada, but today's religious culture is a far cry from the Christian Canada of yesteryear. Reflecting an increasingly diverse Canada, and in many ways shaped by that diversity, religion is expected to be both non-partisan and respectful of pluralism, and has been relegated to the sidelines of Canadian life. Most of the primary public life narratives about health, the economy, racism, and quality of life seldom include the voices of religious groups. Religion has been edited out of most public ceremonies and even private rituals, including marriages and funerals. The 1982 proclamation of the Canadian Charter of Rights and Freedoms that "Canada is founded upon principles that recognize the supremacy of God" sounds anachronistic.

184   Reginald W. Bibby

Rise of the Just Society

With the 1960s came major initiatives in Canada, promoted by Prime Minister Pierre Trudeau and his Liberal government, aimed at creating a more just society (Bibby 1990). They included Royal Commissions on Bilingualism and Biculturalism (1965) and the Status of Women (1970), the adoption of multiculturalism as state policy (1971), and the enactment of the Canadian Charter of Rights and Freedom (1982).

Diversity and pluralism have now been enshrined in Canada. If the 1960s was "the decade in which barriers to Jewish participation in the larger Canadian social, political, and economic mainstream slipped away" (Troper 2010, 4), diversity, pluralism, and choice have now become the axiomatic themes that define Canadian life. A recent survey concludes that Canadian Millennials "recoil at the idea of intolerance. Any negative, let alone vicious targeting of people, particularly those who are disadvantaged in any way ... is deplored and met with aggressive and sometimes angry calls for corrective responses" (Bibby, Thiessen, and Bailey 2019, 230).

Organizational Change

At the level of religious group leadership, dialogue, respect, and acceptance have replaced hostility and efforts at Christian evangelism. Missions and initiatives such as "Jews for Jesus" persist but, in the minds of most Christian groups, are largely things of the past (Davies and Nefsky 1997, 22).

Protestant denominations have increasingly expanded their comfort zones to include, first, other denominations, and then other faiths, so that interdenominational and interfaith organizations have become commonplace. In 1977, the Canadian Christian–Jewish Consultation was created to provide the opportunity for representatives of the Canadian Jewish Congress, the Canadian Conference of Catholic Bishops, and the United, Anglican, and Lutheran churches to meet and enter into dialogue on a number of issues of mutual interest (Canadian Council of Churches n.d.). That was just the beginning.

The Second Vatican Council (1962–5) finally absolved Jews from collective responsibility for the killing of Christ and further acknowledged Christian crimes against the Jewish people. These formal declarations have contributed to an emphasis on interfaith activities on the part of Catholics as well as Protestants (Grant 1988, 195). Today, the official position of the Roman Catholic Church towards Jews is best summed up in the public statement of its foremost national organization, the national Canadian Conference of Catholic Bishops (CCCB n.d.): "The Jewish people are seen by Catholics as 'our elder brothers and sisters' and 'our forbearers in faith.' Christianity's own sacred identity is rooted in the Jewish faith. The Church strives towards deeper reconciliation and friendship with the Jewish People." The CCCB has created a commission that meets regularly with the Canadian Rabbinic Caucus.

Similar initiatives exist for almost all of Canada's major United, Anglican, Presbyterian, and Lutheran denominations. The once-insular Evangelical Fellowship of Canada, an umbrella organization for a range of evangelical groups, signed a declaration of dialogue and partnership with the Centre for Israel and Jewish Affairs (Evangelical Fellowship of Canada 2016).

Some personal, qualitative data: Since the mid-1980s, I have presented research findings on religion in Canada in well over 400 Protestant and Catholic settings that typically have included a large number of one-on-one conversations with leaders and laity. Indicative of what has become normative, I have never encountered a trace of antisemitism. This is not to say such sentiments did not and do not exist; it is to say that, officially, their expression has become unacceptable in Christian settings.

I now turn to a more systematic presentation of survey data on Jews and Christians.

Individual Change

Since 1975, colleagues and I have been conducting a series of surveys on religion in Canada. In the first survey, we found that 24 per cent of Canadians agreed with the statement, "Jews are more likely than Christians to cheat in business." Outside Quebec, the figure was 18 per cent, in Quebec, 42 per cent – increasing to 51 per cent among Quebec Catholics. But the national outlook on such stereotyping has changed, so much so that by 2000, we felt Canadian norms had shifted to the point that asking the question was inappropriate.

The idea that Jews have "too much power in our nation's affairs" declined markedly among both Protestants and Catholics and particularly among Catholics in Quebec. Disapproval of marriages between Jews and Protestants or Catholics also dropped significantly among both Protestant and Catholics, including Catholics in Quebec (see table 13.1).

Yet despite progress in individual attitudes and official norms enshrining equality and pluralism, the realization of such standards remains a work in progress. A 2019 national reading of attitudes towards

186 Reginald W. Bibby

Table 13.1. Attitudes of Canadian Protestants and Catholics towards Jews, 1975 and 2000, in per cent

| | Protestants | | Catholics | | | |
| | | | Quebec | | Rest of Canada | |
	1975	2000	1975	2000	1975	2000
Have too much power in our nation's affairs						
Roman Catholics	32	14	8	2	9	5
Jews	21	11	52	17	23	11
Immigrants	19	30	20	24	17	29
Protestants	4	3	11	7	7	7
Disapprove of marriage between ...						
Roman Catholics and Jews	27	10	24	11	16	10
Protestants and Jews	25	9	28	11	11	8
Protestants and Roman Catholics	17	7	18	9	9	6

Source: Bibby (1975–2000).

Table 13.2. Negative attitudes towards select Canadian religious groups, 2019, in per cent

	Canada	Quebec only
Muslims	39	44
Evangelical Christians	24	18
Sikhs	21	26
Atheists	16	8
Roman Catholics	15	9
Hindus	12	10
Jews	7	15
Buddhists	7	8
Protestants	6	10

Source: Angus Reid Institute (2019).

various religious groups found that 7 per cent of Canadians expressed negative feelings about Jews, with the level rising to 15 per cent in what remains a predominantly Roman Catholic Quebec (Angus Reid Institute 2019). Negative views of Muslims, Evangelical Christians, and Sikhs were also far from uncommon (see table 13.2).

Ira Robinson (2015, 190) maintains that much has changed since the 1950s, but that "it seems that the status of Jews as 'others' to most French Canadians has not." The key difference, he says, "is that in the early twentieth century the Jewish community was the sole significant non-Christian, non-Aboriginal group in Quebec. It has now been joined by Muslims, Hindus, Sikhs, and a host of others." Our 1975 and 2000 comparisons, along with the Angus Reid Institute's recent attitudinal data, suggest that Robinson's assessment is excessively negative. The attitudes of Quebecers towards Jews have become far more positive and strikingly less negative than their views of Muslims and Sikhs, and more positive than their attitudes towards Evangelical Protestants.

Nonetheless, the 2018 Survey of Jews in Canada found that many Jews maintain that they continue to experience discrimination and stigma (Brym, Neuman, and Lenton 2019). Close to four in ten respondents reported that they experienced discrimination in the past five years, a figure that is comparable to the experience of Muslims and well above that of the population at large. Jews between the ages of eighteen and twenty-nine were the most likely to report such incidents.

Two national surveys probing inter-group relations that I carried out with the Maru Group in November 2020 and March 2021 provide corroborating evidence, although it is only suggestive, given the small number of Jews in the sample ($n = 51$). Asked if they face barriers to full participation in Canadian life, 27 per cent of the 3,030 survey participants said they do. The key barriers cited were age, race, and gender. Of the Jews in the sample, 20 per cent indicated that they face barriers due to discrimination. In the Jewish case, however, the religious barrier was perceived as the most salient, albeit by a small margin. Similar to the 2018 Survey of Jews in Canada, adults under thirty years of age were more likely than others to indicate they experience barriers due to discrimination (Bibby and Maru Group 2021).

In short, available data suggest that Canada still has a distance to go before it achieves the level of tolerance towards which most of its citizens aspire. Canadian-Jewish historians agree. Ira Robinson (2015, 175) holds that "at the beginning of the twenty-first century, life has never been better for Canada's Jews." And Irving Abella (2013, 16) remarks that "today's Canada is far different [than in the past] – generous, open, decent, humane."

It is important to remember the role that numbers might play. Sheva Medjuck (1993, 364) offered this provocative observation some three decades ago: "Jews in small communities tend to be fairly well-accepted and integrated into the large society. Indeed, because they are more likely to interact with their non-Jewish neighbours, they are often more integrated into the communities in which they live than are their co-religionists in larger communities." Maybe, maybe not. Some Jewish colleagues who have lived in smaller cities disagree. But, for the record, Medjuck's impression is consistent with my impressions growing up with Jewish school friends in Edmonton in the 1950s and 1960s and interacting with Jewish friends, colleagues, and associates in the

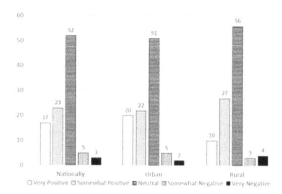

Figure 13.1. Negative attitudes towards Jews by residence, in per cent
Source: Angus Reid Institute (2019).

small city of Lethbridge, Alberta, from the 1970s through to the present day. Jewish lawyers, doctors, and academics have lived life fairly seamlessly in this city that only recently reached a population of 100,000 and has been too small to have a synagogue. The asterisk: over the years, I have observed overt antisemitic attitudes expressed by some European immigrants.

Beyond impressions, the 2019 Angus Reid Institute national survey probing attitudes towards groups found little difference between urban and rural residents in their attitudes towards Jews (see figure 13.1). Perhaps reflecting actual contact with Jews, urban Canadians were slightly more likely to express "very positive" attitudes, while those in rural areas were somewhat more inclined to be "somewhat positive" or hold "neutral" views. The size of Jewish populations over time, nationally and in specific places, large and small, remains a potentially important variable that needs to be better understood.

Religious Polarization in Canada

Despite the pronounced post-1960s decline in religious participation, Canadians across the board have not abandoned religion. Nor, for that matter, will they necessarily continue to abandon religion. On the contrary, considerable empirical evidence supports the thesis that Canadians (like people in other countries) are increasingly polarized when it comes to religion. They variously embrace faith, reject it, or take a position somewhere between the two extremes. I have suggested that their inclinations might be labelled "pro-religious," "no religious," and "low religious" (Bibby 2017).

In a national poll I conducted with the Maru Group in December 2020 (n = 3,029), 25 per cent of Canadians said they are inclined to embrace religion, 31 per cent to reject it, and the remaining 44 per cent indicated they are somewhere in between. The corresponding figures for the Jews in the sample (n = 43) – again, the results are only suggestive because of the small number of Jewish respondents – were 33 per cent embracing, 21 per cent rejecting, and 46 per cent in between (Bibby and Maru Group 2020).

That reality is reflected in attendance: only 13 per cent of Canadians attend services every week, and 19 per cent at least once a month. But among those who embrace religion, the weekly figure is 39 per cent, and the monthly-plus number is 54 per cent. Of particular importance, for all the publicity given to the growth in the "no religion" category, the fact of the matter is that more than 65 per cent of Canadians continue to identify with a religion of some kind (Statistics Canada 2022).

Religious Polarization among Canadian Jews

Over time, Jews who have come to Canada and elsewhere have tended to gravitate towards Orthodox, Conservative, and Reform orientations that seemingly have reflected their adjustment to host cultures rather than their particular European origins or theological inclinations (Mol 1985, 82). Almost five decades ago, sociologist Evelyn Kallen (1977, 52) wrote that "from Orthodox to Conservative to Reform, the emphasis on acculturation increases and the emphasis on distinctive ethnic socialization decreases."

Kallen (1976, 286–7) predicted a trend towards Conservatism: "For the majority of contemporary North American Jews, traditional Orthodox codes and patterns are too far removed ... to provide a positive focus for ethnic identification. Reform, on the other hand, is too ambivalent to provide a positive for most Jews." She concluded that "Conservativism, the middle-of-the-road, has the widest appeal in that it combines tradition and change."

Brym, Neuman, and Lenton (2019, 23) have documented such religious polarization. They note that most Canadian Jews identify as Conservative (25 per cent), Orthodox or Modern Orthodox (17 per cent), and Reform (17 per cent). About 10 per cent say they are part of smaller Jewish movements (e.g., Reconstructionism, Humanistic, Renewal, Hasidism), while the remainder (about 30 per cent) are not affiliated with any particular denomination or movement.

In a seminal article, American sociologist Stephen Steinberg (1965) addressed the complexity of Jewish identity. He suggested that it has several dimensions. The first is the tribal dimension or consciousness of kind tied to a common past, traditions, and values. Second is the religious dimension, which includes components such as beliefs, practices, experiences, knowledge, and behaviour. A third component is the communal dimension, particularly important, according to Steinberg, in the face of secularization, where the synagogue has responded by expanding its activities and offering an array of educational, recreational, and cultural opportunities for children, youth, and adults. Fourth, the secular dimension involves Jews rejecting most of religious and organized communal life but continuing to identify with Judaism and associating with other Jews and giving expression to elements of traditional culture such as Yiddish words, Jewish food, and Jewish humour. Fifth is the intellectual dimension, which involves maintaining interest in and knowledge about Jewish affairs.

These dimensions are all evident among Canada's Jews. About three in ten say that religion is very important to them. Synagogue attendance is consistent with that figure, with 29 per cent attending services at least once a month, 56 per cent yearly, and 15 per cent never (slightly higher than the respective 25 per cent, 43 per cent, and 32 per cent figures for Christians). Salience and attendance are highest among the Conservative and Orthodox (Brym, Neuman, and Lenton 2019, 15–16). That said, a wide range of religious beliefs and rituals persist (Brodbar-Nemzer et al. 1993). A much higher proportion of Canada's Jews than Christians, some seven in ten, say their religion is important to them. Here, Orthodox and Conservative Jews are joined by many who affiliate with Reform or with no denomination or movement and emphasize culture and ancestry rather than religion. Only 8 per cent of Jews say that being Jewish is either "not very important" (6 per cent) or "not important at all" (2 per cent) (see figure 13.2). The 2018 Survey of Jews in Canada found that "one of the most important expressions of Jewish identity involves families getting together over a meal to mark a Jewish holiday...with the religious significance less important than it was in the past" (Brym, Neuman, and Lenton 2019, 5). In addition, about one-half say all or most of their friends are Jewish. Overall, essential aspects of being Jewish include leading a moral life, remembering the Holocaust, and celebrating Jewish holidays (Brym, Neuman, and Lenton 2019, 6, 28; cf. Shaffir 1993, 123).

Morton Weinfeld astutely notes that, in general, an inverse relationship exists between an ethnic group's socio-economic achievements and its maintenance of ethnic culture. Yet "Jews, more than any other group, have somehow been able to fashion a workable synthesis from these two contradictory objectives," enjoying socio-economic success while "boasting high levels of communal organization and identification" (Weinfeld 1993, 168). Brym (2022, 8) corroborates Weinfeld's assertion. In his extensive analysis of Statistics Canada data, he has found that "Canadian Jews are well integrated economically and socially, yet are able to maintain relatively strong ties with other Canadian Jews."

Ongoing Identification and Resilience

So it is that, in 2021 in Canada as a whole, Christians continue to hold a numerical monopoly (about 53 per cent of the population), with other religions accounting for about 12 per cent, and the remaining 35 per cent or so of people indicating they have no religion (Statistics Canada 2022). Identification remains relatively high, whereas participation in religious group life varies significantly.

What has intrigued many observers of religious life in Canada is the inclination of most people to continue to identify with religious traditions, even when they are not actively involved in religious groups. For Canadians overall, religious identification currently stands at about 75 per cent, the valuing of one's religious group at close to 50 per cent, and monthly-plus service attendance at around 20 per cent. In the case of Jews, the proportion who say religion is very important in their lives is similar to that of Christians. But polarization is also evident, with Conservative and Orthodox Jews differing significantly from Reform and unaffiliated Jews, just as Protestant evangelicals differ significantly from mainline Protestants.

However, beyond religious polarization, Canadians Jews reflect the range of dimensions of identification noted by Steinberg in being far more inclined than Christians to place a high level of importance on identity: 65 per cent vs. 23 per cent (see figure 13.2). The importance of being Jewish in Canada and elsewhere is tied to culture and family history and the importance placed on interpersonal relations. But those factors by themselves do not account for the large differences between Jews and Christians. After all, Christians have innumerable multinational and national organizations, and considerable history, culture, and collective experience that work to instill and sustain religious identification.

Bernard Vigod (1984, 16–17) may have isolated two major elements, beyond religion per se, that sustain and intensify Jewish identity: "One is the Holocaust, which speaks to all Jews," he writes. "The second element is the state of Israel, for whose security and well-being most Canadian Jews accept great responsibility." Both are central features of what Steinberg refers to as "the tribal dimension" of Jewish identification, complete with subjective feelings, which, he says, take on a life of their own.

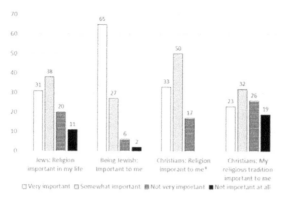

Figure 13.2. Importance of religion/identity, Canada, Jews 2018 and Christians 2019, in per cent
* "Embracing religion, in-between, rejecting religion"
Sources: Brym, Neuman, and Lenton (2019); Bibby (2020).

I conclude that, in the foreseeable future, it is likely that most Jews and Christians will continue to value identity over active religious participation, supplementing identity with a wide range of fragments of beliefs and practices. But most will not be saying goodbye to their identification groups. In addition to the cohesive and adhesive impact of social, cultural, and emotional sources, there simply is negligible value in doing so.

REFERENCES

Abella, Iriving. 1990. *A Coat of Many Colours: Two Centuries of Jewish Life in Canada*. Toronto: Lester & Orpen Dennys.
Abella, Irving. 2013. "Never Again May Be None Too Many." *Globe and Mail*, 26 February 2013, A15.
Abella, Irving, and Harold Troper. 1982. *None Is Too Many: Canada and the Jews of Europe, 1933–1948*. Toronto: Lester & Orpen Dennys.
Angus Reid Institute. 2019. "Crisis of Faith? Even Practicing Catholics Say Church Has Done a Poor Job Handling Sexual Abuse Issue." 28 May 2019. https://angusreid.org/catholic-church-canada/.
Baum, Gregory. 1975. "Salvation Is from the Jews." In *Disputation and Dialogue: Readings in the Jewish-Christian Encounter*, edited by F.E. Talmage, 313–19. New York: KTAV Publishing House.
Betcherman, Lita-Rose. 1975. *The Swastika and the Maple Leaf: Fascist Movements in Canada in the Thirties*. Toronto: Fitzhenry and Whiteside.

Bibby, Reginald W. 1975–2000. Project Canada Survey (PCS) Series. Information available from the author.

Bibby, Reginald W. 1987. *Fragmented Gods: The Poverty and Potential of Religion in Canada*. Toronto: Irwin.

Bibby, Reginald W. 1990. *Mosaic Madness: Pluralism without a Cause*. Toronto: Stoddart

Bibby, Reginald W. 2002. *Restless Gods: The Renaissance of Religion in Canada*. Toronto: Stoddart.

Bibby, Reginald W. 2017. *Resilient Gods: Being Pro-Religious, Low Religious, or No Religious in Canada*. Vancouver: UBC Press.

Bibby, Reginald W., and Maru Group. 2020. "Omnibus Polls on Religion and Barriers to Participation in Canadian Life." Information available from the author.

Bibby, Reginald W., and Maru Group. 2021. "Omnibus Polls on Religion and Barriers to Participation in Canadian Life." Information available from the author.

Bibby, Reginald W., Joel Thiessen, and Monetta Bailey. 2019. *The Millennial Mosaic: How Pluralism and Choice Are Shaping Canadian Youth and the Future of Canada*. Toronto: Dundurn.

Brodbar-Nemzer, Jay, Steven M. Cohen, Allan Reitzes, Charles Shahar, and Gary A. Tobin. 1993. "An Overview of the Canadian Jewish Community." In *The Jews in Canada*, edited by Robert Brym, William Shaffir, and Morton Weinfeld, 39–72. Toronto: Oxford University Press.

Brym, Robert. 2022. "The Occupational and Social Integration of Jews in Canada." In *American Jewish Year Book 2021*, Vol. 121, edited by Arnold Dashefsky and Ira M. Sheskin, 299–312. Cham, Switzerland: Springer.

Brym, Robert, Keith Neuman, and Rhonda Lenton. 2019. *2018 Survey of Jews in Canada: Final Report*. Toronto: Environics Institute for Survey Research. https://bit.ly/3ooSj9F.

Brym, Robert, Anna Slavina, and Rhonda Lenton. 2020. "Qualifying the Leading Theory of Diaspora Jewry: An Examination of Jews from the Former Soviet Union in Canada and the United States." *Contemporary Jewry* 40 (3) 367–85. https://doi.org/10.1007/s12397-020-09315-5.

Canadian Conference of Catholic Bishops (CCCB). n.d. "Religious Relationship with the Jewish People." Accessed 4 July 2022, http://bitly.ws/t4mG.

Canadian Council of Churches. n.d. "Christian Jewish Dialogue." Accessed 4 July 2022, http://bitly.ws/t4mI.

Davies, Alan, and Marilyn Nefsky. 1997. *How Silent Were the Churches? Canadian Protestantism and the Jewish Plight during the Nazi Era*. Waterloo, ON: Wilfrid Laurier Press.

Eliefja, Chaya. 1987. "Jewish-Christian Relations in Canada: The United Church Observer Controversy." MA thesis, Carleton University. https://curve.carleton.ca/dc21778a-e96c-4cb2-a74e-e7966a75a50d.

Evangelical Fellowship of Canada. 2016. "The EFC and CIJA Launch Dialogue." Press release, 13 December 2016. https://bit.ly/3kKEY92.

Grant, John Webster. 1988. *The Church in the Canadian Era*. Updated ed. Burlington, ON: Welch Publishing.

Kallen, Evelyn. 1976. "Synagogue in Transition: Religious Revival or Ethnic Survival?" In *Religion in Canadian Society*, edited by Stewart Crysdale and Les Wheatcroft, 278–88. Toronto: Macmillan.

Kallen, Evelyn. 1977. *Spanning the Generations: A Study in Jewish Identity*. Don Mills, ON: Longman Canada.

Medjuck, Sheva. 1993. "Jewish Survival in Small Communities in Canada." In *The Jews in Canada*, edited by Robert Brym, William Shaffir, and Morton Weinfeld, 363–78. Toronto: Oxford University Press.

Mol, Hans. 1985. *Faith and Fragility: Religion and Identity in Canada*. Burlington, ON: Trinity Press.

Poulin, Hugues, and Jean-V. Dufresne, dirs. 1973. *The Quiet Revolution*. Ottawa: National Film Board of Canada.

Robinson, Ira. 2015. *A History of Antisemitism in Canada*. Waterloo, ON: Wilfrid Laurier Press.

Shaffir, William. 1993. "Culture: Introduction." In *The Jews in Canada*, edited by Robert Brym, William Shaffir, and Morton Weinfeld, 120–5. Toronto: Oxford University Press.

Statistics Canada. 2022. "The Canadian Census: A Rich Portrait of the Country's Religious and Ethnocultural Diversity." *The Daily*, 26 October 2022. http://bitly.ws/xAfD.

Steinberg, Stephen. 1965. "The Anatomy of Jewish Identification: A Historical and Theoretical View." *Review of Religious Research* 7 (1): 1–8. https://doi.org/10.2307/3509829.

Troper, Harold. 2010. *The Defining Decade: Identity, Politics, and the Canadian Jewish Community in the 1960s*. Toronto: University of Toronto Press.

Truth and Reconciliation Commission of Canada. 2015. *Honouring the Truth, Reconciling for the Future: Summary of the Final Report of the Truth and Reconciliation Commission of Canada*. Ottawa: Truth and Reconciliation Commission of Canada. https://bit.ly/3ia5UgX.

Vigod, Bernard L. 1984. *The Jews in Canada*. Ottawa: Canadian Historical Association. https://cha-shc.ca/_uploads/5c3747d8f1333.pdf.

Weinfeld, Moroton. 1993. "Intercommunal Relations: Introduction." In *The Jews in Canada*, edited by Robert Brym, William Shaffir, and Morton Weinfeld, 168–70. Toronto: Oxford University Press.

14 Are the Chinese Canada's New Jews?

FENG HOU AND ROBERT BRYM

Jews started out as outsiders; Asians did too. Jews dedicated themselves to schooling; Asians too. Jews climbed the barriers and crowded the Ivies; Asians too. Jews climbed faster than any other minority in their time; Asians too.

– Eric Liu (1998, 145)

Two Narratives about Asian Canadians

In the early 1980s, two narratives about Asian Canadians crystallized. The first focused on discrimination. The second drew attention to upward mobility.

Those who favoured the discrimination narrative may have borne in mind the thousands of people who gathered outside Vancouver's city hall on the evening of 7 September 1907, waving little flags inscribed with "A White Canada for Us" before they rioted in the city's Chinatown and its Japanese quarter, destroying property and beating and occasionally stabbing their residents. They may have thought, too, about the Chinese head tax meant to discourage immigration between 1885 and 1923, the deportation of more than 28,000 Chinese residents between 1929 and 1939, the Japanese internment camps on the West Coast between 1942 and 1945, and the blockage of almost all Asian immigration until the early 1960s.

They were certainly concerned about contemporary discrimination against Asian Canadians in the paid labour force. Discussions began at Statistics Canada in the early 1980s about creating a new concept that, once operationalized in censuses and labour force surveys, could be used to implement employment equity and related programs. The new concept – "visible minority" – included people who self-identified as Chinese, South Asian (East Indian, Pakistani, Sri Lankan, etc.), Black,

Filipino, Latin American, Southeast Asian (Vietnamese, Cambodian, Malaysian, Laotian, etc.), Arab, West Asian (Iranian, Afghan, etc.), Korean, Japanese, and anyone else who thought the label applied to them. Proponents of the concept believed that counting members of visible minority groups would allow policy makers to demonstrate that Asian Canadians, among others, were under-represented in the middle and upper reaches of Canada's occupational structure, leading to corrective action.

In contrast, proponents of the mobility narrative noted that students of Asian origin were acing a disproportionately large number of national spelling bees, pulling in high school science awards hand over fist, and surging into the top Canadian universities and professional schools – as Harold Troper noted, "the same way Jewish immigrants did in the 1920s and 30s" (quoted in Ottawa Citizen 1986). Some observers started referring to East Asian Canadians in particular (mainly those of Chinese and South Korean origin) as "new Jews." From this perspective, the discriminatory treatment of Asian Canadians was largely a matter of historical interest. Asian Canadians were supposedly marching rapidly up the socio-economic hierarchy, and one could look forward to the time, fast approaching, when Asian Canadians would be widely considered part of the Canadian mainstream.

The discrimination narrative undoubtedly has some validity as a description of the Asian-Canadian reality today. But so does the mobility narrative. True, the mobility narrative is less applicable to visible minority immigrants than to their offspring born in Canada. It applies better to some visible minority groups than to others. And even within the visible minority groups to which it best applies, there are population categories that buck the trend. Nonetheless, recent research demonstrates that some visible minority groups, notably the Chinese, one of the largest visible minority groups in the country, have on average experienced exceptional upward educational, income, and occupational mobility in recent decades (Abada, Hou, and Ram 2009; Bonikowska and Hou 2010; Boyd 2017; Chad and Brym 2020; Lautard and Guppy 2014; Picot and Hou 2011; Reitz 1990).

Notwithstanding this finding, a question remains: Is it accurate to refer to Chinese Canadians as Canada's new Jews in terms of their socio-economic characteristics? That is the issue we tackle here.

Who We Sampled

We base our investigation on the 1981, 1991, 2001, and 2016 Canadian censuses – specifically, data comparing the educational attainment, occupational distribution, and market income of Chinese, Jewish, and non-Jewish White Canadians. Market income derives from wages, salaries, self-employment, and investments. We occasionally use non-Jewish White Canadians as a benchmark to assess the relative position and mobility of Chinese and Jewish Canadians in the country's socio-economic hierarchy.

In 2016, Canada's population was 34.46 million. That year's long-form census asked respondents if they were members of a visible minority group as defined earlier. They could indicate more than one visible minority category if applicable. Respondents who identified as Chinese or Chinese and one or more other visible minority categories are considered Chinese in our analysis.

A second census question asked respondents to note the ethnic or cultural origin(s) of their ancestors. Twenty-eight ethnic or cultural groups were listed as examples: Canadian, English, Chinese, French, East Indian, Italian, German, Scottish, Cree, Mi'kmaq, Salish, Métis, Inuit, Filipino, Irish, Dutch, Ukrainian, Polish, Portuguese, Vietnamese, Korean, Jamaican, Greek, Iranian, Lebanese, Mexican, Somali, and Colombian. Respondents who indicated they were not Jewish or members of a visible minority or Indigenous group are defined as White in our analysis.

By the criteria just outlined, about 1.6 million Canadians considered themselves partly or wholly Chinese and 24.9 million considered themselves non-Jewish White in 2016. Because the long-form census is delivered to 25 per cent of the population, and the response rate tends to be around 95 per cent, the effective sample size of these two groups in our analysis ranges from 58,103 to 355,548 Chinese in 1981 and 2016, respectively, and from 4,410,153 to 6,009,368 non-Jewish White Canadians in 1981 and 2016, respectively.

For reasons that have not been well explored, the number of Canadians defining themselves as Jewish by ethnicity has been declining gradually since the 1991 census. In 2016, for the first time since 1941, the census did not list "Jewish" as an example of an ethnic group in the ethnic question stem.[1] Officials acknowledge that this omission was largely responsible for a sudden and precipitous drop of nearly 54 per cent in the count of Canadian Jews by ethnicity, from 309,650 in 2011 to just 143,665 five years later (Smith and McLeish 2019; Statistics Canada 2019a, 2019b).

To partly correct the undercount, Statistics Canada subsequently increased its estimate of the 2016 Canadian Jewish population by adding individuals who (1) claimed Jewish ancestry in the 2011 National Household Survey (NHS), (2) completed the 2016 census, but (3) failed to claim Jewish ancestry in 2016 (Smith and McLeish 2019).[2] In drawing our sample, we followed this procedure, which gave us an estimate of 183,300 Jews by ethnicity in the population in 2016. The effective sample size for Jews in our analysis ranges from 56,535 in 1981 to 44,045 in 2016. Note that the Jewish sample does not include the considerable number of Canadians who identify as Jewish by religion but not by ethnicity. That is because the question on religion was not included in the 2016 census. It reappears in the 2021 census, unfortunately too late for the present analysis.

The exclusion from our sample of individuals who identify as Jewish by religion alone is a potential source of bias in our findings. To assess this possibility, we created sample 2, composed of the individuals in sample 1 plus those who identified as Jewish by religion alone in the 2011 NHS and participated in the 2016 census. Results from the two samples are almost identical, bolstering confidence in the validity of the findings presented below.[3]

A second potential source of bias in sample 1 is that it includes Jews by ethnicity who identify with a religion other than Jewish. Usually, such individuals are not considered "core" Jews (DellaPergola 2020). We removed these individuals to create sample 3. We found differences between sample 1 and sample 3, but not enough to impugn the tendencies analysed below.[4]

What We Measured

Regarding educational attainment, we restrict our analysis to young adults (25–34 years of age) because most Canadians complete their formal education by the time they are in that age range. Regarding occupations and earnings, we confine our enquiry to members of the paid labour force in their prime earning years (35–54 years of age).

We restrict group comparisons of median market income to individuals with positive market income in the full year preceding each census. Our examination of differences in the occupational distribution of different groups is restricted to individuals who were currently working or had recently worked and reported an occupation at the time of each census. Part of our analysis focuses on the share of workers in the top ten occupations for each ethnic group. We measure educational attainment by the percentage of individuals with at least a bachelor's degree because completion of a university degree is a key prerequisite for employment in a skilled job in Canada. Since Jews are highly overrepresented as lawyers and physicians, we also examine the share of individuals with a degree in those professions for Jews, Chinese, and non-Jewish White Canadians.

We conduct separate analyses for women and men because of gender differences in educational attainment, occupational distribution, and median income. Gender differences in all three dimensions were very large in the past. They have narrowed over time, with women overtaking men in terms of completing at least a bachelor's degree, but the differences remain large enough to require separate analyses. Finally, we present data separately for entire ethnic groups, immigrants, and the Canadian-born, allowing us to occasionally reveal important differences in all three of our focal measures for these different population categories. In the text, percentages are rounded to the nearest integer.

Educational Attainment

We begin by comparing the educational attainment of Jewish, Chinese, and non-Jewish White Canadians. Table 14.1 displays the percentage of those with at least a bachelor's degree, those with a law degree, and those with a medical degree. To reveal the main story we want to tell, we calculated Jewish vs. Chinese representation in each category of educational attainment for women and men in 1981 and 2016. Table 14.2 shows the results of this exercise.

In 1981, Jewish men were 53 per cent more highly represented than Chinese men among those with at least a bachelor's degree. However, by 2016, Chinese men were 7 per cent more highly represented than Jewish men in this category of educational attainment. Among those with a medical degree, over-representation of Jewish men compared to Chinese men fell from 210 per cent to 0 per cent, while for those with a law degree Jewish over-representation fell from 1,767 per cent to 683 per cent. We thus find a dramatic convergence in the educational attainment of Chinese and Jewish men over the thirty-five-year period under consideration, albeit less so among those with a law degree. The trends for women are similar.

A more detailed examination of table 14.1 shows that in 1981, 56 per cent of Jewish men between the ages of twenty-five and thirty-four had at least a bachelor's degree, substantially higher than the comparable rate for Chinese and non-Jewish White men (36 per cent and 16 per cent, respectively). In the following thirty-five years, the university completion rate among Jewish men fluctuated without exceeding the 1981 level. Meanwhile, the university completion rate increased steadily among Chinese men, reaching 58 per cent in 2016, four percentage points higher than the rate for Jewish men. The university completion rate increased for non-Jewish White men from 1991 on, although at a much slower pace.

200 Feng Hou and Robert Brym

Table 14.1. Educational attainment of Jewish, Chinese, and non-Jewish White Canadians between the ages of 25 and 34 by gender and immigration status, 1981–2016, in per cent

	All			Canadian-born			Immigrants		
Year/attainment	Jewish	Chinese	White	Jewish	Chinese	White	Jewish	Chinese	White
					Men				
1981									
Bachelor's +	55.6	36.3	16.0	58.8	39.3	15.6	48.8	35.9	18.7
Degree in law	5.6	0.3	0.1	6.7	0.7	0.7	3.2	0.3	0.5
Degree in medicine	6.5	2.1	0.7	7.6	2.7	0.6	4.2	2.0	0.9
1991									
Bachelor's +	49.3	37.2	15.0	51.5	41.1	14.9	41.4	36.3	16.8
Degree in law	5.8	0.4	0.5	6.7	0.9	0.5	2.5	0.3	0.5
Degree in medicine	5.1	1.8	0.5	5.0	2.8	0.5	5.2	1.6	0.7
2001									
Bachelor's +	54.3	52.5	20.3	55.9	52.9	19.7	50.3	52.4	29.0
Degree in law	5.1	0.5	0.6	5.8	1.2	0.6	3.3	0.3	0.6
Degree in medicine	3.4	1.5	0.5	3.7	2.8	0.4	2.6	1.2	0.9
2016									
Bachelor's +	53.7	57.9	24.0	54.0	59.0	22.8	52.8	57.2	40.2
Degree in law	4.7	0.6	0.7	5.5	0.9	0.6	2.5	0.5	1.2
Degree in medicine	1.8	1.8	0.5	2.1	2.5	0.4	1.0	1.4	1.0
					Women				
1981									
Bachelor's +	44.2	22.1	11.9	46.3	32.8	11.8	40.0	21.2	13.0
Degree in law	1.3	0.2	0.2	1.6	0.7	0.2	0.7	0.1	0.1
Degree in medicine	1.1	0.5	0.2	1.1	0.0	0.2	1.2	0.6	0.3
1991									
Bachelor's +	45.2	28.5	15.2	46.5	38.5	15.1	41.2	26.4	16.8
Degree in law	2.7	0.4	0.5	3.0	0.4	0.5	1.8	0.4	0.4
Degree in medicine	2.5	0.9	0.4	2.4	1.4	0.4	2.8	0.8	0.7
2001									
Bachelor's +	56.7	49.1	26.3	59.3	61.1	25.9	50.3	46.9	31.7
Degree in law	3.8	0.6	0.7	4.5	1.3	0.7	2.1	0.4	0.8
Degree in medicine	2.6	1.4	0.6	2.5	2.9	0.5	2.7	1.1	1.2
2016									
Bachelor's +	64.3	66.0	37.6	63.4	72.2	36.5	66.4	63.4	51.6
Degree in law	3.5	1.0	0.9	4.1	1.1	0.8	1.9	0.9	1.9
Degree in medicine	2.2	1.9	0.9	2.5	3.2	0.8	1.3	1.4	1.4

Source: Statistics Canada (1981, 1991, 2001, 2016).

Table 14.2. Jewish vs. Chinese representation by educational attainment category for men and women between the ages of 25 and 34, 1981 and 2016, in per cent

Year	Men			Women		
	Bachelor's +	Medicine	Law	Bachelor's +	Medicine	Law
1981	53	210	1,767	100	120	550
2016	−7	0	683	−3	16	250

Note: The cells in this table were populated by (1) subtracting the percentage of Chinese from the percentage of Jews, (2) dividing the difference by the percentage of Chinese, and (3) multiplying the result by 100. The larger the absolute number in each cell, the bigger the difference between Jewish and Chinese representation. A negative sign indicates Chinese over-representation relative to Jews, while no sign indicates Jewish over-representation relative to Chinese. Percentages are rounded to the nearest integer. Source: Statistics Canada (1981, 2016).

Similarly, the advantage of young Jewish women over young Chinese women disappeared. In 1981, young Jewish women were twice as likely as young Chinese women to receive at least a bachelor's degree. In the following thirty-five years, the university completion rate increased twenty percentage points among young Jewish women, but forty-four percentage points among Chinese women. As a result, Chinese women had a higher university completion rate than Jewish women in 2016. Increased educational attainment was especially striking among Canadian-born Chinese women, nearly three quarters of whom had a university degree in 2016. Over the same period, non-Jewish White women also experienced a faster increase in the university completion rate than Jewish women did. As a result, the gap between the two groups narrowed over time, although the level was still considerably higher among Jewish women.

Jews between the ages of twenty-five and thirty-four lost their leading position in educational attainment to the Chinese not only in the university completion rate but also in the rate of completing a degree in medicine. In 1981, about 1 in 20 Jewish men had a degree in medicine, compared to 1 in 50 Chinese men and fewer than 1 in 100 non-Jewish White men. Thirty-five years later, the level of concentration was reduced among Jewish men but remained stable among Chinese men. By 2016, the percentage with a degree in medicine was the same in both groups. Among the Canadian-born, the percentage who completed a degree in medicine was higher among Chinese men than among Jewish men. The percentage of non-Jewish White men completing a degree in medicine remained far below the comparable percentages for Chinese and Jewish men.

The percentage of women holding a medical degree increased in all three groups between 1981 and 2016, but for the most part the patterns we discovered for men mirror those for women. In 1981, Jewish women between the ages of twenty-five and thirty-four were far more likely to have a degree in medicine than Chinese and non-Jewish White women in the same age range. The rate of completing a degree in medicine increased for Jewish women until 2001, then declined.

Among Chinese women, the increase was faster, particularly among the Canadian-born, and it continued in 2016. While hardly any Canadian-born Chinese women held a medical degree in 1981, by 2001 Canadian-born Chinese women had surpassed Canadian-born Jewish women in the percentage holding a medical degree. The proportion of non-Jewish White women with a medical degree remained below 1 per cent in 2016.

Relative to the Chinese, Jewish men maintained their high concentration in the field of law. About 1 in 20 Jewish men between the ages of twenty-five and thirty-four had a law degree in 1981, and this proportion decreased only slightly over time. Meanwhile, the proportion of Jewish women completing a law degree increased from about 1 in 80 in 1981 to 1 in 30 in 2016. The tendency to complete a law degree grew among Chinese and non-Jewish White women over the period under consideration, but their completion rates remained much lower than the comparable rate for Jewish women.

Occupational Attainment

The Canadian census allows each respondent to report their job title according to one of about 500 occupations in the National Occupational Classification. Table 14.3 presents the percentage of workers in the ten most common occupations for each of the population groups under consideration. The results are shown separately by gender and immigration status. The higher the percentage in each cell, the greater the concentration in the group's ten most common occupations.

The degree of concentration among non-Jewish White men provides a frame of reference, and it reveals stability over time. In 1981, the top ten occupations of non-Jewish White men accounted for 22 per cent of all non-Jewish White male workers. Over the period of interest, this level decreased only slightly to 19 per cent in 2016. In 1981, the top ten occupations consisted mostly of trades (8 per cent truck drivers, carpenters, and auto mechanics), low-skilled jobs (6 per cent salespersons, farmers, and janitors), and junior managers (6 per cent sales managers, general managers, and foremen). The only high-skilled occupation among the top ten was that of secondary-school teachers (2 per cent). Thirty-five years later, the list of most common occupations had changed little. Thus, in 2016, the top occupations were still trades (7 per cent truck drivers, carpenters, and auto mechanics), low-skilled jobs (7 per cent salespersons, construction labourers, janitors, and material handlers), and junior managers (4 per cent trade managers and agricultural managers). The only high-skilled occupation was information system analysts (about 1 per cent).

In contrast, Jewish men experienced significant decline in occupational concentration and substantial change in the most common jobs. The top ten occupations accounted for 48 per cent of Jewish male workers in 1981 but only 24 per cent in 2016. The decrease resulted mainly from a decline in low-skilled sales occupations and junior management combined with a persistently high concentration in professional occupations. In 1981, the top ten occupations among Jewish men included junior managers (18 per cent general managers, sales managers, and sales supervisors), professions (17 per cent lawyers, accountants, physicians, and university teachers), and sales occupations (12 per cent salespeople, commercial travellers, and real estate salespeople).

Thirty-five years later, seven of the ten top occupations were professionals (17 per cent lawyers, information systems analysts, computer programmers, university professors, software engineers, financial senior managers, and specialist physicians). The other three top occupations (7 per cent of all occupations) were trade managers, truck drivers, and salespersons. Interestingly, truck drivers, the top occupation among non-Jewish White men through most of the thirty-five-year period under consideration, emerged as the fourth most common occupation for Jewish men in 2016. This is a telling sign of occupational convergence towards the mainstream. At the same time, however, Jewish men were still highly over-represented as lawyers and physicians in 2016, especially among the Canadian-born. The emergence of information technology professionals among the top ten occupations was driven mostly by Jewish immigrants.

Like Jewish men, Chinese men experienced decreased occupational concentration and a shift away from low-skilled occupations over time. In 1981, 39 per cent of male Chinese workers were employed in the top ten occupations, compared to 27 per cent in 2016. In 1981, the top ten occupations were predominately low-skilled food service jobs (21 per cent chefs and cooks, food servers, and salespersons) and junior managers (12 per cent food supervisors, service managers, sales managers, and sales supervisors). Only three occupations were high-skilled (6 per cent physicians, accountants, and civil engineers). The high concentration in food service occupations was due to the large share of immigrants among the Chinese.

By 2016, five of the top ten occupations were high-skilled (14 per cent information systems analysts, computer programmers, software engineers, accountants, and electronics engineers). The remaining occupations were junior managers (5 per cent trade managers and food service managers) and low-skilled jobs (8 per cent cooks, chefs, and salespersons). While both Canadian-born and immigrant men displayed a strong tendency to work as information technology professionals, Canadian-born Chinese were over-represented as physicians and financial officers, while immigrants were over-represented in food services occupations.

Non-Jewish White women became much less concentrated in low-skilled office and sales occupations between 1981 and 2016. In 1981, 42 per cent of female non-Jewish White workers were employed in the top ten occupations (34 per cent secretaries, bookkeepers, salespersons, cashiers, janitors, food servers, office clerks, and sewing jobs). Only two high-skilled occupations were among the top ten (8 per cent elementary school teachers and nurses). By 2016, 28 per cent of female non-Jewish White workers were employed in the top ten occupations. Most of the top ten jobs were still low-skilled office and service jobs (16 per cent administrative officers, administrative assistants, salespersons, office support workers, nursing aids, and light-duty cleaners), but the share of high-skilled and junior management occupations increased (12 per cent elementary school teachers, registered nurses, and trade managers).

Relative to female non-Jewish White workers, the decrease in the concentration in low-skilled occupations was larger among female Jewish workers. In 1981, 47 per cent of female Jewish workers were employed in the top ten occupations. Most of these occupations were low-skilled office and sales jobs (37 per cent bookkeepers, salespersons, secretaries, office clerks, real estate salespeople, and typists). The remaining occupations were high-skilled jobs and junior managers (10 per cent elementary school teachers, secondary school teachers, sales supervisors, and sales managers).

Thirty-five years later, only 24 per cent of female Jewish workers were in the top ten occupations. Most of these top occupations were high-skilled or junior managers (15 per cent elementary school teachers, lawyers, registered nurses, university professors, software engineers, and trade managers). The remaining top occupations (9 per cent) were administrative officers, salespersons, early childhood educators, and administrative assistants.

Table 14.3. Jewish, Chinese, and non-Jewish White workers between the ages of 35 and 54 in the ten most common occupations in each ethnic group, by gender and immigration status, 1981–2016, in per cent

	All			Canadian-born			Immigrants		
Year	Jewish	Chinese	Non-Jewish White	Jewish	Chinese	Non-Jewish White	Jewish	Chinese	Non-Jewish White
					Men				
1981	47.7	39.2	22.0	53.2	30.6	23.3	39.8	40.3	20.2
1991	34.7	27.7	20.6	38.4	22.5	21.2	29.8	28.2	18.2
2001	30.3	25.7	20.0	34.6	22.9	20.5	25.9	26.2	17.7
2016	24.0	26.6	19.4	22.5	22.4	19.5	29.5	27.9	20.2
					Women				
1981	47.3	47.6	42.1	50.5	48.2	43.4	45.2	48.4	39.4
1991	36.3	33.9	34.8	36.5	34.7	35.9	36.2	34.6	31.7
2001	28.9	29.7	29.4	28.9	28.6	29.8	30.4	30.5	27.0
2016	24.3	26.1	27.5	26.0	24.7	27.7	26.0	27.4	25.7

Source: Statistics Canada (1981, 1991, 2001, 2016).

Like female Jewish workers, female Chinese workers experienced a sharp decline in concentration in low-skilled jobs. In 1981, 48 per cent of female Chinese workers were employed in the top ten occupations. Sewing was their top occupation, employing 13 per cent of female Chinese workers. Another seven of the top occupations were also low-skilled: unskilled labourers, chefs and cooks, bookkeepers, secretaries, salespeople, food servers, and cashiers. The other top occupations were food supervisors and nurses. Sewing and food service–related occupations were mostly dominated by immigrants, while low-skilled office and sales jobs were prevalent among Canadian-born Chinese women.

In 2016, the top ten occupations employed 26 per cent of female Chinese workers. Seven of the top occupations were still low-skilled (17 per cent salespeople, food servers, accounting clerks, food service helpers, office support workers, cashiers, and administrative officers). The remaining top occupations were accountants, trade managers, and information system analysts. Again, food service and sales occupations were prevalent among immigrant women, while Canadian-born Chinese women were over-represented as elementary and secondary school teachers, accountants, and nurses.

Overall, between 1981 and 2016, Jewish and Chinese workers experienced similarly large decreases in concentration in low-skill jobs, particularly sales jobs among Jewish men and food service jobs among

206 Feng Hou and Robert Brym

Table 14.4. Top ten occupations for Jewish, Chinese, and non-Jewish White men and women between the ages of 35 and 54, 2016, in per cent

Jewish		Chinese		Non-Jewish White	
		Men			
Lawyers	3.5	Information systems analysts	4.3	Truck drivers	3.6
Information systems analysts	3.3	Trade managers	3.8	Trade managers	3.0
Computer programmers	2.8	Computer programmers	3.4	Carpenters	1.8
Trade managers	2.4	Cooks	2.8	Sales persons	1.8
Truck drivers	2.4	Chefs	2.7	Construction labourers	1.7
Sales persons	2.2	Software engineers	2.4	Auto mechanics	1.7
University professors	2.0	Sales persons	2.1	Janitors	1.6
Software engineers	2.0	Accountants	1.8	Material handlers	1.4
Financial senior managers	1.9	Food service managers	1.8	Information systems analysts	1.4
Specialist physicians	1.5	Electronics engineers	1.6	Agricultural managers	1.3
Total	24.0		26.6		19.4
		Women			
Elementary school teachers	4.1	Accountants	5.1	Elementary school teachers	4.0
Lawyers	2.8	Sales persons	3.0	Administrative officers	3.3
Registered nurses	2.7	Food servers	2.6	Administrative assistants	3.3
Administrative officers	2.7	Accounting clerks	2.5	Registered nurses	3.3
Sales persons	2.5	Food service helpers	2.4	Sales persons	2.6
Early childhood educators	2.1	Office support workers	2.3	Office support workers	2.4
University professors	1.9	Cashiers	2.2	Trade managers	2.3
Administrative assistants	1.8	Trade managers	2.1	Early childhood educators	2.3
Trade managers	1.8	Administrative officers	2.0	Nurse aids	2.1
Software engineers	1.8	Information systems analysts	1.9	Light-duty cleaners	1.8
Total	24.3		26.1		27.5

Note: Some column totals do not add up precisely due to rounding error.
Source: Statistics Canada (2016).

Chinese men. However, they remained distinct in their top occupational choices. Jewish men were still over-represented in traditional high-paying, prestigious jobs, including lawyers, physicians, university professors, and financial managers. Jewish men, especially the immigrants among them, also became prominent among information technology professionals. Chinese men, both Canadian-born and immigrants, became prominent among information technology professionals. Canadian-born Chinese men were also over-represented as physicians, financial officers and accountants, while Chinese immigrants were still over-represented in food services.

Like their male counterparts, both Jewish and Chinese women experienced a significant decrease in concentration in low-skilled occupations, a trend shared by non-Jewish White women. In 2016, high-skilled jobs featured more prominently among Jewish women's top ten occupations than among Chinese women's top ten occupations.

Table 14.4 provides a detailed breakdown for the top ten occupations in each population group in 2016.

Earnings

Jews are often seen as relatively well-to-do. The reality is more complex. For one thing, the percentage of Jews below Statistics Canada's low income cut-off is almost exactly the same as the percentage for the entire Canadian population (see chapter 3 in this volume). Moreover, as will soon become clear, convergence of occupational trends between Jews and non-Jewish White Canadians since 1981 has produced a convergence of income levels between these two groups.

Table 14.5 presents median market income (adjusted for inflation) for individuals with positive earnings for the three population groups. Over the thirty-five-year period under consideration, median market earnings of non-Jewish White men between the ages of thirty-five and fifty-four increased less than 6 per cent. Canadian-born Chinese men experienced a 13 per cent increase in real income, but Chinese male immigrants experienced an 8 per cent decrease. Jewish men experienced a 19 per cent drop in real income, with both immigrants and the Canadian-born registering a decline.

As a result of divergent trends between groups, the earnings advantage of Jewish men over non-Jewish White men diminished steadily. In 1980, the median income of Jewish men was 43 per cent higher than that of non-Jewish White men, but this lead was reduced to 10 per cent in 2015. In 1980, the gap in median earnings between Jewish and Chinese men was 68 per cent but was reduced to 41 per cent in

2015. The earnings gap between Jewish and Chinese male immigrant workers remained stable over the thirty-five-year period, but among the Canadian-born, the gap between Jewish and Chinese men reversed. In 1980, median income was 32 per cent higher among Canadian-born Jewish men, but by 2015 Canadian-born Chinese men had 5 per cent higher median earnings.

Between 1980 and 2015, real median earnings increased among all Canadian women as the range of educational and occupational opportunities available to them grew. However, gains varied by ethnic group. Earning grew steeply among non-Jewish White women (77 per cent), moderately among Jewish women (39 per cent), and modestly among Chinese women (17 per cent). Accordingly, the advantage of Jewish women over non-Jewish White women decreased from 41 per cent in 1980 to 10 per cent in 2015, while the lead of Jewish women over Chinese women increased from 25 per cent to 48 per cent over that same period. The decline in the relative position of Chinese women was driven entirely by immigrants. Among the Canadian-born, Chinese women had earnings growth similar to that of non-Jewish White women, and both experienced much faster earnings growth than Jewish women did. By 2015, Canadian-born Jewish women had median earnings 20 per cent below their Chinese counterparts. Among immigrant women, median earnings grew considerably among non-Jewish White Canadians and Jews, but only slightly among Chinese.

Change in the relative earnings positions of Jewish and Chinese Canadians over the thirty-five-year period differed greatly by immigration status. Among the Canadian-born, the median earnings of Chinese Canadians surpassed the median earnings of Jewish Canadians in 2015, particularly among women. Among immigrants, the advantage of Jews over Chinese in median earnings was large and stable among men, and increased considerably among women. Since immigrants accounted for most of the Chinese Canadian population, there was still a large earnings gap between the entire Jewish and Chinese populations. It seems reasonable to expect that if the percentage of immigrants in the Chinese population declines, so will the earnings gap between Jews and Chinese.

Visible and Audible Minorities

Canada's dominant ethnic groups have a long history of discrimination against Chinese and Jewish Canadians. Nonetheless, both minority groups have experienced considerable upward mobility over the long run and are now converging in terms of their socio-economic

Table 14.5. Median annual market income in dollars for Jewish, Chinese, and non-Jewish White workers between the ages of 35 and 54 by gender and immigration status, 2015 constant dollars

	All			Canadian-born			Immigrants		
Year	Jewish	Chinese	Non-Jewish White	Jewish	Chinese	Non-Jewish White	Jewish	Chinese	Non-Jewish White
				Men					
1980	85,600	51,000	59,800	91,300	69,100	59,400	71,900	48,900	60,400
1990	78,800	48,400	58,100	80,900	62,200	57,700	71,100	46,800	61,300
2000	74,400	39,800	55,700	81,100	63,700	55,700	64,600	39,300	57,100
2015	69,500	49,300	63,100	74,100	77,900	63,400	64,900	44,800	60600
				Women					
1980	34,500	27,600	24,500	34,500	35,800	24,200	31,700	27,100	25,900
1990	42,000	30,700	31,300	43,600	38,900	31,200	40,000	30,300	31,500
2000	44,700	27,600	35,000	46,400	48,500	35,100	39,800	26,500	34,500
2015	47,800	32,400	43,300	50,000	63,500	43,700	45,300	29,400	40,300

Source: Statistics Canada (1981, 1991, 2001, 2016).

characteristics. Their successes are partly due to the weakening of labour market prejudice against them since the mid-twentieth century. Their successes are also partly attributable to many of them entering occupations in which they can function as independent professionals and businesspeople rather than having to rely on the goodwill of majority-group employers.

Chinese and Jewish Canadians have been able to choose such occupations disproportionately because, as immigrants, they have tended to be more urbanized, literate, numerate, and skilled than members of many other immigrant groups, and they were less likely than were members of most other immigrant groups to have had working-class and farming jobs in their countries of origin. These circumstances gave them a leg up; they tended to have access to the human capital needed to create close-knit families and home environments emphasizing the importance of hard work and higher education. This situation helped to ensure continued upward mobility on the part of their offspring (Chad and Brym 2020; cf. Steinberg 1989).

When occasional waves of hostility recur – most recently during and after the Trump presidency for the Jews and the COVID-19 epidemic for the Chinese – Jewish Canadians have been relatively well organized and effective in publicizing their outrage and defending their interests, Chinese Canadians less so. Their different levels of vocality may be due to their different stages of integration into Canadian society (cf. Brym 2022; Gilman 2008; Leman 1996). After all, in 2016, 35 per cent of

Canadian Jews were foreign-born while the comparable percentage for Chinese Canadians was 72 per cent (Statistics Canada 2016). In terms of their socio-economic characteristics, Chinese Canadians are indeed becoming Canada's new Jews.[5] We expect that as their level of social and cultural integration comes to resemble more closely that of Canadian Jews, they will be more inclined to think of themselves less as a visible minority and, like Canada's Jews, more of an audible minority.

Appendix

Table 14.6. Sample 3 minus sample 1 Jewish–Chinese differences

	Bachelor's degree (%)		Top ten occupations (%)		Median annual income ($)	
Year	Men	Women	Men	Women	Men	Women
1981	1.5	1.3	1.1	0.7	700	0
1991	4.3	4.4	2.2	1.1	2,200	1,000
2001	2.6	4.5	2	0.9	5,200	1,700
2016	−0.2	0.8	0.4	0	300	200

Source: Statistics Canada (1981, 1991, 2001, 2016).

NOTES

1 Since 1996, ethnic origins listed in the question stem have been determined by the frequency of single responses to the ethnic question in the preceding census. This procedure is prejudicial to Jews. Where Greek immigrants will be inclined to state their ethnic origin as Greek, Jewish immigrants from, say, Russia, are inclined to state their ethnic origin as Jewish and Russian (Smith and McLeish 2019). This propensity likely continues beyond the immigrant generation. Thus, in 2011, multiple responses indicated 252,960 Greek Canadians and 309,650 Jewish Canadians, yet "Greek" was retained in the 2016 ethnicity question stem while "Jewish" was dropped because single responses indicated 141,755 Greek Canadians and 115,640 Jewish Canadians (Statistics Canada 2019b).
2 The National Household Survey (NHS) replaced the 2011 census but was voluntary. It had a collection response rate of 68.6 per cent, compared to the 2016 census collection response rate of 97.8 per cent.
3 For sample 2, $n = 49,104$ with the estimated population size being 201,493. The biggest difference in the two samples concerns annual median income in 2015. In sample 2, Jewish men earned $500 more than Jewish men in sample 1, while Jewish women earned $600 less than Jewish women in sample 1.

This difference may reflect a higher level of gender stratification among the Orthodox, who are likely more numerous in sample 2.

4 To create sample 3, we removed individuals who declared a religion other than Jewish in 1981, 1991, 2001, and 2011. Because the religion question was not asked in 2016, for that year we could only remove individuals who declared a non-Jewish religion in 2011 and participated in the 2016 census. This means an unknown number of ethnic Jews in the 2016 sample had a non-Jewish religion. Table 14.6 in the appendix shows sample 3 minus sample 1 Chinese–Jewish differences in education and occupational concentration, and dollar difference in median annual income. In general, Jews in sample 3 had a higher educational level, a higher level of occupational concentration, and higher median incomes than Jews in sample 1 in 1981, 1991, and 2001, although the differences are not large. However, the across-the-board decline in differences between 2001 and 2016 suggests that the presence of some ethnic Jews who declared a religion other than Jewish in 2016 makes Jewish and Chinese respondents appear somewhat more alike than they actually were in 2016.

5 Convergence in values and intermarriage between Jewish and Chinese Canadians may therefore be expected (see Kim and Leavitt 2012).

REFERENCES

Abada, Teresa, Feng Hou, and Bali Ram. 2009. "Ethnic Differences in Educational Attainment among the Second Generation of Immigrants." *Canadian Journal of Sociology* 34 (1): 1–28. https://doi.org/10.29173/cjs1651.

Bonikowska, Aneta, and Feng Hou. 2010. "Reversal of Fortunes or Continued Success? Cohort Differences in Education and Earnings of Childhood Immigrants." *International Migration Review* 44 (2): 320–53. https://doi.org/10.1111/j.1747-7379.2010.00808.x.

Boyd, Monica. 2017. "Second Generation Educational and Occupational Attainment in Canada." In *Immigration and the Future of Canadian Society*, edited by Robert Brym, 58–80. Oakville, ON: Rock's Mills Press.

Brym, Robert. 2022. "The Occupational and Social Integration of Jews in Canada." In *American Jewish Yearbook 2021*, Vol. 121, edited by Arnold Dashefsky and Ira M. Sheskin, 299–312. New York: Springer.

Chad, Jordan A., and Robert Brym. 2020. "Jewish Intellectual Exceptionalism? The Sociological Roots of Ethnic Diversity at the University of Toronto Medical School." *Contemporary Jewry* 40 (3): 387–402. https://doi.org/10.1007/s12397-020-09344-0.

DellaPergola, Sergio. 2020. "World Jewish Population, 2019." In *American Jewish Year Book 2019*, Vol. 119, edited by Arnold Dashefsky and Ira M. Sheskin, 263–353. Cham, Switzerland: Springer.

Gilman, Sander L. 2008. "Are Jews Smarter Than Everyone Else?" *Mens Sana Monographs* 6 (1): 41–7. https://doi.org/10.4103/0973-1229.34526.

Kim, Helen K., and Noah S. Leavitt. 2012. "The Newest Jews? Understanding Jewish American and Asian American Marriages." *Contemporary Jewry* 32 (2): 135–66. https://doi.org/10.1007/s12397-012-9078-y.

Lautard, Hugh, and Neil Guppy. 2014. "Multiculturalism or Vertical Mosaic? Occupational Stratification among Canadian Ethnic Groups." In *Society in Question*, 7th ed., edited by Robert Brym, 137–51. Toronto: Nelson Education.

Lemann, Nicholas. 1996. "Jews in Second Place: When Asian-Americans Become the "New Jews," What Happens to the Jews?" *Slate*, 25 June 1996. https://bit.ly/3ewkU6h.

Liu, Eric. 1998. *The Accidental Asian: Notes of a Native Speaker*. New York: Vintage.

Ottawa Citizen. 1986. "East Asian-Canadians Top Students in B.C." *Ottawa Citizen*, 11 October 1986, H6.

Picot, Garnett, and Feng Hou. 2011. *Preparing for Success in Canada and the United States: The Determinants of Educational Attainment among the Children of Immigrants*. Ottawa: Statistics Canada. http://bitly.ws/sCx8.

Reitz, Jeffrey G. 1990. "Ethnic Concentrations in Labour Markets and Their Implications for Ethnic Inequality." In *Ethnic Identity and Equality: Varieties of Experience in a Canadian City*, edited by Raymond Breton, Wsevolod W. Isajiw, Warren E. Kalbach, and Jeffery G. Reitz, 135–95. Toronto: University of Toronto Press.

Smith, Trevor, and Scott McLeish. 2019. *Technical Report on Changes in Response Related to the Census Ethnic Origin Question: Focus on Jewish Origins, 2016 Census Integrated with 2011 National Household Survey*. Ottawa: Statistics Canada. https://bit.ly/3vkHjdE.

Statistics Canada. 1981. *1981 Census of Canada*. Ottawa: Statistics Canada. Machine readable file.

Statistics Canada. 1991. *1991 Census of Canada*. Ottawa: Statistics Canada. Machine readable file.

Statistics Canada. 2001. *2001 Census of Canada*. Ottawa: Statistics Canada. Machine readable file.

Statistics Canada. 2011. *2011 National Household Survey*. Ottawa: Statistics Canada. Machine readable file.

Statistics Canada. 2016. *2016 Census of Canada*. Ottawa: Statistics Canada. Machine readable file.

Statistics Canada. 2019a. "Data Tables, 2016 Census: Ethnic Origin (279), Single and Multiple Ethnic Origin Responses (3), Generation Status (4), Age (12) and Sex (3) for the Population in Private Households of Canada, Provinces and Territories, Census Metropolitan Areas and Census Agglomerations, 2016 Census - 25% Sample Data." Catalogue no. 98-400-X2016187. https://bit.ly/33l8WXK.

Statistics Canada. 2019b. "2011 National Household Survey Data Tables: Ethnic Origin (264), Single and Multiple Ethnic Origin Responses (3), Generation Status (4), Age Groups (10) and Sex (3) for the Population in Private Households of Canada, Provinces, Territories, Census Metropolitan Areas and Census Agglomerations, 2011 National Household Survey." Catalogue no. 99-010-X2011028. https://bit.ly/3aC0xU7.

Steinberg, Stephen. 1989. *The Ethnic Myth: Race, Ethnicity, and Class in America*. Updated and expanded ed. Boston: Beacon.

15 Jews and Métis in Canada: Ethnic Mobility and the Politics of Counting

DAVID S. KOFFMAN AND PAUL L. GAREAU

Introduction

Public and scholarly discussions comparing Jews and First Nations peoples or examining their interactions have been expanding recently (Glowacha 2019; Koffman 2017, 2021), but the conversation about or between Jews and Métis is scant. Yet this intersection offers unique possibilities for insight about the nature of "difference" in Canada. Moreover, these curiously similar yet dramatically different in-between, sometimes-racialized, middling peoples of roughly the same population size might offer useful mirrors to one another.

This chapter considers numbers, because one outcome of the flawed 2016 Canadian census was the contrasting impact it had on these two communities. The count of Jews fell by about 50 per cent since the 2011 count, while the Métis population grew by about 50 per cent. Statistics Canada's enumeration practices misconstrued both groups in distinct ways, with each miscount adding another layer atop distinct histories of enumeration. Both communities have been preoccupied with population estimates and the social and political recognition that supposedly comes with state enumeration. The 2016 census exacerbated already palpable tensions of misrecognition of "disappearing Jews" on the one hand, and "making Métis everywhere" (Gaudry and Leroux 2017) on the other.

The meaning of this misrecognition was interpreted and responded to in distinct ways by Jewish and Métis scholars and community leaders. The Jewish response was to take ownership over collective statistics by producing its own technology of enumeration in the 2018 Survey of Jews in Canada (Brym, Neuman, and Lenton 2019), which asked about identity matters of concern to North American Jewry to be put to use by its academic and policymakers, and to advocate for changes to be made to Statistics Canada's future censuses. The Métis response was to repeat its request that the federal agency reframe census questions so they ask about Métis nationhood self-determination rather than stoke the fire of settler self-indigenization by permitting respondents who believe they have mixed First Nations ancestry to claim Métis identity (Andersen 2008, 2017).

Using the misrecognition of Jews and Métis in the 2016 census as a flashpoint, we describe the divergent sociologies of data collection around these two groups, reveal the contrasting self-definitions of these communities, and speak to the broader politics of self-determination/ recognition that undergirds their respective interests. We also highlight the identity issues in the state's efforts to capture data about these two peoples. What the dramatic miscounts of Jews and Métis in the 2016 census and the responses they have engendered show is that numerical misrepresentations have been a consistent, if sometimes unrecognized, issue that reveal something important about how settler-ethnic communities' and Indigenous communities' group identities are construed in distinctly Canadian ways. The statistical representation of self-identifying people tends to reify "minority groups," turning them into single, bounded "things" that neither represent their more fluid nature nor accurately describe these communities' own self-definitions. These numeric technologies create different sorts of "thing-communities" out of "minority groups" (i.e., settlers) and Indigenous peoples. With this comparison in mind, we provide insights on the nature and practice of group differentiation in Canada seen through the prism of counting practices.

Problems Counting Jews and Métis in Canada

The ethnicity question on the 2016 census created a puzzle for persons contemplating identifying as Jewish or Métis. Jewish communal leaders have tended to want Statistics Canada to capture the largest possible number of Jewish persons to help hedge against a sense of losing assimilating Jews. Métis leaders have tended to want Statistics Canada to capture a more exclusive population, limiting the count to individuals who meet the community's stricter definition of belonging so as to leverage its position in nation-to-nation negotiations. Leaders from each community responded to the 2016 misrecognition in distinct ways, but the shortcomings of Statistics Canada's logic of enumerating minorities was revealed in the fact that its errors were so large. When Statistics Canada produces misrepresentative population numbers that reify communities, the state misses its mandate to collect data that support communities' capacities to access its resources and stymies the ability of government agencies, communal agencies, and researchers to use data for their own ends (Curtis 2002).

Who are these peoples who are counted? Jews are a religious and ethnic minority (or collection of minorities) in Canada whose difference is a product of identity choices and immigrant histories – an immigrant/settler community that is often misrecognized and racialized as exclusively White (or Ashkenazi), despite the presence of Jews who present as phenotypically non-White, whose parents, grandparents, or great-grandparents emigrated from Algeria, the Caribbean, Ethiopia, India, Iraq, Iran, Morocco, Yemen, and so on. "Ethnicity" is similarly variable among Jews, where the cultural differences among Jews who immigrated from different countries can be enormous. There is likewise tremendous variation among Canadian Jews in terms of religious adherence and political beliefs. While the numerically and culturally dominant Ashkenazi Jews have arguably long enjoyed the cultural privileges of Whiteness, there are many Canadian Jews born of "mixed" Jewish marriages, and many born of unions between Jews and Gentiles of every conceivable combination of ethnic, racial, and cultural blends. The 2011 National Household Survey (NHS) even found that 1,730 respondents self-identified as Jewish *and* Métis, though we know nothing about their self-understandings or the extent to which they are linked to the communities or the Métis Nation formally.[1] The coarseness of the aggregate population numbers and the likelihood that many people who might identify as Jewish or Jewish+ but did not do so on the census also speak to the question of policy implications of current recognition and enumeration practices.

Métis are similarly diverse, but, in contrast to Jews, they are an Indigenous people/nation. Indigenous peoples or First Peoples living in Canada understand themselves as discrete socio-political collectivities with kin-based, relational engagements through diplomacy and reciprocity with other nations, human and more-than-human. Indigenous peoples are also legally recognized by Canada as *Aboriginal* through the Constitution Act, 1982, section 35 (2), which defines Aboriginals as Indian, Inuit, and Métis peoples. The Métis are a post-contact Indigenous nation located in the Métis Homeland, which includes prairie and parkland areas in what we now call Western Canada and the Northern United States. The Métis Nation has a unique cultural, linguistic, and political identity that sees its relationship with the Canadian state in nation-to-nation terms, not as a cultural minority under the aegis of multiculturalism, politically organized into provincial jurisdictions from British Columbia to Ontario, with the Métis Nation of Canada (MNC) representing Métis concerns to the federal government. Alberta is the only province with Métis settlements: eight tracts of land governed by members of the settlements as a collective land base. In 2017, the Métis Nation signed the Canada–Métis Nation Accord, a bilateral agreement allowing greater state recognition and Métis self-governance over education, health, social services, and employment (Government of Canada 2017). Though there has been recent progress in terms of Métis self-determination, they are not a homogenous community. Métis run the gamut of coded-White to coded-Brown, with a corresponding array of political leanings, from conservative views that affirm the values, actions, and institutions of the settler Canadian state to asserting socio-political self-determination as an Indigenous nation separate from Canada. The main issue for Métis is that they are largely misrepresented by the settler state and the public at large on two counts. First and foremost, Métis are misperceived in racialized terms between Whiteness and Brownness as a mixed-race people because of an idealization of racial mixedness between European settlers and Indigenous people in the fur trade era (Andersen 2014). Second, and somewhat contradictorily, Métis are seen as a cultural minority among others and not exactly Indigenous. Seen to be "hiding in plain sight," or "the forgotten people" (Lischke and McNab 2007), these misrecognitions have had the effect of erasing Métis political distinctiveness and sovereignty as an Indigenous nation.

Why did the 2016 census misrecognition of these two communities happen? The misrepresentative numbers, we argue, were the result of both how Statistics Canada construed ethnicity on the survey around questions of self-identification, and the broader ambiguities of the language we use for group identities – language that is less stable and more contested than we normally recognize. Even the term "ethnicity" has only recently gained traction as part of Canada's official discourse (Day 2000). As a technology of modern nation states, the census has been tied to government interests in centralizing information on diverse socio-political communities and collectivities to turn them into manageable populations (Curtis 2002). As Métis scholar Chris Andersen (2008, 357) explains, "population [numbers] and the census data used to construct them are fundamentally socio-political processes and are ... most fruitfully understood not as technical instruments passively recording data 'out there' but, rather, as an aggressive and centralising technique of 'looking' at a (nation-)state's citizenry." In Canada, this technology has, historically, served different purposes for Jews and Métis at various moments in Canadian history, from pre-Confederation to the twenty-first century.

Technologies of Counting Jews and Métis

The Canadian state has counted Jews in many ways for different ends, applying vastly different assumptions than have been used to count Indigenous peoples. British colonial authorities enforced Hardwicke's Act of 1753, "An Act for the Better Preventing of Clandestine Marriage," to prevent Jews and Quakers marrying into the Church of England, and when the Canadian census started recording religion in 1831 in Lower Canada, it counted the "number of Jews in each household" but just heads of families for other religions, likely to magnify the risk of de-Christianization (Cherkesly, Dillon, and Gagnon 2019). Since then, governments have put statistics on Jews to use with respect to immigration restrictions, profiling non-citizen aliens during the Second World War, refugee policy, eugenic measures focused on crime, language literacy, and access to education (Abella and Troper 2012; Fraser 2015; Meister 2020, 2021). Since the 1970s, census data has also been used to allocate support for Jewish cultural and health care purposes.

Canadian Jewish leaders have paid careful attention to the state's enumeration practices and used state statistics for their own purposes. The Canadian Jewish Congress (CJC) established a research department in 1934 with the "cordial cooperation of the Canadian Census department," according to its leading researcher Louis Rosenberg (n.d.), and consulted data that the state shared on Jewish military enlistment, education, crime, immigration, births, deaths, marriage, social integration, and race relations. In their circulars and newsletters, CJC officials debated what to do with statistics on college admissions, displaced persons, Soviet Jewry, disparities between ethnic and religious groups, language use, country of birth, occupation, and small communities. Jewish (and French Canadian) leaders voiced concerns about adding "Canadian" and "American" as ethnicities during the Diefenbaker administration, fearing it would disadvantage their numbers (Lacasse 2020, 334–8). Yet for the most part, Jewish community leaders wanted to be counted, particularly by religion, which consistently tallied larger figures than "Jewish by ethnicity" (or "race" before the term was dropped in 1951), and they trusted the state to produce accurate numbers. Being counted signalled inclusion and enfranchisement, ensuring that communal concerns had been heard and would be considered in public policy issues around religion as much as ethnicity.

Canadian Jews have also used official statistics for planning and policy purposes in myriad community agencies and organizations. Data inform the allocation of community resources based on geographic location, age, and gaps between religiously and ethnically identified Jews

(Weinfeld 2021). Settlement agencies have examined data on Jewish residential distribution to determine catchment areas for services, and rights activists have used government data to fight antisemitic rental covenants, and to fight reported hate crimes.

The state has counted Indigenous peoples for centuries. Census rolls, reserve censuses, and a battery of numeric analyses of Indigenous communities by the state and social scientists have been deployed in military, legal, reformist, eugenic, and other harmful ways (Trovato and Romaniuk 2014; Walter and Andersen 2013). The Métis were caught up in the politics of counting with many pre-Confederation censuses centred on the fur trade metropolis of Red River (currently Winnipeg) and surrounding areas. The Métis Resistance of 1869–70 against Canadian expansionism into the North-West prairie and parkland regions gave cause for Canada to deploy the 1885 Census of the North-West Territories and the 1886 Census of Manitoba that sought to enumerate specifically "French Métis and Anglo Halfbreeds" (Goldmann and Delic 2014, 65). Subsequent censuses identified "Indians" as either status or non-status, and "Métis as Half-breeds, breeds, and Indian" as a means to distinguish non-status, Indigenous individuals (i.e., individuals who are of mixed-marriages who have lost status based on exogamous rules outlined by the Indian Act). Through enfranchisement, individuals lost "Indian status" and therefore access to fiduciary duties of the state. Therefore, by the early and mid-twentieth century, enumeration became less about counting Métis and more about counting status and non-status Indians (Goldmann and Delic 2014, 70).

Nonetheless, Indigenous peoples continue to be a major focus in terms of data-gathering. Recent data come from a range of sources including instruments concerned with labour and community health services (Statistics Canada 2007), but the most important vehicle for recognizing and locating Indigenous peoples remains the census, which tries to define Aboriginals. The census has also been supplemented by the Aboriginal Peoples Survey (APS), which gathers additional data on health, language, employment, income, schooling, housing, and mobility in an addendum Statistics Canada added to each census year since 1991. These instruments, and the data gathered on First Nation, Inuit and Métis, shape policy in multiple sectors (private and public) and jurisdictions (federal, provincial, and municipal). Although Indigenous peoples are governed by these numeric technologies, data about them was gathered in the 2011 National Household Survey from just four questions: (1) First Nation (North American Indian), Inuk (Inuit), and Métis; (2) registered or treaty status; (3) membership in First Nation band; and ethnicity (Statistics Canada 2013, 5).

In contrast, Jewish identity was recognized in the census principally under the questions on religion (every ten years) and ethnic origin (every five years), though Jewishness could also be recognized in questions on language, birth place, and visible minority status. Options for respondents to identify themselves as Jewish were further complicated by two factors. First, "Jewish" is a boundary-resisting identity category, sometimes referring to religion, sometimes to ethnicity, sometimes to culture, and sometimes to national origins. Second, respondents whose own identities might be plural or intersectional might have reasonably chosen to identify themselves in a host of ways other than Jewish in any one or more of these categories. Increasing the odds of a Jewish miscount was the fact that though "Jewish" could be something a respondent might have indicated for the ethnicity question, most of the examples listed were demonyms for countries, and "Jewish" is not a geographic origin. The 2016 census numbers suggest that many Jews identified themselves as "Russian," "Polish," and "Canadian" in terms of ethnicity (Smith and McLeish 2019).

Like Jewish identity, Indigenous identity also fell under the ethnicity question. Unlike Jewish identity, however, the census afforded no opportunity for Métis respondents to identity their religious identity as Métis other than under the generic category "Traditional (Aboriginal) Spirituality." This steering of answers in the census's examples had the effect of further misrecognizing Métis experiences of religion (Gareau 2021).

Another distinction in the language and optionality of enumeration for Métis people came in the 2016 census, where Métis identification, like Jewish identity, was based solely on self-identification. This stood in marked contrast to First Nation respondents whose recognition in terms of status or band affiliation came under the question on "Registered or Treaty Indian status" or under the question on "Membership in a First Nation or Indian band."

In addition, the question on Aboriginal group further defined Aboriginal people as: (1) people whose ancestors resided in North America before European contact and settlement; (2) excluding persons of East Indian or Asian Indian descent or with ethnic roots in the Indian subcontinent; and (3) excluding persons of mixed-race descent but who are not Aboriginal from North America (Statistics Canada 2018, 18). This note sought to iron out issues related to misreporting by non-Indigenous individuals, but its framing failed to grasp the way Indigenous identity and Métis identity in particular is commonly defined. Statistics Canada's definition of Métis blends together people who claim allegiance to the Métis Nation and people who see Métis defined as mixed race. To make matters still more problematic, since Métis people do not hold status defined by the Indian Act, Métis identity was solely a matter of self-identification based on a list of named ethnicities when in fact it need not be a matter of choice. Métis identification could – many argue should – parallel First Nation status as an exclusive category. As with Jewish identity, the framing of choice in identifying Métis as an ethnic identity accounts for much of the misrecognition of Métis communities, which leads to drastically skewed results.

Ethnic Mobility and the Misrecognition of Jewish and Métis Peoples

The 2016 census data summaries spawned frustration in both Jewish and Métis communities. Statistics Canada responded to the Jewish and Métis misrepresentations by suggesting that the changes observed were due to "ethnic mobility," the phenomenon of survey takers answering identity questions differently from how they self-identified on earlier censuses. Statistics Canada produced a technical report focusing on changes to Jewish identifications, and though it also wrote an "Aboriginal Peoples Technical Report" on the 2016 data (Statistics Canada 2019), it did not publish an official comment about its dramatically faulty Métis math (Andersen 2014).

Analysing the apparent decrease in the number of ethnic Jews between 2011 and 2016, the report noted that 143,665 individuals living in Canada reported Jewish as an ethnic origin, a number 53.6 per cent lower than those reporting Jewish ethnic origins in the 2011 National Household Survey. The authors suggested that since the ethnic question is a "reflection of the respondent's perception of their ancestor's ethnicity at the time of the census," the difference between answers over these five years might reveal that "changes in the social environment, changes in individuals' understanding of the concept [of ethnicity], and changes in awareness of family history" help explain the massive gap (Smith and McLeish 2019, 5). While this explanation seems highly unlikely, the report also suggested, more sensibly, that the drop in the count of Jews by ethnicity was "likely driven by the fact that 'Jewish' did not appear on the list of 28 example ethnic origins on the 2016 Census questionnaire while it was present as an example on the 2011 NHS questionnaire" (Smith and McLeish 2019, 18).

Canadian Jews reacted to the 2016 census misrecognition with a mixture of alarm, bemusement, and action. Canada's most powerful Jewish advocacy group, the Centre for Israel and Jewish Affairs (CIJA), issued several statements that aimed to end "this drastic underreporting of the

Jewish population" (CIJA 2019). CIJA argued that if "Jewish" was not reinstated on the 2021 census, "the work of Jewish charities will be drastically undermined," and that "Jewish Federations and Federation-funded social service agencies [which] collectively spend tens of millions annually on charitable work throughout Canada, including on projects to support seniors, alleviate poverty, educate students, and integrate new Canadians ... requires access to accurate census data providing a clear portrait of Jewish communities across Canada" (CIJA 2020). "The only acceptable solution," CIJA noted in a third statement, "is to more clearly define ethnic origin, using 'Jewish' and multiple other non-country examples as explanatory guides in the question itself. Having a precise and clear question is uniquely crucial for Jewish respondents, given the multi-faceted nature of Jewish identity" (Fogel 2017).

Community responses noted that Jews increasingly identify as ethnically "Canadian," with many Jews being third- or fourth-generation citizens, that an increasing number report more than one ethnic origin, and that marriages and common-law unions, increasingly between people from different cultural and ethnic groups, have created more internal diversity among Jews and have made collecting accurate data about Jews all the more challenging. In view of these challenges, CIJA also recommended that Canada "create (and thus fund) a national survey, similar to the Pew study on American Jews conducted in 2013" (CIJA 2017), an outcome that came to pass with the 2018 Survey of Jews in Canada. Although the initiative for the survey came from academics at two Toronto universities and a major public opinion firm, not from the government, Jewish federations and foundations were also eager to provide financial support for the largest community survey of Canadian Jews to date. This fact speaks to the agency of the community and its investment in data for policy, planning, and budgeting – and for quality scholarship in and of itself, distinct from needs that the state may have for enumerating Jews.

The story of Métis ethnic mobility followed a different path. The first indication of significant anomalies in Métis population numbers emerged in the 2001 census, with an apparently rapid rise of those self-identifying as Métis since the prior census in 1996, especially in Ontario (124.5 per cent increase), PEI (100 per cent), Nova Scotia (280 per cent), and New Brunswick (351.1 per cent) (Statistics Canada n.d.). These numbers exceeded the maximum natural annual increase (5.5 per cent) by an absurd amount (Andersen 2014). Demographic expansion continued in the 2016 census with an overall 51 per cent growth of the Métis population, with the most startling increases in Quebec (149.2 per cent) and the Atlantic provinces (124.3 per cent) (Statistics Canada 2017).

In 2016, Ontario seemed to have become home to the largest population of Métis (80.3 per cent) with a growth of 64.3 per cent, while the Prairie provinces remained at a consistent but "unnatural" growth pattern of 32.9 per cent. The ballooning number of Métis was due largely to respondents who called themselves Métis but resided outside the Métis Homeland or historical Métis communities in the prairie and parkland regions in Western Canada and the Northern US. The problem is that censuses have allowed non-status Indigenous people, people of mixed Indigenous and non-Indigenous identity, and even non-Indigenous people to choose this identity category, thereby misrepresenting the Métis people and the Métis Nation (Andersen 2014, 2017).

Though Statistics Canada did not offer an explanation for its clearly anomalous numbers, Métis scholars and critics responded to them. Though no single explanation has emerged for why so many individuals changed their identity ascriptions between 2011 and 2016, Andersen (2014) suggested two main reasons why more people reported Métis identity. First, a 2003 Supreme Court decision in the Powley case (*R. v. Powley*) outlined a formal test to enable state recognition of Métis self-government and hunting and land rights. This decision spawned a flurry of court cases from people of mixed Indigenous-settler ancestry seeking political recognition from Canada for Indigenous rights as Métis (Adese 2016; Andersen 2012). Second, public reckoning with the Truth and Reconciliation Commission in 2015 – a national discussion that exposed the extent of state-sponsored genocide of Indigenous peoples through "education" – enabled broad socio-political recognition from the Canadian public of Indigenous sovereignty and self-determination. Andersen (2017, 6) argues that these events "created an ecosystem within which individuals have felt more confident to self-identify on the census as Métis."

An additional explanation for the increased numbers is the biologically based, racialized thinking inherent in all settler societies. Today, many people undergo genetic testing and pursue genealogical research that show a measure of Indigenous ancestry. This leads to self-indigenization (Sturm 2011; Tallbear 2013), including identifying as "Métis" (Kolopenuk 2018, 335). The assertion of biological descent – as opposed to kinship relations tied to long-standing, storied places – is almost certainly responsible for much of the Métis population explosion, and "making Métis everywhere" (Gaudry and Leroux 2017). Here, the gap between official numbers and accurate (but absent) population figures lies between identification based on dead ancestors versus living in Métis communities (Macdougall 2021).

The fundamental problem of misidentified ascriptions is that the census does not recognize Indigenous sovereignty in the manner Métis see themselves as a nation. When the state implicitly or explicitly wishes to see the Métis as an ethnic or racialized group among other ethnic or racialized groups, or perhaps, more passively, simply permits such identifications, it sidesteps Métis demands for nation-to-nation recognition and relations with the Canadian state. It also commits an error that Andersen (2014, 279) characterizes as one resulting from "administrative utility" and "fuzzy categories" over considered "ethnic affiliation," an insight that applies to Jews, and many other communities in Canada, as much as it does to Métis.

Accounting for Jewish and Métis Self-Determination

After the 2016 census, Statistics Canada consulted with stakeholders and academics on how to better ask questions that represent communities and ethnic groups. Though this was a step in the right direction, there remains an institutional myopia unable to focus on the unique details of either Jewish or Métis identity.

Statistics Canada was somewhat responsive to the Jewish community's concern over the 2016 misrepresentation. The religion question on the 2021 long-form census questionnaire listed "Jewish" as an example of religious affiliation, as in past years, but for the first time, respondents were invited to click on a web link allowing them to specify their denominational identification. The stem of the ethnicity question allowed multiple responses, as in past years, but it no longer listed any examples. Instead, it provided a web link to a list of 510 ethnic labels, the 417th of which was "Jewish." In fact, as a direct result of the Jewish miscount, Statistics Canada removed the examples of ethnic origins from the 2021 census altogether, understanding that including any prompts or models influences respondents and causes more confusion than clarity (Statistics Canada 2020a, 2020b).

The 2021 census will shed light on the nature and extent of intra-Jewish pluralism, on ethnic and religious blending, Jewish religious diversity, and perhaps on Jews of Colour. Still, an important question remains: Should data gathered by Jews about themselves be provided to Statistics Canada or to federal, provincial, or municipal bodies to help Jews design more effective policies and services for the Jewish community? Would this procedure solve the issue of state socio-political recognition of Canada's Jewish community?

Statistics Canada addressed one of the problems raised in 2016 reporting on Métis populations and ethnic mobility with a new question: "Is this person a registered member of a Métis organization or settlement?" Respondents who answered "yes" could further identify themselves as "a signatory of the Canada–Métis Nation Accord," or provide their own response in the write-in box (Statistics Canada 2020b). The purpose of this question was to link Métis identification to membership in either the Métis settlements (again, unique only to Alberta) or citizenship to the Métis Nation organizations (i.e., the Métis Nation of Ontario, Manitoba Metis Federation, Métis Nation-Saskatchewan, Métis Nation of Alberta, and Métis Nation British Columbia) that have signed the 2017 nation-to-nation Canada–Métis Nation Accord (Government of Canada 2017). The wording of this question sought to mitigate ethnic mobility by curtailing the reporting of people who self-identify as Métis but are not citizens of the signatory Métis organizations or residents of the Métis settlements.

This concession on reporting Métis citizens corresponds almost exactly to the recommendation Chris Andersen made to Statistics Canada in 2008. His question read, "Are you a member of the 'Métis Nation,' i.e. the Aboriginal people whose ancestors historically self-identified as Métis and who resided in the Historic Métis Nation Homeland of western Canada?" (Andersen 2008, 362). Yet, though the questions appear to be nearly identical, there is an important if subtle difference. In Andersen's phrasing, "membership in" the Métis Nation pertains to Métis connected to living Métis communities or residing in the Métis Homeland. His interpretation did not imply solely citizenship in the provincial organizations or membership in a Métis settlement because not all Métis claim an affiliation to these political entities. For Andersen, Métis identity necessarily implies links to the socio-political body that represents Métis interests, ties of kinship with other Métis people, and some connection to collective history in storied places within the Métis Homeland. To drive this point home, Andersen defined Métis identity in socio-political, kinship terms that challenge settler colonialism: "I'm Métis because I belong (and claim allegiance) to a set of Métis memories, territories, and leaders who challenged and continue to challenge colonial authorities' unitary claims to land and society" (Andersen 2011, 165). In an interesting twist, in choosing the wording it did, the Statistics Canada 2021 census drafters may have relied too much on membership in Métis organizations or settlements as a gauge for Métis identity in the same way it focused on status to identify reporting on First Nations peoples. Fundamentally, the problem is that the state remains the authority defining "recognized" Indigenous identity. Indigenous nations are still not free to define themselves as they wish.

Towards Self-Definition

Our analysis does not imply that Canada's Jewish and Métis communities are of one mind regarding numerated claims of Jewish or Métis identity. These communities are diverse and sometimes divided on how to define their contours – even on whether "to count their members" at all (cf. Kravel-Tovi 2020; Walter and Andersen 2013).

We do claim that technologies like the federal census reflect deep historical and structural issues around power and the state, and the construction and racialization of minority group identity, both settler and Indigenous (Andersen 2008; Curtis 2002; Kravel-Tovi 2018). We believe our discussion helps us move away from a debate on how to recognize ethnic communities and identity within a multicultural paradigm. For both Jewish and Métis communities, this discussion necessarily includes engagement with the socio-political and racial pluralism of Canada by asking questions about what it means to be counted Jewish or Métis – and the anxieties that ensue from "disappearing" Jews and "making Métis everywhere." It also invites critical reflection on the recognition and experience of BIPOC Canadians (those who identify as Black, Indigenous, and People of Colour) as we move away from reifying racialist and colonial constructs and towards the self-definition of recognizable collective identities.

NOTE

1 We thank Feng Hou (Statistics Canada) and Robert Brym (University of Toronto) for this information.

REFERENCES

Abella, Irving, and Harold Troper. 2012. *None Is Too Many: Canada and the Jews of Europe, 1933–1948*. 3rd ed. Toronto: University of Toronto Press.

Adese, Jennifer. 2016. "A Tale of Two Constitutions: Métis Nationhood and Section 35(2)'s Impact on Interpretations of Daniels." *Topia* 36: 7–19. https://doi.org/10.3138/topia.36.7.

Adese, Jennifer. 2021. "Restoring the Balance: Métis Women and Contemporary Nationalist Political Organizing." In *A People and a Nation: New Directions in Contemporary Métis Studies*, edited by Jennifer Adese and Chris Andersen, 115–45. Vancouver: UBC Press.

Andersen, Chris. 2008. "From Nation to Population: The Racialisation of 'Métis' in the Canadian Census." *Nations and Nationalism* 14 (2): 347–68. https://doi.org/10.1111/j.1469-8129.2008.00331.x.

Andersen, Chris. 2011. "'I'm Métis, What's Your Excuse?' On the Optics and the Ethics of the Misrecognition of Métis in Canada." *Aboriginal Policy Studies* 1 (2): 161–5. https://doi.org/10.5663/aps.v1i2.11686.

Andersen, Chris. 2012. "Settling for Community? Juridical Visions of Historical Métis Collectivity in and after *R. v. Powley*." In *Contours of a People: Metis Family, Mobility, and History*, edited by Nicole St-Onge, Carolyn

Podruchny, and Brenda Macdougall, 392–421. Norman: University of Oklahoma Press.

Andersen, Chris. 2014. "Ethnic or Categorical Mobility? Challenging Conventional Demographic Explanations of Métis Population Growth." In *Aboriginal Populations: Social, Demographic, and Epidemiological Perspectives*, edited by Frank Trovato and Anatole Romaniuk, 263–84. Edmonton: University of Alberta Press.

Andersen, Chris. 2017. "Who Can Call Themselves Métis?" *The Walrus*, last updated 23 September 2021. https://thewalrus.ca/who-can-call-themselves-metis.

Brym, Robert, Keith Neuman, and Rhonda Lenton. 2019. *2018 Survey of Jews in Canada: Final Report*. Toronto: Environics Institute for Survey Research. https://bit.ly/2QWl13a.

Centre for Israel and Jewish Affairs (CIJA). 2017. "Disappearing Jews: Understanding the Ethnic Origin Question." Accessed 23 May 2021, https://www.cija.ca/disappearing-jews. Page no longer available.

Centre for Israel and Jewish Affairs (CIJA). 2019. "Update: Resolving the Census Challenge for Jewish Canadians." Accssed 23 May 2021, https://www.cija.ca/update-resolving-the-census-challenge-for-jewish-canadians. Page no longer available.

Centre for Israel and Jewish Affairs (CIJA). 2020. "Fix the Census to End the Underreporting of Jewish Canadians." Accessed 27 May 2021, https://www.cija.ca/fix-the-census-to-end-the-underreporting-of-jewish-canadians. Page no longer available.

Cherkesly, Isabelle, Lisa Dillon, and Alain Gagnon. 2019. "Creating the 1831 Canadian Census Database." *Historical Methods: A Journal of Quantitative and Interdisciplinary History* 52 (2): 110–27. https://doi.org/10.1080/01615440.2019.1567419.

Curtis, Bruce. 2002. *The Politics of Population: State Formation, Statistics, and the Census of Canada, 1840–1875*. Toronto: University of Toronto Press.

Day, Richard J.F. 2000. *Multiculturalism and the History of Canadian Diversity*. Toronto: University of Toronto Press.

Fogel, Shimon. 2017. "Statement: 2016 Census." Centre for Israel and Jewish Affairs. Accessed 23 May 2021, https://www.cija.ca/statement-2016-census. Page no longer available.

Fraser, David. 2015. *Honorary Protestants: The Jewish School Question in Montreal, 1867–1997*. Toronto: University of Toronto Press.

Gareau, Paul L. 2021. "Mary and the Métis: Religion as a Site for New Insight in Métis Studies." In *A People and a Nation: New Directions in Contemporary Métis Studies*, edited by Jennifer Adese and Chris Andersen, 188–212. Vancouver: UBC Press.

Gaudry, Adam, and Darryl Leroux. 2017. "White Settler Revisionism and Making Métis Everywhere: The Evocation of Métissage in Quebec and

Nova Scotia." *Critical Ethnic Studies* 3 (1): 116–42. https://doi.org/10.5749/jcritethnstud.3.1.0116.

Glowacha, Dorota. 2019. "'Never Forget': Intersecting Memories of the Holocaust and the Settler Colonial Genocide in Canada." In *Holocaust Memory and Racism in the Postwar World*, edited by Shirli Gilbert and Avril Alba, 386–418. Detroit: Wayne State University Press.

Goldmann, Gustave J., and Senada Delic. 2014. "Counting Aboriginal People in Canada." In *Aboriginal Populations: Social, Demographic, and Epidemiological Perspectives*, edited by Frank Trovato and Anatole Romaniuk, 59–78. Edmonton: University of Alberta.

Government of Canada. 2017. "Canada–Metis Nation Accord." Prime Minister of Canada. https://pm.gc.ca/en/canada-metis-nation-accord.

Koffman, David S. 2017. "Suffering and Sovereignty: Recent Canadian Jewish Interest in Indigenous People and Issues." *Canadian Jewish Studies* 25 (1): 28–59. https://doi.org/10.25071/1916-0925.40013.

Koffman, David S. 2021. "The Unsettling of Canadian Jewish History: Towards a Tangled History of Jewish–Indigenous Encounters." In *No Better Home? Jews, Canada, and the Sense of Belonging*, edited by David S. Koffman, 81–115. Toronto: University of Toronto Press.

Kolopenuk, Jessica. 2018. "'Pop-Up' Métis and the Rise of Canada's Post-Indigenous Formation." *American Anthropologist* 120 (2): 333–7. https://doi.org/10.1111/aman.13044.

Kravel-Tovi, Michal. 2018. "Accounting of the Soul: Enumeration, Affect, and Soul Searching among American Jewry." *American Anthropologist* 120 (4): 711–24. https://doi.org/10.1111/aman.13123.

Kravel-Tovi, Michal. 2020. "The Specter of Dwindling Numbers: Population Quantity and Jewish Biopolitics in the United States." *Comparative Studies in Society and History* 62 (1): 35–67. https://doi.org/10.1017/S0010417519000409.

Lacasse, Simon-Pierre. 2020. "Les Juifs de la Révolution tranquille: Regards d'une minorité religieuse sur le Québec de 1945 à 1976." PhD diss., Université d'Ottawa. http://dx.doi.org/10.20381/ruor-24678.

Lischke, Ute, and David T. McNab, eds. 2007. *The Long Journey of a Forgotten People: Métis Identities and Family Histories*. Waterloo, ON: Wilfrid Laurier University Press.

Macdougall, Brenda. 2021. "How We Know Who We Are: Historical Literacy, Kinscapes, and Defining a People." In *Daniels v. Canada: In and Beyond the Courts*, edited by Nathalie Kermoal and Chris Andersen, 233–67. Winnipeg: University of Manitoba Press.

Meister, Daniel R. 2020. "'Anglo-Canadian Futurities': Watson Kirkconnell, Scientific Racism, and Cultural Pluralism in Interwar Canada." *Settler Colonial Studies* 10 (2): 234–56. https://doi.org/10.1080/2201473X.2020.1726148.

Meister, Daniel R. 2021. *The Racial Mosaic: A Pre-history of Canadian Multiculturalism*. Montreal: McGill-Queen's University Press.

Rosenberg, Louis. n.d. "Jewish Community – People and Attitudes." Canadian Jewish Congress Organizational Records. Series DA 02, Box 1, File 38.

Smith, Trevor, and Scott McLeish. 2019. "Technical Report on Changes in Response Related to the Census Ethnic Origin Question: Focus on Jewish Origins, 2016 Census Integrated with 2011 National Household Survey." Catalogue no. 89-657-X. Ottawa: Statistics Canada. http://bitly.ws/t4oj.

Statistics Canada. n.d. "Aboriginal Peoples of Canada." Ottawa: Statistics Canada. http://bitly.ws/t4of. Page no longer available.

Statistics Canada. 2007. "How Statistics Canada Identifies Aboriginal Peoples." Catalogue no. 12-592-XIE. Ottawa: Statistics Canada. http://bitly.ws/t4oi.

Statistics Canada. 2013. "Aboriginal Peoples Reference Guide, National Household Survey, 2011." Catalogue no. 99-011-XWE2011006. Ottawa: Statistics Canada. http://bitly.ws/t4ok.

Statistics Canada. 2017. "Aboriginal Peoples in Canada: Key Results from the 2016 Census." *The Daily*, 25 October 2017. http://bitly.ws/t4om.

Statistics Canada. 2018. "National Household Survey Dictionary, 2011." Catalogue no. 99-000-X2011001. Ottawa: Statistics Canada. http://bitly.ws/t4oo.

Statistics Canada. 2019. "Aboriginal Peoples Technical Report, Census of Population, 2016." Catalogue no. 98-307-X2016001. Ottawa: Statistics Canada. http://bitly.ws/t4ou.

Statistics Canada. 2020a. "Ethnic or Cultural Origins: Technical Report on Changes for the 2021 Census." Catalogue no. 98-20-0002, issue 2020001. Ottawa: Statistics Canada. http://bitly.ws/t4ow.

Statistics Canada. 2020b. "Updated Content for the 2021 Census of Population: Indigenous Peoples." Catalogue no. 98-20-0001, issue 2020003. Ottawa: Statistics Canada. http://bitly.ws/t4ox.

Sturm, Circe. 2011. *Becoming Indian: The Struggle over Cherokee Identity in the Twenty-First Century*. Santa Fe, NM: School for Advanced Research Press.

Tallbear, Kim. 2013. *Native American DNA: Tribal Belonging and the False Promise of Genetic Science*. Minneapolis: University of Minnesota Press.

Trovato, Frank, and Anatole Romaniuk, eds. 2014. *Aboriginal Populations: Social, Demographic, and Epidemiological Perspectives*. Edmonton: University of Alberta.

Walter, Maggie, and Chris Andersen. 2013. *Indigenous Statistics: A Quantitative Research Methodology*. Walnut Creek, CA: Taylor & Francis Group.

Weinfeld, Morton. 2021. "A Privileged Diaspora: Canadian Jewry in Comparative Perspective." In *No Better Home? Jews, Canada, and the Sense of Belonging*, edited by David S. Koffman, 19–32. Toronto: University of Toronto Press.

16 Jewish Intellectual Exceptionalism? Ethnic Representation at the University of Toronto Medical School

JORDAN A. CHAD AND ROBERT BRYM

Jewish Intellectual Exceptionalism?

In 2020, Jews represented 0.2 per cent of the world's population.[1] At the same time, they accounted for 23.9 per cent of Nobel Prize recipients, 21.5 per cent of Fields Medal recipients for mathematics, 27.1 per cent of Turing Award recipients for computer science, 39 per cent of the 100 most eminent psychologists of the twentieth century, 42.9 per cent of world chess championship winners, and 52.5 per cent of Pulitzer Prize recipients for general nonfiction (A.M. Turing Award n.d.; Haggbloom et al. 2002; International Mathematical Union n.d.; NobelPrize.org n.d.; The Pulitzer Prizes n.d.; Wikipedia 2020).[2] This record of attainment has resulted in the popular conception of Jewish intellectual "exceptionalism" (Gilman 2008).

Significantly, however, Jewish intellectual attainment seems to have declined in recent decades. For example, the proportion of Jewish recipients of the Fields Medal, awarded to mathematicians under the age of forty, is 65.3 per cent lower thus far in the twenty-first century than in the twentieth century. Prior to 2000, Jews won most world chess championships; since 2000, not a single world chess champion has been of Jewish origin. The number of American PhD recipients with distinctive Jewish names has been falling since the 1970s, and the declining rate of Jewish winners of middle school spelling bees and high school science Olympiads in the United States leads us to anticipate a continuation of the trend into the next generation (Chiswick 2009; International Mathematical Union n.d.; Simon 2019; Unz 2012a; Wikipedia n.d.).[3]

Existing theories of Jewish intellectual exceptionalism are of little use in explaining this change. One such theory focuses on genetic factors. It asserts that genes prevalent among Ashkenazi Jews (roughly three quarters of world Jewry) contribute to relatively efficient neural functioning and abnormally high intelligence (Dunkel et al. 2019).[4] The evolutionary mechanisms presumably responsible for inherited intelligence among Jews include the following:

1 Traditional Jewish practice promoted marriage between members of intellectual families, thus increasing the probability of intelligent offspring (MacDonald 1994).
2 While religious tradition encouraged Jews to "be fruitful and multiply," the most intelligent Christians in medieval Europe were encouraged to become celibate monks and were thus removed from the non-Jewish gene pool (Van den Haag 1969).
3 Less intelligent Jews were less likely to survive widespread persecution and were thus removed from the Jewish gene pool (Darlington 1969).
4 Jews were constrained by medieval authorities to engage in mercantile activities, which required greater intelligence to survive than did agricultural labour, the dominant occupation among Christians in the Middle Ages (Cochran, Hardy, and Harpending 2006).

The notion that genetics govern Jewish intellectual attainment has been disputed. While genetics certainly influence intelligence, intelligence is a complex polygenic trait that varies widely within populations, and no single genetic polymorphism has been found to be individually associated with intelligence in the normal IQ range (Carson and Beckwith 2016; Deary, Johnson, and Houlihan 2009; Ferguson 2008; Freese et al. 2020; Nisbett et al. 2012; Plomin and von Stumm 2018; Sternberg, Grigorenko, and Kidd 2005). Little credible evidence thus supports the notion that genetic differences between ethnic groups can give rise to appreciable differences in intelligence.

The second theory of Jewish intellectual exceptionalism focuses on cultural factors. In this view, Jews developed an especially strong tradition of learning after the destruction of the Second Temple in the first century CE, when temple rituals were replaced by legalistic rabbinic scholarship (Botticini and Eckstein 2012). Over the centuries that followed, intense Talmudic study led Jews to develop a book-centred culture emphasizing critical reasoning skills. Additionally, the thrift, sobriety, and ambition engendered by laws compelling Jews to perform mercantile functions yielded a potent combination of practices and values that, according to many scholars, favour high intellectual attainment (Ferguson 2008; Glazer 1955, 31; Gordon 1964, 185; Levinson 1957, 138–40; Sowell 2008, 280).

The main problem with both the genetic and the cultural theories is their inability to explain *variation* in Jewish intellectual attainment over time. When the US Army administered intelligence tests to 1.75 million potential recruits during the First World War, Jews, many of whom were immigrants, scored below average (Gould 1996, 255). Yet, in the course of the twentieth century, average Jewish IQ scores in the US rose with linguistic assimilation and upward educational mobility. Other ethnic groups have experienced similar improvements in average IQ scores over relatively short time periods as their mean educational attainment increases. This observation suggests that social circumstances play a larger role than do genetic factors in determining average IQ scores (Fischer et al. 1996; Gould 1996; Schiff and Lewontin 1986; Roivainen 2012; Steinberg 2001; Unz 2012b, 2012c). Therefore, instead of speculating about the proximate causal effects of nearly invariant traits like nebulous polygenic scores and ancient cultural practices on variation in the intellectual performance of Jews, we identify proximate sociological circumstances that are plausibly associated with intellectual attainment. We then present evidence of a rise and decline in Jewish intellectual attainment over time that is consistent with change in these circumstances – and inconsistent with the genetic and cultural theories of persistent Jewish intellectual exceptionalism.

The University of Toronto Medical School

Our analysis concerns patterns of change in the ethnic composition of graduates from the University of Toronto Medical School (UTMS) (see table 16.1). We justify the selection of this case on two grounds. First, Jewish over-representation among physicians is often used by genetic and cultural theorists of Jewish intellectual exceptionalism as an indicator of high intellectual attainment, and UTMS is one of the world's leading medical schools, ranked sixth globally by *Times Higher Education* (2021). Second, UTMS provides a relatively large amount of data (hundreds of graduates per year) on the intellectual attainment of young Jews, and comparable data are generally unavailable from other indices such as over-representation among prestigious award winners.

The idea of Jewish intellectual exceptionalism derives from Jewish over-representation in intellectual attainment relative to the number of Jews in the global population. However, every intellectual attainment is associated with a more or less distinct catchment area from which recruits are typically selected. Intellectual disciplines tend to be concentrated in urban centres where Jews are disproportionately concentrated. Therefore, to properly examine over-representation, it is appropriate to assess Jewish intellectual attainment with regard to Jewish concentration in specific urban centres. For our case study, the

Jewish Intellectual Exceptionalism? 233

Table 16.1. Ethnic representation, University of Toronto Medical School, 1918–2018

Year	Graduates	White (%)	Jewish (%)	East Asian (%)	South Asian (%)	Middle Eastern (%)	Black (%)	Total (%)
1918	92	94.6	5.4	0.0	0.0	0.0	0.0	100.0
1928	105	91.4	8.6	0.0	0.0	0.0	0.0	100.0
1938	109	75.2	24.8	0.0	0.0	0.0	0.0	100.0
1948	128	76.6	21.9	0.8	0.0	0.0	0.8	100.1
1958	121	70.2	26.4	2.5	0.0	0.0	0.8	99.9
1968	179	67.4	25.8	4.5	0.0	0.0	2.2	99.9
1978	248	52.0	26.2	19.4	0.9	0.4	1.2	100.1
1988	245	47.8	18.0	21.6	9.4	2.0	1.2	100.0
1998	167	42.5	16.8	23.4	11.4	4.2	1.8	100.1
2008	190	40.5	13.7	23.2	17.4	4.2	1.1	100.1
2018	278	30.6	10.8	31.7	17.6	9.0	0.4	100.1

Note: For details on how ethnicity was identified, see the appendix. White, East Asian, South Asian, Middle Eastern, and Black do not include Jewish individuals. Some percentages do not add up to 100.0 because of rounding.
Sources: Medical Alumni Association Database (2019); Ontario Medical Association (2008, 2018); University of Toronto Medical School (1918–2018); University of Toronto Students' Administrative Council (1918–58).

preponderant catchment area for UTMS is the Toronto census metropolitan area (CMA). Therefore, our analysis draws attention to the relationship between characteristics of the Toronto CMA and the ethnic composition of UTMS graduates between 1918 and 2018.

Jewish over-representation at UTMS – measured by the ratio of per cent Jewish UTMS graduates to per cent Jewish population in the Toronto CMA – stood at just 1.1 in 1918, approximately reflecting Jewish representation in Toronto's population. Toronto's Jewish population grew more than 260 per cent in the 1920s, thanks largely to immigration. Between 1928 and 1938, the over-representation of Jewish UTMS graduates jumped to 8.9 – nearly one in four students. To deal with what the UTMS administration regarded as "the serious problem" of Jewish over-representation, a quota on Jewish admissions was imposed from 1942–59 (Friedland 2013, 352; Levi 2003). Paradoxically, however, the over-representation of Jews among UTMS graduates started to fall not long after the removal of the quota, reaching 3.2 in 2018. Overall, Jewish over-representation at UTMS has not been uniform over the century under examination. It rose and fell.

The data further indicate that Jews are not the only group at UTMS to follow this pattern (see figure 16.1). Other over-represented non-Jewish groups are primarily from East Asia, South Asia, and the Middle

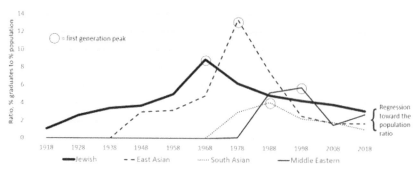

Figure 16.1. Ethnic over-representation among UTMS graduates, Jews vs. selected non-Jewish Asian and Middle Eastern groups, 1918–2018
Note: Ethnic over-representation of a group is calculated by dividing the group's representation in table 16.1 by its corresponding representation in the Toronto census metropolitan area population at the beginning of each decade.
Sources: Canadian Census Analyser (2019); Canada Census and Statistics Office (1913); Dominion Bureau of Statistics (1924, 1935, 1946, 1953, 1962); Statistics Canada (1973, 2019); Medical Alumni Association Database (2019); University of Toronto Medical School (1918–2018); University of Toronto Students' Administrative Council (1918–58); Ontario Medical Association (2018).

East. Non-Jewish White, Black, and Indigenous Canadians have been under-represented at UTMS. A theory of Jewish intellectual exceptionalism must be consistent with a rise and decline in Jewish intellectual attainment over time, and a general theory of intellectual exceptionalism must be consistent with such variation in other ethnic groups.

Towards a Sociological Theory of Intellectual Attainment

We contend that variation in Jewish intellectual attainment over time can be explained by variation in proximate social circumstances. If a group possesses the resources needed to take advantage of expanding employment opportunities, its offspring will tend to be socialized in a culture emphasizing thrift, sobriety, and ambition. The first generation provides a foundation for the next generation to realize its potential (Steinberg 2001). Examples include the first generation of emancipated Jews in Western and Central Europe in the late nineteenth century and the immigrant generation of North American Jews in the early twentieth century.

Important resources for the first generation included comparative advantages in literacy and numeracy (Dilmaghani and Dean 2016). In 1931, the Canadian ethnic groups with the highest rates of literacy traced their ancestry to countries in Northwestern Europe with compulsory public education systems – plus Jews, mostly from Eastern Europe (Rosenberg 1939, 262). It is likely that Jewish numeracy was also comparatively high given that about 35 per cent of the Eastern European Jewish labour force had been involved in mercantile activities at the end of the nineteenth century (Leshchinsky [1928] 2020). In Canada in 1931, 36 per cent of Jews were employed in trade and merchandizing, mainly as small shopkeepers and peddlers. The comparable figure for the entire Canadian population was 8 per cent (Rosenberg 1939, 185).

Another important resource for members of a first generation is skill. More than 35 per cent of the Eastern European Jewish labour force at the end of the nineteenth century were employed in craft and factory jobs, the great majority as skilled workers (Leshchinsky [1928] 2020). Unsurprisingly, therefore, in 1931, while one third of gainfully employed Canadian men were unskilled workers, only 6 per cent of Jewish workers were unskilled (Rosenberg 1939, 164). And while another one third of Canadians worked in primary industries (farming, mining, logging, and the like), the proportion of Jews in these industries was only about 1 per cent. Canadian Jews were twelve times more likely than all other Canadians to work in the clothing industry and twenty-one times more likely to work in the fur industry (Weinfeld with Schnoor, and Shames 2018, 91).

The relatively high levels of literacy, numeracy, and skill of the immigrant generation provided start-up human capital that gave young Canadian Jews advantages in early socialization and intellectual support, thereby launching their upward trajectory. Already in 1931, Jews were 1.9 times as likely to be dentists as were all other Canadians, 2.2 times as likely to be physicians or surgeons, and 2.7 times as likely to be lawyers or notaries (calculated from Rosenberg 1939, 191).[5]

While Jews possessed the resources needed to reach an especially high level of intellectual attainment in post–Second World War Canada, competitors arrived on the scene in the 1960s. Until 1961, immigration policy admitted Europeans on a strongly preferential basis. Thereafter, country of origin was removed as a selection criterion. In 1967, Canada introduced a "points system" of immigrant selection. Possession of skills needed by the Canadian economy thus became the chief criterion for admission. By 2018, 58 per cent of immigrants were in the "economic class," having achieved a minimum score of 67 out of 100 points on proficiency in English or French, level of formal education, amount of work experience, age between eighteen and forty-six, pre-arranged employment in Canada, and an assessment of adaptability. The remaining immigrants were in the family reunification class (26 per cent), consisting largely of the parents of immigrants, and the refugee class (15 per cent) (Mendicino 2020).

Among the first to take advantage of immigration reform in the 1960s were East Asians, particularly Hong Kong Chinese and, a little later, South Koreans (Li 1988). South Asians followed, beginning with Indians expelled from Uganda in 1972 and later a substantial number of Pakistanis (Buchignani 2010). The 1979 Iranian Revolution initiated a substantial wave of immigration from the Middle East, later including Arabs (Rahnema 2011). On average, immigrants from these regions were comparatively well educated and skilled. Thus, while Canada boasts the world's highest percentage of college and university graduates, the points system ensured that among Canadians between the ages of fifteen and sixty-four, the percentage holding at least a bachelor's degree would be twice as high among immigrants as in the population as a whole (Government of Canada 2018; Statistics Canada 2017).

It thus became possible for members of non-Jewish Asian minority groups to effectively compete with Jews in intellectual attainment. The UTMS data are consistent with our contention that Jewish upward mobility into intellectual disciplines like medicine was based on the immigrant generation's above-average literacy, numeracy, and skill levels. Beginning in the 1970s, it was the Asians' turn to benefit from similar advantages.

Intellectual Attainment in Decline

A theory of intellectual attainment based on proximate social circumstances is useful not only because it can explain over-representation in intellectual attainment. It is useful also because it can explain variation in intellectual attainment over time. Jewish over-representation at UTMS declined as non-Jewish Asian and Middle Eastern over-representation rose. This pattern indicates that the latter groups began to outcompete Jews. How was this possible?

Variation in over-representation at UTMS is associated not only with the relative weight in the UTMS catchment area of groups possessing the resources needed to take advantage of employment and educational opportunities. It is also associated with the proportion of group members who form the first generation to have access to these opportunities. The effect of the immigrant generation and its children is evident from figure 16.1. After the Second World War, a surge in immigration occurred at different times for different groups. Jews were first. Next came a surge of East Asians, then South Asians, and finally non-Jewish Middle Easterners. Significantly, for each group, peak over-representation occurs about two decades after an immigration surge, that is, once the children of immigrants are in university or have completed it. After peak over-representation, regression of all groups towards 1.0 (representation equal to the population proportion) is evident.

Recent Canadian studies find that immigrants tend to have higher educational aspirations for their children than do non-immigrants. That is partly because immigrants are on average more highly educated than non-immigrants, and their children have tended to acquire the educational aspirations of their parents (Taylor and Krahn 2005). Among Canada's visible minority groups in 2011, Chinese, South Asian, Southeast Asian, and Arab immigrants had the highest percentage of 25–39-year-olds with at least a bachelor's degree (Boyd 2017, 64). Even immigrants with a relatively low level of educational attainment tend to promote university education for their children. As the authors of one study note, "somehow the idea of going to university is so ingrained in these youth by their immigrant parents that they find the means to attend, even when, statistically speaking, they should not" (Childs, Finnie, and Mueller 2017, 3).

The over-representation of each ethnic group at UTMS can be better understood by comparing it with the proportion of immigrants in each ethnic group in Canada, remembering that Canadian immigrants settle disproportionately in major urban areas, particularly metropolitan Toronto. Only about 10 per cent of non-Jewish, non-Asian Canadians are immigrants.[6] It is likely that about one half of Canadian Jews were immigrants in 1960, while today the figure is around 30 per cent. Fully 65 per cent of Canadians of Asian origin are immigrants today (estimated from Brym, Neuman, and Lenton 2019, 12; Rosenberg 1939, 118–50; Statistics Canada 2019; Weinfeld, with Schnoor and Shames 2018, 55–66). Thus, a large percentage of members of the latter group are immigrants who expect their children to attend university and do everything within their power to ensure that they do. Such expectations tend to be lower among non-Jewish, non-Asian Canadians, 90 per cent of whom are non-immigrants. Accordingly, non-Jewish, non-Asian Canadians are under-represented among UTMS graduates. In 1918, when few Jews and Asians lived in Canada, the ratio of per cent UTMS graduates to per cent non-Jewish, non-Asians in the Toronto CMA was 1.0. As Jewish and Asian immigration rose, the corresponding ratio for non-Jewish, non-Asians fell to 0.5 in 2018.

Discussion

Among the opportunities that influence intellectual attainment are those that result from admission policies. Medical schools across Canada are revising their admission policies to substantially increase racial, socio-economic, and sexual diversity (Friesen 2019; University of Toronto Faculty of Medicine n.d.). Echoing sentiments expressed about

Jewish over-representation in the 1940s and 1950s, the dean of UTMS has expressed concern about Chinese and South Asian over-representation, stating that "Toronto is one of the most ethnically diverse cities in the world, and as its only medical school, we have an obligation to reflect its diversity" (Young 2016). Asians may thus be in the process of becoming Canada's "new Jews" (cf. Gilman 2008; Lemann 1996; Liu 1998; chapter 14 in this volume) not only because of their over-representation among UTMS graduates but because of policies effectively restricting their enrolment (cf. Poon and Segoshi 2018).

UTMS implemented a Black Student Application Program in 2017, leading to a significant rise in Black student admissions following historic Black under-representation. As of this writing, relative to the proportion of Black people in the Toronto CMA, Black students are no longer under-represented among students enrolled at UTMS (Collie 2020). This development again highlights the importance of the structure of opportunities with respect to ethnic representation in intellectual attainment.

An admission policy emphasizing non-Jewish visible minority groups may contribute to the continued regression of Jewish representation among UTMS graduates towards 1.0. Such regression is consistent with our theory of Jewish intellectual attainment based on changing social circumstances – and inconsistent with theories based on relatively invariant ethnic traits.

In sum, our data suggest that the reasons for ethnic intellectual attainment need to be sought in mundane, contemporaneous social forces rather than constants or near-constants such as presumably enduring genetic or cultural traits. Variables can be explained only by other variables – in the present case, by the ethnic composition of the relevant catchment area, the degree to which the ethnic groups have access to resources enabling them to raise children who effectively compete for available opportunities, and the extent to which immigrants and their children predominate among various ethnic groups. These factors are germane to any standard measure of intellectual exceptionalism. Genetics and culture may provide individuals with certain potentials, but social circumstances allow potentials to be realized.

We emphasize the preliminary nature of our effort. A rigorous assessment of the proposed theory would require individual-level data on the ethnic self-identification of UTMS graduates and multivariate analysis of an array of socio-economic and motivational factors that may contribute to occupational choice. It would require comparative data on the degree to which expanding opportunities in various fields have drawn Jews away from pursuits requiring relatively high intelligence (cf. Chiswick 2009). And it would require testing over many more times and places.

Our work has involved only what engineers call "proof of concept." That is, we have merely constructed a theory and rendered it plausible by making two observations. First, the theory is consistent with a century of data on the representation of Jews in a single prestigious school of medicine. Second, popular theories of Jewish intellectual exceptionalism are inconsistent with the data we collected insofar as they cannot account for fluctuations in representation that we have identified.

Despite the shortcomings we mentioned, our analysis leads us to question whether Jewish intellectual exceptionalism exists as a transhistorical phenomenon. After all, the predominance of Jews in intellectual pursuits varies over time and place. Throughout history, many groups other than Jews – ancient Greeks, Andalusian Muslims, Renaissance Italians, contemporary Asian-origin North Americans, and so on – have predominated in intellectual attainment. Jews are just one group among others that have sometimes enjoyed circumstances encouraging extraordinary intellectual attainment. Their future trajectory will depend on how those circumstances unfold.

Appendix

Names and photos of UTMS graduates were retrieved from graduating class photos displayed at the University of Toronto's Medical Sciences Building. For 1918–58, names and photos were retrieved from the University of Toronto Student Yearbook, *Torontonensis*. For 1968–2018, names of graduates were provided by the University of Toronto Medical Alumni Association. For 2008–18, names are also listed in the *Ontario Medical Review*.

A graduate was coded as Jewish if any of the following conditions were met:

1 The graduate was found to speak Hebrew or Yiddish (as long as there were no indicators that these languages were unrelated to their ethnic origin). This information was largely retrieved from profiles of the College of Physicians and Surgeons of Ontario.
2 The graduate was listed as the deceased or relative of the deceased in a Jewish obituary. The majority of obituaries were retrieved from Benjamin's Park Memorial Chapel, Steeles Memorial Chapel, and legacy.com.
3 The graduate was listed in *Canadian Jewish Review* or *Canadian Jewish News*.
4 The graduate was listed in a yearbook or on a website indicating their affiliation with a Jewish organization or institution such as a synagogue or Jewish school or fraternity.

5 The graduate was listed as being of Jewish heritage on a web page or a public family tree.
6 In rare cases, when the ethnicity of the individual could not be otherwise identified, the graduate's given name was of strictly Hebrew or Yiddish origin and the surname was distinctly Jewish (for example, the mock individual Ilan Silverberg would be labelled as Jewish even if no corroborating information was available).
7 The graduate was known to be of Jewish heritage through the authors' personal contact with the graduate or the graduate's family.

The most likely limitation of our procedure involves incorrectly identifying a Jew as non-Jewish White due to a lack of public information confirming the individual's Jewish heritage. It is also possible that a graduate who is not of Jewish heritage was mischaracterized as Jewish if both Jewish and non-Jewish graduates with the same first and last name lived in the same locality at the same time.

Coding of visible minorities is considered reliable because graduating photos were available for cross validation. In conjunction with photos, East Asian and South Asian individuals were primarily identified by surname (Shah et al. 2010). Other conditions for coding a graduate as East Asian were as follows:

1 The graduate was found to speak, or had a name derived from, Cantonese, Tagalog, Japanese, Korean, Mandarin, or Vietnamese (as long as there were no indicators that these languages were unrelated to their ethnic origin).
2 The graduate was listed as East Asian on a web page or public family tree, or found to come from China, Indonesia, Japan, Malaysia, the Philippines, South Korea, Singapore, Thailand, or Vietnam (as long as there were no indicators that these places were unrelated to the graduate's ethnic origin).
3 The graduate was known to be of East Asian heritage through the authors' personal contact with the graduate or the graduate's family.

Other conditions for coding an individual as South Asian were as follows:

1 The individual was found to speak, or had a name derived from, Bengali, Gujarati, Hindi, Punjabi, Sanskrit, Tamil, or Urdu (as long as there were no indicators that these languages were unrelated to their ethnic origin).
2 The individual was listed as South Asian on a web page or public family tree, or found to come from Bangladesh, India, Pakistan, or

Sri Lanka (as long as there were no indicators that these places were unrelated to the graduate's ethnic origin).

3 The graduate was known to be of South Asian heritage through the authors' personal contact with the graduate or the graduate's family.

Other conditions for coding an individual as non-Jewish Middle Eastern were as follows:

1 The graduate was found to speak, or had a name derived from, Arabic or Farsi (as long as there were no additional indicators that these languages were unrelated to their ethnic origin).

2 The graduate was listed as being Middle Eastern on a web page or public family tree of non-Jewish Middle Eastern heritage, or was found to come from Egypt, Iraq, Iran, Jordan, Kuwait, Lebanon, Oman, Palestine, Qatar, Saudi Arabia, Syria, Turkey, United Arab Emirates, or Yemen (as long as there were no other indicators that these places were not related to their ethnic origin – for example, several graduates from the United Arab Emirates met criteria to require coding them as South Asian).

3 The graduate was known to be of non-Jewish Middle Eastern heritage through the authors' personal contact with the graduate or the graduate's family.

Language information was retrieved mainly from profiles of the College of Physicians and Surgeons of Ontario.

NOTES

1 This is a modified version of an article that first appeared in *Contemporary Jewry* (see Chad and Brym 2020). We are grateful to Harriet Hartman, editor of the journal, and Springer Nature Switzerland, the publisher, for permission to reprint.

2 We identified Jews using online biographies that are cited mainly on Wikipedia. Nobel Prizes include the Nobel Memorial Prize in Economic Sciences but exclude the Nobel Peace Prize.

3 The decline is not yet evident among recipients of prestigious awards like Nobel Prizes because recipients of these honours are usually older individuals, often recognized for attainments in their youth (Efron 2013).

4 For convenience, we subsequently refer to Jews in general, despite the fact that researchers analysing Jewish intellectual exceptionalism typically refer only to Ashkenazim. Rise and decline in Jewish intellectual attainment also occurred among Sephardim, with the so-called Golden Age in Muslim

Spain and the subsequent decline following the Christian *reconquista* perhaps being the outstanding example (see Juif, Baten, and Pérez-Artés 2019).

5 Forty years later in Toronto, Jews were 10.2 times as likely as non-Jews to be in medical and health occupations, 7.9 times as likely to be lawyers and notaries, 6.0 times as likely to be physicians and surgeons, and 3.5 times as likely to be university professors (Reitz 1990, 166).

6 Statistics Canada does not consider Jews to be members of a visible minority group, but since Jews represent only 1.4 per cent of the non-Jewish, non-Asian population, they have a negligible effect on the percentage of non-Jewish, non-Asian immigrants.

REFERENCES

A.M. Turing Award. n.d. "Chronological Listing of A.M. Turing Award Winners." Accessed 6 July 2022, https://bit.ly/1rNuhgZ.

Botticini, Maristella, and Zvi Eckstein. 2012. *The Chosen Few: How Education Shaped Jewish History*. Princeton, NJ: Princeton University Press.

Boyd, Monica. 2017. "Second Generation Educational and Occupational Attainment in Canada." In *Immigration and the Future of Canadian Society*, edited by Robert Brym, 58–80. Oakville, ON: Rock's Mills Press.

Brym, Robert, Keith Neuman, and Rhonda Lenton. 2019. *2018 Survey of Jews in Canada: Final Report*. Toronto: Environics Institute for Survey Research. https://bit.ly/2PP4YA2.

Buchignani, Norman. 2010. "South Asian Canadians." *The Canadian Encyclopedia*, last modified 10 February 2020. https://bit.ly/2lESHCm.

Canada Census and Statistics Office. 1913. *Fifth Census of Canada 1911*, Vol. 2. Ottawa: C.H. Parmelee. http://bitly.ws/sE5G.

Canadian Census Analyser. 2019. Computing for the Humanities and Social Sciences (CHASS), University of Toronto.

Carson, Michael, and Jon Beckwith. 2016. "'Race,' IQ and Genes." *Encyclopedia of Life Sciences*. https://doi.org/10.1002/9780470015902.a0005689.pub3.

Chad, Jordon A., and Robert Brym. 2020. "Jewish Intellectual Exceptionalism? The Sociological Roots of Ethnic Diversity at the University of Toronto Medical School." *Contemporary Jewry* 40 (3): 387–402.

Childs, Stephen, Ross Finnie, and Richard E. Mueller. 2017. "Why Do So Many Children of Immigrants Attend University? Evidence for Canada." *Revue de l'integration et de la migration internationale* 18 (1): 1–28. https://doi.org/10.1007/s12134-015-0447-8.

Chiswick, Barry R. 2009. "The Rise and Fall of the American Jewish PhD." *Contemporary Jewry* 29 (1): 67–84. https://doi.org/10.1007/s12397-008-9000-9.

Cochran, Gregory, Jason Hardy, and Henry Harpending. 2006. "Natural History of Ashkenazi Intelligence." *Journal of Biosocial Science* 38 (5): 659–93. https://doi.org/10.1017/S0021932005027069.

Collie, Megan. 2020. "24 Black Medical Students Accepted to U of T Medicine – The Most in Canadian History." *Global News*, 2 June 2020. https://bit .ly/2YBppFV.

Darlington, Cyril D. 1969. *The Evolution of Man and Society*. New York: Simon & Schuster.

Deary, Ian J., W. Johnson, and L.M. Houlihan. 2009. "Genetic Foundations of Human Intelligence." *Human Genetics* 126 (1): 215–32. https://doi .org/10.1007/s00439-009-0655-4.

Dilmaghani, Maryam, and Jason Dean. 2016. "Labor Market Attainment of Canadian Jews during the First Two Decades of the 20th Century." *Contemporary Jewry* 38 (1): 49–77. https://doi.org/10.1007/s12397-017-9210-0.

Dominion Bureau of Statistics. 1924. *Sixth Census of Canada, 1921*. Vol. 1, *Population*. Ottawa: F.A. Acland. https://bit.ly/2TREx15.

Dominion Bureau of Statistics. 1935. *Seventh Census of Canada, 1931*. Vol. 3, *Ages of the People*. Ottawa: J.O. Patenaude. https://bit.ly/2k7PDhH.

Dominion Bureau of Statistics. 1946. *Eighth Census of Canada, 1941*. Vol. 3, *Ages of the Population*. Ottawa: E. Cloutier. https://bit.ly/2kqBwEA.

Dominion Bureau of Statistics. 1953. *Ninth Census of Canada, 1951*. Vol. 1, *Population*. Ottawa: E. Cloutier. https://bit.ly/2lGYaIS.

Dominion Bureau of Statistics. 1962. *1961 Census of Canada*. Series 1.2, *Population, Ethnic Groups*. Ottawa: R. Duhamel. https://bit.ly/2m73zcy.

Dunkel, Curtis S., Michael A. Woodley, Jonatan Pallesen, and Emil O.W. Kirkegaard. 2019. "Polygenic Scores Mediate the Jewish Phenotypic Advantage in Educational Attainment and Cognitive Ability Compared with Catholics and Lutherans." *Evolutionary Behavioral Sciences* 13 (4): 366–75. https://doi.org/10.1037/ebs0000158.

Efron, Noah. 2013. "The Real Reason Why Jews Win So Many Nobel Prizes." *Haaretz*, 21 October 2013. https://bit.ly/2CQ3Y8D.

Ferguson, R. Brian. 2008. "How Jews Became Smart: Anti-'Natural History of Ashkenazi Intelligence.'" *Semantic Scholar*. https://bit.ly/2kxTwN9.

Fischer, Claude S., Michael Hout, Martín S. Jankowski, Samuel R. Lucas, Ann Swidler, and Kim Voss. 1996. *Inequality by Design: Cracking the Bell Curve Myth*. Princeton, NJ: Princeton University Press.

Freese, Jeremy, Ben Domingue, Kamil Sicinski, Sam Trejo, and Pam Herd. 2020. "Problems with a Causal Interpretation of Polygenic Score Differences between Jewish and Non-Jewish Respondents in the Wisconsin Longitudinal Study." *SocArXiv* (July): 1–6. http://doi.org.10.31235/osf.io/eh9tq.

Friedland, Martin. 2013. *The University of Toronto: A History*. Toronto: University of Toronto Press.

Friesen, Joe. 2019. "In a Push for Diversity, Medical Schools Overhaul How They Select Canada's Future Doctors." *Globe and Mail*, 29 July 2019. https:// tgam.ca/2KgcvEL.

Gilman, Sander L. 2008. "Are Jews Smarter Than Everyone Else?" *Mens Sana Monographs* 6 (1): 41–7. https://doi.org/10.4103/0973-1229.34526.

Glazer, Nathan. 1955. "Social Characteristics of American Jews, 1654–1954." *The American Jewish Yearbook* 56: 3–41. https://www.jstor.org/stable/23604870.

Gordon, Milton M. 1964. *Assimilation in American Life: The Role of Race, Religion, and National Origins.* New York: Oxford University Press.

Gould, Stephen J. 1996. *The Mismeasure of Man.* Rev. and expanded ed. New York: Norton.

Government of Canada. 2018. "Six Selection Factors – Federal Skilled Worker Program (Express Entry)." Last modified 9 March 2020. https://bit.ly/2MtOucY.

Haggbloom, Steven J., Renee Warnick, Jason E. Warnick, Vinessa K. Jones, Gary L. Yarbrough, Tenea M. Russell, Chris M. Borecky, Reagan McGahhey, John L. Powell III, Jamie Beavers, and Emmanuelle Monte. 2002. "The 100 Most Eminent Psychologists of the 20th Century." *Review of General Psychology* 6 (2): 139–52. https://doi.org/10.1037/1089-2680.6.2.139.

International Mathematical Union. n.d. "Fields Medal." Accessed 6 July 2022, https://bit.ly/2kyQ052.

Juif, Dácil, Joerg Baten, and Mari Carmen Pérez-Artés. 2019. "Numeracy of Religious Minorities in Spain and Portugal during the Inquisition Era." *Revista de Historia Económica: Journal of Iberian and Latin American Economic History* 38 (1): 147–84. https://doi.org/10.1017/S021261091900034X.

Lemann, Nicholas. 1996. "Jews in Second Place: When Asian-Americans Become the 'New Jews,' What Happens to the Jews?" *Slate Magazine,* 25 June 1996. https://bit.ly/2uGSj7S.

Leshchinsky, Yakov. (1928) 2020. "The Development of the Jewish People over the Last 100 Years." Translated by Robert Brym. *East European Jewish Affairs* 50 (1/2): 157–242. https://doi.org/10.1080/13501674.2020.1793279.

Levi, Charles. 2003. "'There Is a Definite Limitation Imposed' (Robin Ross to Claude Bissell, December 4, 1959): The Jewish Quota in the Faculty of Medicine, University of Toronto: Generational Memory Sustained by Documentation." *Historical Studies in Education/Revue d'histoire de l'éducation* 15 (1): 131–8. https://doi.org/10.32316/hse/rhe.v15i1.477.

Levinson, Boris M. 1957. "The Intelligence of Applicants for Admission to Jewish Day Schools." *Jewish Social Studies* 19 (3/4): 129–40. https://www.jstor.org/stable/4465552.

Li, Peter. 1988. *The Chinese in Canada.* Toronto: Oxford University Press.

Liu, Eric. 1998. *The Accidental Asian: Notes of a Native Speaker.* New York: Random House.

MacDonald, Kevin B. 1994. *A People That Shall Dwell Alone: Judaism as a Group Evolutionary Strategy.* Westport, CT: Praeger.

Medical Alumni Association Database. 2019. University of Toronto.

Mendicino, Marco E.L. 2020. *2019 Annual Report to Parliament on Immigration.* Catalogue no. Ci1E-PDF. Ottawa: Minister of Immigration Refugees and Citizenship. https://bit.ly/2QFbcpD.

Nisbett, Richard E., Joshua Aronson, Clancy Blair, William Dickens, James Flynn, Diane F. Halpern, and Eric Turkheimer. 2012. "Intelligence: New Findings and Theoretical Developments." *American Psychologist* 67 (2): 130–59. https://doi.org/10.1037/a0026699.

NobelPrize.org. n.d. "All Nobel Prizes." Accessed 6 July 2022, https://bit.ly/2kqBixd.

Ontario Medical Association. 2008. "The Ontario Medical Association Is Honoured to Congratulate the 2008 Medical Graduates." *Ontario Medical Review* 75 (7): 70–1.

Ontario Medical Association. 2018. "Ontario Doctors Congratulate the 2018 Medical Graduates." *Ontario Medical Review* 85 (4): 29–30.

Plomin, Robert, and Sophie von Stumm. 2018. "The New Genetics of Intelligence." *Nature Reviews Genetics* 19: 148–59. https://doi.org/10.1038/nrg.2017.104.

Poon, OiYan A., and Megan S. Segoshi. 2018. "The Racial Mascot Speaks: A Critical Race Discourse Analysis of Asian Americans and Fisher vs. University of Texas." *The Review of Higher Education* 42 (1): 235–7. https://doi.org/10.1353/rhe.2018.0029.

The Pulitzer Prizes. n.d. "General Nonfiction." Accessed 6 July 2022, https://bit.ly/2lJj5Lg.

Rahnema, Saeed. 2011. "Iranian Canadians." *The Canadian Encyclopedia*, last modified 23 January 2020. https://bit.ly/2k9aph2.

Reitz, Jeffrey G. 1990. "Ethnic Concentrations in Labour Markets and Their Implications for Ethnic Inequality." In *Ethnic Identity and Equality: Varieties of Experience in a Canadian City*, edited by Raymond Breton, Wsevolod W. Isajiw, Warren E. Kalbach, and Jeffrey G. Reitz, 135–95. Toronto: University of Toronto Press.

Roivainen, Eka. 2012. "Economic, Educational, and IQ Gains in Eastern Germany 1990–2006." *Intelligence* 40 (6): 571–5. https://doi.org/10.1016/j.intell.2012.07.007.

Rosenberg, Louis. 1939. *Canada's Jews: A Social and Economic Study of the Jews in Canada*. Montreal: Bureau of Social and Economic Research, Canadian Jewish Congress.

Schiff, Michel, and Richard Lewontin. 1986. *Education and Class: The Irrelevance of IQ Genetic Studies*. Oxford: Clarendon Press.

Shah, Baiju R., Maria Chiu, Shubarna Amin, Meera Ramani, Sharon Sadry, and Jack V. Tu. 2010. "Surname Lists to Identify South Asian and Chinese Ethnicity from Secondary Data in Ontario, Canada: A Validation Study." *BMC Medical Research Methodology* 10 (42): 1–8. https://doi.org/10.1186/1471-2288-10-42.

Simon, Johnny. 2019. "The Champions and Winning Words from 20 Years of Spelling Bees." *Quartz*, 31 May 2019. https://bit.ly/2lEypZK.

Sowell, Thomas. 2008. *Ethnic America: A History*. New York: Basic Books.

Statistics Canada. 1973. *1971 Census of Canada, Population: Ethnic Groups.* Catalogue no. 92-723. Ottawa: Statistics Canada. https://bit.ly/2kzCb6x.

Statistics Canada. 2017. "Education in Canada: Key Results from the 2016 Census." *The Daily*, 29 November 2017. https://bit.ly/2VrFkly.

Statistics Canada. 2019. "Visible Minority (15), Immigrant Status and Period of Immigration (11), Age (12) and Sex (3) for the Population in Private Households of Canada, Provinces and Territories, Census Metropolitan Areas and Census Agglomerations, 2016 Census – 25% Sample Data." Catalogue no. 98-400-X2016191. http://bitly.ws/sE7a.

Steinberg, Stephen. 2001. *The Ethnic Myth: Race, Ethnicity, and Class in America.* Boston: Beacon Press.

Sternberg, Robert J., Elena L. Grigorenko, and Kenneth K. Kidd. 2005. "Intelligence, Race, and Genetics." *American Psychologist* 60 (1): 46–59. https://doi.org/10.1037/0003-066X.60.1.46.

Taylor, Alison, and Harvey Krahn. 2005. "Aiming High: Educational Aspirations of Visible Minority Immigrant Youth." *Canadian Social Trends* 79: 8–12.

Times Higher Education. 2021. "Best Universities for Medicine 2020." *Times Higher Education*, 16 September 2021. https://bit.ly/2tnhEV6.

University of Toronto Faculty of Medicine. n.d. "Equity, Diversity and Inclusion at the Temerty Faculty of Medicine." Accessed 6 July 2022, https://bit.ly/2FK6Wfs.

University of Toronto Medical School. 1918–2018. Graduation Photographs. Medical Sciences Building, Toronto, ON.

University of Toronto Students' Administrative Council. 1918–58. *Torontonensis.* Toronto: Students' Administrative Council. https://bit.ly/3x1yFlT.

Unz, Ron. 2012a. "The Myth of American Meritocracy." *The American Conservative*, 28 November 2012. https://bit.ly/2ECNofP.

Unz, Ron. 2012b. "Race/IQ: Super-Flynn Effects in Germans, Jews, and Hispanics." *The Unz Review*, 10 September 2012. http://bitly.ws/sMyE.

Unz, Ron. 2012c. "Race, IQ, and Wealth." *The Unz Review*, 18 July 2012. http://bitly.ws/sMyH.

Van den Haag, Ernest. 1969. *The Jewish Mystique.* New York: Stein and Day.

Weinfeld, Morton, with Randal Schnoor and Michelle Shames. 2018. *Like Everyone Else but Different: The Paradoxical Success of Canadian Jews.* 2nd ed. Montreal: McGill-Queen's University Press.

Wikipedia. n.d. "List of World Chess Championships." Accessed 6 July 2022, https://bit.ly/2lEwUL6.

Young, Trevor. 2016. "We're Not That Diverse, but We're Working on It." University of Toronto, Faculty of Medicine, 26 October 2016. https://bit.ly/2FPKnHl.

PART D

Comparing Jews in Canada and Other Countries

17 Jewish Demography and Identity in Nine Countries

SERGIO DELLAPERGOLA

Introduction

This chapter explores aspects of the demography and Jewish identity of Jews in Canada in comparative perspective. This statement implies several theoretical and methodological choices that cannot be taken for granted given ongoing debates about the contemporary Jewish experience.

The first postulate of Jewish comparative research is that there must exist entities – in this case Jewish communities, most often relatively small minorities within total society – with sufficient commonalities to allow for assessing the nature of residual differences. As this chapter focuses on the Jewish population and community in Canada, the assumption is that Jews in other countries, even in different continents, have enough in common with Jews in Canada to allow for relevant comparisons. This entails the assumption of the existence of a transnational entity – the Jews – sharing significant past and present traits (DellaPergola 2013). This assertion may not be obvious to all readers. A rival assumption is that within a given country, Jews constitute part of local reality and are influenced by the local culture, hence the main prism for comparison should be other local minorities, not other Jewish communities. The two objectives do not contradict each other, and both should be pursued. Here I deal with the intra-Jewish aspect.

From this perspective, the historical and sociological processes of formation of Judaism as a cluster of norms, beliefs, rituals, sanctions, institutions, and social networks were accompanied by significant geographical mobility, including large-scale continental and intercontinental migration. Jews coming from a variety of lands, mainly in the Middle East, and later in Europe and North Africa, settled new lands, eventually reaching the Americas. These migrants diffused similar cultural and social-structural backgrounds to different places. The fact that Jews everywhere came to constitute small minorities within larger and pre-constituted societal contexts generated similar conditions of entrance in the new countries, lack of symmetry vis-à-vis the majority, and distinct mobility patterns. Over time, exposure to different local political and institutional environments and different cultural and economic conditions enhanced emergent differences across Jewish communities. Those differences reveal each country's performances in terms of the opportunity range that was available to immigrant Jews and in terms of the development of independent resources and initiatives inside the Jewish collective (DellaPergola 2009).

In this chapter, I compare selected aspects of Canada's Jewish population and community with eight other relevant cases. The countries chosen for comparison are the United States, Australia, the United Kingdom, France, Germany, Russia, Argentina, and Israel. The focus is on the nine largest Jewish populations worldwide, most in highly developed societies in different continents, but whose migration, demographic, and Jewish identification profiles are bound to feature a blend of significant similarities and differences. It should be noted that the data presented here come from different sources of unequal quality and are not always synchronous. These limitations do not prevent me from drawing inferences about the position of Canadian Jewry in global perspective.

Jewish Population Size and Human Development

The geographical distribution of Jews worldwide was decisively influenced by large-scale migrations that reflected major transformations of the global geopolitical system and existing or emerging opportunities in countries of origin and potential countries of destination. As the Habsburg, Prussian, Tsarist, and Ottoman empires fell, countries in the Middle East and Eastern Europe contributed large masses of Jewish emigrants to countries in North America, the southern hemisphere, and Western Europe. Canada was involved in the population redistribution, which reached its peak during the first half of the twentieth century but did not lose momentum until the second half, when the British, French, and Soviet empires collapsed. These events shaped population trends in Israel, which, since 1948, became the main beneficiary of Jewish international migration, even though Israel also constantly featured a negative migration balance vis-à-vis the main democratic countries in the West.

In recent years, a finer analysis of world Jewish geographical distribution reveals its high correlation with the human development levels of the respective countries of emigration and immigration. One correlate of the intensity and direction of Jewish population mobility is the UN's Human Development Index (HDI) (United Nations Development Programme 2020). The HDI incorporates measures of a country's population health (such as life expectancy), education (such as average years of education attained), and income (measured in the US dollar's real purchasing power in a given country). A strong positive correlation exists between a country's HDI and the number, and especially the percentage, of Jews in the country's total population. A strong negative correlation exists between a country's HDI and the rate of emigrants per 1,000 Jewish residents.

The Canadian Jewish migration experience and its influence on Jewish population size unfolded in the shadow of the United States and other Western countries during the first half of the twentieth century (Brym, Shaffir, and Weinfeld 1993; Weinfeld with Schnoor and Shames 2018). Incentives, but above all limitations and quotas, strongly affected the possibility of growth. In recent decades, Jewish population trends have reflected more flexible migration policies but also the natural increase or decrease of communities through birth and death rates, and the balance of those who joined (by conversion or otherwise) and those who left the Jewish group.

Table 17.1 reports the estimated Jewish population for Canada and the eight countries selected for comparison from 1980 to 2020. The data refer to the core Jewish population: those who, in censuses or surveys, declare themselves Jewish by religion and/or ethnicity, or who have no religion, have Jewish parents, and do not identify with a non-Jewish religion. Pending the 2021 Canadian census, the 2020 estimate reflects the 2011 National Household Survey plus estimated effects of subsequent net migration and the balance of births and deaths. Canadian Jewry grew steadily, but total intercensal growth was usually lower than the total intercensal migration balance, hinting at internal attrition. Reporting of Jewish ethnicity in Canada collapsed over the last twenty years, even apart from the unreliable 2016 census results, indicating apparent erosion among the more secular fringes of the group with Jewish ancestry (Shahar 2019).

There was a significant discrepancy between Jewish population size and the pace of growth from 1980 to 2020. Israel grew most in absolute terms, and after 2010 it became the world's largest Jewish collectivity. In relative terms, however, growth was fastest in Germany, which attracted immigrants, mostly from the former Soviet Union (FSU). Israel was second fastest (more than doubling thanks to large-scale immigration and a comparatively high, steady, and increasing fertility rate).

Table 17.1. Jewish population and HDI, Canada and eight other countries, 1980–2020

Year	Canada	US	Australia	Israel	UK	France	Germany	Russia	Argentina
				Jewish population[a]					
1980	308,000	5,690,000	70,000	3,282,700	390,000	535,000	34,500	713,400	242,000
1990	310,000	5,700,000	88,000	3,946,700	315,000	530,000	40,000	470,000	215,000
2000	358,600	5,800,000	97,000	4,882,000	297,000	521,000	96,700	275,000	200,000
2010	373,900	5,900,000	107,500	5,701,900	291,400	483,000	117,400	200,000	182,300
2020	393,000	6,000,000	118,000	6,773,400	292,000	448,000	118,000	155,000	179,500
Ratio 2020/1980	1.28	1.05	1.69	2.06	0.75	0.84	3.42	0.22	0.74
				HDI[b]					
1980	0.789	0.810	0.791	0.748	0.737	0.711	0.777	0.692	0.656
1990	0.850	0.860	0.866	0.792	0.775	0.780	0.801	0.734	0.707
2000	0.868	0.881	0.898	0.853	0.867	0.842	0.869	0.721	0.770
2010	0.895	0.911	0.926	0.887	0.905	0.872	0.920	0.780	0.818
2020	0.929	0.926	0.944	0.919	0.932	0.901	0.947	0.824	0.845
Change 1980–2020	0.140	0.116	0.153	0.171	0.195	0.190	0.170	0.132	0.189

[a] Source: Division of Jewish Demography and Statistics, Avraham Harman Institute of Contemporary Jewry, Hebrew University of Jerusalem; DellaPergola (2021).
[b] Source: United Nations Development Programme (2020).

Australia was third, followed by Canada. Canada, with an increase of 28 per cent, grew more rapidly than the US (5 per cent, based on estimates revised in the light of the 2020 Pew Research Center survey of Jewish Americans). All other Jewish communities reported here shrank – Russia conspicuously more than the others.

Table 17.1 also reports HDIs for each country between 1980 and 2020. The US had the highest index in 1980, but by 2020 it had been surpassed by Germany, Australia, the UK, and Canada. Israel's HDI was slightly lower, but its pace of growth was faster than in Canada and the US.

Overall, there was an association between change in a country's level of development and its changing Jewish population size. Five of seven countries with HDIs above 0.900 in 2020 (Israel, the US, Canada, Germany, and Australia) had growing Jewish populations. The UK's Jewish population declined while its HDI was below 0.900, but it stabilized once it reached that threshold. France's HDI was barely above 0.900 in 2020, but Jews in France experienced higher levels of antisemitism than Jews in English-speaking countries and had to cope with serious terrorist attacks, leading to significant out-migration and declining population size. Russia and Argentina, with HDIs below 0.900, also featured declining Jewish populations. Jews in Argentina suffered the traumatic destruction of the AMIA (Asociación Mutual Israelita Argentina) Jewish community building in 1994 (following the bombing of the Israeli embassy in 1992) and the bankruptcy of the central bank in 2001. With the collapse of the Soviet Union, Russia experienced a temporary decline in their HDI and allowed unlimited Jewish emigration.

The general lesson about the socio-economic environment preferred by Jewish communities is clear: better conditions attract Jewish populations. One can also hypothesize that in more developed countries political regimes are more democratic, tolerant of diversity, and hence more open to the autonomous development of Jewish communities. In Canada, local conditions permitted steady growth. Assuming the continuation of present circumstances, Canada will in the foreseeable future likely surpass France as the country with the largest Jewish community in the world after Israel and the US.

Migration to Israel

An aspect of Jewish population change of broad interest in comparative analysis concerns propensity to emigrate. Other than Israel, no country has an annual database on Jewish immigrants from each country of the world. Although limited in scope, these data allow for extended comparison over time.

Between 1991 and 2020, 1,275,590 immigrants arrived in Israel (DellaPergola 2020; Israel Central Bureau of Statistics 2020). The high point, 1991, coincided with the collapse of the Soviet Union. Thereafter, a decline persisted until 2008, followed by a gradual increase until 2019, and a sharp reduction in 2020, the year of the COVID-19 pandemic. The total was strongly affected by Russia (with a total of 343,349 immigrants) and other FSU republics. Canada contributed a total of 6,860 immigrants over this period, with the gradient slightly increasing over time. The US Jewish community contributed about nine times as many immigrants (61,739), although its Jewish population is nearly fifteen times larger than that of Canada. In contrast, France contributed nearly ten times as many immigrants as Canada (67,252) with a Jewish population only 14 per cent larger. Argentina, with 22,154 immigrants over the period under consideration, contributed a rising number of immigrants until 2002, in conjunction with a catastrophic financial crisis, followed by a sharp decline. France had a major emigration increase in 2014–16, apparently attributable to terrorist attacks but actually due to a surge of unemployment. The UK (14,751 immigrants to Israel), Australia (3,245, including New Zealand), and Germany (3,157) witnessed only minor fluctuations over the years. The number of immigrants from all countries except France and Argentina declined in 2020.

The data just summarized represent absolute numbers out of populations of widely different size. A more revealing measure of trends is the immigration rate per 1,000 Jews in each country of origin.

Between 1991 and 2020, Canada's average annual migration rate to Israel was the second lowest in the world (0.6 per 1,000 Jews in Canada). The lowest rate was registered by the US (0.4 per 1,000). Among the countries examined here, migration rates were moderately higher for Australia (1.0 per 1,000 on average), Germany (1.2), and the UK (1.7). All five of these countries have HDIs over 0.900 and Jewish populations that are stable or growing. Average migration rates were higher for Argentina (3.8 per 1,000) and France (4.6). Russia, with an average migration rate of 41.3 per 1,000, stood in an entirely different category, as did other FSU countries not shown here, not to mention Ethiopia, nearly the entire Jewish population of which was transferred to Israel during this same period. Low and stable levels of migration point to the relatively minor impact of negative push forces in the countries of origin. Thus, the ranking of migration rates, from low to high, provides a powerful inverse indication of the amount of socio-economic prosperity and stability in a society, often accompanied by a compatible ranking of political stability.

A separate analysis (DellaPergola 2020) reveals a correlation between the unemployment rate in the country of origin and in Israel, on the

Jewish Demography and Identity in Nine Countries 255

one hand, and each country's rate of migration to Israel, on the other. In general, higher unemployment rates in the countries of origin were associated with a higher rate of migration to Israel. Among the countries examined, Canada was least responsive to the unemployment rate, pointing to the overriding importance in Canada of a unique pattern of relatively high societal stability and political uneventfulness in contributing to its low rate of out-migration to Israel.

Age Composition

The age composition of a population at a given moment is a composite of several processes of population change that preceded that point in time. The size of different age cohorts reflects the intensity of the birth rate in previous years, namely in the years of birth of the respective cohorts, but it also reflects the intensity of mortality at various ages in response to general health conditions and special intervening factors. Age composition is also sensitive to past migration movements since immigrants are typically young adults. Age composition also provides important insights regarding possible future development of the population, as all lifecycle events like births and deaths, but also migration, are strongly related to age. Table 17.2 demonstrates the evolution of the Jewish population in Canada and in other countries by main age groups over a span of nearly 100 years between 1925 and 2020.

According to the variable proportion of children and elders, country age profiles can be classified along a continuum, from those with a relatively high proportion of children below age fifteen and few elders above age sixty-five to those with a growing dominance of older adults and elders over children. Over time, the proportion of Jewish children has tended to diminish in each country, reflecting fertility decline over time. As a consequence, in a context of relatively high and growing life expectancy, the share of elders has increased. The Jewish communities chosen for comparison display different age composition models. Jews in immigration countries like Canada, the US, and Australia followed roughly similar paths of ageing, but Jews in Australia were older on average than in North America, reflecting a higher share of older immigrants. Jews in the UK, France, and Argentina (represented here by the Greater Buenos Aires metropolitan area) had relatively similar age structures. Ageing was significantly more advanced in Russia and in Germany, where the Jewish population eventually consisted mostly of FSU immigrants.

Over the long run, age profiles reflect the wave-like succession of cohorts of different magnitudes. Thus, the post–Second World War baby boom in North America and elsewhere was bound to generate an echo twenty-five to thirty-five years later. This occurred as expected, but it was of smaller magnitude than the original boom. Jews in France at the beginning of the 2000s were still affected by the succession of heavier and thinner cohorts determined by the large immigration of the late 1950s and early 1960s, which comprised many younger adults. The more recent profile of Jews in the UK indicates a cessation of the ageing trend and a rejuvenation produced by the higher birth rate of the more Orthodox sections of the population, whose weight relative to the total Jewish population is growing. Israel was a clear exception, with a persistently higher percentage of children and a lower percentage of elders.

Careful inspection of table 17.2 reveals that, in the 1920s and 1930s, most countries had similar Jewish age structures. Over time, Germany and Russia reached exceedingly high percentages in the sixty-five and older age cohort, announcing a sharp reduction in Jewish population size (as in Russia), unless somewhat compensated by continuing immigration (as in Germany). Migration to Germany, however, did not seem to stop the ongoing growth in the proportion of elders. At the other extreme, the Jewish population aged more slowly in Israel than in other countries. The estimate for Israeli elders in 2020 was similar to that of Canada, the US, and France in the late 1970s. That said, Canada's Jewish population aged more than did the Jewish population of most other countries. As far as the percentage of children under the age of fifteen is concerned, we observe a concomitant decline over time, with temporary exceptions in Israel, France, the UK, and Germany.

The Israeli family model implied by these data is exceptional. The main determinant of a high and quite stable proportion of children was the high total fertility rate (TFR) – still above three children in 2020. In addition, intermarriage in Israel is infrequent (around 5 per cent of all married Jews in 2008), largely reflecting couples one of whose members is a non-Jewish immigrant – mostly people born in the FSU or born in Israel from a FSU-born non-Jewish mother. In most other countries, Jews have TFRs of two or lower. There was also a large gradient of intermarriage frequencies. The rate of intermarriage in Canada (where the overall per cent out-married was 23 per cent in 2018) was slightly higher than in Australia (19 per cent in 2011), almost the same as in the UK (24 per cent in 2018), lower than in France (31 per cent in 2018), and significantly lower than in the US (42 per cent in 2020), Argentina (43 per cent in 2004), Germany (46 per cent in 2018), or Russia (54 per cent as far back as 1994). These data refer to total married Jews of all ages. The corresponding percentages for the more recent marriage cohorts were often substantially higher.

Table 17.2. Age composition of Jews in Canada and eight other countries, 1925–2019, in per cent[a]

Country	0–14	15–29	30–44	45–64	65+
Canada 1931	27	**34**	21	15	3
Canada 1971	21	25	15	**27**	12
Canada 2001	18	19	18	**27**	18
Canada 2011	18	19	18	**28**	17
US 1957	24	17	21	**28**	10
US 1970	22	24	17	**26**	11
US 1990	19	19	26	19	17
US 2001	16	20	19	**26**	19
US 2013	16	19	17	**31**	17
Australia 2001	17	18	19	**27**	19
Australia 2016	17	16	18	**26**	23
Palestine 1931	**33**	32	19	11	4
Israel 1948	**29**	26	**26**	15	4
Israel 1961	**34**	22	19	20	5
Israel 1970	**30**	27	16	20	7
Israel 1985	**30**	24	20	16	10
Israel 2000	**26**	24	18	20	12
Israel 2008	**26**	23	19	21	11
Israel 2019	**27**	20	19	20	14
UK 1975–9	20	21	18	**23**	18
UK 1986	17	19	19	21	**24**
UK 2001	16	17	19	**26**	22
UK 2011	19	17	18	**25**	21
France 1975–8	19	**26**	18	24	13
France 2002	21	17	21	**22**	19
Prussia 1925	18	**25**	24	**25**	8
Germany 1970	11	17	16	**35**	21
Germany 1989	12	15	22	25	**26**
Germany 2001	10	15	18	**30**	27
Germany 2009	7	14	15	29	**35**
Germany 2019	7	11	15	26	**41**
USSR 1926	29	**34**	18	15	4
Russia 1959	14	19	23	**36**	9
Russia 1970	10	16	23	**31**	20
Russia 1979	8	15	21	**31**	25
Russia 1994	6	10	17	**35**	32
Russia 2002	5	11	14	33	**37**
Greater Buenos Aires 1960	20	21	22	**29**	8
Greater Buenos Aires 2004	15	21	16	**28**	20

[a] The highest value in each row is underlined and bold.
Source: Division of Jewish Demography and Statistics, Avraham Harman Institute of Contemporary Jewry, Hebrew University of Jerusalem.

258   Sergio DellaPergola

All in all, these patterns confirm Canada's membership in the group of countries with large-scale Jewish immigration over the years. However, Canada has demonstrated more robust Jewish demographic resilience than other Jewish populations in that group, standing as it does between the obviously exceptional case of Israel, and the terminally ageing Jewish communities of Eastern Europe and their derivatives in the West.

Markers of Jewish Identity

In this section, I examine similarities and dissimilarities in the structure of Jewish identity in Canada and other countries. Jewish identity can be compared transnationally based on questions about identity markers included in surveys. Identity markers refer to perceptions and behaviours of respondents in relation to the meaning of being Jewish (such as religion, ethnicity, and culture), the mode of expressing one's Jewishness (such as Orthodox, Conservative, Reform, and agnostic), and the contents of personal Jewish identity (such as memory of the Holocaust, caring for Israel, and belief in God).

Respondents in several recent national surveys were asked to rate the importance of each item in a list of identity markers for defining their Jewish identity. The percentage indicating the strongest level of identification is analysed here. Table 17.3 summarizes responses to thirteen questions on essential components of Jewish identity. The responses were in many cases remarkably similar across countries. At the top of the list, we find "remembering the Holocaust," followed by "leading a moral and ethical life" and "combatting antisemitism." These are followed by "supporting social justice causes" (*tikun olam* in Hebrew) and feeling part of the Jewish people. Other options chosen with intermediate frequency include participating in Jewish festivals with family members and supporting Israel. Options related to observing religious traditions and law and believing in God generally command less support. The frequent consistency in the strength of Jewish identity markers across countries points to the persistence of a coherent global Jewish outlook despite different local experiences.

Beyond the ranking of options, it is important to determine whether the mutual relations between the different preferences are the same or different in various countries. This can be ascertained by creating maps of the similarity or dissimilarity between various Jewish identity markers. Here, I employ similarity structure analysis (SSA) to explore this issue (Guttman 1968; Amar and Levy 2014; DellaPergola, Keysar, and Levy 2019).

SSA computes the covariations between identity markers. The covariations are then graphically processed so that each variable appears as a point on a map. The more strongly associated two or more variables are in the minds of respondents, the closer the respective points are on the map. The opposite is true for points that appear distant from each other. Neighbouring variables with similar contents can be regrouped under broader, conceptual labels, providing a quick intuitive view of the overall structure of Jewish identity and of its internal partitions into major regions of content. These broader categories help when somewhat different though conceptually similar questions are asked in different surveys, thus permitting comparisons and easy grasping of the overall internal logic of the system.

Figure 17.1 uses the correlations between the items in table 17.3 (and occasionally several others not reported here) to provide SSA maps for eight countries, all investigated between 2013 and 2018. Insufficient data were available for Russia to allow for a similar display.

In general, points appear in a radial configuration, at the centre of which stands one variable. The central item is not necessarily the one with the highest frequency. It is the item whose overall correlation with all other items is the highest. In other words, in terms of proximity and distance it can be considered the variable around which, in the given local context, it may be possible to reach some consensus between persons otherwise separated by different appreciations of the other Jewish identity options.

Starting with Canada, in clockwise sequence from the upper-right corner of the map, we identify a region of variables related to Jewish community, family, and friends; followed by Jewish normative/ritual items; followed by ethics and social justice; memory of the Holocaust; and attention to Jewish culture. At the map's centre – between the more secular items on the left part of the map and the more traditional ones on the right – we find "caring for Israel." Such concern is shared by people with otherwise different Jewish outlooks.

All other country maps follow approximately the same circular sequence of main identification domains, with only minor differences in part caused by the lack of uniformity in the questions covered by the various surveys. We see everywhere a cluster of Jewish normative/ritual items, as well as the overlap of memory of the Holocaust and combating antisemitism.

The intriguing difference concerns the central part of the maps. In three countries (Canada, Australia, and Germany), the central region is occupied by support for Israel. In two cases (Israel and Latin America), the central spot is occupied by belonging to the Jewish people. Two

Table 17.3. Per cent stating items are a very important component of their Jewish identity, Canada and seven other countries, 2013–2018

Item	Canada 2018[a]	USA 2013[b]	Australia 2017[c]	Israel 2015[d]	UK 2018[e]	France 2018[e]	Germany 2018[e]	Latin America 2013[f]
Remembering the Holocaust	69	72	73	65	78	84	76	60
Leading a moral and ethical life	72	72	75	47	n/a	n/a	n/a	n/a
Combating antisemitism	n/a	n/a	62	n/a	68	80	71	62
Feeling part of the Jewish people worldwide	n/a	81	56	88	64	77	63	66
Sharing Jewish festivals/traditions with family	58	n/a	64	53	55	60	42	49
Supporting social justice causes	52	57	37	28	n/a	n/a	n/a	49
Supporting/caring for Israel	53	47	26	19	48	59	53	60
Belonging to a Jewish community	40	28	57	32	n/a	n/a	n/a	55
Living in Israel	n/a	n/a	n/a	33	n/a	n/a	n/a	15
Donating money to charity	80[g]	56[g]	39	7	38	34	24	35
Jewish cultural experiences/activities	14	n/a	26	n/a	33	49	39	n/a
Believing in God	62[g]	36	27	58	35	38	37	57
Observing *halacha* (Jewish law)	22	24	14	42	n/a	n/a	n/a	30

Note: n/a = not available.

[a] Source: Brym, Neuman, and Lenton (2019).
[b] Source: Pew Research Center (2013).
[c] Source: Graham and Marcus (2018).
[d] Source: Pew Research Center (2016).
[e] Source: DellaPergola and Staetsky (2021).
[f] Source: Bokser Liwerant et al. (2015).
[g] Total positive responses, not just "very important."

more countries (the UK and France) centrally display a combination of Israel and the Jewish people. The only country with a centreless configuration is the US; this is a finding of major importance because it outlines a basic difference between Jewish identity in the US and the rest of the world. Internal Jewish identity polarization in the US is not mediated by an element of shared peoplehood, of which attention to Israel is a notable manifestation. In the words of Jennifer Thompson (2014, 173), "the category of peoplehood does not exist in American culture, even though it is an important concept for Judaism."

It should be added that the Israel here portrayed as a Jewish identity marker is not necessarily the same Israel discussed above as a possible country of emigration. The symbolic and the operational constitute two separate perceptual domains.

Conclusion

In recent social scientific debate, the observation that most Jewish populations outside Israel are characterized by ongoing processes of demographic stagnation, if not erosion, has been interpreted and criticized as a deterministic affirmation (Brym, Slavina, and Lenton 2020). In reality, there is no place for determinism in socio-demographic studies that rely on empirical observation and comparison over time and space. Trends should be assessed case by case in the light of a broader conceptual framework whose elements must comprise evaluations of individual demographic perceptions and behaviours facing community, national, and global interactions, constraints, and opportunities, hence causal determinants (DellaPergola 2014). Comparative cross-national research is crucially important in the attempt to assess local situations. To the extent that several locales share similar conditions, in relation to the political, socio-economic, and cultural environment, and/or in relation to the internal composition of the Jewish community, it can be expected that parallel trends may develop.

In this chapter, selected aspects of the demography and corporate identity of Canadian Jewry were examined. The conclusion from the data presented here is that Canada has perhaps offered its Jews a more favourable and resilient setting than any other country in the Jewish diaspora. This circumstance has allowed for Jewish population growth and high retention of Jewish human capital. In Canada, a high and growing level of human development and liberal immigration policies created attractive conditions for absorbing new Jewish immigrants and for retaining the resident Jewish population. Rates of intermarriage among Jews in Canada are at the lower end of the range of diaspora

262   Sergio DellaPergola

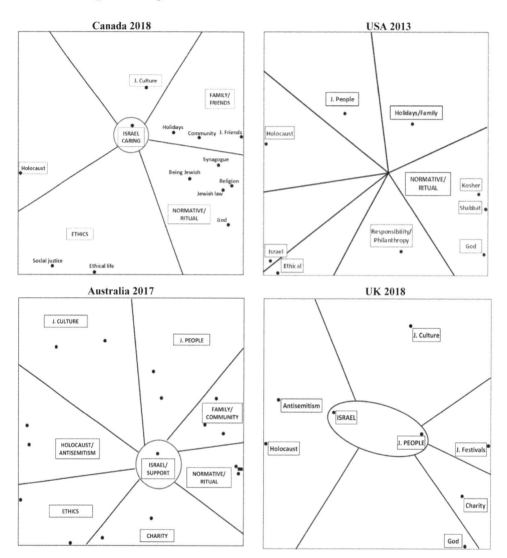

Figure 17.1. Identity maps of Jewish identity markers, Canada and seven other countries, 2013–2018

Jewish Demography and Identity in Nine Countries 263

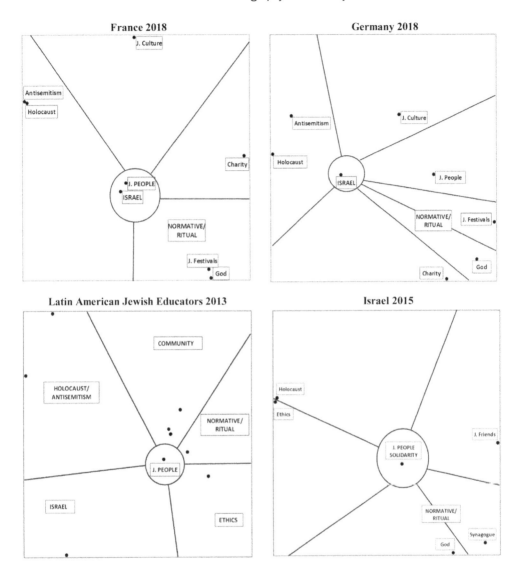

Figure 17.1. Identity maps of Jewish identity markers, Canada and selected other countries, 2013–2018 (*Continued*)

Jewry. A relatively high retention of the younger Jewish generation has preserved a population structure that is younger than in other countries with similar migration histories. The country's relatively greater sensitivity to cultural pluralism and attitude to diversity is compatible with the Jewish community maintaining its religious, ethnic, and cultural predilections and keeping more than elsewhere to a model of Jewish identification with an emphasis on caring for Israel's fate. And in relation to another variable not discussed in this chapter, the level of antisemitism in Canada is in the bottom decile of the world's countries (Anti-Defamation League 2014).

When comparing Canada and the US, it appears that the two countries and their Jewish communities share many historical experiences, but at least over the last forty years Canadian Jewry has revealed a much higher degree of Jewish identity resilience. Perhaps the most crucial difference is the much higher solvent power of US national identity at the expense of particularistic group identities. In the US, Jewish identity has tended to become subordinate to Americanness, while in Canada, full acculturation and participation of the Jews in public and civil life has not exacted the same price in terms of keeping their own distinct cultural profile. Demographic and identity patterns and trends described here make modest Jewish population increase in Canada a likely prospect, unlike the situation in many other Jewish diaspora communities.

ACKNOWLEDGMENTS

The author wishes to thank Robert Brym of the University of Toronto for providing unpublished data from the 2018 Survey of Jews in Canada. Andrew Marcus of Monash University (Melbourne) and David Mittelberg of Oranim Academic College (Kiryat Tiv'on, Israel) provided unpublished data from the 2017 Australian Jewish Community Survey. Ariela Keysar of Trinity College (Hartford, Connecticut) helped with data processing from the 2013 Pew Survey of Jewish Americans and the 2015 Pew Survey of Religion in Israel. Daniel Staetsky of the Institute of Jewish Policy Research (JPR) in London helped with data processing from the 2018 European Union Agency for Fundamental Rights (FRA) Survey on experiences and perceptions of antisemitism, discrimination, and hate crimes against Jews in the European Union. Maya Shorer Kaplan of Bar Ilan University (Ramat Gan, Israel) helped with data processing from the 2013 Survey of Transnational Jewish Educators in Latin America undertaken by the Liwerant Center for the Study of Latin America, Spain, and Portugal and their Jewish communities at the Hebrew

University of Jerusalem. Evgueny Andreev and Evgueny Soroko of the Research Institute of Goskomstat (Moscow) helped with data processing of the 1994 Microcensus of the Russian Federation. Heike von Bassewitz of the Zentralwohlfahrtsstelle der Juden in Deutschland (Frankfurt am Main) provided the data on the Jewish population in Germany. Eilat Cohen-Kastro of Israel's Central Bureau of Statistics provided unpublished data on immigration to Israel. Responsibility for the contents of this chapter is solely that of the author.

REFERENCES

Amar, Reuven, and Shlomit Levy. 2014. "SSA: Similarity Structure Analysis." In *Encyclopedia of Quality of Life and Well-Being Research*, edited by Alex C. Michalos, 6306–13. Dordrecht, Netherlands: Springer.

Anti-Defamation League. 2014. "ADL Global 100: An Index of Anti-Semitism." https://global100.adl.org/map.

Bokser Liwerant, Judit, Sergio DellaPergola, Leonardo Senkman, and Yosi Goldstein. 2015. *El educador judío latinoamericano en un mundo transnacional*. Vol. 1, *Informe de investigación*. Vol. 2, *Síntesis, conclusiones y recomendaciones del informe de investigación*. Jerusalem: Centro Liwerant para el estudio de América Latina, España, Portugal y suyas comunidades judías, Hebrew University of Jerusalem; Mexico City: Universidad Hebraica; Buenos Aires: AMIA.

Brym, Robert, Keith Neuman, and Rhonda Lenton. 2019. *2018 Survey of Canadian Jews: Final Report*. Toronto: Environics Institute for Survey Research. https://bit.ly/2PP4YA2.

Brym, Robert, William Shaffir, and Morton Weinfeld. 1993. *The Jews in Canada*. Toronto: Oxford University Press.

Brym, Robert, Anna Slavina, and Rhonda Lenton. 2020. "Qualifying the Leading Theory of Diaspora Jewry: An Examination of Jews from the Former Soviet Union in Canada and the United States." *Contemporary Jewry* 40 (3): 367–85. https://doi.org/10.1007/s12397-020-09315-5.

DellaPergola, Sergio. 2009. "International Migration of Jews." In *Transnationalism: Diasporas and the Advent of a New (Dis)order*, edited by Eliezer Ben-Rafael and Yitzhak Sternberg, 213–36. Leiden: Brill.

DellaPergola, Sergio. 2013. "National Uniqueness and Transnational Parallelism: Reflections on the Comparative Study of Jewish Communities in Latin America." In *Judaica Latinoamericana: Estudios históricos, sociales y literarios*, Vol. 7, edited by Margalit Bejarano, Florinda Goldberg, and Efraim Zadoff, 73–100. Jerusalem: AMILAT.

DellaPergola, Sergio. 2014. "Jewish Demography: Fundamentals of the Research Field." In *The Social Scientific Study of Jewry: Sources, Approaches, Debates*, edited by Uzi Rebhun, 3–6. New York: Oxford University Press.

DellaPergola, Sergio. 2020. *Diaspora vs. Homeland: Development, Unemployment and Ethnic Migration to Israel, 1991–2019*. Jerusalem: Avraham Harman Institute of Contemporary Jewry, Hebrew University of Jerusalem.

DellaPergola, Sergio. 2021. "World Jewish Population, 2020." In *American Jewish Year Book 2020*, Vol. 120, edited by Arnold Dashefsky and Ira M. Sheskin, 273–370. Cham, Switzerland: Springer.

DellaPergola, Sergio, Ariela Keysar, and Shlomit Levy. 2019. "Jewish Identification Differentials in Israel and in the United States: Similarity Structure Analysis." *Contemporary Jewry* 39 (1): 55–90. https://doi.org/10.1007/s12397-019-09283-5.

DellaPergola, Sergio, and L. Daniel Staetsky. 2021. *The Jewish Identities of European Jews: What, Why and How*. London: Institute for Jewish Policy Research. http://bitly.ws/sF3g.

Graham, David, and Andrew Markus. 2018. *Gen17 Australian Jewish Community Survey: Preliminary Findings*. Melbourne: Australian Centre for Jewish Civilisation and JCA. http://bitly.ws/sF3d.

Guttman, Louis. 1968. "A General Nonmetric Technique for Finding the Smallest Coordinate Space for a Configuration of Points." *Psychometrika* 33: 469–506. https://doi.org/10.1007/BF02290164.

Israel Central Bureau of Statistics. 2020. "Population: Statistical Abstract of Israel 2020 – No. 71." http://bitly.ws/sMyN.

Pew Research Center. 2013. *A Portrait of Jewish Americans: Findings from a Pew Research Center Survey of U.S. Jews*. Washington, DC: Pew Research Center. http://bitly.ws/sF3K.

Pew Research Center. 2016. *Israel's Religiously Divided Society*. Washington, DC: Pew Research Center. http://bitly.ws/sF3Q.

Pew Research Center. 2021. *Jewish Americans in 2020*. Washington, DC: Pew Research Center. http://bitly.ws/sF49.

Shahar, Charles. 2019. "Canadian Jewish Population, 2018." In *American Jewish Year Book 2018*, Vol. 118, edited by Arnold Dashefsky and Ira M. Sheskin, 349–60. Cham, Switzerland: Springer.

Thompson, Jennifer A. 2014. *Jewish on Their Own Terms: How Intermarried Couples Are Changing American Judaism*. New Brunswick, NJ: Rutgers University Press.

United Nations Development Programme. 2020. *Human Development Report 2020: The Next Frontier: Human Development and the Anthropocene*. New York: United Nations Development Programme.

Weinfeld, Morton, with Randal Schnoor and Michelle Shames. 2018. *Like Everyone Else but Different: The Paradoxical Success of Canadian Jews*. 2nd ed. Montreal: McGill-Queen's University Press.

18 Intermarriage in Canada and the United States: Déjà Vu or Different?

FERN CHERTOK AND MATTHEW A. BROOKNER

The Complexity of Intermarriage

On 6 June 1963, the Jewish Telegraphic Agency reported that, according to a study by the Canadian Jewish Congress, the rate of intermarriage of Canadian Jews had increased "alarmingly" from 3.8 per cent to 18.5 per cent between 1931 and 1963 (Jewish Telegraphic Agency 1963). The report concluded that connections among Canadian Jews were weakening and the continued upward climb of the rate of intermarriage would soon endanger the vitality of the Canadian Jewish community. A year later, the American popular magazine *Look* featured an infamous cover story titled "The Vanishing American Jew," raising concerns about the "soaring" rate of marriages between Jews and non-Jews and the potential loss of up to 70 per cent of children born to intermarried couples (Morgan 1964).

In the early 1960s, the rates of intermarriage in both Canada and the US were similar and already cause for communal concern. In the following decades, these demographic trends have continued to rise in both countries, but have also diverged. The 2018 Survey of Jews in Canada indicated that 21 per cent of Jewish adults in Canada were married to or partnered with a non-Jew (Brym, Neuman, and Lenton 2019), less than half the 47 per cent rate of intermarriage reported for the US Jewish community five years earlier (Pew Research Center 2013). One common refrain is that the Jewish intermarriage rate in Canada is just a generation behind the rate in the United States and will inevitably match US levels. Looking at intermarriage across generations within Canada supports this perspective. For example, Shahar and Schnoor (2015) note that in the Greater Toronto Area, the intermarriage rate is higher among young Jews, and approximately 35 per cent of recently married Jews have a non-Jewish spouse.

However, intermarriage rates in Canada and the US do not capture the entirety of this comparative story. Multiple factors influence the rate of marriage between Jews and non-Jews, as well as the ensuing connections of interfaith couples and their children to Jewish life and identity. For example, research in both countries indicates that access to formal and informal Jewish education and home practice can substantially minimize the Jewish identity gap between children with one or two Jewish parents. Canadian adult children of intermarriage who experience full-time Jewish schooling have the same likelihood of marrying a Jewish partner as peers raised by two Jewish parents (Brym and Lenton 2020). Among US Reform Jews, children of in-marriage and children of intermarriage who had similar experiences of Jewish home ritual, education, and social networks were found to have grown up to look very much alike Jewishly (Chertok, Phillips, and Saxe 2008). Research on American young adults found that children of intermarriage who had Jewish experiences – even as late as college – were more likely to identify as Jewish and participate in Jewish community life as compared with peers with intermarried parents but without such formative experiences (Sasson et al. 2015).

This chapter explores the communal experiences and patterns of Jewish engagement of Canadian and American couples where one partner is Jewish and the other is from another background.[1] Our discussion is premised on the assumption that the trajectories of intermarried families are embedded within and influenced by multiple environmental levels including immediate and extended family and the larger social and national context (Bronfenbrenner 1977; Hartman 2020). Of the myriad factors at each level, we focus on a set of influences the significance of which emerged from our research. Looking at the family, we explore how couples think about religious identity, their connections with extended family, and their preferences for communal engagement. Looking at the broader cultural context we discuss similarities and differences in the Canadian and US Jewish communities regarding Jewish identity and patrilineal descent, access to Jewish education, and the movement of young families out of historically Jewish neighbourhoods. Some factors we discuss pertain mainly to the likelihood of Jews selecting partners from other religious backgrounds. Other factors relate to how interfaith couples connect to Jewish identity and life and raise their own children. Many social forces influence both outcomes. Our examination of intermarriage in Canada and the US considers how trajectories of intermarriage in the two national contexts differ and how they are similar.

Our comparative analysis weaves together data from multiple sources to understand how interfaith couples in Canada and the US navigate

Table 18.1. Data collection by city

Target area	Couples interviewed	% married	% with children in home	Couples surveyed*	Interview period
Boston	32	88	47	n/a	Nov. 2018–Feb. 2019
Pittsburgh	29	86	62	n/a	Mar. 2019–Jun. 2019
Toronto	40	55	50	436	Oct. 2019–Feb. 2020

*An online survey was conducted in Toronto only.

their religious backgrounds and think about decisions regarding participation in Jewish life and the religious upbringing of children. We draw on our research with young interfaith couples in Toronto, Boston, and Pittsburgh. In each of these three cities, we focused on committed couples with one Jewish and one non-Jewish partner. Couples eligible to participate in our research had children no older than early primary school age or had no children. As table 18.1 shows, across the three cities we interviewed more than 100 couples. Interviews were conducted in person, over the phone, and online. In Toronto, we also conducted an online survey of young interfaith couples.[2] This chapter also draws on data reported in the 2018 Survey of Jews in Canada and the 2013 Pew Survey of US Jews (Brym, Neuman, and Lenton 2019; Pew Research Center 2013). We limit our comparison of results from these surveys to variables with equivalent, or near-equivalent, wording and response options.

Divergence

In this section, we discuss how the differing socio-cultural contexts of Canada and the US may influence interfaith couples' experiences of Jewish life. We focus on the two countries' historical and current approaches to the preservation of distinctive cultural groups, the accessibility of Jewish educational experiences, the determination of Jewish identity, and the propensity to live near family members.

The National Context of Intermarriage: Multiculturalism or Melting Pot?

Conventional sociological wisdom is that "unmarried people do not just wander around a region looking for a spouse" (Kalmijn 1998, 403). Instead, people find partners in the same settings where they already live – in schools, workplaces, and friendship groups. Even with the rise of internet dating, local "marriage markets" remain powerful determinants of which potential partners will have contact with each other.

In the first half of the twentieth century, significant barriers prevented the full integration of Jews into Canadian and American societies. Absent conversion, non-Jewish marriage markets were largely closed to Jews. Explicit and implicit restrictions limited options in housing and professional employment, and Jews were disqualified from entry to many institutions of higher education (Kolko 2003; chapters 4 and 16 in this volume). This picture changed dramatically in the aftermath of the Second World War (Sarna 2004). With their full entry over the last half century into communities, campuses, and the workplace, unmarried Jews in Canada and the US now have access to more diverse marriage markets than ever before. The rise in intermarriage rates in both countries over the last few decades is an expected result.

Proximity is not the only factor at play in the selection of a partner. The stronger the sense of belonging to a distinctive group, the more likely it is that members will marry within that group. A potent sense of group identification has the potential to counter the pull of increasing social integration. Group ties affect not only the selection of a partner but also the salience collective identity has in the families and homes that people create.

The national contexts of Canada and the US are markedly different with regard to the emphasis placed on collective group identity. Codified in the Canadian Constitution is the value of multiculturalism and emphasis on the importance of the survival of distinctive ethnic groups and their cultures. By contrast, the American approach, typically referred to as the "melting pot," focuses on the assimilation of diverse cultural and religious groups into a homogenized "American" identity and national culture (Barrett 1992). The differing approaches to culturally distinctive groups combined with a historically less complete separation of church and state in Canada has important implications for the maintenance of the collective group identity of Jewish citizens. As noted by Morton Weinfeld (1987, 1), in Canada "the state has become an ally of the community in both the struggle against anti-Semitism and in the struggle to prevent cultural assimilation."

Using data from the 2018 Survey of Jews in Canada and the 2013 Pew Survey of US Jews, we compared indicators of connection to the Jewish community of intermarried couples in the US and Canada. As shown in table 18.2, intermarried Jews are less involved in Jewish life than their in-married counterparts in both countries. This echoes research findings that on a variety of indices of communal, religious, and cultural Jewish engagement, American interfaith couples are less involved than their in-married peers (Shain et al. 2019; Sasson et al. 2015).

Table 18.2. Indicators of Jewish communal connection in Canada and the US, in per cent

	Intermarried Jews, Canada (n = 239)	Intermarried Jews, US (n = 749)	In-married Jews, Canada (n = 1,361)	In-married Jews, US (n = 1,565)
Raising at least one child Jewish*	68[b]	62[c]	98[b]	98[c]
Attended services in past year	63[b]	62[c]	92[b]	92[c]
Lit Shabbat candles in past year	36[b]	25[c]	83[b]	72[c]
Household belongs to a synagogue	25[b]	16[c]	70[b]	68[c]
Household belongs to a non-synagogue Jewish organization	26[a,b]	12[a,c]	55[b]	49[c]
Donated to Jewish organization	54[a,b]	40[a,c]	91[b]	87[c]
Importance of being Jewish in your life (very important)	40[b]	31[c]	73[b]	68[c]

* This row excludes non-parents.
[a] Confidence intervals do not overlap between intermarried Jews in both countries.
[b] Confidence intervals do not overlap between intermarried and in-married Jews in Canada.
[c] Confidence intervals do not overlap between intermarried and in-married Jews in the US.

However, marked differences exist between US and Canadian intermarried couples. A larger portion of intermarried Canadians than intermarried Americans participate in each type of communal engagement measured. We found statistically significant differences for involvement with Jewish organizations, with 26 per cent of Canadian intermarried couples vs. 12 per cent of US peers belonging to non-synagogue organizations, and 54 per cent vs. 40 per cent donating to Jewish organizations. At the same time, intermarried Jews in both countries attended services, lit Shabbat candles, and belonged to synagogues at similar rates.

Access to Jewish Ethnic and Religious Capital-Building Experiences

Research has repeatedly shown that Jews in the US who intermarry have less intense Jewish upbringings than those who marry other Jews: they have fewer years of Jewish education and come from households with fewer Jewish practices (Phillips 1997). Intermarried Jews are thus less likely to have accumulated "Jewish ethnic and religious capital."

Ethnic capital refers to "an individual's knowledge of and skill at the cultural practices of a given ethnicity" (Phillips and Fishman 2006, 488) while religious capital consists of knowing the content and choreography of religious rituals (Stark and Finke 2000; chapter 22 in this volume).

One of the implications of differences in national policy is that Jewish day schools receive significant public funding in Quebec, Manitoba, Alberta, and British Columbia, where 41 per cent of Canada's Jewish population reside (see chapter 5 in this volume). In addition, the federal government supports other types of Jewish ethnic and religious capital-building organizations nationwide (Weinfeld 1987). This type of government support is not available to Jewish organizations in the US, making their services and programs more expensive to access. Thus, our comparison of intermarried couples in the two countries showed that a larger share of intermarried Jews in Canada as compared with those in the US attended Jewish day schools and Jewish summer camps and were more likely to be *b'nai mitzvah* (see table 18.3). In fact, on these indicators, intermarried Jews in Canada have Jewish backgrounds that are similar to the backgrounds of in-married Jews in the US. A significantly greater portion of Canadian as compared with American intermarried Jews also come from households with two Jewish parents and the exposure to Jewish home life that implies.

Access to opportunities to build Jewish ethnic and religious capital, or lack thereof, has implications for the Jewish engagement of intermarried couples. Those with a history of formal and informal Jewish education bring a storehouse of memories, knowledge, and skills into their marriage, regardless of whom they marry. They can be expected to have a positive orientation towards providing their own children with similar Jewish ethnic and religious capital-building experiences and, in Canada, these decisions will often be subsidized by the government. Intermarried Jews without a history of ethnic and religious capital-building may be disinclined to engage in Jewish events or settings because they feel uncomfortable doing so. In a circular path of reinforcement, their Jewish identity can be further diminished (Osherson 2001).

Who Is a Jew? The Question of Patrilineal Descent

Perhaps the key difference between communal responses to intermarriage in the two countries concerns the definition of who is a Jew. Traditional interpretation of Jewish religious law defines a Jew as a person with a Jewish mother. However, in the US, the Reform and Reconstructionist movements have had a policy for more than four decades of

Table 18.3. Jewish ethnic and religious capital-building in Canada and the US, in per cent

	Intermarried Jews, Canada ($n = 239$)	Intermarried Jews, US ($n = 749$)	In-married Jews, Canada ($n = 1,361$)	In-married Jews, US ($n = 1,565$)
Attended day school in childhood	38[a]	16[a,c]	46	31[c]
Attended Jewish camp in childhood	50[a,b]	29[a,c]	61[b]	52[c]
B'nai mitzvah as a child	63[a]	44[a,c]	58	63[c]
Parents in-married	81[a,b]	67[a,c]	96[b]	94[c]

[a] Confidence intervals do not overlap between intermarried Jews in both countries.
[b] Confidence intervals do not overlap between intermarried and in-married Jews in Canada.
[c] Confidence intervals do not overlap between intermarried and in-married Jews in the US.

accepting people as Jews if they have a Jewish father and a non-Jewish mother. Moreover, people in the US who do not want their non-Jewish spouse or their offspring to go through a conversion process have the option of belonging to a liberal denomination and having their children educated in it. In contrast, few Canadian rabbis and synagogues accept that patrilineal descent is sufficient to determine Jewishness. These policies typically reflect the boundaries and understandings of Jewish law established by the national bodies of denominational movements and central rabbinic governing bodies. Although there has been some evolution in Jewish communal policy in Canada, the implication for most intermarried families is that unless the mother is Jewish, children are unlikely to be accepted as Jewish and have access to Jewish education.

Toronto interfaith parents we spoke with expressed concern about the Jewish status and acceptance of their children. Some grappled with the implications of the matrilineal descent rule and the requirement it implies for child conversion, including circumcision. Families with non-Jewish mothers worried their children would be viewed as "not Jewish" by Jewish peers and institutions and would not be accepted by synagogues. As one Toronto Jewish father remarked:

I feel like [child's name] is fully Jewish, but I know Judaism puts a lot of value on the mother being Jewish. So that's a fear that I have that [child's name] won't be fully included by other Jews. That's something that makes me sad because I want [child's name] to feel like he's Jewish if he wants to be, and not feel like the community's stopping him from feeling fully Jewish.

Many interfaith couples in Toronto described pressure from family, friends, and religious leaders for the non-Jewish partner to convert to Judaism, especially when the partner was female. Although some couples in the US reported attempts to influence the non-Jewish partner to convert, this was less pronounced and common than in Canada. Pressure to convert from religious leaders in the community felt unwelcoming and intrusive to these couples and pushed some away from Jewish involvement. One intermarried Torontonian noted that

> [the] *shul* that we belong to, I loved it there until [non-Jewish partner's name] started coming to events with me. There was just this huge pressure on him. At one point the rabbi was probing him about converting and trying to convince him to do conversion classes, and he was so upset. Then we weren't engaged [there anymore].

The non-Jewish partners we interviewed in Toronto described their focus on maintaining their personal values in the face of conversion pressures on the part of Jewish religious leaders, family, or the broader community. For many, this was a matter of "authenticity" and respect for their own identity and choices. They viewed conversion as a serious religious act, which did not align with their personal, often secular, views. An intermarried non-Jewish partner from Toronto put it this way: "I feel that it's just disingenuous to convert if I don't necessarily believe in a higher spiritual power that way. Because you're not converting to the culture you're converting to the religion." And in the words of an intermarried non-Jewish partner from Boston:

> Some people just convert and they don't know what their responsibilities are. It's all wonderful that you feel welcomed by this particular community that you're about to join. There are a lot of aspects that one should think about before making this decision because it doesn't come just with the gifts of community. It also comes with responsibility ... towards yourself and towards others.

Access to Local Family

Our research suggests that in both the Canadian and American contexts, local extended family members often served as portals into Jewish life (Chertok, Brookner, and Minkin 2019; Chertok et al. 2020). Young intermarried couples described how family members "curated" Jewish programming options, alerting them to opportunities that might be particularly attractive. In each of the cities we studied, ties from extended families to local Jewish communities made it easier for intermarried couples to know about and access local Jewish resources, including participation in synagogue programming, before they became members. Here is what a respondent from Pittsburgh said: "We've benefited in a lot of ways from the fact that my siblings are here and they're engaged, my parents are here and they're engaged. We have a big social network here that is largely engaged in the Jewish communities."

Having family nearby also increased opportunities to engage in Jewish home rituals and celebrations. A non-Jewish husband in Pittsburgh described how meaningful it was to help his Jewish mother-in-law prepare the Passover Seder; a respondent in Boston emphasized that, despite not being very observant, family meals for Jewish holidays, especially Passover, were routine; and a respondent from Toronto remarked that "now that we're back in Toronto and see my family more regularly, [Jewish living] fits into our life more easily."

Just as the presence of local Jewish family enhanced the Jewish connections and activities of interfaith households, couples without local ties experienced less access to Jewish life. For example, according to our survey data, Toronto couples who did not have local Jewish family were less likely to celebrate Passover or the High Holidays than were peers who had local family connections. As one Toronto respondent lamented, "We don't have our extended families around us and it would be really meaningful and feel very welcoming if we were to be invited to celebrate Passover somewhere so that we could learn how to do this."

One relevant differences between US and Canadian societies is the lower rate of residential mobility in the latter. According to the 2006 Canadian census, 4 per cent of households moved to a new census metropolitan area in the previous five years as compared with 11.4 per cent who made similar moves in the US (Molloy, Smith, and Wozniak 2011; Pendakur and Young 2013). Living near extended families contributes positively to the Jewish engagement of intermarried families in both countries, but in Canada couples are, overall, more likely to be living in the same geographic area as their immediate relatives. One of the striking features of the couples we spoke with in Toronto was the high proportion who had ties to their local Jewish families. Fully 78 per cent of surveyed couples with local Jewish families reported seeing them frequently.

Convergence

We turn now to similar influences on interfaith experience among Jews in Canada and the US. We limit our discussion to young couples' need for community, their deeper interest in cultural over religious

Searching for Community, Not Membership

People strive for a sense of community, the experience "that one is part of a readily available, mutually supportive network of relationships upon which one [can] depend and as a result of which one [does] not experience sustained … loneliness" (Sarason 1974). Many of the young couples we spoke with, in both Canada and the US, were looking for Jewish peers with whom they could feel a sense of community. Both the Jewish and non-Jewish partners we interviewed often mentioned the strong sense of community among Jews as one of the most attractive features of Jewish living. "A community, where you can build relationships with people. That to me is being Jewish," said one respondent in Boston. That sentiment was echoed in Pittsburgh: "For us it wasn't about religion, but just being in an environment, in a community, where we know that there are like-minded people, we know that we are going to be welcomed with open arms." Views were not different in Toronto: "A lot of my closest friends are Jewish. It's more about community and celebrating holidays and things like that. That's what Judaism is for me."

Jewish and non-Jewish partners in both countries often mentioned wanting their children to feel embedded in a community and to have family and friends with whom they could share the experience of Jewish home celebrations. What one Toronto partner in an intermarriage told us was echoed in Boston and Pittsburgh: "We both want an understanding of the Jewish religion, history, and traditions, but are more interested in the community. We both grew up with a strong sense of family and community, which is what we want to pass on to our family."

Many of the couples we interviewed, across cities and national borders, described being warmly welcomed by Jewish institutions. However, some couples in both countries felt an undercurrent of disapproval rather than acceptance as integral and valued members of the community. For example, some couples were offended by language that suggested intermarriage is a "challenge" to the Jewish community. They did not see themselves as a problem and wanted to be known for who they were and not for what they were not. "The language at synagogues and in denominations isn't necessarily welcoming," remarked a Boston respondent, and a Jewish respondent in Toronto told us the following: "A rabbi said to me that when interfaith families come into Jewish spaces, they're there for the Jewish part and not to have any other part of them acknowledged, so they hang it up when they come in. I just don't see how that's possible."

In some instances, the authenticity of the welcome seemed to fade over time. Some couples recounted being regularly welcomed when they first attended synagogue activities but never really progressing to the point where they felt they belonged in the community. Interfaith couples, especially non-Jewish partners, wanted to be seen as valuable members in their own right rather than as a means for ensuring Jewish continuity. Some commented that there was much curiosity about how they were raising their children but little concern with them as individuals with their own talents, interests, and needs. "It feels like they only want me for our kids. 'We'll be nice to you so your children will be Jewish – we don't condone it, but we want your kids.'" That was now a non-Jewish partner in Boston felt.

Identifying with Culture, Not Religion

Intermarried families do not live in a hermetically sealed cultural bubble. Similar changes in the social and cultural contexts of Canada and the US influence and perhaps truncate the relationship of intermarried couples with Jewish identity and engagement. Most notable among these social trends is the receding salience of institutionalized religious engagement among contemporary young adults (Chaves 2017; Bibby 2019, 173–200; chapter 13 in this volume). Millennials and members of Generation Z appear less connected with the institutions that sustained previous generations. The proportion of Canadians who say they have no religion or are religiously unaffiliated has risen from 4 per cent in 1971 to 29 per cent in 2019 (Lipka 2019). The same trend is seen in the US with a growing number of adults describing themselves as atheists, agnostics, or "nothing in particular" religiously (Pew Research Center 2015).

Jewish young adults pulling away from conventional institutions, including those related to religious life (Levine 2015; Pew Research Center 2014), are using culture and tradition instead of religion as ways to express their Jewish identity (Kelman et al. 2017). They are comfortable and proud to be Jewish but increasingly disconnected from institutionalized religious Judaism.

Much like their generational peers, many of the couples we interviewed in Canada and the US described themselves as "cultural" Jews. The religious aspects of Judaism were, at best, peripheral to their lives. Jewish partners often told us that, for them, Judaism was a source of pride and meaning because it connected them with their family's heritage. In Toronto we heard that "the word religion is what trips me up because the religious aspect of it I still struggle with. But the identity aspects, the cultural aspects … it's a huge part of my life right now." This sentiment was echoed in Boston: "I feel like both of us want the family and the connection and everything that we had growing up absent the religion."

In many cases, individuals we spoke with told us they chose partners whose stance on religion in general was similar to theirs even though the partner had a different religious background. Couples in both the US and Canada talked about how similar they were to each other in terms of the relevance, or more frequently the lack of relevance, of religion in their lives and the values they wanted to impart to their families. As a respondent from Boston said: "Going into our first date, we already knew that neither of us were particularly religious in any way. … I think if one of us had been really observant and the other one wasn't, that probably would have been a challenge to overcome."

Many of the intermarried parents we interviewed talked about wanting to give their children a sense of membership in the Jewish people and provide them with the cultural knowledge to feel at home with members of the "tribe." For some couples, this meant providing their children with religious education and the experience of home rituals. However, even parents who did not plan to involve their children in Jewish worship or religious practice wanted them to have a strong and unequivocal cultural Jewish identity. We heard this in Pittsburgh, and similar sentiments in Boston and Toronto: "I look back at my childhood and see the things that I did … Seders or dinners at Rosh Hashanah. To me there's more than just a religious aspect to it, it is a family communal thing, and I don't want to deprive my children of that."

Changing Residential Patterns: Moving to the Suburbs

Each of the communities we studied has a historic Jewish core area (the Bathurst corridor in Toronto, Squirrel Hill in Pittsburgh, and Brookline and Newton in the Boston area). However, rising prices for housing in these areas means that young couples, including those that are intermarried, are increasingly moving to other, more affordable urban and suburban areas. In each of the communities we studied, the location of programs was an inhibiting factor for people who lived outside the historic Jewish core area. Interfaith families that had moved to suburban areas recounted challenges in locating Jewish neighbours or finding local options for engaging in Jewish life. "There's a real physical barrier for me getting to things these days because it just takes so long to get there and, at the end of the week, I'm tired and I don't want to go," remarked one Toronto respondent. Another Torontonian remarked that "most of the stuff is happening in [the Jewish core neighbourhood], and I'm not willing to trek with young children all the way out there for a program. Even if I know they're going to have a great time."

Summary and Conclusions

The title of this chapter poses a false dichotomy. The Canadian experience of Jewish intermarriage compared to intermarriage in the US is less a case of "déjà vu *or* different" than a case of "déjà vu *and* different." That is, Jewish intermarriage in Canada is different from Jewish marriage in the US in some respects, and similar in other respects. It seems that Canadian values and policies regarding support for ethnic and religious groups, and the propensity to live near extended family, positively influence the salience of Jewish identity and the accessibility of Jewish experiences, factors demonstrated to affect the likelihood of intermarriage and Jewish engagement of children raised by intermarried parents. Intermarried Jews in Canada have much higher rates of formal and informal childhood Jewish education. Strikingly, intermarried Canadian Jews have Jewish backgrounds more in line with in-married rather than intermarried Jews in the US. At the same time, Jewish communal approaches to defining Jewish identity and patrilineal descent in Canada might serve to limit the engagement of interfaith families. Without the acceptance of patrilineal descent by at least one of the major Jewish denominations in Canada, it is difficult – though certainly not impossible – for interfaith couples to maintain deep connections to Jewish communal life. In both countries, we noted that the movement of young families out of historically Jewish neighbourhoods coupled with their desire for a sense of community and preference for cultural rather than religious ways of expressing their Jewish identity are influencing their Jewish choices.

The value of comparing Jewish communities in different countries, particularly Canada and the US, seems clear. Jewish communities are embedded in larger socio-cultural frameworks. One of the advantages of cross-country comparison is that it illuminates the role played by national context (see chapter 19 in this volume). Research on intermarriage typically focuses on the intimate partners as the unit of interest – their backgrounds, preferences, choices, and community participation. While important, such a narrow, individual-level focus obscures the role played by ecological systems including the extended family and the local and national landscape of opportunities for Jewish involvement. The lesson of this exploration may be that although the intermarriage rate in the US and Canada may continue to converge or diverge, the experiences of intermarried couples will certainly continue to reflect the communal and national contexts in which they take place.

NOTES

1 Throughout this chapter, we refer to legally married and cohabitating couples jointly as being "intermarried." We also count as Jews not only those whose religion is Judaism but also those who consider themselves Jewish or partially Jewish aside from religion and who have Jewish backgrounds.
2 Survey recruitment included two sources: the local PJ Library contact list and the Canada Israel Experience (CIE) database of Birthright Israel participants. Although the sample may not be fully representative of all interfaith couples in Toronto, it includes all levels of involvement in organized Jewish life, both parents and non-parents, and people across multiple life stages. The experiences of these respondents therefore provide context to the circumstances of the larger population of interfaith couples in the Toronto area.

REFERENCES

Barrett, James R. 1992. "Americanization from the Bottom Up: Immigration and the Remaking of the Working Class in the United States, 1880–1930." *The Journal of American History* 79 (3): 996–1020. https://doi.org/10.2307/2080796.
Bibby, Reginald W. 2019. *The Millennial Mosaic: How Pluralism and Choice Are Shaping Canadian Youth and the Future of Canada.* Toronto: Dundurn.
Bronfenbrenner, Urie. 1977. "Toward an Experimental Ecology of Human Development." *American Psychologist* 32 (7): 513–31. https://doi.org/10.1037/0003-066X.32.7.513.
Brym, Robert, and Rhonda Lenton. 2020. "Jewish Religious Intermarriage in Canada." *Canadian Jewish Studies* 30 (2): 67–82. https://doi.org/10.25071/1916-0925.40184.
Brym, Robert, Keith Neuman, and Rhonda Lenton. 2019. *2018 Survey of Jews in Canada: Final Report.* Toronto: Environics Institute for Survey Research. https://bit.ly/2W6Fuoj.
Chaves, Mark. 2017. *American Religion: Contemporary Trends.* 2nd ed. Princeton, NJ: Princeton University Press.
Chertok, Fern, Matthew A. Brookner, and Rachel Minkin. 2019. *We'll Cross That Bridge When We Come to It: Life Stage and the Needs of Interfaith Couples*

in Greater Boston. Waltham, MA: Maurice and Marilyn Cohen Center for Modern Jewish Studies, Brandeis University. http://bitly.ws/sFna.

Chertok, Fern, Matthew A. Brookner, Rachel Minkin, and Tzvi Glazer. 2020. *Swimming Upstream: Interfaith Families in Greater Toronto*. Waltham, MA: Maurice and Marilyn Cohen Center for Modern Jewish Studies, Brandeis University. http://bitly.ws/sFn5.

Chertok, Fern, Benjamin Phillips, and Leonard Saxe. 2008. *It's Not Just Who Stands under the Chuppah: Intermarriage and Engagement*. Waltham, MA: Maurice and Marilyn Cohen Center for Modern Jewish Studies, Brandeis University. https://hdl.handle.net/10192/23017.

Hartman, Harriet. 2020. "The 2019 Sklare Address: How Gender and Family Still Matter for Contemporary Jewry." *Contemporary Jewry* 40 (2): 161–85. https://doi.org/10.1007/s12397-020-09338-y.

Jewish Telegraphic Agency. 1963. "Large Rise in Intermarriage of Jews in Canada Reported; Data Given." *Daily News Bulletin*, 6 June 1963. http://bitly.ws/sFnC.

Kalmijn, Matthijs. 1998. "Intermarriage and Homogamy: Causes, Patterns, Trends." *Annual Review of Sociology* 24: 395–417. https://doi.org/10.1146/annurev.soc.24.1.395.

Kelman, Ari Y., Tobin Belzer, Ilana Horwitz, Ziva Hassenfeld, and Matt Williams. 2017. "Traditional Judaism: The Conceptualization of Jewishness in the Lives of American Jewish Post-Boomers." *Jewish Social Studies* 23 (1): 134–67. https://doi.org/10.2979/jewisocistud.23.1.05.

Kolko, Valerie B. 2003. "A History of Jews in American Higher Education." *Journal of the Indiana University Student Personnel Association* (2003): 20–32. http://bitly.ws/sMyZ.

Levine, Peter. 2015. "Talking about This Generation: The Millennials and Politics." *Extensions* (Summer): 4–9. http://bitly.ws/xKN6.

Lipka, Michael. 2019. "5 Facts about Religion in Canada." Pew Research Center, 1 July 2019. http://bitly.ws/sMz7.

Molloy, Raven, Christopher L. Smith, and Abigail Wozniak. 2011. "Internal Migration in the United States." *Journal of Economic Perspectives* 25 (3) 173–96. https://doi.org/10.1257/jep.25.3.173.

Morgan, Thomas. 1964. "The Vanishing American Jew." *Look* 28 (May): 42–6.

Osherson, Samuel. 2001. *Rekindling the Flame: The Many Paths to a Vibrant Judaism*. New York: Harcourt.

Pendakur, Ravi, and Nathan Young. 2013. "Putting on the Moves: Individual, Household, and Community-Level Determinants of Residential Mobility in Canada." *Demographic Research* 29: 767–96. https://doi.org/10.4054/DemRes.2013.29.28.

Pew Research Center. 2013. *A Portrait of Jewish Americans: Findings from a Pew Research Center Survey of U.S. Jews*. Washington, DC: Pew Research Center. http://bitly.ws/sF3K.

Pew Research Center. 2014. *Millennials in Adulthood: Detached from Institutions, Networked with Friends*. Washington, DC: Pew Research Center. http://bitly.ws/sFt2.

Pew Research Center. 2015. *America's Changing Religious Landscape*. Washington, DC: Pew Research Center. http://bitly.ws/sFt5.

Phillips, Benjamin T., and Sylvia B. Fishman. 2006. "Ethnic Capital and Intermarriage: A Case Study of American Jews." *Sociology of Religion* 67 (4): 487–505. https://doi.org/10.1093/socrel/67.4.487.

Phillips, Bruce A. 1997. *Re-examining Intermarriage: Trends, Textures and Strategies*. New York: Susan and David Wilstein Institute of Jewish Policy Studies and American Jewish Committee.

Sarason, Seymour. 1974. *The Psychological Sense of Community: Prospects for a Community Psychology*. San Francisco: Jossey-Bass Publishers.

Sarna, Jonathan D. 2004. *American Judaism: A History*. New Haven, CT: Yale University Press.

Sasson, Theodore, Leonard Saxe, Fern Chertok, Michelle Shain, Shahar Hecht, and Graham Wright. 2015. *Millennial Children of Intermarriage: Touchstones and Trajectories*. Waltham, MA: Maurice and Marilyn Cohen Center for Modern Jewish Studies, Brandeis University.

Shahar, Charles, and Randal Schnoor. 2015. *2011 National Household Survey: The Jewish Community of Toronto*. Part 5, *The Jewish Family*. Part 6, *Intermarriage*. Toronto: Jewish Federations of Canada – UJA. http://bitly.ws/sFum.

Shain, Michelle, Leonard Saxe, Fern Chertok, Graham Wright, Shahar Hecht, and Theodore Sasson. 2019. *Beyond Welcoming: Engaging Intermarried Couples in Jewish Life*. Waltham, MA: Maurice and Marilyn Cohen Center for Modern Jewish Studies, Brandeis University.

Stark, Rodney, and Roger Finke. 2000. *Acts of Faith: Explaining the Human Side of Religion*. Berkeley: University of California Press.

Weinfeld, Morton. 1987. "Canadian Cultural Pluralism and Its Implications for the Jewish Community." *Shofar* 5 (2): 1–7. https://www.jstor.org/stable/42940853.

19 Qualifying the Leading Theory of Diaspora Jewry: Jews from the Former Soviet Union in Canada and the United States[1]

ROBERT BRYM, ANNA SLAVINA, AND RHONDA LENTON

The Leading Theory of the Jewish Diaspora

The leading theory of the Jewish diaspora claims that Jewish communities outside Israel are shrinking due to a low birth rate; an aging population; a high and rising intermarriage rate; and out-migration to Israel, though much moderated in recent decades. Due to these factors, the population of the Jewish diaspora stood at 10.5 million in the middle of the twentieth century and declined to 8.2 million in 2000. According to DellaPergola, Rebhun, and Tolts (2000), the Jewish diaspora population can be expected to fall to just 5 million by 2080, with no Jews left in the former Soviet Union (FSU) by that date.

Gitelman (1998, 2013) is among the leading proponents of this theory. He argues that nationalism and religion are the only enduring bases for Jewish existence, so diaspora Jews who are neither ardent Zionists nor religiously observant are bound to diminish in number and find the strength of their Jewish identity weakening. The results of multiple surveys in various countries add weight to his claim. For example, surveys conducted in Russia, Ukraine, and Belarus show that Jews who do not plan on emigrating from the FSU tend to be more religiously and ethnically assimilated to non-Jewish cultural norms than are those who decide to emigrate, while Jewish *émigrés* choosing to go to the West tend to be more religiously and ethnically assimilated than those choosing Israel as their destination (Brym and Ryvkina 1994; Gitelman 2013; Shrayer 2017).

To be sure, the research literature identifies exceptions to the general trend. For example, unlike the Jewish community of the former Soviet Union, the Jewish communities of Western Europe and the United States have not experienced mass out-migration. The relatively high level of formal education achieved by diaspora Jews and their concentration in relatively high-status socio-economic locations has increased opportunities for intra-ethnic interaction and thus mitigated assimilation (Goldscheider and Zuckerman 1984; Hartman and Hartman 2009; Rebhun 2015). Still, in most of the diaspora, total fertility and in-migration rates have been low enough to lead to population decline, while the permeability of ethnic boundaries and the thinning out of cultural content has been made possible by increasing intermarriage and other forms of close association with non-Jews. As Gitelman (2013) wrote, "American Jews, who had all the cultural and religious facilities during the 70 years that their Soviet brethren had very few, are 'catching up and overtaking,' as Nikita Khrushchev liked to say." Nor does he restrict his generalization to American Jewry. Provocatively, he claims that "we are all Russians now."

Canadian Exceptionalism?

The leading theory of the Jewish diaspora notwithstanding, Canada seems to be bucking the global trend. For one thing, the Canadian Jewish population is growing. In 2021, it stood at about 393,500. If current trends persist, Canada's Jewish population may be larger than that of France before 2030, making it second in size only to the United States among diaspora communities (Brym, forthcoming; DellaPergola 2017, 2018).

Beyond the population count, behavioural indicators suggest that Canadian Jews tend to be significantly less assimilated than their American counterparts. The 2018 Survey of Jews in Canada (Brym, Neuman, and Lenton 2019) and the 2013 Pew Survey of US Jews (Pew Research Center 2013) provide numerous comparable measures of ethnic retention, nine of which are listed in table 19.1. The 2,335 Jews in the Canadian survey score higher than the 3,475 Jews in the American survey on in-marriage, friendship ties with fellow Jews, attending full-time Jewish school, and other forms of Jewish ethnic and religious identification and participation. On average across all nine indicators, Canadian Jews score 26 percentage points higher than do American Jews. Despite sampling differences between the two surveys, we are convinced that most of the observed difference reflect the Canadian Jewish community's greater ethnic cohesiveness.[2]

These data suggest that the Jewish communities of the United States and Canada are substantially different. What accounts for the difference? We believe three main factors are at play.

First, in proportionate terms, Jewish immigration has been considerably more robust in Canada than in the United States since the Second

Qualifying the Leading Theory of Diaspora Jewry 285

Table 19.1. Indicators of Jewish religious and ethnic retention, Canada, 2018, and the US, 2013, in per cent

	US (n = 3,475)	Canada (n = 2,335)	Difference
Endogamous, 18–29-year-olds[a]	29	68	39
Non-synagogue Jewish organization membership (yes)	18	47	29
Synagogue membership (yes)	31	58	27
Endogamous[a]	50	77	27
All or most friends Jewish	32	57	25
Lights Shabbat candles weekly or usually	22	46	24
Financial donation to Jewish cause in past year (yes)	56	80	24
Attended Jewish summer camp[b] (yes)	38	58	20
Attended full-time Jewish school[b] (yes)	23	43	20
Average			26

[a] Canadian figures based on 2011 population data.
[b] In the US survey, asked only of people who said they were brought up Jewish or who have at least one Jewish parent.
Sources: Pew Research Center (2013); Brym, Neuman, and Lenton (2019).

World War. Consequently, about 30 per cent of Canadian Jews are immigrants compared to just 14 per cent of American Jews. Canadians therefore tend to have stronger ties to "old country" traditions and languages than do American Jews.

The second factor accounting for Canadian Jewry's higher level of religious and ethnic retention is that Canadian national identity is weaker than American national identity; raucous displays of national pride, so frequent in the United States, are considered unseemly in Canada, except during some international sports tournaments (Adams 1997, 171). Because of their strong American patriotism, American Jews have historically been less enthusiastic than Canadian Jews about Zionism. This tendency has mitigated the assimilation of Canadian Jews for more than a century.

The Canadian/American difference in strength of national identity exists partly because the United States was first settled by Europeans a century earlier and has therefore had more time for a national identity to crystallize. In addition, Canadian national identity emerged gradually with the peaceful evolution of independence from Great Britain, while American national identity was forged in an anti-colonial war that, like all group conflict, sharpened and hardened group identity. Consequently, when Zionism appeared on the scene in the late nineteenth century, it conflicted with American patriotism, particularly for Reform Jews, members of the country's largest Jewish denomination by far. Many Reform Jews thought Jewishness should be based on religion, not a national movement, and so were opposed to the Zionist idea (Kolsky 1990). Not so in Canada, where the Reform movement was weaker than the Orthodox and especially Conservative denominations. Already by the beginning of the First World War, Zionism was a core element of Jewish identity for the great majority of Canadian Jews (Tulchinsky 1992, 201). Zionism thus facilitated the retention of religious and ethnic identity by providing a new basis for Jewish identification that became even more compelling after the Holocaust.

The third main reason for Canadian-Jewish exceptionalism is that, out of political necessity, fostering the growth of ethnic institutions has been Canadian public policy since the British conquest of New France in 1760. Part of the British strategy for dominating the relatively large French population was not to quash French Catholic culture but to allow the conservative Catholic Church to maintain religious, educational, and cultural control of the French population (while reserving for the English control of trade and, later, industry). The eventual establishment of separate school systems in Quebec – Catholic for the French, Protestant for the English – did not easily accommodate Jewish immigrants. It thus fostered the growth of a private Jewish school system and other Jewish community institutions that promoted the retention of Jewish ethnic identity. For instance, according to Canada's leading historian of Yiddish, in the early twentieth century, while the "mainstream American Yiddish press promoted Americanization, Montreal intellectuals ... advocated ... *yidishkayt*" (Margolis 2011, 31). Then, beginning in the late 1950s, a substantial number of French-speaking Sephardic Jews immigrated to Montreal. They now comprise about one quarter of the city's Jewish population. A distinct Canadian-Jewish bilingual sub-identity crystallized among them, pulling Canadian Jewry even farther from the unilingual and assimilationist American model of Jewishness (Bérubé-Sasseville 2017).

Canada was officially proclaimed a bilingual and bicultural country in the 1960s. Shortly thereafter, numerous minority ethnic groups argued that they, too, deserved official recognition and funding. The era of multiculturalism had arrived. Since the early 1970s, strong state support for ethnic institutions has helped all Canadians, Jews among them, to ward off religious and ethnic assimilation. Support for ethnic diversity has become a key component of Canadian identity – some would say the key component (Adams 1997). In contrast, opposition to ethnic diversity has been stronger in the United States historically and has, if anything, strengthened in recent years with the rise of White nationalism and its political offshoots.

Significantly, survey research suggests that the only other diaspora country with a Jewish community as cohesive as Canada's on a wide range of demographic and behavioural measures is Australia (Graham and Markus 2018). The Jewish populations of both countries are growing. And the two communities seem to be similarly cohesive for similar contextual reasons. Thus, while immigrants make up 30 per cent of Canada's Jewish immigrant population, they make up as much as 48 per cent of Australia's. Like Canada, Australia gained independence from Great Britain peacefully rather than through an anti-colonial war, which, in the United States, led to intense patriotism that conflicted with Zionism. And like Canada, but unlike the United States, Australia developed a vibrant multicultural policy in the early 1970s that undergirds religious and ethnic identity retention among its citizens (for details regarding Australia, see chapter 22 in this volume).

In short, the Canadian case teaches us that context matters. In this case, "context" means the timing and volume of immigration and the nature of ideologies and institutions relevant to ethnic identity. The Canadian Jewish community is relatively cohesive, and its Jewish population is growing – a rarity among diaspora communities. Beyond that, the Canadian case suggests that, while the American and Soviet-era/FSU Jewish communities have without question been the dominant actors on the diaspora stage for the past century, they should not be allowed to monopolize the narrative concerning the future of the Jewish diaspora. Assimilation is taking place among Canadian Jews, but at a relatively attenuated pace. As we will now argue, this circumstance has important implications for Canadian Jews born in the former Soviet Union.

National Contexts of FSU Jews

If, as we have suggested, historical and institutional contexts matter, it follows that Jewish *émigrés* from the former Soviet Union arriving in different countries should develop religious and ethnic tendencies influenced by the characteristics of their host countries. That seems to be the case.

For example, Judaism is Israel's state religion, pervading the lives of its Jewish citizenry. We would expect Israel's strong Jewish religious environment to push Soviet Jewish *émigrés* towards substantially greater Jewish religious observance over time. And that is in fact just what 2015 Pew Research Center data show (see table

Table 19.2. Indicators of religious assimilation, FSU Jews, Israel, 2014–2015, in per cent (*n* ≈ 568)[a]

	FSU first gen.	FSU second gen.	All Israeli Jews	FSU first–second gen. difference
Keep kosher at home (yes)	24	50	63	26
Light Chanukah candles (always)	26	43	52	17
Keep kosher outside home (yes)	19	35	52	16
Believe in God (yes)	55	70	77	15
Light Shabbat candles (weekly)	19	34	43	15
Average				18

[a] The Pew Research Center survey included 3,789 Jews, but the number of individuals from the FSU is not specified in their published report. Based on population data from Israel's Central Bureau of Statistics, we estimate that about 15 per cent of the sample consisted of Jews born in the FSU and their offspring.
Source: Theodorou (2016).

19.2). On five measures of assimilation to Jewish religious norms, second-generation FSU Jews score an average of 18 percentage points higher than do first-generation FSU Jews. Even if this behaviour is largely "an adaptive response aiming at social inclusion in the Israeli Jewish mainstream rather than actually emerging religiosity," it testifies to the existence of a strong contextual effect (Remennick and Prashizky 2012, 55).

We might also anticipate a difference in this regard between Jews from the former Soviet Union arriving in the US and those arriving in Canada. That is because Jewish religious observance is more widespread in Canada. However, in neither country is Judaism anything like the pervasive force it is in Israel, so we would expect such Canadian/American differences to be relatively small. In this connection we can compare three indicators from the 2018 Survey of Jews in Canada and the 2013 Pew Survey of US Jews, bearing in mind that we are dealing here with just 515 respondents total between the two surveys. Any inferences drawn from such a small subsample must be regarded as no more than suggestive. That said, the data in table 19.3 follow expectations. Religious differences between FSU Jews in the two countries average 9 percentage points – less than one-third the magnitude of the average cross-national *ethnic* difference we are about to observe.

On non-religious dimensions of ethnicity, we would expect larger differences between Soviet Jewish *émigrés* arriving in the United States

Qualifying the Leading Theory of Diaspora Jewry 289

Table 19.3. Indicators of religious retention, FSU Jews in Canada and the US, in per cent (*n* = 515)

	US (*n* = 366)	Canada (*n* = 149)	Difference
Synagogue member (yes)	21	37	16
Attend religious services (once a week+)	8	17	9
Light *Shabbat* candles (weekly)	23	26	3
Average			9

Sources: Pew Research Center (2013); Brym, Neuman, and Lenton (2019).

and Canada. That is because, as noted earlier, the Canadian and American social contexts – that is, their institutional structures, government policies, and cultural environments – differ sharply in the degree to which they offer material and symbolic support to ethnic groups.

We concede that it is not always easy to distinguish religious from non-religious dimensions of Jewish ethnicity. For example, endogamy may be based on religious or non-religious considerations, or a mix of the two. To minimize overlap between the religious and non-religious dimensions of ethnicity, table 19.4 refers to indicators of ethnicity that do not have an *explicitly* religious focus. Again, as anticipated, we find a large difference between FSU Jews in Canada and the United States. On six measures of ethnic retention, FSU Jews in Canada out-score FSU Jews in the US by an average of 29 percentage points.

Objections

Two objections may be raised to our claim that Canada is exceptional in terms of its effects on the ethnic identification of Jews in general and Jews born in the FSU in particular. First, it is often held that Canada lags behind the United States on a whole range of dimensions and that, in due course, Canada will "catch up" to the US. From this point of view, Canada's Jews, including its FSU Jews, will eventually be as assimilated as their counterparts in the US today. For example, if current trends in intermarriage persist, Canadian Jewry may reach the current intermarriage rate of American Jewry in roughly three decades.[3]

On the other hand, the Pew Research Center (2015) projects that while the US Jewish population will continue to shrink between 2010 and 2050, the Canadian Jewish population will continue to grow. It seems entirely possible that Canadian Jewish population increase, due mainly to immigration, combined with the country's institutional and cultural

Table 19.4. Indicators of ethnic retention, FSU Jews in Canada and the US, in per cent (*n* = 515)

	US (*n* = 366)	Canada (*n* = 149)	Difference
Aside from religion, does spouse consider him/herself Jewish? (yes/ partly)	18	62	44
Member of Jewish organization other than a synagogue? (yes)	13	43	30
Religious intermarriage rate	42	14	28
How important is being Jewish in your life? (very)	22	50	28
Financial donation to Jewish charity or cause in past year? (yes)	48	71	23
How emotionally attached are you to Israel? (very)	37	56	19
Average			29

Sources: Pew Research Center (2013); Brym, Neuman, and Lenton (2019).

context, which we have briefly described, may prevent the level of Jewish assimilation that the United States is witnessing.

The second objection to the claim that the Canadian and American social contexts affect FSU Jews differently is that divergence between the two groups may not be due to contextual so much as compositional factors. That is, FSU Jews in Canada may differ from FSU Jews in the United States because individual-level characteristics influencing propensity to assimilate differ between the two populations. For example, proportionately more FSU Jews in Canada may have been socialized in more robust Jewish environments. To discover whether that is in fact the case, we conducted a multivariate analysis of pooled data on FSU Jews drawn from the 2018 Survey of Jews in Canada and the 2013 Pew Survey of US Jews. The appendix provides details concerning our multivariate analysis. Here we focus on the big picture.

Multivariate Analysis

We began by combining multiple questionnaire items, including those found it table 19.1 and table 19.3, to form separate scales of Jewish religious retention and Jewish ethnic retention. After testing the scales for statistical reliability, we determined how well ten variables commonly used to explain religious and ethnic retention influence Jewish religious and ethnic retention among FSU Jews. That is, we calculated the unique effect of each of the ten variables and the combined effect of all ten variables on each scale. The variables include the respondent's (1) gender, (2) age, (3) highest educational degree,

(4) household income, and (5) year of immigration (if applicable); whether the respondent had (6) a non-Jewish partner, (7) a Jewish partner, and (8) at least one Jewish parents; and if the respondent (9) was raised Jewish and (10) resided in Canada or the United States at the time of the survey.

We found that only the last of these variables had a statistically significant effect on Jewish *religious* retention. This means that, with one exception, none of the ten variables just listed influenced Jewish religious retention when respondents were matched on the nine other variables. The one exception was whether the respondent lived in Canada or the United States.

We believe that having one or two Jewish parents, having a Jewish or non-Jewish spouse, being raised Jewish, and all the other variables we included in our analysis (except for country of residence) had no discernible effect on Jewish religious retention because Jewish religious identification was weak among most FSU Jews in our sample when they arrived in North America. The USSR aimed to eliminate religion and promote atheism. Religious institutions including schools were shut down, property owned by religious bodies was appropriated by the state, atheism was taught in schools and universities, religious practices were officially stigmatized, and public displays of religiosity were prohibited. As a result, the Jewish religion was not extinguished but the flame guttered, with urbanization and education probably having as much or more of an effect on religious assimilation as government campaigns had. A representative 1993 survey of Jews in Moscow, Kiev, and Minsk found that just 16 per cent of Jews were bringing up their children with Jewish traditions, and a mere 10 per cent regularly celebrated Shabbat (Brym with Ryvkina 1994, 25). A minor religious revival began in the 1980s, but it was strongly associated with the emigration movement and in many cases failed to endure (Beizer 2019). There is more evidence of a religious revival in the post-Soviet era, but the resurgence is not strong. For instance, only about 100 families in Moscow and St. Petersburg are deeply involved in the Lubavitcher Hasidic movement, which is sanctioned by the Putin regime (Shrayer 2017). A 2004 survey in St. Petersburg asked Jews which religious doctrine they found most attractive. More than 35 per cent answered "none" and more than 20 per cent answered "Christianity," with just over 10 per cent replying "don't know." "Judaism" attracted only 27 per cent of the respondents (Gitelman 2012, Table 5.4). We suspect that in the context of such weak religious socialization, a person who has a Jewish partner or a Jewish parent, or even someone who has been raised Jewish, is on average unlikely to be much more religious than someone who lacks these characteristics. Hence the non-significant social and demographic variables in our multivariate models.

In contrast, whether FSU Jews lived in Canada or the United States *did* significantly influence Jewish religious retention. We contend that Jews from the FSU in Canada tended to score higher on the Jewish religious retention scale because the Canadian context is more congenial to that outcome than is the American context.

With respect to Jewish *ethnic* retention, a somewhat different picture emerges. Several socio-demographic variables influence ethnic retention. Specifically, having a Jewish partner, having a Jewish parent and being raised Jewish are significantly associated with Jewish ethnic retention. Apparently, respondents who are single, intermarried, or lack a Jewish parent have little access to support networks that can sustain ethnic identification and are more assimilated than people who enjoy such support. These relationships exist even when country of residence is introduced into our multivariate model. Even so, residing in Canada versus the United States is the most powerful single variable mitigating ethnic assimilation. As is the case for religious retention, context matters.

The Advantage of Comparative Analysis

Most social scientific research on Jews focuses on particular cities or countries and the individuals who reside in them. While such research is without question of great academic and practical value, it is deficient in one respect: it ignores how features of cities and countries themselves influence thought and action independent of individual-level characteristics. The methodological significance of this chapter and, indeed, much of this book is that examining such macro-sociological factors greatly enhances our understanding of Jewish religious and ethnic retention – and, by implication, other features of Jewish life.

Comparative social scientific research on Jews exists. Much of it is of high quality. We are thinking here principally of the work associated with Sergio DellaPergola and Daniel Staetsky. Yet even their careful cross-national examinations of Jewish population size, identification, perceptions of antisemitism, and other important issues tend to neglect analysis of how specific structural and cultural features of the social contexts in which individuals are embedded influence their beliefs, values, attitudes, and behaviours.

The migration of Jews from the former Soviet Union to Israel, the United States, Germany, Canada, Australia, and other countries since the 1970s offers researchers a golden opportunity to study individual- and country-level effects and their interactions. The challenges associated with such research are undoubtedly considerable. However, we believe that inquiries of this type would enhance our understanding of the wide variation in what being Jewish means today, making it well worth the effort.

Appendix

Sample and Measures

Our multivariate analysis pools data on all respondents from the 2013 Pew Survey of US Jews and the 2018 Survey of Jews in Canada who identified as fully or partially Jewish and who immigrated to Canada or the United States from the FSU since 1970, when the modern wave of Jewish emigration from the FSU began. Respondents in both surveys were asked about their level of engagement with diverse religious and ethnic practices, Jewish upbringing, institutional and cultural connectedness, and social and economic location. Our statistical models are based on complete case analyses of the subsample. That is, only respondents with valid responses on all independent variables are included in the analysis. Accordingly, our effective sample size is 398 respondents.[4]

To examine the extent of Jewish religious and ethnic retention in Canada and the United States, we constructed two measures of retention based on ten survey items tapping respondents' level of attitudinal, cognitive, and behavioural affinity with the Jewish community.

The index of Jewish religious retention includes measures of the importance of the Jewish religion in the respondent's life, synagogue membership, frequency of attending religious services, and frequency of lighting Shabbat candles. The index of Jewish ethnic retention includes items tapping membership in Jewish organizations other than synagogues, donating money to Jewish organizations, the proportion of one's friends who are Jewish, self-assessed knowledge of the Hebrew alphabet, and emotional attachment to Israel. Both indices also include country of residence. Cronbach's alpha (α) measures the internal consistency or reliability of questionnaire items, that is, how closely related the items are. A Cronbach's α of 0.7 or greater usually indicates a reliable scale. For the religious retention scale, Cronbach's $\alpha = 0.769$. For the ethnic retention scale, Cronbach's $\alpha = 0.751$.

Because the number of response options in questionnaire items varied, items were standardized before scales were constructed. The indices were then standardized again in the pooled data to have a mean of 0 and a standard deviation of 1. Therefore, the b coefficients in our models measure the average estimated effect of a one-unit change in each independent variable on a one-standard-deviation difference in the religious and ethnic retention scales.

We performed factor analyses for each outcome variable as an additional check to ensure that the items making up our scales measure single, internally consistent constructs. For both outcomes, constitutive items loaded strongly (> 0.4) on one factor in both the pooled and country-segmented data. Because factor analysis results support the structure of both scales, and because removal of any item lowers the Cronbach α associated with each scale, we retained the structure of our outcome variables.

After constructing the Jewish religious and ethnic retention scales, we estimated a series of ordinary least squares (OLS) regressions on each of the outcome variables.[5] Table 19.5, model 1 and model 3, test the effects of demographic and socio-economic variables that are commonly used to explain religious and ethnic retention (or their opposites: religious and ethnic assimilation). Model 2 and model 4 add a dummy variable for country of residence to examine whether country context affects religious and ethnic retention among FSU Jews (US = 0, Canada = 1).

Our socio-economic and demographic controls include respondents' gender (male = 0, female = 1); age in years; level of educational attainment, operationalized as the highest degree attained in eight categories; annual household income in six categories; year of immigration; and couple composition, distinguishing respondents who are single, those who have a Jewish spouse or partner, and those who have a non-Jewish spouse or partner (included in the models as dummy variables with "single" as the reference category). We also control for level of religious upbringing by including dichotomous measures capturing whether respondents were raised Jewish and whether they have at least one Jewish parent.

Findings

Table 19.5 presents OLS regression results for the religious and ethnic retention models. Both unstandardized coefficients (b) and standardized coefficients (β) are presented.

A striking finding that first emerges from our modelling exercise is that standard socio-economic and demographic measures account for little variation in religious retention. In model 1, having a Jewish spouse or partner is the only variable that is significantly associated with religious retention; people in endogamous unions experience a higher level of religious retention than do single respondents. However, the relationship between having a Jewish spouse or partner and religious retention becomes non-significant once we include country of residence in the analysis. Thus, in model 2, none of the socio-economic or demographic predictors are significantly associated with religious retention. Said differently, in our sample of FSU Jews who immigrated to Canada or the United States since 1970, religious retention does not vary across categories of gender, age, education, income, or childhood upbringing, net of the country effect. Context alone matters, with Canadian Jews from the FSU scoring significantly higher on religious retention than do American Jews from the FSU.

We investigated the possibility that these non-significant results were driven by low variation on religious retention. However, coefficients of variation and box plots showed considerable variation in religious retention in both the pooled and country-segmented data. We also investigated the possibility that standard social and demographic variables were non-significant because our models were handicapped by insufficient statistical power due to small sample size. To explore this possibility, we conducted a stepwise regression analysis with backward elimination to see if the removal of the most non-significant variables in succession would improve model fit. Stepwise regression analysis with backward elimination left only Jewish partnership and country of residence in the model. We conclude that the non-significant results cannot be attributed to small sample size.

Socio-economic and demographic factors explain considerably more variation in respondents' level of ethnic retention. Table 19.5, model 3, indicates that having a Jewish partner, having a Jewish parent, and being raised Jewish are significantly associated with ethnic retention. These relationships hold even when country of residence is introduced into the regression equation in model 4. However, the β coefficients in model 4 show that residing in Canada versus the United States is the strongest single variable mitigating ethnic assimilation net of other variables in the regression equation.

Table 19.5. Ordinary least squares (OLS) regression predicting Jewish religious retention and Jewish ethnic retention

	Jewish religious retention scale				Jewish ethnic retention scale			
	Model 1		Model 2		Model 3		Model 4	
	b (se)	β	b (se)	β	b (se)	β	b (se)	β
Female	−0.174 (0.172)	−0.089	−0.206 (0.172)	−0.105	0.245* (0.017)	0.143*	0.204 (0.114)	0.119
Age	−0.006 (0.004)	−0.110	−0.006 (0.004)	−0.107	0.001 (0.004)	0.022	0.001 (0.004)	0.026
Highest degree	0.018 (0.058)	0.032	−0.005 (0.056)	−0.008	0.037 (0.041)	0.071	0.007 (0.036)	0.014
Household income	−0.069 (0.065)	−0.108	−0.092 (0.064)	−0.143	0.037 (0.042)	0.066	0.008 (0.042)	0.014
Jewish partner (ref.: single)	−0.539* (0.218)	0.274*	0.416 (0.216)	0.211	0.614*** (0.150)	0.355***	0.456*** (0.141)	0.263***
Non-Jewish partner (ref.: single)	−0.273 (0.200)	−0.104	−0.292 (0.199)	−0.111	−0.137 (0.203)	−0.059	−0.161 (0.202)	−0.070
Year of immigration	−0.008 (0.009)	−0.079	−0.010 (0.009)	−0.097	0.018** (0.006)	0.199**	0.016** (0.006)	0.174**
Raised Jewish	0.167 (0.227)	0.068	0.169 (0.230)	0.069	0.411** (0.145)	0.191**	0.413** (0.145)	0.192**
Jewish parent	−0.128 (0.263)	−0.018	−0.283 (0.281)	−0.040	0.917** (0.317)	0.146**	0.717* (0.310)	0.114*
Canada			0.395** (0.144)	0.192**			0.509*** (0.119)	0.281***
Constant	16.292 (18.502)		19.969 (18.244)		−37.622*** (11.649)		−32.884** (11.483)	
n	398		398		398		398	
R^2	0.128		0.153		0.362		0.416	

*$p < 0.05$; **$p < 0.01$; ***$p < 0.001$.
Note: This table reports OLS regression coefficients (b), robust standards errors (se), and standardized regression coefficients (β).

NOTES

1 This is an abbreviated version of an earlier paper published in *Contemporary Jewry* (see Brym, Slavina, and Lenton 2020). We are grateful to Harriet Hartman, editor of *Contemporary Jewry*, and the publisher, Springer Nature Switzerland, for permission to reprint.

2 The Canadian survey includes only cities with a Jewish population of about 13,000 or more. The US survey includes Jews in communities of all sizes and rural areas. However, roughly 85 per cent of Jews in both countries live in cities with Jewish populations of about 13,000 or more. Rural areas in both countries are typically devoid of Jews. And cities with small Jewish populations seem to be more ethnically cohesive in Canada than in the United States. For example, Calgary, Alberta, and Alexandria, Virginia, each have Jewish populations of about 5,000, but Calgary has three synagogues while Alexandria has two; Halifax, Nova Scotia, and Charlottesville, Virginia, each have Jewish populations of about 2,000, but Halifax has two synagogues while Charlottesville has one.

3 Because the intermarriage rates may be calculated in different ways, comparison of intermarriage statistics across time and between countries is hazardous. With this proviso in mind, we note that the 1990 National Jewish Population Survey in the United States found that 27 per cent of married people who were born Jewish were not married to a person who was born Jewish or who had converted to Judaism. In the 2018 Survey of Canadian Jews, 23 per cent of married respondents reported that their spouse or common-law partner did not identify as Jewish at the time of the survey (Brym, Neuman, and Lenton 2019, 39; Goldstein 1992, 126).

4 Descriptive statistics for all variables are in Brym, Slavina, and Lenton (2020).

5 Models were estimated using weighted data. Weights for the US data were constructed by the Pew Research Center to adjust for various aspects of the survey design and demographic characteristics (educational attainment, census region, stratum, age, gender, and race/ethnicity). The Canadian weights adjust the sample for the age and gender distribution of Jews in the respondent's city, the national age cohort–specific exogamy rate for respondents who are married or have a common-law partner, and the size of the Jewish population in each city. Country-level weights were normalized to centre at 1 to facilitate comparison in the pooled dataset.

REFERENCES

Adams, Michael. 1997. *Sex in the Snow: Canadian Social Values at the End of the Millennium*. Toronto: Penguin.

Beizer, Michael. 2019. "Religious Life among the Leningrad 'Refuseniks' in the 1980s." Paper presented at the Symposium in Honour of Dr. Mark Tolts on His Retirement, Hebrew University of Jerusalem, 27 June 2019.

Bérubé-Sasseville, Olivier. 2017. "La construction d'une mémoire commune." In *Les sépharades du Québec: Parcours d'exils nord-africains*, edited by Yolande Cohen, 113–43. Montreal: Del Busso.

Brym, Robert. Forthcoming. "Canadian Jewish Population 2021: New Estimates." *American Jewish Year Book 2022*, Vol. 122, edited by Arnold Dashefsky and Ira M. Sheskin. Cham, Switzerland: Springer.

Brym, Robert, Keith Neuman, and Rhonda Lenton. 2019. *2018 Survey of Canadian Jews: Final Report*. Toronto: Environics Institute for Survey Research. http://bitly.ws/sK4N.

Brym, Robert, with Rozalina Ryvkina. 1994. *The Jews of Moscow, Kiev and Minsk: Identity, Antisemitism, Emigration*. New York: New York University Press.

Brym, Robert, Anna Slavina, and Rhonda Lenton. 2020. "Qualifying the Leading Theory of Diaspora Jewry: An Examination of Jews from the Former Soviet Union in Canada and the United States." *Contemporary Jewry* 40 (3): 367–85. https://doi.org/10.1007/s12397-020-09315-5.

DellaPergola, Sergio. 2017. "World Jewish Population, 2016." In *American Jewish Year Book 2016*, Vol. 116, edited by Arnold Dashefsky and Ira M. Sheskin, 253–332. New York: Springer.

DellaPergola, Sergio. 2018. "World Jewish Population, 2017." In *American Jewish Year Book 2017*, Vol. 117, edited by Arnold Dashefsky and Ira M. Sheskin, 297–377. New York: Springer.

DellaPergola, Sergio, Uzi Rebhun, and Mark Tolts. 2000. "Prospecting the Jewish Future: Population Projections, 2000–2080." In *American Jewish Year Book 2000*, Vol. 100, edited by David Singer and Lawrence Grossman, 103–20. New York: The American Jewish Committee.

Gitelman, Zvi. 1998. "The Decline of the Diaspora Jewish Nation: Boundaries, Content, and Jewish Identity." *Jewish Social Studies* 4 (2): 112–32. https://doi.org/10.2979/JSS.1998.4.2.112.

Gitelman, Zvi. 2012. *Jewish Identities in Postcommunist Russia and Ukraine: An Uncertain Ethnicity*. Cambridge: Cambridge University Press.

Gitelman, Zvi. 2013. "We Are All Russians Now." *Forward*, 4 November 2013. https://bit.ly/2KX0K7d.

Goldscheider, Calvin, and Alan S. Zuckerman. 1984. *The Transformation of the Jews*. Chicago: University of Chicago Press.

Goldstein, Sidney. 1992. "Profile of American Jewry: Insights from the 1990 National Jewish Population Survey." In *American Jewish Year Book 1992*, Vol. 92, edited by David Singer and Ruth R. Seldin, 77–173. New York: The American Jewish Committee.

Graham, David, and Andrew Markus. 2018. *Gen 17 Australian Jewish Community Survey: Preliminary Findings*. Melbourne: Australian Centre for Jewish Civilisation and JCA. http://bitly.ws/sF3d.

Hartman, Harriet, and Moshe Hartman. 2009. *Gender and American Jews: Patterns in Work, Education and Family in Contemporary Life*. Waltham, MA: Brandeis University Press.

Israel Central Bureau of Statistics. 2021. "Erev yom ha-zikaron l'sho'a v'l'gvura." Press release, no. 115/2021, 6 April 2021. https://bit.ly/3uZz9qF.

Kolsky, Thomas A. 1990. *Jews against Zionism: The American Council for Judaism, 1942–1948*. Philadelphia: Temple University Press.

Margolis, Rebecca. 2011. *Jewish Roots, Canadian Soil: Yiddish Culture in Montreal, 1905–1945*. Montreal: McGill-Queen's University Press.

Pew Research Center. 2013. *A Portrait of Jewish Americans: Findings from a Pew Research Center Survey of U.S. Jews*. Washington, DC: Pew Research Center. http://bitly.ws/sF3K.

Pew Research Center. 2015. "The Future of World Religions: Population Growth Projections, 2010–2050." Pew Research Center, 2 April 2015. https://pewrsr.ch/2HQ9igj.

Rebhun, Uzi. 2015. "Assimilation in American Life: An Empirical Assessment of Milton Gordon's Multi-dimensional Theory." *Journal of Contemporary Religion* 30 (3): 473–96. https://doi.org/10.1080/13537903.2015.1081350.

Remennick, Larissa, and Anna Prashizky. 2012. "Russian Israelis and Religion: What Has Changed after 20 Years in Israel?" *Israel Studies Review* 27 (1): 55–77. https://doi.org/10.3167/isr.2012.270104.

Shrayer, Maxim D. 2017. *With or Without You: The Prospect for Jews in Today's Russia*. Boston: Academic Studies Press.

Theodorou, Angelina E. 2016. "Israeli Jews from the Former Soviet Union Are More Secular, Less Religiously Observant." Pew Research Center, 30 March 2016. https://pewrsr.ch/2TEIYMu.

Tulchinsky, Gerald. 1992. *Taking Root: The Origins of the Canadian Jewish Community*. Toronto: Lester.

20 Perceptions and Realities of Antisemitism: Canadian, British, and French Jews

L. DANIEL STAETSKY

In the contemporary Western world, negative opinions of Jews are distinctly a minority view. In the anglophone world, including Canada, Australia, the UK, and the US, it is especially low. Pew Research Center surveys indicate that at most 10 per cent of people in these countries reveal strong negativity towards Jews. Furthermore, during the late twentieth and early twenty-first centuries, negativity towards Jews has remained stable or declined in prevalence, and no state-sponsored violence is inflicted on Jews at present (Bergmann 2008; Jikeli 2017; J. Cohen 2018; Staetsky 2019b). Antisemitic incidents are rare: in Canada and the UK, recorded antisemitic incidents are at a level of 550–600 incidents per 100,000 Jewish population per year, while in France the comparable figure is about 120 per 100,000 Jewish population per year. Nationally, the level of total police-recorded crime in Canada and the UK is at 6,000–10,000 incidents per 100,000 population.[1] Even if one accounts for very significant levels of under-reporting of antisemitic incidents and differential reporting by country (Enstad 2017), the overarching conclusion regarding rarity remains unchanged. The nature of trends in antisemitic incidents remains uncertain; increases in the volume of antisemitic victimization – reported recently across many Western countries, including Canada and the UK – owe significantly to improvements in the scope of the reporting of such incidents (Brym 2019; European Union Agency for Fundamental Rights 2018a, 2020).

These facts notwithstanding, a significant proportion of Jews living in the diaspora continue to see antisemitism as a serious problem. Recent research in Canada, for example, has shown that about 85 per cent of Jews in Canada believe that Jews experience discrimination and about one third say discrimination against Jews occurs often (Brym, Neuman, and Lenton 2019). In the 2018 survey of Jewish communities conducted by the European Union Agency for Fundamental Rights

(EU-FRA) in twelve European countries, about 85 per cent of the respondents indicated that antisemitism, in their view, is a problem in their societies, and about 45 per cent said it is a very big problem. Specifically, in France the respective proportions were 95 per cent and 65 per cent, and in the UK 75 per cent and 30 per cent (EU-FRA 2018b). The situation in the US is no different, as indicated by the 2019 American Jewish Committee (AJC) survey of American Jews: almost 90 per cent defined antisemitism as a problem and nearly 40 per cent said it was a big problem (Mayer 2019).

Note that the different measures mentioned above are not correlated. The survey-based evaluation of negativity towards Jews, the number of recorded antisemitic incidents captured by the police and Jewish security organizations, and the extent of Jewish anxieties captured by surveys of Jews do not reveal the same country hierarchy of "antisemitism as a problem." Canada, France, and the UK are pretty indistinguishable from each other when it comes to the (low) prevalence of negativity towards Jews in the general population. France has the lowest levels of recorded antisemitic incidents, while Canada and the UK are at about the same level. Jewish anxieties, on the other hand, are highest in France while Canada and the UK look very similar.

The discrepancy between Jewish perceptions and other metrics of antisemitism has not gone unnoticed. It has been suggested that the usual metrics of antisemitism are a mixture of "signal" and "noise," and the amount of noise (measurement issues) is such that it prevents the clear signal (level of severity of antisemitism) from coming through. Some analysts have suggested, with respect to surveys of the general population, that antisemitism may be high and rising in specific, small segments of the non-Jewish population (Islamists, the far right), something that population-level surveys cannot capture. Others suggest that recording antisemitic incidents is very partial and that the scope of under-reporting varies by country. It has also been hypothesized, with respect to Jewish anxieties, that the visibility of pre-existing antisemitic views may have increased, rather than their prevalence as such, and that this may have happened due to the development of the online culture. It could also be that Jewish anxiety is a response to "softer" forms of negativity or ambiguity about Jews rather than hard-core, murderous antisemitism (Brym 2019; Enstad 2017; Staetsky 2017, 2019b; Jikeli 2017; Fireberg 2020).

How, then, do we understand Jewish anxieties? How are they connected to the objective level of threat to Jews in a given context? Do Jews sense something that conventional measures of levels and trends in antisemitism cannot register? Is the Jewish perspective on the seriousness of antisemitism coloured by factors other than the objective level of threat? To many established scholars of antisemitism, these questions appear intractable. Yet the normative assumption of policymakers in the area of combatting antisemitism is that Jewish views matter for policy development. This is evidenced by the willingness of policymakers to conduct large-scale and expensive surveys of Jewish views and experiences (EU-FRA 2013, 2018b). Should Jewish perceptions of antisemitism be taken into account in policy development in this area and, if so, in what way? Before this can be done, Jewish perceptions and the relationship between them and other metrics of antisemitism should be understood considerably better than they are at present.

I do not offer instant answers to any of the questions just posed. I do two things, however, to prepare the ground for future research in this area. First, I position the question of discrepancy between Jewish perceptions and other metrics of antisemitism at the centre of the social scientific research agenda on antisemitism. Second, I explore in-depth variation in Jewish perceptions of antisemitism in three Western societies (Canada, France, and the UK) in an attempt to identify patterns and regularities in perceptions. Do certain subgroups of Jews harbour a more or less strong perception of antisemitism as a problem? Does antisemitic victimization play a role in shaping Jewish anxieties? What other factors, over and above victimization, play a role? Of all metrics of antisemitism presented above, Jewish perceptions of it are perhaps the most under-researched. This is in part simply because the first large-scale surveys of Jewish views are still novel research products.

Sources

This paper brings together recent surveys of Jews in Canada, France, and the UK. The survey of Jews in Canada was carried out in 2018 by the Environics Institute for Survey Research together with sociologists from the University of Toronto and York University. The survey of Jews in France and the UK was conducted by Ipsos MORI and the London-based Institute for Jewish Policy Research (JPR) on behalf of EU-FRA, also in 2018. Both surveys included questions on Jewish perceptions and experiences of antisemitism as well as a wide range of demographic, socio-economic, and Jewish identity items.

The Canadian Jewish sample includes 2,335 respondents. It was obtained by a combination of probability sampling (based on lists of common Jewish names) and convenience sampling (designed to ensure representation of the hard-to-reach subgroups within the Jewish population). The French and British samples include 3,869 and 4,731 respondents, respectively. Both European samples were obtained by convenience sampling that started with selected "seed" lists of members/affiliates/subscribers supplied by Jewish organizations across the French and British Jewish communities and continued with chain referral to Jewish contacts of the initial "seeds." Upon completion of the fieldwork, the three samples were compared to known socio-demographic profiles of Jews in their respective countries and weighted to adjust for the (typically moderate) deviations from the expected distributions (Brym, Neuman, and Lenton 2019, 77–80; EU-FRA 2018b, 73–8). The Canadian survey was predominantly competed by telephone (80 per cent, landline or mobile), with small subgroups completing it online (about 20 per cent). The European survey was conducted exclusively online.

No survey is perfect. Surveys of Jews outside Israel are especially difficult to carry out because Jews constitute a very small proportion of the general population. They are impossible to capture in significant numbers in conventional nation-wide probability samples; so severe is the "rarity problem" of Jews that oversampling them is also impractical. Surveys of Jewish populations often rely on convenience samples, either partly or fully. I judge the Canadian and European surveys as sufficiently robust with respect to representation. The selectivity of the European surveys of the French and British Jewish populations was investigated and deemed insignificant for the study of antisemitism or the differences between subgroups of the Jewish population (Staetsky 2019a).

Who Is in the Samples?

All three samples underlying the analysis represent demographically mature, medium-sized Jewish populations, with Canada at 393,500, the UK at about 300,000, and France at 446,000 (DellaPergola 2022, 334).[2] The socio-demographic profiles of these populations are rather similar. In all three populations, those aged fifty years and over constitute a majority among the adults, and women form a small majority over men.[3] All three populations are geographically concentrated in and around major urban centres/capitals: about 60 per cent of Canadian Jews reside in southern Ontario (mainly Toronto), about 60–70 per cent of British Jews live in and around London, and a similar proportion of French Jews live in and around Paris. All three Jewish populations are highly educated: the proportion of adults with university-level qualifications in all three groups is in the range of 70–80 per cent. Alongside these broad similarities, differences exist.

Native-born Jews (adult population) constitute under 70 per cent in Canada, and 75–80 per cent in France and the UK. The foreign-born minorities in all three populations consist of American, Israel-born, and former Soviet Union (FSU) Jews but in different proportions. In Canada, it is convenient to think of each of these groups numerically as being about 9 per cent of the adult Jewish population in Canada. In France and the UK, the proportion of Jews from the FSU is less than 1 per cent. The share of Israel-born and American Jews in the adult British population is around 5 per cent each, while in France the share of these subgroups is lower (1–2 per cent each). A unique feature of the French Jewish population is the significant presence of Jews born in North Africa, probably around 20 per cent of adult French Jews. In Canada, the proportion of Sephardic Jews is about 10 per cent, including many who were born in Canada.

In terms of patterns of Jewish identity, Canadian Jews are more similar to British Jews than they are to French Jews. About 20 per cent of all adult Jews in Canada and in the UK self-identify as Orthodox (either mainstream or strictly Orthodox). In the UK, the share of strictly Orthodox Jews is higher than in Canada: they are nearly one half of all self-identified adult Orthodox. In France, the proportion of Orthodox Jews among adult Jews is about 10 per cent. About 80 per cent of Canadian Jews, 75 per cent of French Jews, and around 60 per cent of British Jews are strongly (or very strongly) attached to Israel.

Politically, Canadian Jews can be characterized as centrists: nearly equal proportions think of themselves as Liberal (36 per cent) or Conservative (32 per cent) with respect to the major political parties in Canada. French and British Jews can be characterized as centre-right. Although the European surveys did not ask questions about political affiliations, other sources can help in this respect. Surveys of voting intentions and behaviour have indicated that about 60 per cent of Jews in France belong to the right and centre-right (Fourquet 2012; Institut d'études opinion et marketing en France at à l'international 2014; E. Cohen 2015, 74). About 65 per cent of British Jews support the Conservative Party (Staetsky 2019c).

All three surveys included questions on negative experiences based on religion and/or ethnicity. The Canadian Jewish picture is not perfectly comparable to the European due to differences in formulation of survey questions, yet it is possible to form a broad impression of the scope of antisemitic victimization. In Canada, 15 per cent of Jews said that in the twelve months preceding the survey they had been called offensive names or snubbed in a social setting due to their Jewishness, and 26 per cent maintained that they experienced discrimination due to religion or ethnicity in the past five years. In France and the UK, about 16 per cent of Jews said they heard antisemitic comments in person in the past twelve months, a proportion similar to that observed in Canada. The European surveys included detailed questions on different types of antisemitic experiences. Putting all these experiences together leads to the conclusion that about 25 per cent of Jews in France and the UK experienced antisemitic harassment (comments in person and online, threatening or offensive calls or messages, physical violence, or vandalism) in the twelve months preceding the survey.

Methodology

The focus of this article is on the differences between subgroups of Jews with respect to the perceptions of antisemitism or negativity towards Jews. The formulation of questions relating to Jewish perceptions of negativity differed somewhat between the Canadian and the European surveys. Scholars and institutions responsible for the surveys did not coordinate their efforts. The imperfect comparability of the questions is worth bearing in mind, yet it is not detrimental to the attempt to conduct comparative analysis. Ultimately, the questions have been designed to capture the same world of meaning: the "Jewish diagnosis" of the severity of anti-Jewish sentiment in the general population of the countries Jews reside in.

In the sections that follow, I present in detail the Jewish diagnosis of antisemitism in each country, the connection of the diagnosis with other views and opinions that Jews hold, and the extent to which one can speak of a "single Jewish opinion." Nearly all attitudes and views have many determinants and correlates that tend to operate simultaneously. In the Canadian Jewish context, for example, immigrants from the FSU tend to have a rather positive view of Canadian society; they see less antisemitism compared to their non-immigrant counterparts. Why is this so? Is it an intrinsic feature of this migrant population that, for cultural reasons, has lessened sensitivity towards the Western version of antisemitism? Or is it, for example, because of their patterns of residence – distant from more antisemitic districts? It is because this type of immigrant is typically not religious and not visible as a Jew?

I work around this problem by resorting to regression analysis, which isolates the unique effect of each characteristic by examining it while holding other characteristics constant. For the benefit of the non-technical reader, the results are presented graphically; for the technical readership, the features of the statistical models are described in footnotes when appropriate.

Canadian Jewish Perceptions in Perspective

"For each of the following groups, please tell me whether you think they are often, sometimes, rarely or never the subject of discrimination in Canadian society today." Such was the prompt given to the Canadian Jewish survey respondents about the following groups: Jews, Blacks, South Asians (from India and Pakistan), Muslims, Indigenous or Aboriginal People, gays, and lesbians. "To what extent do you think the following are a problem in [country]?" – this was the question presented to French and British Jewish respondents, with antisemitism, crime level, unemployment, racism, immigration, government corruption, and intolerance towards Muslims listed as possible responses.

Table 20.1 compares Jewish responses in the three contexts. Eighty-six per cent of Canadian Jews think that Jews are often or sometimes the subject of discrimination in Canada, and about one third think that they are discriminated against often. In the UK, the situation is essentially the same. In France, the proportion of Jews perceiving antisemitism as a big problem – 65 per cent – is much higher than in Canada or the UK.

Let us now examine the extent to which actual experiences of antisemitism shape these perceptions. In Canada, exposure to antisemitism was captured by questions on whether respondents (1) had been called offensive name or snubbed/left out in social settings because of their Jewishness in the year preceding the survey, or (2) experienced discrimination/unfair treatment in the past five years in Canada. In table 20.2, respondents who answered "yes" to one of these questions are included among those who experienced antisemitism. In France and the UK, detailed questioning on victimization was implemented due to the specialized nature of the survey. Those with experience of antisemitism include respondents who experienced antisemitic harassment (antisemitic comments received in person, online, or via messages), threats, physical attacks, and acts of vandalism in the past twelve months. Canada, France, and the UK are not directly comparable here, but comparison is not the purpose of this part of my analysis. Rather, the purpose is examining the correlation between victimization and perceptions.

The existence of such a correlation is evident. In all three countries those with experience of antisemitism perceive the problem of antisemitism in society as more widespread than those without such experience. Nearly half of those who experienced antisemitism in Canada think Jews in Canada are often discriminated against and about one third of those who did not experience antisemitism think so. In France and the UK, the proportion of those who think that antisemitism is a very big problem are almost 80 per cent and 45 per cent, respectively;

Table 20.1. Perception of the seriousness of discrimination against Jews/antisemitism by country, in per cent

	Canada: frequency of discrimination	UK: antisemitism a problem	France: antisemitism a problem
Often/very big problem	36	28	65
Sometimes/fairly big problem	50	45	29
Rarely/not a very big problem	12	25	5
Never/not a problem at all	3	3	1
Total	100	100	100

Note: Results are weighted. Some columns do not add up to 100 because of rounding.

among those who did not experience antisemitism, the proportions are about 60 per cent and 20 per cent, respectively.

Note in addition that if Jews experienced no antisemitism whatsoever, the levels of anxiety about it would not have been nil. In the absence of experiencing antisemitism, the proportion of those who think that Jews are often discriminated against in Canada would stand at 31 per cent instead of the current 36 per cent. In the other two countries, the expected drops are from 65 per cent to 60 per cent (France) and from 27 per cent to 21 per cent (UK). Perceptions are not driven just by experience – far from it.

Apart from questions relating to discrimination against Jews or antisemitism, all three surveys included questions on perceptions of negativity towards other groups (Muslims, Blacks, and so on) and related phenomena such as racism. This creates an opportunity to examine the broader domain of Jewish social and political concerns. In this respect, the position of Canadian Jews is unique among the three countries under consideration. First, the percentage of Canadian Jews who think that Muslims and Blacks are discriminated against often (about 50 per cent) is higher than the percentage who think the same about Jews (36 per cent). Second, those who see Jews as a frequent object of discrimination display a tendency to see others as being discriminated against. As table 20.3 shows, among Jews who think Jews are often discriminated against, 76 per cent think the same of Muslims and 77 per cent think the same of Blacks. In contrast, among Jews who think Jews are rarely or never discriminated against, just 25 per cent think the same of Muslims and 23 per cent think the same of Blacks. The tendency (not shown here) to see Jews as frequently discriminated against is also correlated with the tendency to see groups such as South Asians, Indigenous Canadians, and gays and lesbians as the objects of discrimination. Thus, Jewish anxieties about negativity towards Jews

308   L. Daniel Staetsky

Table 20.2. Connection between antisemitic victimization and perception of discrimination against Jews/antisemitism as a problem

Per cent who think that …	Experienced	Did not experience	Total
Canada			
Jews are often discriminated against	48	31	36
Jews are sometimes discriminated against	43	53	49
Jews are never/rarely discriminated against	8	16	15
Total	100	100	100
UK			
Antisemitism is a very big problem	45	21	27
Antisemitism is a fairly big problem	44	44	44
Antisemitism is not a big problem/no problem at all	11	34	28
Total	100	100	100
France			
Antisemitism is a very big problem	78	60	65
Antisemitism is a fairly big problem	20	33	29
Antisemitism is not a big problem/no problem at all	2	7	5
Total	100	100	100

Note: Results are weighted. Some columns do not add up to 100 because of rounding.

in Canada seem to be embedded in the underlying structure of anxieties about negativity towards religious, ethnic, and racial groups, and groups defined by lifestyle. They are not specific to Jews.

In France and the UK the situation is different. In both countries, intolerance towards Muslims is seen as a very big problem by only a minority of Jews: 13 per cent of Jews in France and 20 per cent of Jews in the UK. Racism features higher as a cause of concern: it is perceived as a very big problem by 47 per cent of French Jews and 27 per cent of British Jews. In the UK this level of anxiety is close to the level of anxiety about antisemitism. In France it is far below. Another difference with Canada is that, in France and the UK, thinking that antisemitism is a very big problem is not associated with thinking that intolerance towards Muslims is a big problem. At the same time, as in Canada, thinking that antisemitism is a very big problem is correlated with anxiety about racism. In sum, in France and the UK, antisemitism is not an isolated area of concern among Jews but part of a broader area of concerns, yet intolerance towards Muslims does not constitute a part of this broader area.

Differences of Opinion?

With respect to many major political and social issues, consensus is rare. The situation with perceptions of antisemitism by Jews is no different. The usual focus of reporting on Jewish perceptions of antisemitism is on intercountry differences (EU-FRA 2013, 2018b), yet a small number of studies delved into internal differences between various categories of Jews in Europe. They found, for example, that more religious and less educated Jews perceive antisemitism as a problem more than their less religious and more educated counterparts (Staetsky and Boyd 2014; DellaPergola and Staetsky 2015). Differences by age and gender are inconsistent, suggesting that these differences may be small. The relationship between the perceptions of antisemitism and political positions/social attitudes of Jews remains unexplored.

Here I document differences of opinion across different categories of Jews. To do so, I calculate the probability of thinking that Jews are often discriminated against for men and women, young and old, those with a university degree and those without, those born in Canada or elsewhere, and those of different Jewish denominations and regions of residence (see figure 20.1). In addition to these socio-demographics, I also explore differences between voters for different political parties, those more or less attached to Israel, and those more or less sensitive to discrimination against Blacks. The last characteristic can be understood as describing a degree of sensitivity towards racism and/or a critical position towards the problem of racism in Canadian society. I present probabilities independently associated with each characteristic – for example, the probability of thinking that Jews are often discriminated against in Canada for those born in Canada and immigrants, holding all other characteristics (age, political views, country of birth, and so on) constant. This procedure clarifies how much each factor matters by itself.

For expository ease and convenience, I calculate a benchmark: a middle-aged, Canadian-born Jewish woman, highly educated, and residing in Toronto. She is Orthodox in Jewish denominational terms and has not experienced discrimination as a Jew. She votes for the Liberal Party, does not think that discrimination against Blacks occurs often in Canada, and is attached to Israel. The probability for this benchmark person thinking that discrimination against Jews often occurs in Canada is 17 per cent.

Let us now change just one characteristic of the benchmark: gender. A man with all other characteristics of the benchmark would have a somewhat lower probability of thinking that Jews in Canada are often discriminated against (11 per cent). And if the benchmark is transformed from a middle-aged woman to a young adult woman (between eighteen and twenty-nine years of age), but otherwise remains the same, she would have an even lower probability of perceiving anti-Jewish discrimination as often occurring (7 per cent).

The most interesting finding in this analysis is the apparent association between perceiving anti-Jewish discrimination as often occurring and

Table 20.3. Connection between perception of discrimination against Jews/antisemitism as a problem and perception of discrimination against Blacks and Muslims

Per cent who think that …	Blacks are often discriminated against	Blacks are not often discriminated against	Total	Muslims are often discriminated against	Muslims are not often discriminated against	Total
		Canada				
Jews are often discriminated against	77	23	100	76	24	100
Jews are sometimes discriminated against	37	63	100	40	60	100
Jews are never/rarely discriminated against	23	77	100	25	75	100

	Racism is a very big problem	Racism is not a very big problem	Total	Intolerance towards Muslims is a very big problem	Intolerance towards Muslims is not a very big problem	Total
		France				
Antisemitism is a very big problem	62	38	100	14	86	100
Antisemitism is a fairly big problem	19	81	100	9	91	100
Antisemitism is not a big problem/no problem at all	23	77	100	21	79	100
		UK				
Antisemitism is a very big problem	56	44	100	23	77	100
Antisemitism is a fairly big problem	17	83	100	16	84	100
Antisemitism is not a big problem/no problem at all	14	86	100	23	77	100

Note: Results are weighted. Some rows do not add up to 100 because of rounding.

direct experience of discrimination, on the one hand, and political and social views, on the other hand. The leading correlate is perception of anti-Black discrimination as often occurring. If the benchmark held this view, the probability of her seeing Jews as often discriminated against would jump to 64 per cent. No other characteristic has the same strength of effect. Being a victim of anti-Jewish discrimination understandably elevates the perception of anti-Jewish discrimination as often occurring. Yet even this experience cannot compete with the perception of anti-Black discrimination as often occurring. Supporting the Conservative Party has an effect comparable to experiencing anti-Jewish discrimination (30 per cent). Lack of attachment to Israel lowers the benchmark's probability of perceiving anti-Jewish discrimination as often-occurring (10 per cent).

Based on these findings, I infer that political and social views shape, or at least are related to, perceptions of anti-Jewish discrimination in Canada. Canadian Jews holding the most critical view of Canadian society – perceiving it as having a serious racism problem – also see more anti-Jewish discrimination. Said differently, there is a significant subjective component to perceptions of the seriousness of anti-Jewish discrimination. An objective cause – direct experience of discrimination – is evident too, but it is weaker than the subjective cause. In the conclusion I will return to the policy implications of this reality.

Meanwhile, let us examine the situation in France and the United Kingdom. We proceed with the same method of presentation as before. The British benchmark is a middle-aged, British-born Jewish woman who is highly educated and resides in London. She is Orthodox and has not experienced anti-Jewish harassment or violence in the year preceding the survey. She is attached to the European Union and Israel. She does not think that racism is a very big problem in the UK (see figure 20.2). The French benchmark is identical in all respects but place of birth (France) and residence (Paris) (see figure 20.3).

The first important feature in this comparison is the similarity of the levels of anxiety between Canadian and British Jewry; the probability of thinking that antisemitism is a very big problem in these contexts is in the range of 11–17 per cent, compared to 48 per cent for French Jews. The second notable feature is the similarity of the pattern of correlates. On the whole, age, gender, and place of residence have little effect on believing that antisemitism is a big problem. When we statistically change each of these characteristics in turn, the probability of thinking that antisemitism is a very big problem is only very moderately affected, if at all (figure 20.3). For instance, the young are consistently optimistic, but the difference between them and the middle-aged is relatively small, in the range of 3–10 per cent.

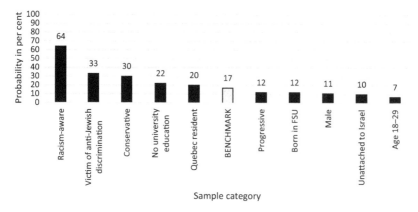

Figure 20.1. Probability of believing that Jews in Canada often face discrimination, by sample category

Note: (1) "Racism-aware" is used for brevity. It relates to perception of anti-Black discrimination as often occurring in Canada. (2) Probabilities are calculated from a logistic regression model with "thinking that Jews are often discriminated against" as the response variable and all variables appearing in figure 20.1 as predictors. Nagelkerke R^2 for the model is 0.345.

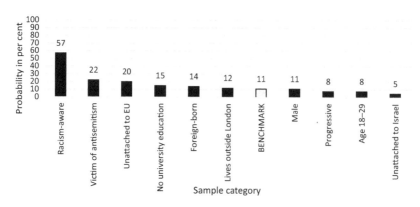

Figure 20.2. Probability of believing that antisemitism in the UK is a very big problem, by sample category

Note: (1) The label "Racism-aware" is used here for brevity. It relates to the perception of racism as a very big problem. (2) Probabilities are calculated from logistic regression models, with "thinking that antisemitism is a very big problem" as the response variable and all variables arrayed on the x-axis as predictors. Nagelkerke R^2 for the model is 0.357. (3) The UK information on voting is implied by the FRA 2018 survey. The latter included a question on degree of attachment to the European Union, which is associated with position on the left-right spectrum. For example, most Conservative voters in the UK have expressed support for Brexit, while most Labour voters have opposed Brexit.

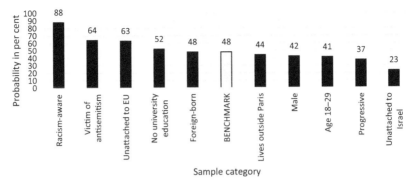

Figure 20.3. Probability of believing that antisemitism in France is a very big problem, by sample category

Note: (1) The label "Racism-aware" is used here for brevity. It relates to the perception of racism as a very big problem. (2) Probabilities are calculated from logistic regression models, with "thinking that antisemitism is a very big problem" as the response variable and all variables arrayed on the x-axis as predictors. Nagelkerke R^2 for the model is 0.343. (3) Information on voting is implied by the 2018 FRA survey. The latter included a question on degree of attachment to the European Union, which is associated with position on the left-right spectrum (stronger attachment leans left, weaker attachment leans right).

The status of political opinions and predispositions is altogether different. As in Canada, what matters most for assessing the seriousness of antisemitism is the perception of the state of racism in general. Those who hold the view that racism is a very big problem tend to think the same about antisemitism. The benchmark person, who does not see racism as a very big problem, has an 11 per cent probability in the UK and a 48 per cent probability in France of thinking that antisemitism is a very big problem. For the benchmark person who sees racism as a very big problem, the probability is about 64 per cent in the UK and 88 per cent in France.

As in Canada, experiencing antisemitism matters too. The probability of perceiving antisemitism as a very big problem by those who experienced antisemitism is 22 per cent in the UK and 64 per cent in France. But as in Canada, these percentages are much lower than the corresponding percentages for the effect of being racism-aware. The effect of political conservatism (approximated here by weak attachment to the EU project) is similar in size and direction to experience of antisemitism. Detachment from Israel is associated with a relatively low probability of perceiving antisemitism as a very big problem. In the two largest European Jewish communities, as in Canada, political and social views are significantly correlated with perceptions of the severity of antisemitism.

Conclusion

Canada belongs to the group of Western countries with especially low antisemitism. The UK belongs to the same group while the situation of France is different. Although France may not be different from Canada and the UK when it comes to the prevalence of negativity towards Jews as registered in surveys of the general population, the Jews of France are very anxious about antisemitism. This is likely due to the fact that France, unlike Canada and the UK, has suffered several violent and highly impactful antisemitic events in recent years.

Ultimately, students of antisemitism lack a decisive explanation for the discrepancy between the objective level of antisemitism in society and the subjective Jewish assessment of it. This caveat aside, it is clear that the levels of concern about antisemitism among Jews in Canada and the UK – low antisemitism countries by objective and subjective measures – are not negligible. Significant minorities of Jews in all three countries think that Jews in their respective countries of residence are often discriminated against or that antisemitism is a very big problem. Personal exposure to antisemitism is linked to these anxieties but does not determine them exclusively. If the Jewish communities of Canada and the UK consisted only of people with no personal exposure to antisemitism, the level of anxiety about it would be lower but not dramatically so.

Alongside personal experience of antisemitism, what else impacts, or is correlated with, Jewish anxieties? I found that a general view of Canadian/French/British society as ridden with racism is associated with perceiving it as antisemitic. This is in fact the strongest correlate of Jewish anxieties I found. I also discovered that a conservative political predisposition has a similar but lesser effect on the perception of antisemitism as a problem. Attachment to Israel is associated with a higher level of anxiety.

Minorities' perspectives are today considered critical in defining the nature of policies affecting minority groups, yet the question of who counts as an authentic voice is rarely raised. Minorities do not speak in a single voice. Subgroups may differ considerably on what is good for the group and what is understood as negativity or insult. Recent comparative research on antisemitism and Islamophobia demonstrates that Western Muslim educational elites differ from the rest of the Muslim population on the definition of Islamophobia (Hargreaves and Staetsky 2020). The difference between more and less educated Jews in the definition of antisemitism or perception of its severity is not as sharp, but the bigger question remains: Which view – and whose view – should be taken into account? Turning specifically to the Jewish communities of Canada, France, and the United Kingdom, whose perspective matters most for policy? Jewish social critics for whom antisemitism is a severe problem alongside other types of ethnic hatred and religious intolerance that are seen as prevalent, or those who do not see antisemitism as a very big problem?

NOTES

1 These calculations are based on data on antisemitic incidents recorded by the Community Security Trust (CST 2020), B'nai Brith Canada (2020), and Service de Protection de la Communauté Juive (SPCJ 2020). The CST recorded 1,805 antisemitic incidents in 2019 and B'nai Brith Canada recorded 2,207 such incidents. Three years average of antisemitic incidents recorded by SPCJ equalled 513. Relating these counts to Jewish population counts for the UK, Canada, and France (292,000; 392,000; and 450,000, respectively) gives a rate of 618 per 100,000 for the UK, 563 per 100,000 for Canada, and 114 per 100,000 for France. In 2019, the annual count of crimes reported to the police in England and Wales was 5.8 million (Office for National Statistics 2020a) and 2.2 million in Canada (Statistics Canada 2020). These counts, coupled with population counts for England and Wales (56 million) and Canada (37.5 million), produce the following rates: 10,375 per 100,000 for England and Wales and 5,866 per 100,000 for Canada (Office for National Statistics 2020b; Statistics Canada 2020).

2 I recently re-estimated the Jewish UK population, bumping it up from 292,000 to above 300,000.

3 The rest of this section draws on the samples used in the analysis as well as on the background socio-demographic literature and census resources of Canada and the United Kingdom (see Brym, Neuman, and Lenton 2019; Office for National Statistics 2011a, 2011b; E. Cohen 2015; Graham 2015).

REFERENCES

Bergmann, Werner. 2008. "Anti-Semitic Attitudes in Europe: A Comparative Perspective." *Journal of Social Issues* 6 (2): 343–62. https://doi.org/10.1111/j.1540-4560.2008.00565.x.

B'nai Brith Canada. 2020. *Annual Audit of Antisemitic Incidents 2019*. North York, ON: B'nai Brith of Canada League for Human Rights. http://bitly.ws/sLk7.

Brym, Robert. 2019. "Antisemitic and Anti-Israel Actions and Attitudes in Canada and Internationally: A Research Agenda." *Patterns of Prejudice* 53 (4): 407–20. https://doi.org/10.1080/0031322X.2019.1614295.

Brym, Robert, Keith Neuman, and Rhonda Lenton. 2019. *2018 Survey of Jews in Canada: Final Report*. Toronto: Environics Institute for Survey Research. https://bit.ly/3hKsXOh.

Cohen, Eric H. 2015. *The Jews of France Today: Identity and Values*. Leiden: Brill.

Cohen, Jeffrey E. 2018. "From Antisemitism to Philosemitism? Trends in American Attitudes towards Jews from 1964 to 2016." *Religions* 9 (4), 107. https://doi.org/10.3390/rel9040107.

Community Security Trust (CST). 2020. "Antisemitic Incidents Report 2019." *CST Blog.* 6 February 2020. http://bitly.ws/t5gG.

DellaPergola, Sergio. 2020. "World Jewish Population, 2019." In *American Jewish Year Book 2019*, Vol. 119, edited by Arnold Dashefsky and Ira M. Sheskin, 263–353. Cham, Switzerland: Springer.

DellaPergola, Sergio. 2022. "World Jewish Population, 2021." In *The American Jewish Year Book 2021*, Vol. 121, edited by Arnold Dashefsky and Ira M. Sheskin, 313–412. Cham, Switzerland: Springer.

DellaPergola, Sergio, and L. Daniel Staetsky. 2015. *From Old and New Directions: Perceptions and Experiences of Antisemitism among Jews in Italy.* London: Institute for Jewish Policy Research. https://archive.jpr.org.uk /object-iti2.

Enstad, Johannes Due. 2017. *Antisemitic Violence in Europe, 2005–2015: Exposure and Perpetrators in France, UK, Germany, Sweden, Denmark and Russia.* Oslo: Center for Research on Extremism (C-REX), University of Oslo. https://bit .ly/3hmXPWg.

European Union Agency for Fundamental Rights (EU-FRA). 2013. *Discrimination and Hate Crime against Jews in EU Member States: Experiences and Perceptions of Antisemitism.* Luxembourg: Publications Office of the European Union. https://bit.ly/3yBBn1c.

European Union Agency for Fundamental Rights (EU-FRA). 2018a. *Antisemitism: Overview of Data Available in the European Union, 2007–2017.* Luxembourg: Publications Office of the European Union. https://bit.ly/3r1OdTZ.

European Union Agency for Fundamental Rights (EU-FRA). 2018b. *Experiences and Perceptions of Antisemitism: Second Survey on Discrimination and Hate Crime against Jews in the EU.* Luxembourg: Publications Office of the European Union. https://bit.ly/3wqH5By.

European Union Agency for Fundamental Rights (EU-FRA). 2020. *Antisemitism: Overview of Antisemitic Incidents Recorded in the European Union, 2009–2019.* Luxembourg: Publications Office of the European Union. https://bit.ly/3xwOd0U.

Fireberg, Haim. 2020. "The Antisemitic Paradox in Europe: Empirical Evidences and Jewish Perceptions. A Comparative Study between the West and East." In *Being Jewish in 21st Century Central Europe*, edited by Haim Fireberg, Olaf Glöckner, and Marcela Zoufala, 269–80. Berlin: DeGruyter Oldenburg.

Fourquet, Jérôme. 2012. *Les électorats sociologiques: Des votes juifs.* Paris: Sciences Po, CEVIPOF. https://bit.ly/3PdeutK.

Graham, David. 2015. *Britain's Israeli Diaspora: A Demographic Portrait.* London: Institute for Jewish Policy Research. https://www.jpr.org.uk /publication?id=4252.

Hargreaves, Julian, and L. Daniel Staetsky. 2020. "Antisemitism and Islamophobia: Measuring Everyday Sensitivity in the UK." *Ethnic and Racial Studies* 43 (12): 2176–98. https://doi.org/10.1080/01419870.2019.1682177.

Institut d'études opinion et marketing en France at à l'international (IFOP). 2014. "Les votes juifs: Poids demographique et comportement electoral des juifs de France." *IFOP Focus* 116 (August): 1–15. http://bitly.ws/t5gQ.

Jikeli, Günther. 2017. "Explaining the Discrepancy of Antisemitic Acts and Attitudes in 21st Century France." *Contemporary Jewry* 37 (2): 257–73. https://doi.org/10.1007/s12397-017-9221-x.

Mayer, Avi. 2019. "American Jews on Antisemitism in America: Insights from the AJC's Landmark Survey." *American Jewish Committee*, 23 October 2019. https://bit.ly/3xseNYW.

Office for National Statistics. 2011a. "Highest Level of Qualification by Religion by Age." Census 2011, Table DC5204EW. NOMIS Official Labour Market Statistics. http://bitly.ws/sMzu.

Office for National Statistics. 2011b. "Religion by Sex and Age." Census 2011, Table DC2107EW. NOMIS Official Labour Market Statistics. http://bitly.ws/sMzx.

Office for National Statistics. 2020a. "Crime in England and Wales: Year Ending in March 2020." http://bitly.ws/sKei.

Office for National Statistics. 2020b. "Population Estimates for the UK, England and Wales, Scotland and Northern Ireland, Provisional, Mid-2019." https://bit.ly/3qRxLpm.

Service de Protection de la Communauté Juive (SPCJ). 2020. *Report on Antisemitism in France*. Paris: SPCJ. https://www.antisemitisme.fr/dl/2020-EN.

Staetsky, L. Daniel. 2017. *Antisemitism in Contemporary Great Britain: A Study of Attitudes towards Jews and Israel*. London: Institute for Jewish Policy Research. https://bit.ly/3wqMkkI.

Staetsky, L. Daniel. 2019a. "Can Convenience Samples Be Trusted? Lessons from the Surveys of Jews in Europe, 2012." *Contemporary Jewry* 39 (1): 115–53. https://doi.org/10.1007/s12397-019-09280-8.

Staetsky, L. Daniel. 2019b. "Global Levels, Trends, and Correlates of Antisemitic Attitudes through the Prism of Modernization Theory: Insights from the Pew Research Center and World Values Surveys." *Journal of Contemporary Antisemitism* 2 (1): 47–64. https://doi.org/10.26613/jca/2.1.22.

Staetsky, L. Daniel. 2019c. "How British Jews Vote and Why They Vote This Way." *Times of Israel*, 5 September 2019. https://bit.ly/3hR7dk5.

Staetsky, L. Daniel, and Jonathan Boyd. 2014. *The Exceptional Case? Perceptions and Experiences of Antisemitism among Jews in the United Kingdom*. London: Institute for Jewish Policy Research. https://bit.ly/36jeJhZ.

Statistics Canada. 2020. "Police-Reported Crime Increases in 2019." *The Daily*, October 29 2020. http://bitly.ws/t5gU.

21 Marriage and Mobility of Moroccan Jews in Montreal and Paris[1]

MARTIN MESSIKA AND YOLANDE COHEN

Editors' Note

Canada's Jewish population is diverse. One of its main divisions is between Ashkenazim, who comprise about 90 per cent of the Jewish population, and Sephardim, who also boast a rich history in Canada.

Ashkenazim are said to derive from the Roman exile in 70 CE, Sephardim from the Babylonian exile, 657 years earlier. Where Muslim Andalusia (the Iberian Peninsula) influenced Sephardi culture, Christian Europe influenced Ashkenazi culture.

When Christians completed their reconquest of the Iberian Peninsula in the late fifteenth century, the Inquisition forced Jews who did not convert to Christianity to flee. Expelled Jews resettled in North Africa, the Netherlands, Italy, the Ottoman Empire, and elsewhere. Some of them eventually made their way to England. Following the British conquest of New France in 1763, a few immigrated to Montreal. Mainly merchants, these immigrants founded Canada's first congregation, Shearith Israel, and the synagogue named after their countries of origin, the Spanish and Portuguese Synagogue, in 1768.

The legacy of the early Sephardic immigration largely dissipated, but a revitalization occurred when Jews from North Africa, mostly Morocco, felt compelled to leave their countries in the context of European decolonization and growing anti-Jewish sentiment following the creation of the State of Israel. Between the late 1950s and the 1980s, about 15,000 French-speaking Moroccan Jews settled in Montreal, with a smaller, mostly Spanish-speaking Moroccan community preferring Toronto.

According to the 2018 Survey of Jews in Canada, about 90 per cent of Canada's Sephardim are divided approximately equally between Toronto and Montreal. In Montreal, they form nearly one quarter of the Jewish population. When respondents were asked in 2018 how connected they feel to Jewish life in their city, the difference between Sephardim and Ashkenazim in *the proportion who said "not very connected," "not at all connected," and "don't know" reached statistical significance (p < 0.01). The immigrant generation did not always see eye to eye with the English-speaking Ashkenazi majority in Montreal, and table 21.1 suggests that the sense of estrangement persists in at least part of the Sephardic community today. About three in ten Sephardim feel less well connected to the Canadian Jewish mainstream than Ashkenazim do.*

For two reasons, these results should be treated cautiously. First, the self-identified Sephardi subsample in the 2018 Survey of Jews in Canada is small and heterogeneous, including, like previous surveys, people of North African and Middle Eastern origin. Second, the findings should be tempered with the observation that a 2017 focus group of twenty young Montreal Sephardim expressed stronger attachment to Judaism than to the Montreal Jewish community. More recent interviews with young Sephardim show the same trend, with a minority active in Hassidic or ultra-Orthodox groups in the Montreal metropolitan area.[2]

Table 21.1. "How connected are you to Jewish life in your city?" 2018, in per cent

	Sephardim (n = 207)	Ashkenazim (n = 1,947)
Very	34	40
Somewhat	38	41
Not very/not at all/don't know	28	20
Total	100	101

Note: The second column does not equal 100 due to rounding. An additional twenty respondents self-identified as "Mizrakhim" (Easterners). Adding them to the Sephardim does not significantly change the findings.
Source: Brym, Neuman, and Lenton (2019).

Introduction

Israel was the main destination of Moroccan-Jewish immigrants in the 1950s, while France and Canada were important secondary centres of immigration. The Jews who immigrated to Canada in the 1960s and 1970s first settled mainly in Greater Montreal. Those who immigrated to France settled mainly in the Paris region. In the latter cases, the immigrants were in their great majority educated in the francophone school system of the Alliance Israélite Universelle and therefore aspired to be part of the middle class in Morocco and in the countries to which they immigrated (Abitbol 2009).

How did the Moroccan-Jewish population adjust to life in Montreal and Paris? Did immigration consolidate the middle class? Or did migration to Montreal or Paris confirm the hope these migrants had of achieving upward occupational mobility? Comparative analysis makes it possible to understand such specificities of Moroccan-Jewish migration in each urban area (Green 2002). The migration took place over several decades, so one can also ask how the occupational profile of the immigrants changed over the years.

For a long time, the historiography of this immigration movement has centred on men, ignoring women's paths. However, Moroccan-Jewish immigrants, who are sometimes not mentioned in general works on Moroccan immigration, included women as well as men. The present analysis allows us to compare the ways in which men and women adjusted to life in the two cities.

Studies conducted in the years following their arrival show that the immigrants quickly became economically independent (Berman, Nahmiash, and Osmer 1970, 5). Based on the 1971 Canadian census, Jean-Claude Lasry and Claude Tapia (1989) emphasize the importance of the category "office workers and sales personnel," which accounted for 40 per cent of North African Jews in Montreal, compared with 14 per cent of the general population at the national level. Using an index of occupational status, Lasry also analysed the career paths of Jews from the Maghreb in Montreal. He established that the early stages of arrival in Montreal corresponded to a period of "prestige loss" and downward mobility. This was particularly the case for individuals who were property owners, members of the liberal professions, and small traders in their country of birth. Nevertheless, opportunities for upward occupational mobility existed for those who became blue-collar workers.

Lasry found that after seven years in Canada, immigrants were employed in an occupation with the same level of occupational prestige as the ones they held in their country of birth (Lasry 1980). This finding is consistent with that of Naomi Moldofsky (1968), who discovered that the percentage of migrants who felt that the job they held was of higher status than the one they had in their country of birth depended on how long they had been in Canada: 15 per cent for those who had been in the country for four years, rising to 40 per cent for newcomers who had been in the country for nine years or more. In addition, analyses of the 2001 census and the 2011 National Household Survey reveal a Sephardic Montreal population, including but not limited to Moroccans, that is well integrated into the working world and with a significant number of managers and professionals. It has therefore become common to consider this population as having migrated relatively successfully in comparison with non-Jewish immigrant groups who settled in Montreal at about the same time, such as Portuguese, Haitians, and Italians.

Analysis of the French case reveals similarities, even if Moroccan natives are more difficult to identify since studies include them in the larger category of North African Jews from Tunisia, Morocco, and Algeria. Thus, in her pioneering work, Doris Bensimon (1972) emphasized their economic integration into the French system – without minimizing the difficulties they encountered culturally and emotionally. Compared to Haitians who arrived in France in the same time period, Moroccan Jews fared better in terms of their socio-economic status (Cohen and Jabouin 2021).

Sources

This chapter provides a fresh perspective on the settlement of Jews from Morocco by focusing on two dimensions indicating their degree of adjustment in the host society: marriage and occupation. It extends previous work on marriages at Montreal's Spanish and Portuguese Synagogue and two Parisian synagogues (rue Copernic and Synagogue des Tournelles), which highlights the high rate of intermarriage between spouses of North African origin in Montreal and Paris (Cohen and Scioldo-Zürcher 2014). Data on the occupations of newcomers upon arrival in Montreal and Paris derive from information collected by the social service agencies from which they received assistance (Messika 2020). Information at the time of marriage (a stage of stabilization in the host country) is based on files and marriage certificates in Parisian and Montreal synagogues.[3] The study covers the period 1961–75 in Paris and 1969–2014 in Montreal. To provide a basis for comparing occupations in the two cities, we used the Canadian National Occupational Classification (NOC). This categorization was refined by identifying job categories not included in the NOC.

Arrival in Montreal and Paris

The profile of Moroccan-Jewish immigrants and the conditions of their settlement differed from the profile and settlement conditions of other immigrants who arrived in Canada after the Second World War. For example, unlike Italians, they almost all arrived with their families, were more highly skilled occupationally, and settled in urban centres. In Montreal, their settlement was supported by Jewish associations such as Jewish Immigrant Aid Services (JIAS), which offered financial assistance and help finding housing and employment. Analysis of social agency files allows us to compose a socio-professional profile of the newcomers and offer a partial assessment of their social situation and professional background.

In their country of birth, the majority of men had been employed as office workers (including accountants; 29 per cent) or craft workers (22 per cent). The majority of women (53 per cent) had at least one previous paying job. Among those who worked in the paid labour force, 48 per cent of Moroccan-born women had been office workers (secretaries or clerks), while 27 per cent worked as dressmakers, hairdressers, and the like (27 per cent).

This snapshot of the Moroccan Jewish population upon arrival in Montreal reveals a relatively skilled population, among which office jobs predominated for both men and women. Nevertheless, during their settlement, men and women followed different paths to paid work, reflecting a period of adjustment in their return to employment. For men, arrival in Montreal was often associated with a change in employment sector. Thus, only 49 per cent of men who were office workers or accountants in Morocco and found their first job in Montreal with the assistance of a social worker were able to work in their previous field of employment. This phenomenon is common among immigrants, testifying to the difficulties they have initially in finding the same kind of job they had in their country of origin.

Women's labour force participation rates fell substantially after they arrived in Montreal.[4] This finding is consistent with other studies that show that the percentage of North African Jewish women without work in the paid labour force is higher in Montreal than in their country of birth. The difference can be explained by the structure of the Montreal labour market, which can be less welcoming for women than for men. In addition, JIAS social workers may have been more concerned with finding a job for the "male head of household" than for their wives and daughters (Néméh-Nombré 2017).

In the French case, analysis of reception files allows us to sketch a profile of the newcomers. In her analysis of social services offered by the Fonds social juif unifié in Toulouse, Colette Zytnicki highlighted the importance of the employed population, comprising 29 per cent of its clients. Workers and service personnel represented 18 per cent of the employed clients, craft workers 14 per cent, and tradespeople 15.7 per cent (Zytnicki 1998, 155). In Paris, at the Comité d'Action sociale israélite de Paris, 35 per cent of Moroccan-born people worked in occupations close to the craft industry, representing a larger percentage than office workers in Montreal. This difference may be related to source bias, but may also be the result of more highly qualified Jewish populations immigrating to Canada, the latter having been selected by Canadian immigration authorities partly for their socio-occupational profile, which was not the case in France.

Marriage Record Samples

Collection of data for the period 1955–70 began at Montreal's Spanish and Portuguese Synagogue and in two Parisian synagogues, a consistorial synagogue on rue des Tournelles and a liberal synagogue on rue Copernic.

The earlier research is developed here in two ways. First, in addition to marriages celebrated at Montreal's Spanish and Portuguese Synagogue, we include marriages that took place at Montreal's Or Hahayim Synagogue, which has a large Moroccan membership. In addition, complementary research was carried out at the Consistoire de Paris for synagogues in the Paris region, bringing together diverse places of worship, including synagogues established as chapels.

The Montreal sample consists of 1,834 marriages celebrated in the Spanish and Portuguese Synagogue and Or Hahayim. Between these two synagogues, 665 marriages were celebrated between 1969 and 1979, another 629 between 1980 and 1989, 261 between 1990 and 1999, and 279 between 2000 and 2014.[5] Of these 1,834 marriages, we count 454 men and 309 women born in Morocco. If we consider the category "Sephardic" to include people born abroad or in Canada,[6] we count 831 Sephardic men and 668 Sephardic women.

Overall, the number of marriages celebrated in the synagogues in our study increased over the years, with a decrease only in the period 1969–89.

The Ile-de-France sample is composed of 2,126 marriage certificates from a variety of synagogues located in Paris and the surrounding area between 1961 and 1975. The presence of people from Morocco in the sample is a consequence of the fact that there are 1,063 records in which at least one of the spouses was born in that country – a total of 561 men and 571 women.

Who Do Moroccan Natives Marry?

Previous work established that 67 per cent of the marriages that took place at the consistorial synagogue on rue des Tournelles were between natives of North Africa. This figure compares to 11 per cent at the rue Copernic synagogue and 18 per cent at the Spanish and Portuguese Synagogue in Montreal (Cohen and Scioldo-Zürcher 2014). The collection of additional data in other Parisian consistorial synagogues and the study of marriages after the 1980s suggest about the same level of geographical in-marriage as in previous work among Moroccan natives in liberal synagogues and a small increase in in-marriage in the Parisian consistorial synagogues and Montreal.

For the Paris region, the most common union among North African natives was between Moroccans and Algerians (40 per cent), followed by Moroccan natives among themselves (29 per cent). The latter percentage is almost ten percentage points higher than in earlier studies. In the case of Montreal's Spanish and Portuguese Synagogue and Or Hahayim, the extension of collection dates does not change the results; unions between Moroccans compose fully 90 per cent of North African marriages. However, among Moroccan natives, most marriages are between Moroccan and Canadian natives (220 marriages compared to 177 marriages between Moroccan natives). For 30 per cent of marriages of men with Canadian natives, the fiancés are French-Canadians who converted from Catholicism to Judaism (Cohen and Guerry 2011). In Paris, there were 256 marriages between individuals born in Morocco and France, which attests to the integration of newcomers into the host society, since this figure is higher than the number of marriages between Moroccan natives.

These data show that living in Montreal or Paris is associated with relative openness in terms of choice of spouse. But if marriage to non-native Moroccans is frequent, even the majority, in the two areas studied, small disparities exist between men and women. In Montreal, 61 per cent of Moroccan-born men marry women who were not born in Morocco. For Moroccan-born women the comparable figure is 58 per cent. The situation is similar in the Paris region, where marriage between the Moroccan-born is common, but not the majority. Some 68 per cent of Moroccan-born men marry non-Moroccan women, compared to 64 per cent of Moroccan-born women. Thus, somewhat greater openness to geographical out-marriage is evident in Montreal and among men. Still, members of this first cohort of migrants, both men and women, tend to marry outside of their group of origin, while retaining their strong identification with Judaism by converting their mostly Catholic fiancés to their own faith.

Occupational Profile of Moroccan Jews in Montreal and Paris

Marriage records also allow us to assess the socio-occupational situation of the migrant populations at the time of their arrival in the two cities. Analysis of these data allows us not only to draw comparisons between the migrations to Canada and France, but also to propose avenues for drawing comparisons within these Jewish communities. The Canadian classification that we have adopted is particularly broad and is mainly concerned with economic sector, not hierarchical position. Applying this classification allows us to conclude that the occupational profiles of Moroccan Jews who married in Montreal and in the rest of Canada are similar, as are the occupational profiles of Moroccan Jews who married in Montreal and in the Paris area. However, the Montreal and Paris samples differ somewhat. Notably, the sample from the Montreal synagogues consists of 418 men and 273 women (a gender ratio of 1.5), while the sample from the Paris area synagogues consists of 573 men and 474 women (a gender ratio of 1.2).

For native Moroccans, the main occupations in Paris are in "sales and services" (126 people) and "business, finance, and administration" (119 people). Students and people in scientific occupations come next, with 87 and 75 people, respectively. The "sales and services" category includes a wide range of occupations associated with sales, but also with craft skills, while the "business, finance, and administration" category also includes some management positions. Technical occupations are included in the "trades, transportation, machinery, and related" and "manufacturing and public utilities" categories. They include workers at various skill levels.

The occupational structure of married men associated with the Montreal synagogues is similar to that of the men living in Paris. In the two Montreal synagogues, most of the men are in "sales and services," "business, finance, and administration," and "trades, transportation, machinery, and related" occupations.

However, an analysis within the main categories reveals a difference between the two populations. If "sales and service" personnel are most numerous in both cases, they include a different mix of occupations in the two cities. In Montreal, the largest group in this category, at 46 per cent, is in sales, while the comparable figure in Paris is 21 per cent. Meanwhile, the percentage of craft workers and those involved in commerce is higher in Paris. Comparing Montreal fiancés born in Morocco with those not born in Morocco also reinforces the idea of a relative concentration of Moroccan natives in the "sales and services" category.

At the time of their marriage in Montreal, 82 per cent of Moroccan-born women had a paying job.[7] This was not the case in the period immediately following their arrival in Montreal, as the JIAS data show. In fact, their labour force participation rate is nearly the same as that of Canadian-born women (83 per cent) and considerably higher than that of women in Canada who were born in a country other than Canada or Morocco (76 per cent).

The occupational profile of women born in Montreal is dominated by two main categories: administrative occupations (28 per cent) and sales occupations (27 per cent), the latter of which also includes some occupations associated with craft work, such as hairdressing. Native Moroccan fiancés are more likely to belong to the latter category than are brides born in other countries, testifying to the relative ease of entry into hairdressing.

This is less the case in the Paris sample, where the concentration is higher in business, finance, and administration (49 per cent) and the student group (20 per cent). The first group includes secretaries and stenographers/typists, the most common occupations. In this respect, the concentration of women in Paris in these professions as well as their weight in Montreal sheds light on the process of entry into the labour market, which was made possible in the occupations associated with secretarial work by the fact that this young and educated population either attended francophone schools in Morocco or had been educated in the host country. In France, these jobs are often the first entry point into the labour market.

Finally, we can consider the place of students in comparing the Montreal and Paris samples. The percentage of female students was higher in Paris (20 per cent) than in Montreal (16 per cent). The latter was close to the percentage of non-Moroccan women who married in the Montreal sample (17 per cent). The discrepancy between male students in Paris (13 per cent) and Montreal (3 per cent) was more substantial.

It is difficult to interpret this important Montreal/Paris difference. It can be considered on two levels. First, it may reflect the relative ease of access to higher education in Paris for a migrant population, schooled in French, in a context where it is difficult for them to find a job and where tuition is free. Second, it may reflect greater confidence among the Parisians that their entry into the paid labour force will be relatively easy after they complete their studies. The fact that the absence of a permanent job does not seem to be an obstacle in some students' decision to marry in Paris supports the latter interpretation.

Upward Mobility and Career Paths

It is difficult to discern much upward mobility for men over the years, but upward mobility is more apparent for women (see table 21.2 for men and table 21.3 for women).

The decade-by-decade figures in table 21.2 and table 21.3 should be read with caution, since the number of people per decade varies

Table 21.2. Occupational distribution of Moroccan-Jewish men in Montreal, 1969–2014, in per cent

	1969–1979	1980–1989	1990–1999	2000–2014	Total
Sales and services	33	22	27	25	28
Business, finance, and administration	10	23	20	13	16
Trades, transportation, machinery, and related	14	11	16	8	13
Management	13	13	10	13	13
Education, law, and social, community, and government services	6	8	8	13	7
Natural and applied sciences and related	8	5	4	13	7
Arts, culture, sports, and recreation	7	7	0	0	6
Health	3	5	6	13	5
Students	5	1	2	0	0
Manufacturing and public utilities	1	4	4	0	2
Pensioners	0	1	2	4	1
Total	100	100	99	102	98
Number of cases	197	148	49	24	418

Note: Some columns do not equal 100 due to rounding.
Sources: Marriage records, Spanish and Portuguese Synagogue and Or Hahayim Synagogue.

substantially. Nevertheless, we can see meaningful change over time. The percentage of men in "sales and services" dropped eight percentage points between the 1970s and the 2000s. For occupations in "arts, culture, sports and recreation," the absolute number of individuals is small, but the decline is seven percentage points between the 1970s and the 2000s. For students, we see a five percentage-point decline over the same period, likely due to the fact that the average age at marriage increased over time and the fact that men who marry do so after their studies. On the other hand, the percentage of individuals in the health field grew by ten points over the period under consideration. Although a total of just twenty people were in the health professions over the entire period, the relative importance of these occupations in the workforce may reflect an increase in professional qualifications overall.

For women, the tendency towards increased professional qualifications is more conspicuous. The professional profile of Moroccan-born women changed over the years. The proportion of women in "business, finance, and administration" fell by nineteen percentage points while the corresponding figure for students was seventeen percentage points. Sales and hairdressing were common occupations in the female

328   Martin Messika and Yolande Cohen

Table 21.3. Occupational distribution of Moroccan-Jewish women in Montreal, 1969–2014, in per cent

	1969–1979	1980–1989	1990–1999	2000–2014	Total
Business, finance, and administration	36	23	18	10	27
Sales and services	28	28	25	19	27
Students	17	22	11	0	16
Education, law, and social, community, and government services	9	11	14	33	12
Health	4	2	29	19	7
Management	4	4	0	14	4
Arts, culture, sports, and recreation	1	2	4	0	1
Manufacturing and public utilities	0	5	0	0	1
Natural and applied sciences and related	1	2	0	0	1
Trades, transportation, machinery, and related	1	0	0	5	1
Pensioners	0	0	0	0	0
Total	101	99	101	100	97
Number of cases	142	82	28	21	273

Note: Some columns do not equal 100 due to rounding.
Sources: Marriage records, Spanish and Portuguese Synagogue and Or Hahayim Synagogue.

population in the 1970s, but the number of hairdressers, for example, fell from twenty-three in the 1970s to ten in the 1980s and then to zero in the 1990s. On the other hand, employment in "education, law, and social, community, and government services" rose from 9 per cent (thirteen people) in the 1970s to 33 per cent (seven people) in the 2000s. Similarly, even though the number of women in the health professions remains modest, it increased between 1970 and 1990 from five to eight people. On the whole, it seems clear that women have improved their professional qualifications over time, partly because of their improved integration into Canadian society, partly because of the rising status of all women in Canadian society over the nearly half-century represented by table 21.3.

Conclusion

In the first years after immigration, some Moroccan Jews experienced difficulties integrating into Montreal's paid labour force. However, their descendants appear to have experienced considerable upward mobility.

Women apparently had more difficulty entering the paid labour force than men did, probably because of the way the work world was structured and the greater emphasis placed on men's work. It is also possible that immigration tightened the family sphere, initially distancing women from paid work. This issue requires more research, especially through the use of surveys and oral histories. Over time, constraints on women's labour force participation faded. The labour force participation rate for women increased the longer families had to adjust to their new country, the longer the presence of women in the paid labour force normalized their taking on paid work, and the larger the proportion of women who attended school in Canada.

The occupational profile of native Moroccans who marry in the Paris region and in Montreal are similar, but not identical. For instance, there have been more students among Moroccan Jews in Paris and more salespeople in Montreal. Improved qualifications and consequent upward mobility has been evident from the beginning of Moroccan-Jewish immigration in Montreal, especially for women of the second generation.

Immigration has also enabled Moroccan-Canadians to out-marry geographically, socially, and even religiously, although women are less likely than men to do so. The results of this survey therefore suggest that marriage strategies reflect a generally positive outlook, especially among men, on the host society. However, it is the acquisition of professional qualifications that allows for upward mobility, especially for women.

NOTES

1 This chapter is a revised version of Messika and Cohen (2017). It was translated from the French by Robert Brym with the assistance of Yolande Cohen and is part of a larger project on postcolonial migrations of Moroccan Jews, supported by the Social Sciences and Humanities Research Council of Canada. The authors thank Robert Brym for his translation, kind assistance, and thorough editing of the text.
2 We are grateful to Yolande Cohen for this information.
3 We thank Veronique Cahen and Christine Chevalier-Caron, who entered data from the marriage certificates.
4 In the sample cited, only 23 per cent of Moroccan-born women (sixty-three people) held a job at least once before their follow-up interview.
5 Data for the years 2008, 2009, and 2011 are missing.
6 Charles Shahar (2015, 49) defines people as Sephardic if they were born in Afghanistan, Albania, Algeria, Bulgaria, Egypt, France, Greece, India, Iran,

Iraq, Jordan, Kuwait, Lebanon, Libya, Morocco, North Yemen, Pakistan, Portugal, Saudi Arabia, South Yemen, Spain, Syria, Tunisia, Turkey, Yemen, or Yugoslavia (Bosnia and Herzegovina, Croatia, Macedonia, Slovenia); if their mother and father were born in those countries; if their mother tongue is French, Arabic, Greek, Bulgarian, or Yugoslavian; or if they are children in a household where both parents fit these criteria.

7 The percentage without a paying job is calculated from mentions of "housewife" and "unemployed" and the absence of any indication that the individual was in the paid labour force.

REFERENCES

Abitbol, Michel. 2009. *Histoire du Maroc*. Paris: Perrin.

Bensimon, Doris. 1972. *L'Intégration des Juifs nord-africains en France*. La Haye: Mouton.

Berman, Gerald, Daphne Nahmiash, and Carol Osmer. 1970. *A Profile of Moroccan Jewish Immigrants in Montreal*. Montreal: McGill University.

Brym, Robert, Keith Neuman, and Rhonda Lenton. 2019. *2018 Survey of Jews in Canada: Final Report*. Toronto: Environics Institute for Survey Research. https://bit.ly/3hKsXOh.

Burgard, Antoine. 2017. "Les Sépharades dans les études démographiques." In *Les sépharades du Québec: Parcours d'exils nord-africains*, edited by Yolande Cohen, 33–56. Montreal: Del Busso.

Cohen, Yolande, and Linda Guerry. 2011. "Mariages et parcours migratoires: Juifs nés au Maroc et mariés à la Spanish and Portuguese Synagogue de Montréal (1969–1981)." *Studies in Religion/Études religieuses* 40 (3): 293–317. https://doi.org/10.1177/0008429811408212.

Cohen, Yolande, and Evens Jabouin. 2021. "Comparer l'incomparable: Haïtiens et Juifs marocains en France (1960–1980)." *Archives juives* 54: 112–32. https://doi.org/10.3917/aj1.542.0112.

Cohen, Yolande, and Yann Scioldo-Zürcher. 2014. "Maghrebi Jewish Migrations and Religious Marriage in Paris and Montreal, 1954–1980." In *Religion in the Public Sphere*, edited by Solange Lefebvre and Lori Beaman, 250–74. Toronto: University of Toronto Press.

Green, Nancy. 2002. *Repenser les migrations*. Paris: Presses universitaires de France.

Lasry, Jean-Claude. 1980. "Mobilité professionnelle chez les immigrants juifs nord-africains à Montréal." *Applied Psychology* 29 (1–2): 17–33. https://doi.org/10.1111/j.1464-0597.1980.tb00879.x.

Lasry, Jean-Claude, and Claude Tapia. 1989. *Les Juifs du Maghreb: Diasporas contemporaines*. Montreal: Presses de l'Université de Montréal.

Messika, Martin. 2020. *Politiques de l'accueil: États et associations face à la migration juive du Maghreb en France et au Canada des années 1950 à la fin des années 1970*. Rennes: Presses universitaires de Rennes.

Messika, Martin, and Yolande Cohen. 2017. "Juifs marocains à Paris et à Montréal." In *Les sépharades du Québec: Parcours d'exils nord-africains*, edited by Yolande Cohen, 57–71. Montreal: Del Busso.

Moldofsky, Naomi. 1968. "The Economic Adjustment of North African Jewish Immigrants in Montreal." PhD diss., McGill University.

Néméh-Nombré, Philippe. 2017. "L'emploi des femmes judéo-marocaines à leur arrivée à Montréal (1956–1978)." In *Les sépharades du Québec: Parcours d'exils nord-africains*, edited by Yolande Cohen, 161–82. Montreal: Del Busso.

Shahar, Charles. 2015. *2011 National Household Survey: The Jewish Community of Montreal*. Part 7, *The Sephardic Community*. Montreal: Jewish Federations of Canada – CJA. http://bitly.ws/sw5h.

Zytnicki, Colette. 1998. *Les Juifs à Toulouse entre 1945 et 1970: Une communauté toujours recommencée*. Toulouse: Presses universitaires du Mirail.

22 Jewish Engagement in Canada and Australia

ADINA BANKIER-KARP

Canadian and Australian Jewry: Similar yet Different

Canadian and Australian Jewry are similar in many respects. They are embedded in English-speaking democracies whose origins derive at least in part from British colonialism (Weinfeld 2021; Levi and Bergman 2002). They both became home to Jewish immigrants in the second half of the eighteenth century. Poverty and political turmoil in Eastern Europe motivated their largest waves of immigration in the twentieth century (Tulchinsky 1993; Rutland 1988). They are among the world's medium-sized Jewish communities, Canada with a Jewish population of 392,000 and Australia with a Jewish population of 118,000 (DellaPergola 2020). The two countries are known for the warmth with which they welcome newcomers, their resilient institutions, their relative prosperity, and their high scores in rankings of citizen happiness – on the last dimension, Canada ranked fifteeth and Australia ranked twelfth in the world in 2020 (Bartrop 1995; Hammerton 2001; Helliwell et al. 2021).

Nonetheless, as will become apparent in the following analysis, the Canadian and Australian Jewish communities differ in an important respect: Australian Jews are more Jewishly engaged than Canadian Jews are. With a more geographically concentrated population, a comparatively higher proportion of immigrants and students of Jewish day schools, and more traditional marriage and endogamy norms, Australian Jews have forged a stronger sense of Jewish kinship and thereby enabled more intense Jewish engagement. I will make this case by analysing data from two recent surveys of Canadian and Australian Jewry – the 2018 Survey of Jews in Canada (Brym, Neuman, and Lenton 2019) and the Gen17 Australian Jewish Community Survey (Graham and Markus 2018).

Jewish Social and Religious Capital

Sociologists distinguish various forms of capital that play a central role in my analysis. *Social capital* refers to the value of social ties. It is accumulated when individuals uphold beliefs and perform actions that are widely approved in given social contexts (Putnam 2000). Social capital engenders trust and support among individuals and thus strengthens social collectivities. *Religious capital* refers to religious belief and behaviour (Iannaccone 1990). Religious capital encompasses intimate knowledge of the central tenets, practices, and customs of a religion. Accumulation of religious capital offers individuals joy and meaning.[1]

Jewish social capital translates social capital into the Jewish sphere (Pomson and Schnoor 2018). It refers to an individual's bonds with Jewish family, Jewish peers, and Jewish community. *Jewish religious capital* refers to the capacities and meaning inspiring and derived from ritual behaviours such as Sabbath observance and prayer. In this chapter, I regard those with higher measures of Jewish social and religious capital as having higher levels of Jewish engagement.

Comparative Jewish Engagement

The 2018 Survey of Jews in Canada and the Gen17 Australian Jewish Community Survey recently interviewed large, carefully weighted, and broadly representative national samples of Jewish adults in the two countries.

According to measures of Jewish social and religious capital in the two surveys, Australian Jews are more Jewishly engaged. For example, with respect to Jewish social capital, Australians are more likely than Canadians to report that all their close friends are Jewish (27 per cent vs. 9 per cent). They are also more likely to say that being part of a Jewish community is essential to their conception of what it means to be Jewish (58 per cent vs. 40 per cent). Australian Jews also have more Jewish religious capital. They are more likely than Canadian Jews to report always lighting Shabbat candles (43 per cent vs. 34 per cent) and attending a synagogue at least once a week (14 per cent vs. 7 per cent).

From the relevant literature, I identify five factors that may account for these differences:

1 *Generation.* Generational erosion theory holds that an ethnic group becomes more acculturated as each successive post-immigration generation broadens and deepens its ties to individuals outside the ethnic group in educational institutions, workplaces, friendship

circles, and families. In due course, this process results in loss of ethnic, cultural, and/or religious distinctiveness and the assimilation of the group into the wider society (Alba 1990; Gans 1979; Waters 1990). It follows that the length of time an immigrant group lives in its new country will be negatively associated with its ethnic or religious distinctiveness. It is significant in this regard that about 30 per cent of Canadian Jews and 47 per cent of Australian Jews are immigrants, and that the largest wave of Jewish immigration to Canada took place between 1900 and 1920, while the largest wave of Jewish migration to Australia occurred between 1934 and 1954 (Rutland 2006; Tulchinsky 1993; Weinfeld 2021).

2 *Jewish education*. Critics of generational erosion theory argue that loss of distinctiveness and group solidarity are not inevitable; Jewish communities may be sustained by "thick" Jewish culture, which is manifest in a strong sense of kinship and shared religious or secular values, both of which articulate and sustain strong group boundaries. In particular, intensive Jewish education mitigates the effects of generation on ethnic group cohesion (Gitelman 1998). From this point of view, Jewish day school education in particular exerts enduring effects on Jewish learning, festival observance, community service, and engagement with Israel, even when controlling for family background (Brym and Lenton 2020; Chertok et al. 2007; Graham 2014; chapter 5 in this volume). In Canada and Australia, Jewish day school education, particularly in each country's two largest cities, is common, as is summer camp attendance and other informal types of Jewish education. However, Australians are more likely than Canadians to participate in some form of informal Jewish education such as a youth trip to Israel (84 per cent vs. 67 per cent) and attend at least one year of Jewish day school (52 per cent vs. 44 per cent), although attendance at Jewish summer camps is somewhat more common among Canadians (58 per cent vs. 52 per cent).

3 and 4 *Spouse/partner religion and childrearing*. Prolonged and permanent singlehood, together with delayed childbearing and childlessness, negatively influence religious participation given that people who are more religiously engaged tend to be more likely to marry and have children than people who are less religiously engaged (Engelberg 2016; Wuthnow 2010). Canadian and Australian Jewish marriage and fertility patterns differ. Significantly, fewer Canadians than Australians are married or in a common-law relationship (69 per cent vs. 80 per cent) and more Canadians reported being never married (16 per cent vs. 11 per cent) or divorced or separated (15 per cent vs. 9 per cent). In addition, fewer Canadians than Australians

report living at home with their child or children under the age of eighteen (71 per cent vs. 80 per cent). Married life is more conducive than single life to Jewish engagement in marriages where both partners are Jewish. It is therefore notable that more Canadians than Australians report that their spouse or common-law partner is not Jewish (15 per cent vs. 10 per cent).

5 *Population concentration.* Population concentration of an ethnic group enhances community-mindedness and increases opportunities for socializing and religious participation within the group (Kadushin 2012; Rossi and Rossi 1990). Canada's Jewish community enjoys high population concentration, with 71 per cent of Jewish adults residing in Toronto or Montreal. However, Australia's Jewish community is even more concentrated, with 84 per cent residing in Melbourne or Sydney (Graham and Narunsky 2019). This factor, too, may account for the higher level of Jewish engagement of Australian Jews compared to Canadian Jews.

The next section tests the five theories I have outlined by analysing data from the Canadian and Australian surveys.

Methodology

Data

The 2018 Survey of Jews in Canada was conducted online and via telephone, with recruitment methods informed by census data and distinctive Jewish name lists in cities with large Jewish populations as well as snowball sampling. The Australian survey was conducted online, drawing on Jewish communal organization membership lists and snowball sampling. The Canadian survey was conducted between 10 February and 30 September 2018, yielding a sample of 2,335 individuals identifying as Jewish by their present religion, or Jewish/partially Jewish in ways other than religion. The Australian survey was conducted between February and May 2017, yielding a sample of 8,621 individuals who identify as "Jewish in any way." The national census in both countries included a question about religious identification, and census data was used to inform the development of post hoc weighting for both surveys by total population size, age, and sex.

The two datasets are comparable because each has a claim to being a representative sample of the Jews in that country (see methodological appendices of Brym, Neuman, and Lenton 2019; Graham and Markus 2018). Therefore, the two datasets were combined for analysis. Because

336   Adina Bankier-Karp

the survey populations are distinct, the original weights for each survey are used in the analysis. For variance estimation, the population is treated as if it were composed of two strata, with 10,956 individuals sampled from the strata.

Variables

I identified variables common to the two surveys. Question wording differed somewhat between some of the variables in the Canadian and Australian questionnaires, but I deemed them sufficiently similar to be comparable for the purposes of this chapter. After conducting internal tests of consistency on the common questionnaire items to determine their reliability, I determined that eight Jewish engagement variables and seven independent variables could be used to test the theories outlined earlier.

Distinct Jewish social capital and Jewish religious capital scales emerged from an exploratory factor analysis that was performed on the eight Jewish engagement variables. Each factor consisted of four items with loadings greater than 0.30.

The Jewish social capital scale included questions asking respondents how important being Jewish is to them, what proportion of their close friends are Jewish, how important sharing festivals with family members is to them, and how important belonging to a Jewish community is to their sense of Jewish identity. Questions about importance were coded "not at all important" = 1 to "very important/essential" = 3. The question about friends was coded "none" = 1 to "all" = 3. Responses were scaled and added together, resulting in a scale ranging from 4 to 12 with a high score indicating a high level of Jewish social capital.

The Jewish religious capital scale included questions asking respondents how often they attend synagogue or another form of prayer service, how often they light Shabbat candles, how important observing Halakha (Jewish law) is to their sense of Jewish identity, and whether anyone in their household is a member of a synagogue. Responses were scaled as above, this time resulting in a scale ranging from 3 to 10 with a high score indicating a high level of Jewish religious capital.

Independent variables in the analysis include country (Australia = 0, Canada = 1), generation (born abroad = 0, native born = 1); Jewish education (none = 0, supplemental only = 1, at least day school = 2); partner religion (non-Jewish = 0, single = 1, Jewish = 2); childrearing (no children under eighteen in household = 0, child/children under eighteen in household = 1); population centre (not living in Toronto/Montreal or Sydney/Melbourne = 0, living in Toronto/Montreal or Sydney/

Melbourne = 1). I also included control variables for age (in years) and sex (male = 0, female = 1).[2]

Analysis

I first compared the Canadian and Australian Jewish communities across the two Jewish engagement scales and found small but statistically significant between-country differences. Four linear regression models were then used to determine what might account for differences in Jewish engagement between the two countries. The models examine the association between country and each scale controlling for age, sex, generation, Jewish education, marital status and partner religion, childrearing status, and population concentration. The purpose of this modelling is to determine whether controlling the independent variables has a statistically significant effect on the coefficients of the country variables – in other words, whether differences between Canadian and Australian Jews attenuate when controlling for any of the hypothesized predictors of Jewish engagement.

Results

To determine whether country means on the social and religious scales are significantly different, I ran adjusted Wald tests. As expected, the results show that Canadian Jews have significantly lower levels of Jewish social and religious capital than Australian Jews do (table 22.1). However, the differences between means are substantively small.

Multivariate regression analysis reveals that the independent variables of interest partly explain differences between the two countries in Jewish social and religious capital (table 22.2). Specifically:

Hypothesis 1 – that individuals farther removed from the immigrant experience have reduced levels of Jewish engagement – is not supported. Being an immigrant is not associated with either of the Jewish capital scales at standard levels of statistical significance, net of other variables in the regression equation. Apparently, the cultural and institutional structure of Canadian and Australian Jewry mitigates against much generational erosion (see chapter 19 in this volume).

Hypothesis 2 – that Jewish education is associated with differences between the two communities – is supported. Having a Jewish day school education is significantly and positively associated with Jewish social and religious capital. Conversely, not having any Jewish education is significantly and *negatively* associated with Jewish social and religious capital. The fact that Canadian Jews are less likely than

Table 22.1. Difference between country means for Jewish social and religious capital scales

	Mean	Standard error	95% confidence interval
Jewish social capital***			
Canada	10.031	0.053	9.928–10.134
Australia	10.813	0.018	10.777–10.850
Jewish religious capital***			
Canada	6.334	0.054	6.229–6.440
Australia	6.839	0.023	6.794–6.883

***$p < 0.001$

Australian Jews to have a Jewish day school education and more likely to have no Jewish education partly accounts for these differences.

Hypothesis 3 – that differences between the two communities are associated with marital status and partner religion – is supported. Having a Jewish partner is significantly and positively associated with Jewish social and religious capital. Conversely, having a non-Jewish partner is significantly and *negatively* associated with Jewish social and religious capital. The fact that Canadian Jews are less likely than Australian Jews to have a Jewish partner partly explains this difference.

Hypothesis 4 – that childrearing is associated with differences between the two communities – is not supported. Contrary to hypothesis 4, raising children is not significantly associated with Jewish social and religious capital at standard levels of statistical significance.

Hypothesis 5 – that greater population concentration is associated with a higher level of Jewish engagement – is partly supported. Living in a major population centre is significantly and positively associated with Jewish social capital. The fact that Canadian Jews are less likely than Australian Jews to live in a major population centre partly explains these differences. However, contrary to hypothesis 5, living in a major population centre is not significantly associated with Jewish religious capital.

Discussion

Comparison of country means on Jewish social and religious capital reveals statistically significant differences between Canada and Australia that are consistent with the view that Australian Jews are more Jewishly involved than Canadian Jews are. However, multivariate analysis uncovers a more complex story.

Jewish Engagement in Canada and Australia   339

Table 22.2. Ordinary least squares (OLS) regression predicting Jewish social and religious capital

	Jewish social capital		Jewish religious capital	
	Model 1 (restricted)	Model 2 (unrestricted)	Model 3 (restricted)	Model 4 (unrestricted)
Country = Canada	−0.772***	−0.534***	−0.522***	−0.221***
(ref.: Australia)	(0.055)	(0.057)	(0.058)	(0.062)
Age (in years)	−0.003*	−0.001	−0.003*	−0.003**
	(0.001)	(0.001)	(0.001)	(0.001)
Gender = female	0.319***	0.340***	-0.189***	−0.198***
(ref.: male)	(0.035)	(0.032)	(0.042)	(0.041)
Generation = native born		0.041		0.079
(ref.: born abroad)		(0.032)		(0.043)
Jewish education				
(ref.: supplemental only)				
At least day school		0.312***		0.365***
		(0.039)		(0.048)
None		−0.400***		−0.181*
		(0.060)		(0.073)
Partner's religion				
Jewish		0.574***		0.767***
		(0.044)		(0.055)
Non-Jewish		−1.023***		−1.233***
		(0.094)		(0.089)
Childrearing = rearing		−0.000		0.004
child/children		(0.040)		(0.052)
(ref.: not rearing child/				
children)				
Population centre = big city		0.179*		0.150
(ref.: not big city)		(0.071)		(0.085)
Constant	10.785***	10.147***	7.067***	6.440***
	(0.058)	(0.113)	(0.073)	(0.141)
R^2	0.045	0.171	0.013	0.127

$* p < 0.05; ** p < 0.01; ***p < 0.001$
Note: This table displays regression coefficients, with standard errors in parentheses.
Ref. = reference category. Big city = Toronto, Montreal, Sydney, and Melbourne.

Generation does not significantly contribute to differences in the two communities' levels of Jewish social and religious capital. It is worth noting in this connection that the Australian survey data contains country-of-birth information for three generations of respondents' families; comparable data were not available for Canadian Jewry. Researchers conducting future cross-national analyses may wish to test the generational erosion theory to compare differences between people of different generations where more extensive demographic participant data is available.

Jewish education was a significant and positive contributor to Jewish social and religious capital. Conversely, the absence of a Jewish education was a significant and negative contributor to Jewish social and religious capital.

Partner's religion was significantly associated with both forms of Jewish capital, positively in the case of Jewish partners and negatively in the case of non-Jewish partners. The literature is consistent with these findings.

When controlling for the other independent variables in my models, raising children had no significant effect on Jewish social and religious capital. It is likely that these measures of Jewish capital are a function of the impact of Jewish education and the religion of partners. The increased involvement of parents in ritual, together with the likelihood that communal engagement caters most effectively to families, is not apparent in these results, perhaps because raising children thwarts participation in social or religious activities due to diminished time and economic resources.

Finally, population concentration was significantly and positively associated with Jewish social capital. Population concentration enables more frequent gatherings, thickening social bonds.

I conclude that Australian Jews are more Jewishly engaged on the dimensions of social and religious capital. Australian Jews have higher rates of Jewish education, endogamy, and people living in areas with high population concentration, which partially underpins the greater Jewish engagement of Australian compared with Canadian Jewry. The good news in these findings is that communal policies and education can influence the impact of the socio-demographic variables in my models. Communal leadership may harness them to foster forms of Jewish capital and Jewish engagement more broadly.

NOTES

1 Researchers also discuss *cultural capital*, which refers to the kinds of knowledge, proficiencies, scholarship, and capacities that are valued in a given society, the accumulation of which elevates the esteem in which individuals are held (Bourdieu 2011). Cultural capital was not investigated in this study due to a lack of items in the two surveys that measure Jewish cultural capital.

2 Details of the variables and scale construction are available from the author on request.

REFERENCES

Alba, Richard D. 1990. *Ethnic Identity: The Transformation of White America*. New Haven, CT: Yale University Press.

Bartrop, Paul R. 1995. "Canada, Australia and the Holocaust: Comparing the Refugee Record of the Two Largest Dominions." *Australian-Canadian Studies: An Interdisciplinary Social Science Review* 13 (1): 33–47.

Bourdieu, Pierre. 2011. "The Forms of Capital." In *Cultural Theory: An Anthology*, edited by Imre Szeman and Timothy Kaposky, 81–93. New York: Wiley-Blackwell.

Brym, Robert, and Rhonda Lenton. 2020. "Jewish Religious Intermarriage in Canada." *Canadian Jewish Studies/Études juives canadiennes* 30: 67–82. https://doi.org/10.25071/1916-0925.40184.

Brym, Robert, Keith Neuman, and Rhonda Lenton. 2019. *2018 Survey of Jews in Canada: Final Report*. Toronto: Environics Institute for Survey Research. https://bit.ly/3hKsXOh.

Chertok, Fern, Charles Kadushin, Annette Koren, Graham Wright, Leonard Saxe, and Aron Klein. 2007. *What Difference Does Day School Make? The Impact of Day School: A Comparative Analysis of Jewish College Students*. Waltham, MA: Maurice and Marilyn Cohen Center for Modern Jewish Studies, Brandeis University. http://bir.brandeis.edu/handle/10192/22974.

DellaPergola, Sergio. 2020. "World Jewish Population, 2019." In *American Jewish Year Book 2019*, Vol. 119, edited by Arnold Dashefsky and Ira M. Sheskin, 263–356. Cham, Switzerland: Springer.

Engelberg, Ari. 2016. "Religious Zionist Singles: Caught Between 'Family Values' and 'Young Adulthood.'" *Journal for the Scientific Study of Religion* 55 (2): 349–64. https://doi.org/10.1111/jssr.12259.

Gans, Herbert J. 1979. "Symbolic Ethnicity: The Future of Ethnic Groups and Cultures in America." *Ethnic and Racial Studies* 2 (1): 1–20. https://doi.org/10.1080/01419870.1979.9993248.

Gitelman, Zvi. 1998. "The Decline of the Diaspora Jewish Nation: Boundaries, Content, and Jewish Identity." *Jewish Social Studies* 4 (2): 112–32. https://doi.org/10.2979/JSS.1998.4.2.112.

Graham, David. 2014. "The Impact of Communal Intervention Programs on Jewish Identity: An Analysis of Jewish Students in Britain." *Contemporary Jewry* 34 (1): 31–57. https://doi.org/10.1007/s12397-013-9110-x.

Graham, David, and Andrew Markus. 2018. *Gen17 Australian Jewish Community Survey: Preliminary Findings*. Melbourne: Australian Centre for Jewish Civilisation and JCA. http://bitly.ws/sF3d.

Graham, David, and Leon Narunsky. 2019. *The Jewish Population of Australia: Key Findings from the 2016 Census*. Sydney: JCA. https://jca.org.au/2016-census/.

Hammerton, Anthony James. 2001. "Epic Stories and the Mobility of Modernity Narratives of British Migration to Canada and Australia since 1945." *Australian-Canadian Studies: An Interdisciplinary Social Science Review* 19 (1): 47–63.

Helliwell, John F., Richard Layard, Jeffrey D. Sachs, Jan-Emmanuel De Neve, Lara B. Aknin, and Shun Wang. 2021. *World Happiness Report 2021*. New York: Sustainable Development Solutions Network. http://bitly.ws/sLsv.

Iannaccone, Laurence R. 1990. "Religious Practice: A Human Capital Approach." *Journal for the Scientific Study of Religion* 29 (3): 297–314. https://doi.org/10.2307/1386460.

Kadushin, Charles. 2012. *Understanding Social Networks: Theories, Concepts and Findings*. New York: Oxford University Press.

Levi, John S., and George F.J. Bergman. 2002. *Australian Genesis: Jewish Convicts and Settlers 1788–1860*. 2nd ed. Melbourne: Melbourne University Press.

Pomson, Alex, and Randal F. Schnoor. 2018. *Jewish Family: Identity and Self-Formation at Home*. Bloomington: Indiana University Press.

Putnam, Robert D. 2000. *Bowling Alone: The Collapse and Revival of American Community*. New York: Simon & Schuster.

Rossi, Alice, S., and Peter Rossi H. 1990. *Of Human Bonding: Parent-Child Relations across the Life Course*. New York: Aldine De Gruyter.

Rutland, Suzanne D. 1988. *Edge of the Diaspora: Two Centuries of Jewish Settlement in Australia*. Sydney: Collins.

Rutland, Suzanne D. 2006. *The Jews in Australia*. Melbourne: Cambridge University Press.

Tulchinsky, Gerald. 1993. *Taking Root: The Origins of the Canadian Jewish Community*. Hanover, NH: Brandeis University Press.

Waters, Mary C. 1990. *Ethnic Options: Choosing Identities in America*. Berkeley: University of California Press.

Weinfeld, Morton. 2021. "A Privileged Diaspora: Canadian Jewry in Comparative Perspective." In *No Better Home: Jews, Canada, and the Sense of Belonging*, edited by David S. Koffman, 19–32. Toronto: University of Toronto Press.

Wuthnow, Robert. 2010. *After the Baby Boomers: How Twenty- and Thirty-Somethings Are Shaping the Future of American Religion*. Princeton, NJ: Princeton University Press.

Contributors

Adina Bankier-Karp, Research Associate, Cohen Center for Modern Jewish Studies, Brandeis University, Waltham, MA

Reginald W. Bibby, Professor Emeritus, Sociology, University of Lethbridge, Alberta

Matthew A. Brookner, Associate Research Scientist, Cohen Center for Modern Jewish Studies, Brandeis University, Waltham, MA

Robert Brym, Professor, Department of Sociology and Anne Tanenbaum Centre for Jewish Studies, University of Toronto

Jordan A. Chad, Research Associate, Rotman Research Institute, Baycrest Academy for Research and Education, Toronto

Fern Chertok, Lecturer and Director of Advising and Fieldwork, Hornstein Jewish Professional Leadership Program, Brandeis University, Waltham, MA

Yolande Cohen, Professeure, Département d'histoire, Université du Québec à Montréal

Sergio DellaPergola, Professor Emeritus, The Avraham Harman Institute of Contemporary Jewry, The Hebrew University of Jerusalem

Paul L. Gareau, Associate Professor, Faculty of Native Studies, University of Alberta, Edmonton

Joshua Harold, Professor, Liberal Studies, Humber College, Toronto

344   Contributors

Feng Hou, Principal Researcher, Statistics Canada, Ottawa

Abdolmohammad Kazemipur, Professor and Chair of Ethnic Studies, Sociology, University of Calgary, Alberta

David S. Koffman, Associate Professor and J. Richard Shiff Chair for the Study of Canadian Jewry, Department of History, York University, Toronto

Rhonda Lenton, President and Vice-Chancellor, York University, Toronto

Naomi Lightman, Associate Professor, Department of Sociology, Toronto Metropolitan University

Richard Menkis, Associate Professor, Department of History, University of British Columbia, Vancouver

Martin Messika, Docteur, Département d'histoire contemporaine, Université Paris, Panthéon Sorbonne

Elizabeth Moorhouse-Stein, PhD Candidate, Department of Political Studies, Queen's University, Kingston, Ontario

Marina Morgenshtern, Assistant Professor, Department of Social Work, Trent University, Peterborough, Ontario

Ira Robinson, Professor, Department of Religions and Cultures, Concordia University, Montreal

Randal F. Schnoor, Adjunct Professor, Department of Social Science and Israel and Golda Koschitzky Centre for Jewish Studies, York University, Toronto

Charles Shahar, Chief Researcher, Jewish Community Foundation of Montreal

Anna Slavina, Director, Data Science Program, Research Manitoba, Government of Manitoba, Winnipeg

L. Daniel Staetsky, Senior Research Fellow, European Jewish Demography Unit, Institute for Jewish Policy Research, London, UK

Contributors 345

Harold Troper, Professor, Department of Curriculum Teaching and Learning, Ontario Institute for Studies in Education, University of Toronto

Morton Weinfeld, Professor, Department of Sociology, McGill University, Montreal

Index

Notes, tables, and figures are indicated by lowercase letters following the page numbers: "n," "t," and "f," respectively. FSU stands for former Soviet Union.

Abella, Irving: on antisemitism in Canada, 181, 182, 187; *None Is Too Many*, 42

Aboriginal people. *See* Indigenous people

Aboriginal Peoples Survey (APS), 219

Alberta: Jewish school tuition, 67n3; Métis settlements in, 217

Alesha (immigrant from FSU), 132–3

Alla (immigrant from FSU), 135, 136

Alliance of Christian Schools, 64

American Jewish Committee (AJC), survey of American Jews (2019), 301

American Jewish Year Book, 74

American Pastoral (Roth), 6

AMIA (Asociación Mutual Israelita Argentina), 253

Andersen, Chris, 215, 217, 223, 224, 225

Angus Reid Institute national survey (2019), 188

anti-Asian racism, 195–6, 209–10

anti-Black racism, 307–11

Anti-Defamation League, 2021 report on antisemitism, 46, 48

antisemitism: ancient history of, 39; anti-Israel, 40–1, 45, 46; anti-Zionist, 45, 46, 48–9, 50; anxiety about, 300–2; CJC response to, 15, 17; compared to other forms of discrimination, 46–7, 167–9, 170–1, 173–6; crimes of, 46–7, 300, 315n1; data on, 46–8, 300, 315n1; declining levels of, 185–8; defining, 48, 49; in France, 300, 301, 315n1; Holocaust denial and, 21–2, 45; Jewish identity and, 74, 131–2, 191, 258, 260t; Jewish neighbourhoods and, 86, 88, 92-6, 93t, 94t; Jewish quotas, 42, 131, 233; leading to out-migration, 253; in media, 22, 24, 50–1; responses to, 17, 39, 40, 92, 209; social contact and, 43, 48; Spanish Inquisition, 318; by the state, 42–3, 64, 67n3, 117–18, 130–2; types of, 42–6, 168; in the UK, 300, 301, 305–7, 315n1; urban vs. rural levels of, 187–8; in the US, 300–1. *See also* Holocaust

antisemitism in Canada: data on, 46–8, 264, 300, 315n1; historically, 17, 40–2, 45, 181–2, 218;

348 Index

antisemitism in Canada (*cont.*)
  present-day, 21–2, 39–42, 45–51,
  264, 300, 315n1; in Quebec, 50–1,
  118–19, 185–6; in universities, 40,
  42, 45–6, 47–8, 233
antisemitism, perception of: anxiety
  resulting from, 39, 40, 307; choice
  of neighbourhood and, 92, 93t; in
  criticism of Israel, 40, 45–6, 48–50,
  51, 170, 175; Jewish identity and,
  51; in Quebec nationalism, 117;
  reality vs., 47–8, 300–15
APS (Aboriginal Peoples Survey), 219
Arcand, Adrien, 42
Argentina, Jews in, 252, 253t, 254,
  255, 256
Ashkenazim: genetics, 230–1; in
  Montreal, 119–21; origin of, 318;
  Sephardi vs., 14, 120, 122
Asian Canadians: attainment of,
  196, 199–202, 203–4, 234t, 236–8;
  identifying for study, 240–1;
  immigration of, 236–7; racism
  against, 195–6, 209–10. *See also*
  Chinese Canadians
Asociación Mutual Israelita
  Argentina (AMIA), 253
assimilation: effect of intermarriage
  on, 66–7, 74–6, 78–9, 81; of
  Jewish immigrants into Jewish
  community, 122, 136, 143; of
  Jews into Canadian society,
  5–7; theories of, 87; in the US
  compared to Canada, 264, 270–1,
  284, 285–7. *See also* integration
Associated Hebrew School, 57, 64
attainment: Asian, 196, 199–202,
  203–4, 208–9, 234t, 236–8; Muslim,
  166–7, 171
attainment, Jewish: compared
  to other communities, 100–12,
  166, 199–207, 209, 234, 237;

educational, 75–81, 199–202, 230–
  9; immigration and, 101–12, 132–3,
  136, 138–42, 209, 322–3; Jewish
  identity and, 75–81; lack of, 34–6,
  207; occupational, 130, 202–7, 235,
  242n5; in spite of antisemitism, 47
Australia, Jews in, 252t, 253–7,
  259–60, 287, 332–40
Avrich-Skapinker, Mindy, 134–5

Bais Ya'acov school, 57
Bauman, Zygmunt, 143
BDS (Boycott, Divestment, and
  Sanctions), 40, 45–6, 50, 159
Begin, Menachem, 20
Bensimon, Doris, 321
Bialik, Chaim Nachman, 5
Bialik Hebrew Day School, 57
bilingualism in Canada, 16
Bill 21, 43, 118
Bill 22, 19
Bill 101, 19, 117
Black Student Application Program
  at UTMS, 238
B'nai Brith Canada, 46, 315n1
British Columbia, Jews in, 31, 32, 36.
  See also Vancouver, Jews in
Byers, Michele, 142

Calgary, Jews in, 32, 33t, 34, 67n3,
  297n2
Canada: bilingualism in, 16;
  immigration, 14, 41, 43, 235–6;
  population growth or decline
  across provinces, 31; relations with
  Israel, 24. *See also* antisemitism
  in Canada; Jewish Canadian
  immigrants; Jewish Canadians;
  multiculturalism, Canadian
Canada–Métis Nation Accord, 217
Canadian Baptist, The, 181
Canadian Centre for Diversity, 182

Canadian Charter of Rights and Freedoms. *See* Charter of Rights and Freedoms
Canadian Christian–Jewish Consultation, 184
Canadian Conference of Catholic Bishops (CCCB), 185
Canadian embassy in Israel, 20
Canadian Friends of Peace Now, 20–1, 24–5, 158–9
Canadian Jewish Congress (CJC), 15–17, 24, 40, 218
Canadian Jewish News, 24, 40
Canadian Jewry. *See* Jewish Canadians
Canadian multiculturalism. *See* multiculturalism, Canadian
capital, Jewish, 271–2, 273t, 333–5, 337–40
CCCB (Canadian Conference of Catholic Bishops), 185
censuses in Canada: attempting to recognize ethnicity, 197–8, 214–18, 219–26; as colonialist, 218, 225; efforts to improve, 224–5; questions on, 197, 202, 211n4; value of, 215–16, 218–20, 222. *See also* surveys
Centre for Israel and Jewish Affairs (CIJA), 158, 171, 185, 222
Chambers, Simone, 175
Charter of Rights and Freedoms: Constitution Act (1982), 216; mention of God in, 183; notwithstanding clause, 43; right to free speech, 21, 22, 44
Charter of the French Language (Bill 101), 19, 117
CHAT (Community Hebrew Academy of Toronto), 57, 58, 64–6, 67n2
Chinese Canadians: attainment of, 196, 202–9, 234t; compared to

Jewish Canadians, 195–211, 238; dealing with racism, 195–6, 209–10; population of, 197
Christian antisemitism, 44
Christian Canadians: dominance of, 42–3, 64, 67n3, 179–80, 191; evangelism, 180, 184; genetics, 231; historical importance of religion, 179–80; identity, 191–2; relations with Jews, 180–2
Christian education, state funding of, 42–3, 64, 67n3
CIJA (Centre for Israel and Jewish Affairs), 158, 171, 185, 222
CJC (Canadian Jewish Congress), 15–17, 24, 40, 218
Clark, Joe, 20, 24
CMAs (major census metropolitan areas), 32–3
Cohen, Maxwell, 17
cohesion, social, 6–7, 114–15
Community Hebrew Academy of Toronto (CHAT), 57, 58, 64–6, 67n2
Community Security Trust (CST), 315n1
connectedness to Jewish community. *See* Jewish engagement
Conservative Jews: attitudes towards Israel, 147, 148, 149t, 155t, 156; Jewish schools, 57, 61, 62; population identifying as, 189; synagogue attendance, 183
Conservative Party of Canada, 157
Constitution Act (1982), 216
Crestwood Heights (Seeley, Sim, and Loosley), 41
CST (Community Security Trust), 315n1
cultural antisemitism, 43–4
cultural capital, 340n1
Cummings Centre for Jewish Seniors in Montreal, 120

350 Index

de facto and de jure antisemitism, 42–3
Delisle, Esther (*Myths, Memory and Lies*), 42
Deschênes Commission (1985), 22
discrimination: against Asians, 195–6, 209–10; against Blacks, 307–11; against Jews (*see* antisemitism); against minority languages, 117–18; against Muslims (*see* Islamophobia); awareness of, 307–13; in censuses, 218, 219, 226; in media, 22, 24, 50–1, 169; in Ontario educational system, 42–3, 64, 67n3; in Quebec, 43, 50–1, 117–19, 185–6; statistics on, 47
diversity. *See* multiculturalism, Canadian
dual loyalty, 24, 50

earnings, 34–6, 101–12, 132–3, 207–10
economic status. *See* attainment
Edmonton, Jews in, 32, 33t
educational attainment: of Asians, 196, 199–202, 234t, 236–8; of Jews, 75–81, 199–202, 230–9
education, Jewish. *See* Jewish education
Eichmann, Adolf, 17
Eitz Chaim School, 57, 64
endogamy: Jewish engagement and, 66–7, 74–5, 76, 78–9, 81, 83n4, 295, 338, 339t; rates of, 285t
Eric (immigrant from FSU), 131
ethnic capital, 271–2
ethnic cohesion, 6–7, 114–15
ethnic diversity, 237–8
ethnic mobility, 221–4
ethnic pluralism. *See* multiculturalism, Canadian

ethnic retention, 284–6, 290–5, 296t. *See also* Jewish engagement; Jewish identity
Evangelical Fellowship of Canada, 185

far-right groups, 168–9
Fields Medal, 230
former Soviet Union. *See* Jews from FSU; Jews in FSU
France. *See* Jews in France

Gen17 Australian Jewish Community Survey, 335–6
gender: attainment by, 199, 200t, 201t, 210–11n3; attitudes towards Israel and, 154, 155t; roles, 138–42, *See also* men; women
generational erosion theory, 333–4, 337, 339–40
Generations Trust Scholarship, 65
Germany, Jews in, 40, 251, 252t
ghettos. *See* Jewish neighbourhoods
Gitelman, Zvi, 283, 284
Givens, Phillip, 15
Glickman, Yakov, 134
Goldscheider, Calvin (*The Transformation of the Jews*), 10n1
Gomery, Madeleine, 115
Granovsky family, 65
Grassroots for Affordable Jewish Education (GAJE), 64
Green Party of Canada, 49–50

Hafez, Farid, 167, 173–4
Halifax, Jews in, 32, 33t, 36, 88, 297n2
Hamilton, Jews in, 32, 33t, 34
Hardwicke's Act (1753), 218
Harper, Stephen, 157
Hart, Ezekiel, 41
Hasidim. *See* ultra-Orthodox Jews

hatred: hate crimes, 46–7, 300, 315n1; hate literature, 17, 21, 45, 181; hate speech, 21, 22, 45. *See also* antisemitism; discrimination

HDI (Human Development Index), 250–1

Herzog, Elizabeth (*Life Is with People*), 86

Holocaust: Canadian antisemitism during, 182; denial of, 21–2, 44; effect on Canadian Jewry, 13, 44, 51; effect on Jews of, 39, 40; ignorance of, 44; Jewish Canadian experience after, 13–26; as shaping Jewish identity, 191, 258, 260t; Todorov on, 176

Holocaust survivors: immigrating to Canada, 13–15, 41; in Montreal, 120; population in Canada, 35, 59–60; response to antisemitism, 17

Holy Blossom temple, 121

Human Development Index (HDI), 250–1

Hungarian uprising (1956), 14

Hunter, Ernest, 181

Ignatieff, Michael, 157

IHRA (International Holocaust Remembrance Association), 21, 49

IJV (Independent Jewish Voices), 159

immigrants: Asian, 204, 205, 207, 208, 209, 236–7; attainment, 101–3, 107; educational aspirations, 237; Jewish, history of, 318; lack of recognition of credentials, 132, 139–40, 322; Middle Eastern, 14, 166, 236, 237. *See also* Jewish Canadian immigrants

immigration in Canada, 14, 41, 43, 235–6

income, 34–6, 101–12, 132–3, 207–10

Independent Jewish Voices (IJV), 159

Indian Act, 219, 220

Indigenous people: on censuses, 214–18, 219–21, 222–4; residential schools, 180; self-determination, 225; self-identifying, 223–4, 225. *See also* Métis people

Inna (immigrant from FSU), 136

Inquisition, Spanish, 318

integration: of Jewish immigrants into Jewish community, 122, 136, 143; of Jewish sub-communities into Jewish community, 14, 23, 134–43; of Jews into Canadian society, 87, 187–8, 270. *See also* assimilation

interfaith organizations, 184

intermarriage: attitudes towards, 185, 211n5; effect on assimilation, 66–7, 75, 76–9; historical barriers to, 218, 270; intolerance towards, 273–4, 276–7; Jewish identity of children, 36–7, 268–9; of Moroccan Jews, 324; rates of, 115, 261, 263, 335; as tolerance indicator, 48; in Weimar Germany, 40. *See also* assimilation

intermarriage in Canada compared to the US, 267–80; community connectedness, 274–7, 278; declining interest in religion and, 277–8; Jewish engagement and, 270–1; mobility and, 275, 278–9; rates of, 267, 270, 272, 289, 297n3

International Covenant on Civil and Political Rights, 64

International Holocaust Remembrance Association (IHRA), 21, 49

intersectionality: of antisemitism, 50; of Soviet Jewish identity and experience, 129, 142–3

Iraqi Jews, 14

352 Index

"Islamophilia," 168
Islamophobia: compared to
antisemitism, 167–9, 170–1, 173–6.
See also Muslim Canadians
Israel: age composition, 256–8;
birth rate, 256; conflict with
Palestinians, 169–70, 175;
hostilities with neighbouring
countries, 17–18, 20–1; Jewish
Canadian attitudes towards,
147–59, 191; migration to, 133,
250, 253–5; relations with Canada,
23–4; settlements on West Bank,
24–5; as shaping Jewish identity,
258, 259–64; share of global Jewish
population, 30, 251–3; support for,
16, 20–1, 24–5, 49, 135, 157–9. *See
also* Palestinians
Israel, criticism of: linked to
antisemitism, 40–1, 45, 46; by
organizations, 24; perceived as
antisemitic, 40, 45–6, 48–50, 51,
170, 175; by politicians, 24, 49, 157;
on university campuses, 45–6, 50;
within Jewish community, 20–1,
24–5, 159
Israeli Apartheid Week, 40
Isserman, Ferdinand, 181

Janna (immigrant from FSU), 130,
133
Japanese Canadians, 195
Jerusalem Definition of
Antisemitism, 49
Jesin, Norm, 65
Jewish Americans: access to
Jewish education, 57–61, 272;
antisemitism faced by, 300;
degree of assimilation, 264,
270–1, 284, 285–7; degree of
Jewish engagement, 268, 270–3,
274–80, 284–7; identity, 261, 262f,

264, 272–3; marrying non-Jews
(*see* intermarriage in Canada
compared to the US); population
of, 252t; presumed Whiteness of,
40
Jewish attainment. *See* attainment,
Jewish
Jewish Canadian immigrants: age
composition of, 104–6; attainment
of, 101–12, 132–3, 136, 138–42, 209,
322; children of, 106–7, 109t, 110;
compared to Jewish immigrants in
other countries, 59–60, 287, 333–
40; from FSU, 62, 128–44; history
of, 318; Holocaust survivors,
13–14, 41; from Morocco, 14, 123,
318–29; occupations of, 203, 320–9;
perceptions of antisemitism, 305;
population of, 284–5, 287; waves
of, 23, 25, 236
Jewish Canadians: from abroad (*see*
Jewish Canadian immigrants);
age composition, 255–8, 261,
264; antisemitism faced by
(*see* antisemitism in Canada);
assimilation of (*see* assimilation);
attainment of, 34–3, 100–12, 207;
attitudes towards Israel, 147–59,
191; bilingualism among, 123;
children attending public schools,
41, 179; comparative research on,
7–8; compared to Jews in other
countries, 249–64, 267–80, 284–6,
288–95, 296t, 297n2; compared
to other ethnic communities,
166–7, 176, 199–210, 214–26, 287,
332–40; core Jews, 73, 198, 251;
distribution across provinces,
31–3; from FSU (*see* Jews from
FSU); history of, 13–26, 181–4,
231–2, 235–6, 270; Holocaust
survivors, 13–15, 35, 59–60, 120;

identity (*see* Jewish identity); immigrants (*see* Jewish Canadian immigrants); intellectual exceptionalism, 230–9; Jewish schools (*see* Jewish education); marrying Jews (*see* endogamy); marrying non-Jews (*see* intermarriage); in Montreal vs. Toronto, 114–24; movement within Canada, 19–20, 23; occupations of, 202–7, 235, 242n5, 320–9; participation in Jewish life (*see* Jewish engagement); perception of antisemitism (*see* antisemitism, perception of); population of, 6, 22–3, 29–32, 251–3, 284, 289–90; presumed Whiteness of, 40, 128, 142, 144n2, 216; reaction to mass murder of Palestinians, 20–1; relations with Christians, 180–2; relations with Muslims (*see* Jewish–Muslim relations); religious polarization among, 189–91; residential patterns (*see* Jewish neighbourhoods; Jewish residential concentration); as segregated, 115, 171–2; seniors, 33–4, 35; Sephardi vs. Ashkenazi, 120, 122; social cohesion of, 6 7, 114–15; support for political parties, 49, 157, 304, 311; as urban, 13, 23, 114, 297n2

Jewish Canadian young people: attending Jewish schools, 61; leaving Quebec, 117; living in poverty, 35; perception of antisemitism, 311; rate of intermarriage, 36; view of Israel, 147, 149t, 150

Jewish capital, 271–2, 273t, 333–5, 337–40

Jewish communists, 15

Jewish diaspora: origin of, 39; population of, 5–6, 30, 283–4

Jewish education: affordability, 62–5, 66t, 67; attitudes towards Israel and, 154, 155t; in Canada compared to the US, 57–61, 272; history in Canada, 57–9, 286; Jewish engagement and, 62, 63t, 66–7, 272, 273t, 334, 337–8; Jewish identity and, 56; in Ontario, 57–9, 119; in Quebec, 118, 119, 179; rates of attendance, 58–9, 61–2, 64–5, 66t; state discrimination against, 42–3, 64, 67n3

Jewish engagement: in Canada compared to Australia, 287, 332–40; in Canada compared to the US, 268, 270–3, 274–80, 284–7; choice of partner and, 66–7, 75–9, 267–80, 295, 338, 339t; Jewish attainment and, 75–81, 110–12; Jewish education and, 62, 63t, 66–7, 272, 273t, 334, 337–8; Jewish summer camps and, 56–7, 62, 63t, 334; of Jews from FSU, 136–7, 143–4, 287–95, 296t; in Montreal, 114–15, 116; residential concentration and, 74–5, 78–9, 81–2, 84, 335, 338; of Sephardim, 319, 319t; synagogue attendance, 183, 190. *See also* Jewish identity

Jewish Federations of Canada: Jewish Federation of Montreal, 37; Jewish Federation of Toronto, 57. *See also* Centre for Israel and Jewish Affairs (CIJA)

Jewish Foundation of Greater Toronto, 65

Jewish identity: antisemitism as shaping, 51, 92, 131–2, 191, 258, 260t; in Canada compared to other countries, 258–64, 272–3, 304;

354   Index

Jewish identity (*cont.*)
  conflicting views of, 134, 135–6;
  defining, 37, 73–7, 198, 211n4, 216,
  239–40; degrees and dimensions
  of, 73–83, 90–2, 189–91, 216,
  222, 258–64; descent and, 272–3,
  279; ethnic mobility and, 221–4;
  ethnic vs. religious, 134, 135–6,
  191–2; impact of parents on, 36–7,
  90, 93, 94t, 95; importance, 190,
  191–2; intermarriage and, 272–4;
  intersectionality of, 129, 142–3;
  Jewish Standard Definition, 37; of
  Jews from FSU, 130, 134, 135–7,
  142–3; mapping, 258–61, 262–3f;
  as marker of difference, 142; in
  national censuses, 197–8, 210n1,
  214–16, 218–19, 220, 221–2, 224; as
  shaped by circumstance, 56, 75–83,
  130, 133, 142–3. *See also* Jewish
  engagement
Jewish Immigrant Aid Services
  (JIAS), 13, 322
Jewish immigrants, history of,
  318. *See also* Jewish Canadian
  immigrants
Jewish intellectual exceptionalism,
  230–3. *See also* attainment, Jewish
Jewish Labour Committee, 15
Jewish migration, 62, 249–55
Jewish–Muslim relations: degree of
  interaction, 171–2; difficulties in,
  165, 169–71; historical narratives,
  172–4; ideas for improving, 174–7
Jewish neighbourhoods: defined,
  92–3; degree of segregation,
  171–2; history in Canada, 88–9; in
  Montreal, 33, 87, 89–90, 92–3, 93t,
  94t, 120–1; reasons for creation
  of, 86–8; reasons for living in,
  88, 90, 93–6; as shaping identity,
  74–5, 78–9, 80t, 81–2, 84, 90–6;

  in Toronto, 33, 86, 87, 89, 92–3,
  94t; in Vancouver, 89, 90, 92; in
  Winnipeg, 89, 90, 92, 93
Jewish residential concentration:
  compared to other ethnicities,
  87, 167; as correlated with Jewish
  engagement, 79, 335, 338; as
  influencing choice of partner, 269–
  70; in particular provinces, 31–2;
  reasons for, 87–97; in urban areas,
  13, 23, 32–4, 61. *See also* Jewish
  neighbourhoods
Jewish schools. *See* Jewish education
Jewish Standard Definition, 37
Jewish summer camps: affordability,
  65; Jewish engagement and, 56–7,
  62, 63t, 334; rates of attendance,
  61; in the US and Canada, 272
Jews: age composition, 104–6,
  255–8, 261, 264; diaspora
  population, 5–6, 30, 283; difficulty
  of surveying, 303; in Eastern
  Europe, 235; engaged in trade,
  235; favourability ratings of, 171;
  migration of, 14, 250–3, 254–5,
  318; position of Roman Catholic
  Church on, 16, 181, 184–5;
  prophesied end of, 5; Sephardi vs.
  Ashkenazi, 14, 120, 122; threats to
  (*see* antisemitism; assimilation);
  world population of, 30. *See also*
  specific communities
Jews in Argentina, 252, 253t, 254,
  255, 256
Jews in Australia, 252t, 253–7, 259–
  60, 287, 332–40
Jews in Canada. *See* Jewish
  Canadians
Jews in France: age composition of,
  255–7; antisemitism and, 253, 300,
  301, 305–7, 315n1; identity of, 260t,
  261, 263f, 304–5; migration of,

254; from Morocco, 319–26, 329; perception of antisemitism of, 306, 307, 308, 311–14; political leanings of, 304; population of, 252t, 253

Jews from FSU: accessing Canadian education, 138–41, 141; attainment of, 132–3, 136, 139–40, 141; attending Jewish schools, 62; compared with Canadian-born Jews, 136–8; compared to Jews in FSU, 284; experiencing state-sponsored antisemitism, 130–2; gender roles of, 138–42; identity of, 130, 134, 135–7, 142–4, 287–95, 296t; integration into Jewish community, 23; migration of, 62, 132–4, 251, 253, 254, 287–8; relations with Canadian Jewish community, 134–7, 138f, 143–4; at risk of assimilation, 136; in Toronto, 23, 120, 128

Jews in FSU, 130–2, 251–7, 283–4, 291–2

Jews in Germany, 40, 251, 252t

Jews from Morocco: accessing education, 326; French-speaking, 14, 318–20; marriages of, 323–4; migrating, 14, 119, 123, 318, 319–22; occupations of, 320–9; Spanish-speaking, 123, 318–30. *See also* Sephardim

Jews from North Africa, 14, 122, 319, 322, 324. *See also* Jews from Morocco; Sephardim

Jews in the UK: antisemitism and, 300, 301, 305–7, 315n1; compared to Canada, 304; identity of, 304–5; perception of antisemitism of, 306, 307, 308, 311–14; population of, 303, 315n2

JIAS (Jewish Immigrant Aid Services), 13, 322

Johnstone, Alex, 44
JSpaceCanada, 159

Kallen, Evelyn, 189
Kalmijn, Matthijs, 269
Kattan, Naïm, 115
Keegstra, James, 22, 44
King, Mackenzie W.L., 182
Kingston, Jews in, 32, 33t, 35
Kitchener-Cambridge-Waterloo, Jews in, 32, 33t, 35
Koffman, David S., 114

language discrimination in Quebec, 117–18
Larissa (immigrant from FSU), 130
Lasry, Jean-Claude, 320
Layton, Irving, 182
League for Human Rights (B'nai Brith Canada) reports on antisemitism, 46
l'École Maïmonide, 122
Le Devoir, 42
left-wing antisemitism, 44
Léger, Paul-Émile (Cardinal), 180
Lenin, Vladimir, 130
Leo Baeck school (Reform), 57, 64
Leon (immigrant from FSU), 131
Liberal Party of Canada, 157
LICO (low income cut-off), 34–6, 207
life course theory, 88, 96
Life Is with People (Zborowski and Herzog), 86
LIM-BT (low income measure before tax), 102
London (ON), Jews in, 32, 33t, 34
London (UK), Jews in, 303
Lora (immigrant from FSU), 130, 131, 140–1
Loosley, Elisabeth W. (*Crestwood Heights*), 41
low income, 34–6, 101–12, 207

356   Index

Mailloux, Louise, 51
major census metropolitan areas (CMAs), population distribution across, 32–3
Manitoba, Jews in, 31, 120. *See also* Winnipeg, Jews in
marriage: of Jews from Morocco, 323–4. *See also* endogamy; intermarriage
Maru Group national surveys, 187, 189
McGill University, 42, 45–6
Medjuck, Sheva, 187
Meer, Nasar (and Tarq Modood), 168
men: Chinese and Jewish attainment, 199–201, 202–8, 205t, 206t, 210t; intermarriage of Moroccan Jews, 324; perception of antisemitism, 309, 311; top ten Chinese and Jewish occupations, 202–4
Métis Nation of Canada (MNC), 217
Métis people, 214–26; on censuses, 214–18, 219–21, 222–4; diversity of, 216; identity of, 216–17, 223–4, 225. *See also* Indigenous people
Métis Resistance of 1869–70, 219
Middle Eastern Canadians: attainment of, 234; identifying for study, 241; immigrating, 236–7. *See also* Muslim Canadians
Millennials, 184, 277. *See also* Jewish Canadian young people; young people
MNC (Métis Nation of Canada), 217
Modood, Tariq, 168
Moldofsky, Naomi, 320
Montessori Jewish Day School, 58
Montreal: immigration to, 119. *See also* Quebec
Montreal, Jews in: culture and communities, 20, 115–18,

119–23, 286, 318–21; dealing with antisemitism, 39; dealing with Quebec nationalism, 19, 117–18; history of, 116–18, 119–20; immigrant income of, 102–8, 109t, 110–12; intermarriage rates of, 36; Jewish neighbourhoods, 33, 87, 89–90, 92–3; Jewish schools and summer camps, 59, 60t, 61, 67n3, 118, 119; leaving Montreal, 19–20, 23, 90, 116–18; living in poverty, 35; population of, 32, 116–17, 120; social cohesion of, 114–15. *See also* Quebec, Jews in
Morgan, Thomas ("The Vanishing American Jew"), 267
Moroccan Jews. *See* Jews from Morocco
MS *St. Louis*, 182
Mulroney, Brian, 22, 23
multiculturalism, Canadian: compared to Australian, 287; compared to the US melting pot, 264, 270–1, 284–7; controversy around, 16, 19; history of, 18–19, 60–1, 184, 286; interpreting Charter in context of, 21; in universities, 237–8
Muslim Canadians: attainment of, 166–7, 171, 234, 237; compared to Jewish Canadians, 166–7; degree of segregation of, 171–2, 173t; discrimination against, 167–9, 170–1, 173–6; hate crimes against, 168–9, 175; immigrating, 14, 236–7; "Islamophilia," 168; relations with Jews, 165, 169–77; Sunni–Shia conflict, 169–70; view of Israel–Palestine conflict, 170, 175. *See also* Middle Eastern Canadians
Myths, Memory and Lies (Delisle), 42

Natasha (immigrant from FSU), 141
National Household Survey (NHS), 29, 37, 74–5, 210n2, 220
National Jewish Population Survey (1990), 297n3
National Social Christian Party, 42
Neiman, Susan, 175
Ner Israel school, 57
Neuberger, Edie, 64
New Israel Fund (NIF), 159
NHS (National Household Survey), 29, 37, 74–5, 210n2, 220
NIF (New Israel Fund), 159
None Is Too Many (Abella and Troper), 42
North African Jews, 14, 122, 319, 322, 324. *See also* Jews from Morocco; Sephardim
Nuremberg Laws (1935), 74

occupational attainment, 202–10
Official Language Act (Bill 22), 19
"Olympics of suffering," 175
Ontario, Jews in: antisemitism faced by, 21, 48; Jewish schools and summer camps, 42–3, 57–9, 60t, 61–5, 67n3, 119; living in poverty, 35; population of, 31, 32; view of multiculturalism, 19. *See also* Ottawa, Jews in; Toronto, Jews in
oral history, 144n4
Orthodox Jews: antisemitism faced by, 47; attitudes towards Israel, 148, 149t, 150–3, 155t, 156; birth rate of, 121–2, 256; in Canada compared to the UK and France, 304; in Montreal, 120–1; population of, 189; schools and summer camps, 57–8, 61; synagogue attendance, 183. *See also* ultra-Orthodox Jews

Ottawa, Jews in: attainment of, 35; population, 32, 33t, 89, 90; rate of intermarriage of, 115; senior population of, 34. *See also* Ontario, Jews in

Palestinians: Canadian Jewish support for, 159; framing of conflict with Israel, 169–70, 175; as Indigenous people, 175; Joe Clark on, 24; mass murder of, 20–1. *See also* Israel
Parizeau, Jacques, 23
participation in Jewish life. *See* Jewish engagement
Parti Québécois (PQ), 19, 23
Paul, Annamie, 49
Paul Penna Downtown Jewish Day School, 58
Peace Now, 20–1, 24
Pearson, Lester, 16, 17
Peiladeau, Pierre, 50
Pew surveys of American Jews, 40, 156, 270–1, 287–9, 297n2
Phalange, The (militia group), 20
Phillips, Nathan, 15
"philosemitism," 168
"pink-washing," 50
pluralism. *See* multiculturalism, Canadian
population concentration. *See* Jewish residential concentration
poverty, 34–6, 101–12, 132–3, 207
Powley case, 223
propaganda, 17, 21, 45, 181
Protocols of the Elders of Zion, 44
Proulx, Gilles, 51
Putin regime, 291

Quebec: concerns around multiculturalism, 16, 123–4;

358   Index

Quebec (*cont.*)
  discriminatory legislation in,
  43, 118; immigration to, 119;
  nationalism, 16, 19–20, 23,
  116–18, 123
Quebec, Jews in: antisemitism faced
  by, 42, 48, 50–1, 118–19, 185–6;
  being friends with non-Jews, 43;
  children attending public schools,
  41; concerned about Quebec
  nationalism, 16, 19, 117–18;
  leaving Quebec, 19–20, 23, 116–17,
  123; population of, 31, 116–17. *See
  also* Montreal, Jews in
Quiet Revolution, 117–18
Quran 16:90, 174

racism. *See* discrimination
racist antisemitism, 44
Rawidowicz, Simon, 5
reciprocal solidarity, 50
referendums on Quebec sovereignty,
  20, 23
Reform Jews: attitudes towards
  Israel, 147, 148, 149t, 158–9;
  identity of, 189, 272–3; popularity
  in Toronto, 121; population
  identifying as, 189; schools, 57, 61,
  62; synagogues, 121, 183; in the US
  vs. Canada, 60
religion: as affecting choice of
  partner, 285t, 295, 338, 339t;
  compulsory instruction in,
  21; importance of, 179–83,
  189, 190; lack of, 36, 76t, 180,
  183, 189, 277–8; marrying
  outside of (*see* intermarriage);
  recorded in censuses, 218;
  religious capital, 271–2, 273t,
  333; religious diversity, 183–4;
  religious identification, 191;
  religious observance (*see*

Jewish engagement); religious
  polarization, 188–91; religious
  retention, 289t, 290–5, 296t. *See also
  specific religions/denominations*
residential concentration. *See* Jewish
  residential concentration
residential mixing, 43
residential schools, 180
retention. *See* ethnic retention
Revised Jewish Definition, 37
right-wing antisemitism, 44
Robbins Hebrew Academy
  (Conservative), 57
Robinson, Ira, 186, 187
Rosenberg, Louis, 218
Rosenberg, Stuart, 122
Roth, Philip (*American Pastoral*), 6
Royal Commission (1963), 16
Russia, Jews in. *See* Jews in FSU
R. v. Powley, 223

St. Louis (ship), 182
Sarason, Seymour, 276
Sartre, Jean-Paul, 73–4
Scholem, Gershom, 123
schools, Jewish. *See* Jewish education
Second Vatican Council, 16, 184
Second World War. *See* Holocaust
Security Council of the United
  Nations, 24
Seeley, John R. (*Crestwood Heights*), 41
seniors, 33–4, 35
Sephardim: antisemitism faced by,
  47; Ashkenazi vs., 14, 120, 122;
  connectedness with community,
  319, 319t; identifying for study,
  330n6; immigrating to Canada, 14;
  integration into CJC leadership,
  123; in Montreal, 14, 20, 119, 120,
  122–3, 124, 318–29; occupations of,
  320; in Toronto, 14, 122, 318–19.
  See also Jews from Morocco

Service de Protection de la Communauté Juive (SPCJ), 315n1
Shaar Hashomayim, 121
Sharansky, Natan, 134
Shryock, Andrew, 168
shtetlekh. See Jewish neighbourhoods
similarity structure analysis (SSA), 258–9
Sim, Robert A. (*Crestwood Heights*), 41
Six Day War, 17–18
social capital, 333
social cohesion, 6–7, 114–15
socio-economic status. *See* attainment
sovereignty in Quebec, 19–20
Soviet Jewry campaign, 18
Soviet Jews. *See* Jews from FSU
Spanish Inquisition, 318
spatial assimilation, 87
Special Committee on Hate Propaganda (1965), 17
SSA (similarity structure analysis), 258–9
Stalin, Joseph, 130–1
Stanfield, Robert, 20
Stass (immigrant from FSU), 132, 140
Statistics Canada, 195–6, 197, 214–25. *See also* censuses in Canada
Steinberg, Stephen, 189–90, 191
Stella (immigrant from FSU), 130, 132, 141
Supreme Court of Canada, 15, 22, 45, 64
Survey of Jews in Canada (2018): on antisemitism, 47–8, 187, 302–3; on attitudes towards Israel, 49, 147–8; compared to Pew surveys, 297n2; on identity, 190; on income, 104–6, 110–12; on Jewish school attendance, 61; on language discrimination, 118; methodology of, 335–6; on movement within Canada, 117; participant demographics, 303–4; questions from, 104; on rates of intermarriage, 267, 297n3; reason for, 214–15, 222; on social cohesion, 114–15

surveys: Angus Reid Institute national survey (2019), 188; challenges with surveying Jews, 303; of Indigenous people, 219; of Jews in Australia, 335–6; of Jews in France and the UK, 302–4; of Jews in the US, 40, 156, 270–1, 287–9, 297n2; Maru Group national surveys, 187, 189; National Household Survey (NHS), 29, 37, 74–5, 210n2, 220; National Jewish Population Survey (1990), 297n3. *See also* censuses in Canada; Survey of Jews in Canada (2018)
Sveta (immigrant from FSU), 131, 135, 140
synagogues, 121, 183, 190, 297n2

TanenbaumCHAT (Tanenbaum Community Hebrew Academy of Toronto), 64–6, 67n2
Tanya (immigrant from FSU), 141
testimonio, 144n4
Thornhill (Vaughan), 33, 83, 87, 89
tikun olam, 258
Todorov, Tzvetan, 176
Tolik (immigrant from FSU), 140
Torczyner, Jim, 37
Toronto, Jews in: antisemitism faced by, 42, 46; attainment of, 105t, 106, 109t, 110–12; demographics of, 23, 32, 117, 121; from FSU, 23, 120, 128; immigrants, 14, 110–12, 120, 122; income of, 105t, 106, 109t, 110–12; intermarriage rates of, 36;

360 Index

Toronto, Jews in (*cont.*)
Jewish neighbourhoods, 33, 86, 87, 89, 92–3; Jewish schools and summer camps, 57–9, 60t, 61–5, 119; mobility of, 16, 117; social cohesion of, 114–15; winning elections, 15. *See also* Ontario, Jews in
Transformation of the Jews, The (Goldscheider and Zuckerman), 10n1
Troper, Harold: comparing Asians to Jews, 196; *None Is Too Many*, 42
Trudeau, Pierre E., 18–19, 20, 184
Truth and Reconciliation Commission, 223
Tsarist secret police, 44

UJA (United Jewish Appeal) Federation of Toronto, 64, 67n4
UJPO (United Jewish People's Order), 15
Ulpanat Orot school, 58
ultra-Orthodox Jews: antisemitism faced by, 40; in FSU, 291; in Montreal, 120–2, 124. *See also* Orthodox Jews
United Jewish People's Order (UJPO), 15
United Kingdom. *See* Jews in the UK
United Nations High Commissioner for Refugees, 64
United Nations Human Development Index (HDI), 250–3
United States. *See* Jewish Americans
United Synagogue Day School (Conservative), 57
University of Toronto, 45
University of Toronto Medical School (UTMS), 42, 232, 237–8

Vancouver, Jews in: demographics and population of, 23, 32, 104,
117; income of, 102–3, 105t, 106, 107, 109t, 110–12; Jewish neighbourhoods, 89, 90, 92; Jewish schools and summer camps, 60t, 61, 67n3; Orthodox Jews, 121; social cohesion of, 114–15
"Vanishing American Jew, The" (Morgan), 267
Vegans for BDS, 50
victimhood, 175
Victoria, Jews in, 32, 33t, 34, 36
Vigod, Bernard, 191
visible minorities, identifying for study, 240
Volodya (immigrant from FSU), 130, 131, 136, 138

Weinfeld, Morton, 107, 114, 190–1, 270
Windsor, Jews in, 32, 33t, 34
Winnipeg, Jews in: exodus from, 23, 90; income of, 104, 106, 107, 109t, 110–12; Jewish neighbourhoods, 89, 90, 92, 93, 93t, 94t; Jewish schools, 60t, 67n3; Orthodox Jews, 121; population of, 32, 33t, 34; social cohesion of, 114–15. *See also* Manitoba, Jews in
women: Chinese and Jewish attainment, 201–2, 204–6, 207–8, 210t; intermarriage of Moroccan Jews, 324; Moroccan-Jewish occupations, 320–9; non-Jewish White attainment, 204, 205t, 206t, 208; perception of antisemitism, 309; top ten Chinese and Jewish occupations, 204–5, 205t

Yeshivat Or Chaim school, 58
Yiddish, 121, 131
young people, 44, 184, 277. *See also* Jewish Canadian young people

Zborowski, Mark (*Life Is with People*), 86

Zionism: anti-Zionism, 45, 46, 48–9, 50; differing views on, 15, 16–17; in the US and Canada, 285–6

Zuckerman, Alan S. (*The Transformation of the Jews*), 10n1

Zündel, Ernst: *Did Six Million Really Die?*, 21–2, 44; trial of, 21–2

Zytnicki, Colette, 322

Milton Keynes UK
Ingram Content Group UK Ltd.
UKHW012144210424
441411UK00002B/36